Contents

"Our highest assurance of the goodness of Providence seems to me to rest in the flowers. All other things, our powers, our desires, our food, are all really necessary for our existence in the first instance. But this rose is an extra. Its smell and its colour are an embellishment of life, not a condition of it. It is only goodness which gives extras, and so I say again that we have much to hope from the flowers."

Sir Arthur Conan Doyle, "The Naval Treaty"
in *The Memoirs of Sherlock Holmes*

R.G.H. Cormack
Wild Flowers of Alberta

Hurtig Publishers
Edmonton

i

Illustrated with line drawings by the author
Colour photographs by Alberta's nature photographers

Hurtig Publishers
10560 105 Street
Edmonton, Alberta

ISBN 0-88830-283-5

Printed and Bound in Canada

Dedicated

to

The Boy Scouts

Girl Guides

Cubs and Brownies

of Canada

Acknowledgments

In a book such as this the author finds himself indebted to a great many interested and kind people. All the photographs used in this book were contributed by Alberta photographers and it is their enthusiasm and generosity that has made this book possible. To each and everyone of the following contributors I express my sincere thanks:

Dr. G. Bell, Dr. D. A. Boag, Dr. H. J. Brodie, Mr. J. A. Campbell, Mr. J. Claessen, Mr. D. S. S. Cormack, Mrs. Lucille J. Cossins, Mr. A. H. Dickson, Elk Island National Park, Miss Janette Goodwin, Mr. H. E. Hamly, Dr. C. G. Hampson, Mr. A. Karvonen, Professor J. J. Klawe, Professor R. H. Knowles, Mr. F. Kozar, Dr. H. A. MacGregor, Mr. P. J. Martin, Dr. G. J. Mitchell, Dr. J. R. Nursall, Mr. M. Ostafichuk, Mr. H. Pegg, Mr. A. G. Porcher, Dr. A. M. Revell, Professor W. Ray Salt, Mr. R. J. Schraa, Mr. P. D. Seymour, Mr. B. R. Shantz, Dr. W. H. Vanden Born, Mr. D. Wighton, Mr. A. J. Whyte, Dr. J. H. Whyte, Dr. W. C. Wonders, Edmonton.

Mr. D. Beers, Dr. J. D. Erickson, Mrs. Eva Hackett, Mr. W. J. Hackett, Miss Kathleen Hodges, Miss Julie Hrapko, Miss Alison Jackson, Mr. L. H. Leacock, Mrs. Gladys H. McKillop, Mr. A. G. Saxby, Calgary; Mrs. J. Bassett, Mr. W. M. Brown, Mr. E. Gushul, Dr. G. A. Hobbs, Mr. N. E. Kloppenborg, Dr. and Mrs. D. W. A. Roberts, Dr. R. W. Salt, Mr. J. J. Sexsmith, r. Mr. H. Sivyer, Dr. S. Smoliak, Lethbridge; Miss Aileen Harmon, Mr. C. S. Hunter, Banff; Mrs. Dorthea Calverley, Dawson Creek, B.C.; Mr. R. E. Hahn, Granum; Mr. G. W. Machell, Mr. R. C. Sweet, Islay; Mr. J. D. Grieve, Mr. R. D. Langevin, Jasper; Mr. P. H. Pohlman, Kamloops, B.C.; Mr. B. Godwin, Olds; Mr. R. N. Smith, Seebe; Mrs. Maureen White, Wainwright.

I am greatly indebted to Professor W. Ray Salt of the Department of Anatomy, University of Alberta, Edmonton, for his advice, assistance and friendly encouragement. It was he who promoted the writing of this book and who took upon himself the exacting and tedious task of arranging the photographs with the plant descriptions and paginations. The fact that not one description runs over into the succeeding page speaks for itself. I am grateful to Dr. E. C. May of the Department of Classics, University of Alberta, Edmonton, for translating many of the scientific names and to Dr. Lorene L. Kennedy of the Department of Botany and Mr. Robert Lister of the Department of Zoology, University of Alberta for their interest and helpful suggestions. I am also grateful to Mr. H. E. Hamly of Commercial Printers Limited, Edmonton, for his friendly help and advice. His expert knowledge of colour was indispensable in selecting the colour photographs for reproduction. My sincere thanks go to my wife, Margaret, who read the whole manuscript, making corrections and invaluable suggestions and to Miss Merle Whyte, Botany Department secretary who did all the typing and secretarial work.

Introduction

For a long time now there has been a need for a popular, illustrated book on the wild flowers of Alberta. It is hoped that this present volume will supply this need and the author considers himself privileged to have been given the opportunity to make the attempt. This book is not written for serious students of plant life. Such a volume, "The Flora of Alberta", by the late Professor E. H. Moss exists already. Rather it is written for those, young and old, who love our wild flowers and who wish to know more about them. If it succeeds in doing this or in helping to make a day's outing or a summer's holiday more enjoyable then the objective of the book has been achieved.

To know more about our wild flowers we have first to know their names. Each plant has two names, an English common name and a Latin scientific name. For example, the common name of our best-known wild rose is the Prickly Rose and the scientific name is *Rosa acicularis*. The first word *Rosa* refers to the genus and the second to the species. Out of hundreds of wild roses in the world only one will fit the description for *Rosa acicularis*. As this book is written more for the general public than for botanists, common names are given precedence but scientific names are included for certainty of identification. Where there is no distinctive common name the plant is called by its generic name or by a literal translation of the scientific name.

Quite often when we are introduced to a stranger we are able to relate him or her to another acquaintance with a similar name. The same is true with our wild flowers. Once we know the name of one plant we can relate it to another which it closely resembles. To those who are accustomed to call any yellow cup-shaped flower a buttercup it may come as a surprise to learn that there are hundreds of buttercups, *Ranunculus*, in the world and that twenty-seven of them grow in Alberta. The general practice is to place a number of similar species into a distinctive group called the genus and to clump all genera having certain obvious features in common into a still larger group called the family. For example, the Prickly Rose, *Rosa acicularis*, is placed with all the other roses in the genus *Rosa*. Then because the roses, *Rosa*, have several points in common with the raspberries, *Rubus*, the cinquefoils, *Potentilla*, the cherries, *Prunus*, and many other genera, they are all put into the family *Rosaceae*.

In keeping with the spirit of this book there is no botanical key. Technical terms, with the exception of those dealing directly with plant structure, have been kept to a minimum. Identification is based entirely on comparison of the unknown or unfamiliar plant with a photograph and the accompanying brief description. Hundreds of photographs were contributed and each one was judged solely on its suitability for identification and reproduction. As was to be expected, there were a great many duplicates of our most popular and attractive wild flowers and to decide which was the best Prickly Rose, Common Paint Brush or Prairie Crocus proved to be a most difficult task. A sincere effort was made to use at least one photograph from each photographer but unfortunately this was not possible. In general, the species included in this book are the most familiar and most popular representatives of our native wild flowers and wayside plants. Identification by colour photograph has its limitations, but in most cases each photograph will lead the reader directly to the exact species, or in those instances where a large number of species are involved, to the genus. In the case of the grasses and sedges only one or two of our most familiar species were included and these will have to serve as an example of the whole group.

The description of each species is so arranged that the chief characteristics of flowers, fruit and leaves may be seen at a glance. In the general remarks an attempt is made to point out those details of colour, scent and form which may help to distinguish the plant in question from any other species or from a very similar species for which no photograph is available. However, as in everything else, ease in the identification of our wild flowers comes only with practice.

Under the headings, Habitat and Distribution, and in the general remarks the place in which the species is most likely to be found is briefly described. The excellent photographs which appear in the front of the book show some of the varied habitats and plant associations which can be seen in this large and beautiful province.

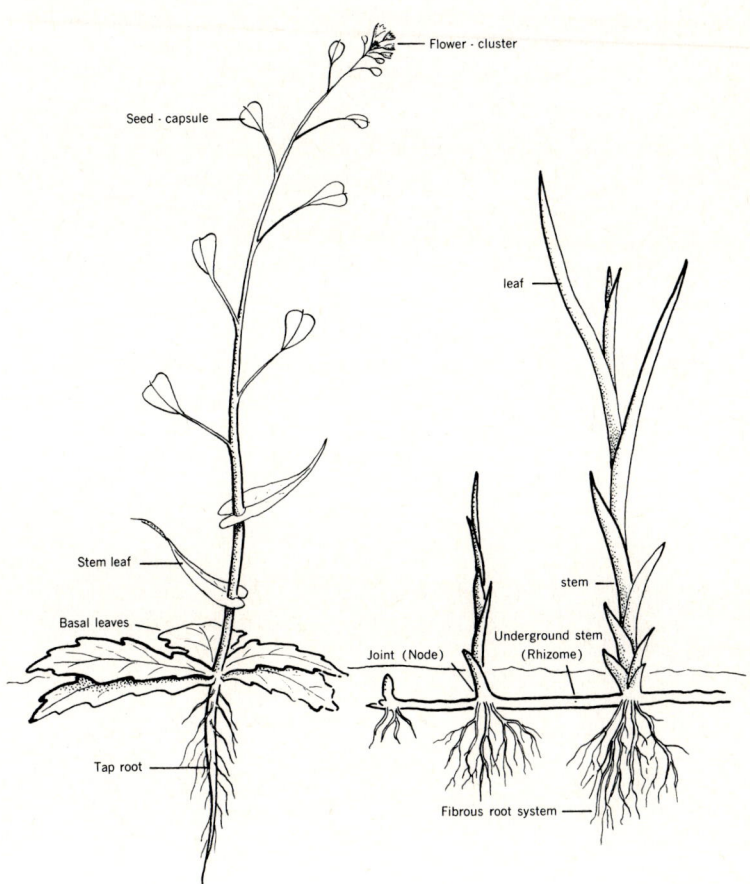

LEAF STRUCTURE

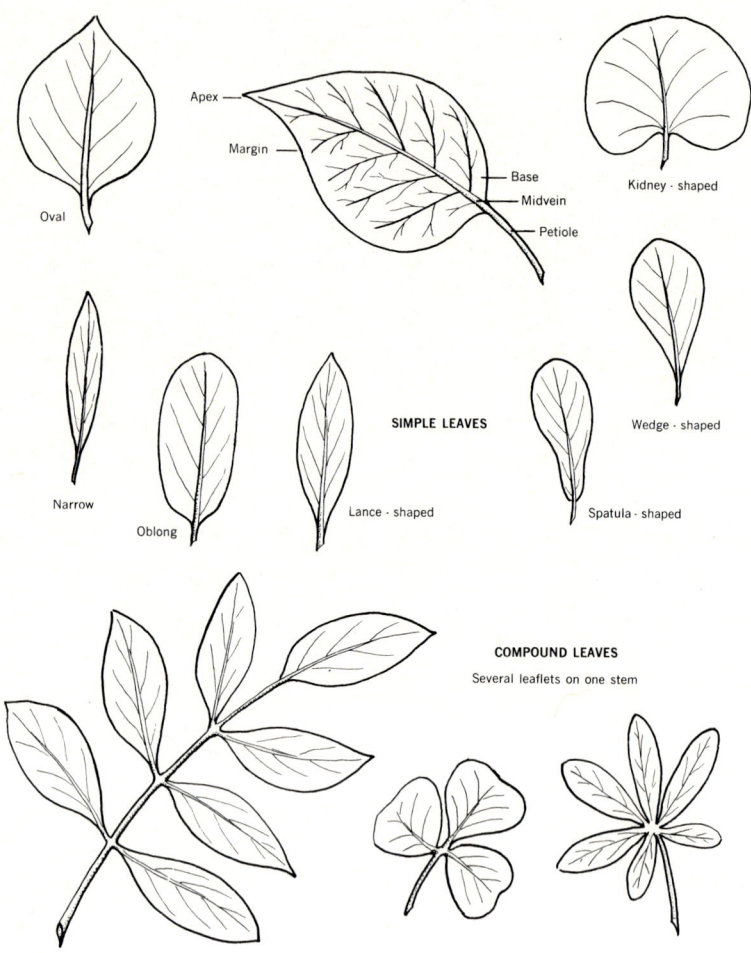

Oval

Apex

Margin

Base

Midvein

Petiole

Kidney - shaped

SIMPLE LEAVES

Narrow

Oblong

Lance - shaped

Spatula - shaped

Wedge - shaped

COMPOUND LEAVES

Several leaflets on one stem

FLOWER STRUCTURE

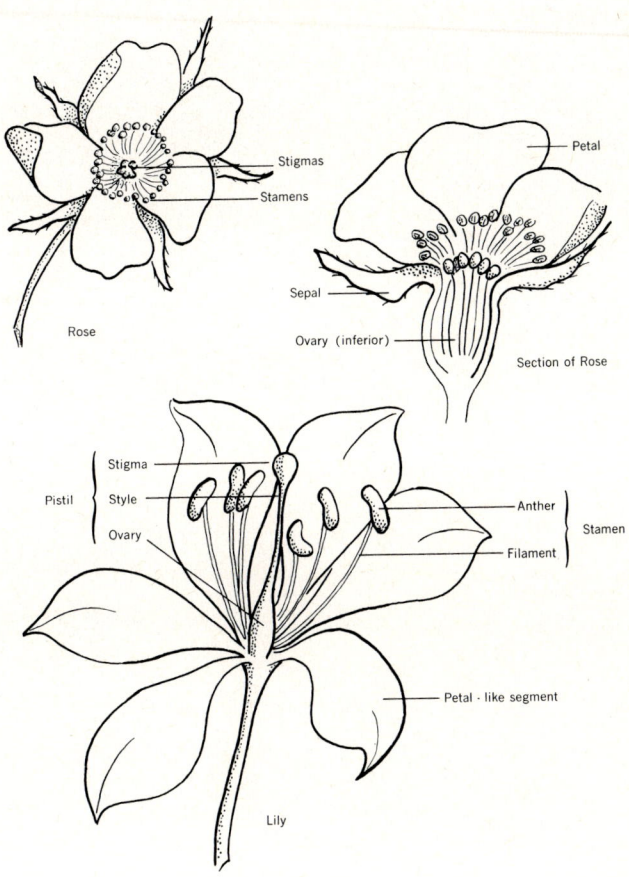

Rose

Stigmas
Stamens

Section of Rose

Petal
Sepal
Ovary (inferior)

Lily

Pistil
Stigma
Style
Ovary

Anther
Filament
Stamen

Petal - like segment

FLOWER STRUCTURE

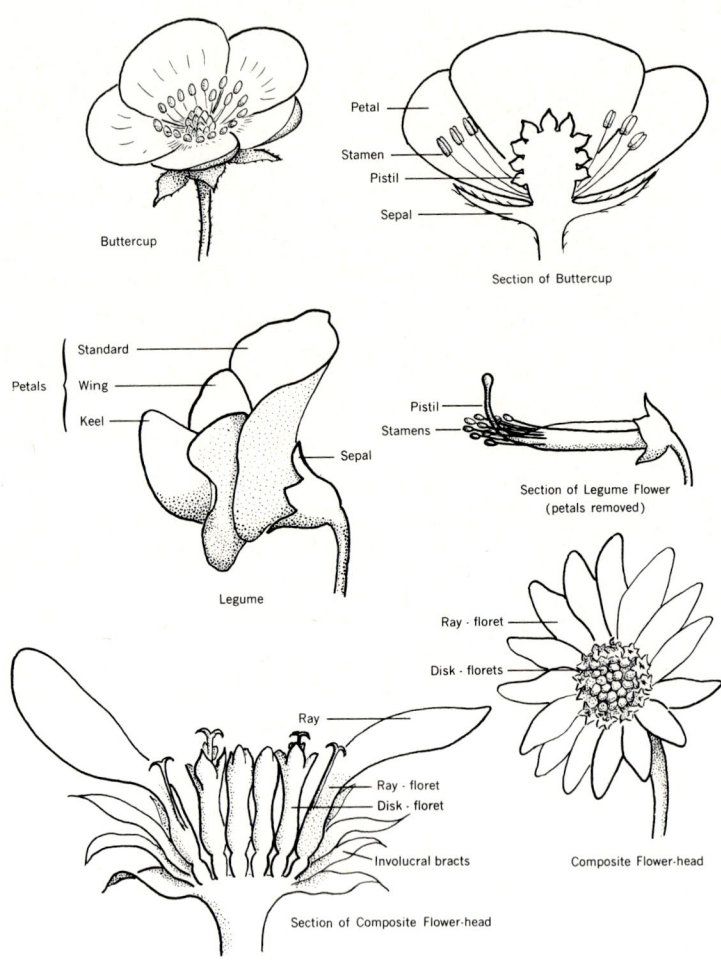

Buttercup

Section of Buttercup

Petal
Stamen
Pistil
Sepal

Petals
Standard
Wing
Keel

Sepal

Legume

Pistil
Stamens

Section of Legume Flower
(petals removed)

Ray · floret
Disk · florets

Composite Flower-head

Ray
Ray · floret
Disk · floret
Involucral bracts

Section of Composite Flower-head

xii

Index by Family

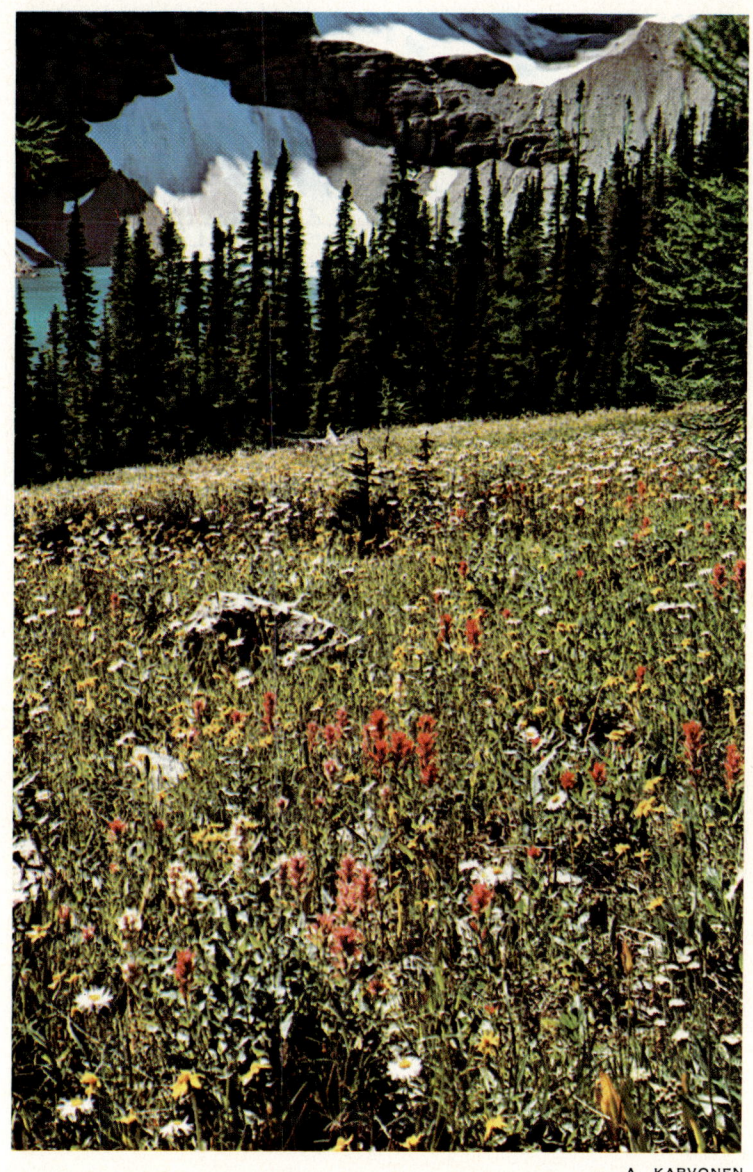

An alpine meadow in midsummer. Some of the wild flowers to be found here are paint brush, fleabane, ragwort, lousewort and gentian. Scarab Lake, Banff National Park.

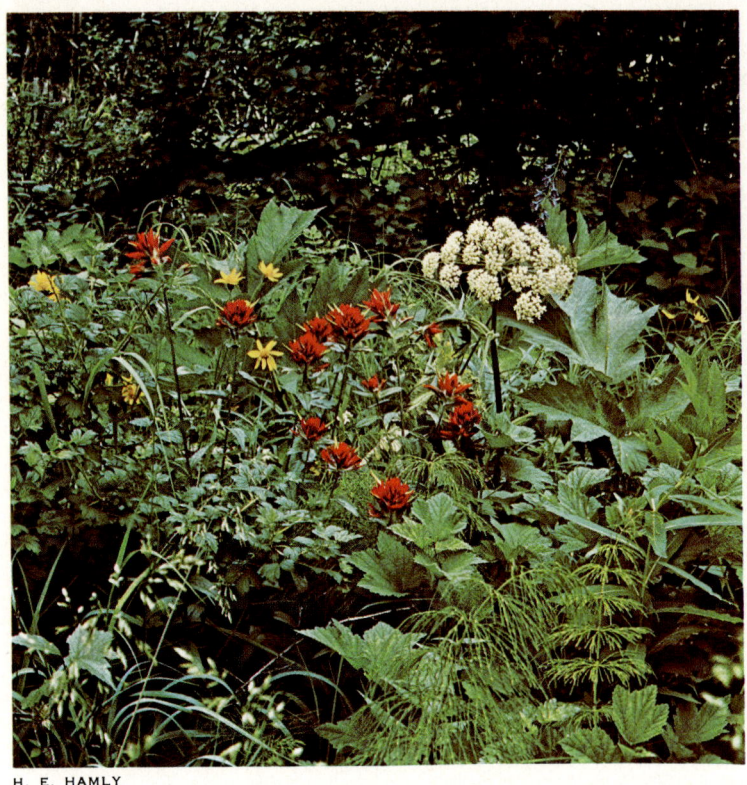

A woodland thicket in late July. Here is a great mixture of familiar wild flowers including Cow Parsnip, Common Red Paintbrush, Arnica, Wild Currant and Woodland Horsetail. Jasper National Park.

A woodland pond in midsummer, with a border of cattails, sedges and willows and with Water Knotweed in the open water.

The foothills in early summer showing a field of yellow buttercups.

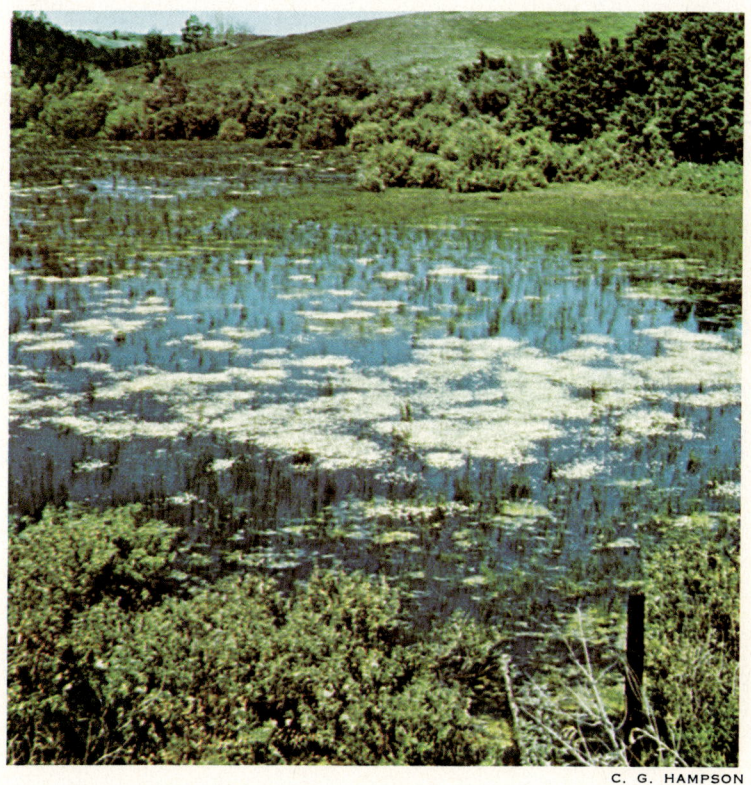

A parkland slough in early summer with White Water Crowfoot and Duck-weed in the open water and sedges and rushes around the edge.

The prairie in midsummer with locoweeds and lupines in full bloom.

The parkland in midsummer. An abandoned field covered with Common Fireweed.

The parkland in late summer. Goldenrod and Fireweed are signs of approaching fall.

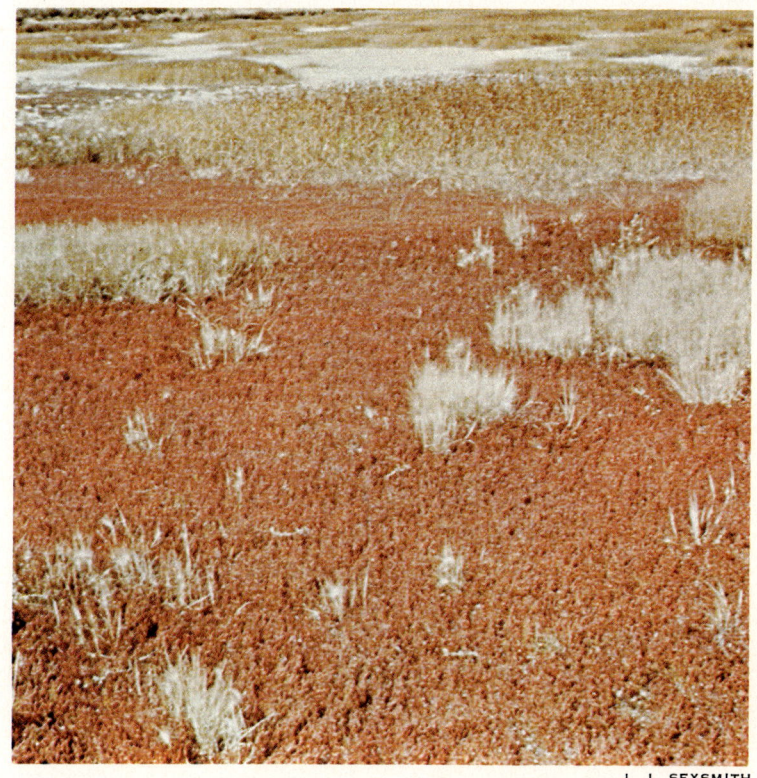

A dried-out alkaline slough on the prairie of Southern Alberta showing a mixture of drought and salt resistant goosefoots and grasses. The most conspicuous of these is the Samphire whose bright red succulent almost leafless stems stand out in sharp contrast to the grey-green fleshy stems and leaves of the Sea Blite, Greasewood and Russian Thistle and to the waving plumes of the Foxtail Barley.

A treeless windswept plateau well above timberline and the home of many beautiful alpine plants including Mountain Avens, Alpine Buttercup, Alpine Cinquefoil and Alpine Forget-Me-Not.

The prairie in spring. A field of prairie crocus.

The parkland in early summer. A country road bordered by the Prickly
Rose — Alberta's floral emblem.

Glacier Lilies at timberline.

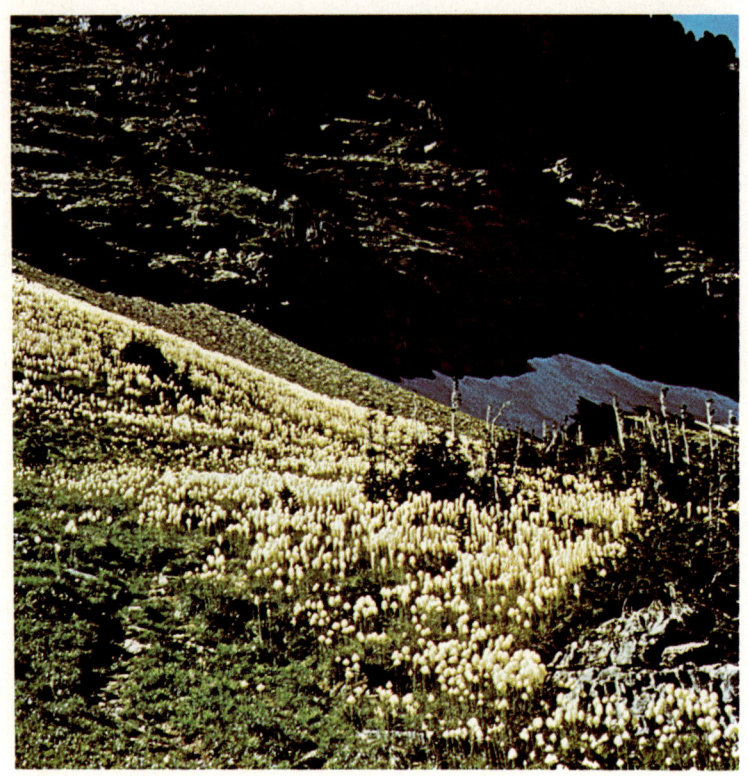

Timberline. Bear Grass and stunted trees.

Another alpine meadow with a profusion of paint brush, fleabane, columbine, lousewort and many other summer wild flowers. Peyto Lake view-
point, Banff National Park.

P. J. MARTIN

Native grasses of the prairie-foothills.

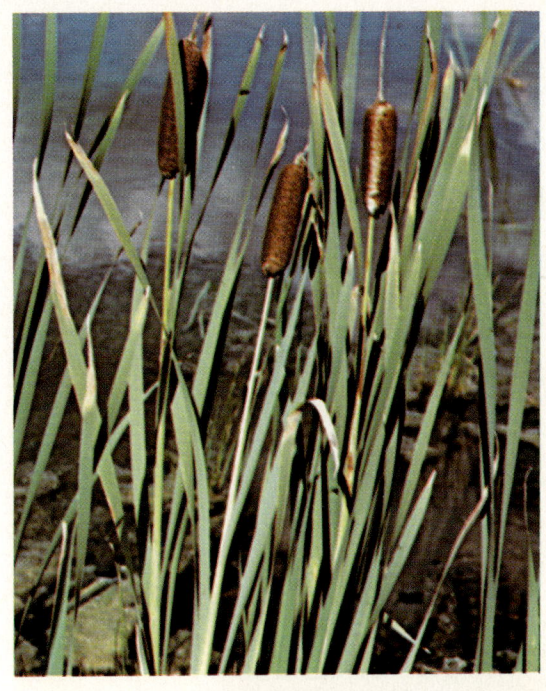

**COMMON
CATTAIL**
(Text p. 18)

R. J. SCHRAA

**GIANT
BUR-REED**
(Text p. 19)

P. D. SEYMOUR

17

CATTAIL FAMILY — *TYPHACEAE*

Members of this family of perennial herbs grow in marshes, pools of shallow water and in low, wet ground. The tall flowering stem and long sheathing leaves spring from a creeping rootstock. Both staminate and pistillate flowers occur on the same stem. Only one species of this family is native to Alberta. This same species is found everywhere else in Canada, in the British Isles and in Northern Europe.

COMMON CATTAIL   Photo. p. 17
Typha latifolia   *Perennial*

FLOWERS: Inconspicuous; minute; innumerable in a dense, cylin-
                  drical spike; the staminate flowers above, the pistillate
                  flowers beneath; sepals and petals absent.

FRUIT: A minute, tufted, 1-seeded achene.

LEAVES: Long, narrow, light olive green, sheathing the base of
                  the flowering stalk.

HEIGHT: 4 - 8 feet.

HABITAT: Swamps, sloughs, ditches, wet marshy ground.

DISTRIBUTION: Common and widely spread throughout Alberta. June-
                  July.

To hunters, birdwatchers, naturalists and to boys who like to investigate around the edge of sloughs for the sheer joy of getting their feet wet, the Common Cattail is by far the best known marsh plant. A slough or road-side ditch would have little attraction without the cattails. This erect plant with its sheath of tall leaves is conspicuous at all seasons, but particularly so in the fall when the last twelve inches of the six foot flowering stalk turn dark brown and resemble that furry object from which it derives its common name. Cattails are so characteristic of wet places that whenever we see a small clump of them growing in a cultivated field, their presence indicates a small pool of water or a wet depression not otherwise visible from the road.

BUR-REED FAMILY — *SPARGANIACEAE*

A small family of aquatic or marsh plants which are closely related to the cattails with which it shares many common features. All the members of this family are characterized by stout perennial rootstocks, erect or floating stems, dark green, slender, basal leaves, both staminate and pistillate flowers and round, bur-like fruits. Six species of bur-reeds are found in Alberta but only three are of common occurrence.

GIANT BUR-REED
Sparganium angustifolium

Photo. p. 17
Perennial

FLOWERS:	Yellowish-green; small; fluffy; in separate staminate and pistillate clusters.
FRUIT:	A round bur-like head of achenes, ¾ - 1¼ inches in diameter.
LEAVES:	Several, all basal, slender, grass-like.
HEIGHT:	2 - 5 feet.
HABITAT:	Shallow water and marshes.
DISTRIBUTION:	Common throughout Alberta. July - August.

The Giant Bur-Reed is one of several species of this group which together with cattails, bulrushes, and other reedy plants make up the vegetation of shallow water, muddy borders of ponds and sloughs. The leaves growing from the perennial rootstock, are long, flat and bayonet-shaped and clasp the long conspicuous flowering stem at the base. The small, fluffy flowers are of two kinds: staminate and pistillate; these are collected in separate, round, dense heads, alternately strung along the stem to the very end. After pollination, the staminate heads fall away while the pistillate ones remain and mature into the characteristic, round bur-like fruits.

WATER PLANTAIN FAMILY — *ALISMACEAE*

Only four members of this family grow in Alberta. They are all aquatic or marsh plants with perennial bulb-like rootstocks, a cluster of long-petioled, dark green, basal leaves and conspicuous leafless flowering stalks.

BROAD-LEAVED WATER PLANTAIN
Alisma plantago - aquatica

Not Illustrated
Perennial

FLOWERS:	White, sometimes pinkish; small, about ⅜ inch across; very numerous in successive whorls on the much-branched flower-stem; each flower on a separate stalk; 3 green persistent sepals; 3 white petals; 6 - 9 stamens; 1 pistil of many carpels.
FRUIT:	A small head of dry, flattened achenes.
LEAVES:	Simple, long-petioled with dark green, oval blades 2 - 7 inches long.
HEIGHT:	Flower-stem up to 30 inches.
HABITAT:	Shallow water in ponds and ditches.
DISTRIBUTION:	Common throughout Alberta. June - July.

The Broad-Leaved Water Plantain is a plant that must be looked for in shallow water along the reedy shores of marshes, ponds and slow-moving streams. It grows from a stocky, fleshy stem-base which sends down fibrous roots into the mud and sends up long-stalked, olive green leaves and an erect leafless flower-stem into the air. The leaves vary greatly in size, shape and form depending on the level of the water; the aerial leaves being broadly oval and the submerged leaves being ribbon or strap-shaped. The flower-stem is tall and symmetrically branched displaying the many spreading whorls of small white flowers. The charm of this plant lies in the symmetry of its much-branched flower-stem, which in flower or fruit relieves the monotony of the reeds and rushes. The only other Alberta species, *Alisma gramineum*, has usually very long ribbon-like leaves and grows in the same marshy locations.

ARROWHEAD
(Text p. 22)

**FOXTAIL
BARLEY**
(Text p. 23)

COTTON
GRASS
(Text p. 23)

DORTHEA CALVERLEY

COMMON
GREAT
BULRUSH
(Text p. 24)

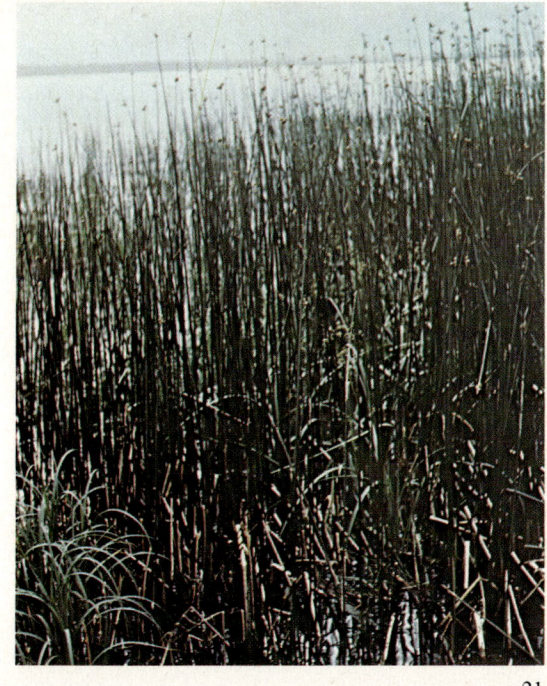

D. S. S. CORMACK

21

WATER PLANTAIN FAMILY — *ALISMACEAE*

ARROWHEAD   Photo. p. 20
Sagittaria cuneata   *Perennial*

FLOWERS: White; showy; several often in whorls of 3 on the leafless flower-stalk; 3 sepals; 3 petals; staminate flowers of 10 - 18 stamens; pistillate flowers of several carpels.

FRUIT: A round, dense head of dry, flattened achenes.

LEAVES: Aerial leaves, simple, arrowhead-shaped; submerged leaves, simple, narrow, strap-shaped.

HEIGHT: 8 - 16 inches.

HABITAT: In mud and shallow water of sloughs and lakes.

DISTRIBUTION: Common throughout Alberta. July - August.

The place to look for the Arrowhead is in the mud or shallow water of small ponds, lakes and slow-moving streams. In mid summer, its beautiful arrow-shaped leaves are fully expanded and its long flowering stalk stands well above the surface of the water. Although the leaves are usually arrow-shaped, they vary greatly in size, shape and form, depending upon the level of the water. The flowers look superficially alike but a closer examination reveals that the upper ones are staminate while the lower ones are pistillate and after pollination the latter grow into rounded heads of flattened achenes. Another distinctive feature is the production of underwater tubers which are used as food by ducks and shore birds.

GRASS FAMILY — *GRAMINEAE*

The Grass Family is one of the largest and most economically important families of flowering plants in the world and its members are found all over the earth's surface. Nearly two hundred native grasses are found in Alberta and many others have been introduced. Because the flowers are small and have no showy parts they are often thought by many not to be flowering plants. As a family they are annual or perennial herbs with hollow stems and long, narrow, strap-shaped leaves which sheath the main stem at the joints. The flowers are variously arranged in small spikelets and these in turn are arranged in spikes or clusters. They have either stamens or pistils or both and a number of small bracts or scales. The flowers are wind-pollinated and during the summer months large quantities of pollen are shaken into the air. After fertilization the flowers are replaced by small, seed-like fruits called grains. Grasses make up the natural grasslands of every continent: the Campos and Pampas of South America, the Veldt of South Africa, the Steppes of Russia and Asia, and the Prairies of North America. Grasses are found on the sandy shores of oceans and beside large inland lakes, on the tundra, on semi-deserts, on the marshy shores of sloughs, ponds, lakes and rivers and in valleys and on high alpine meadows. Oats, wheat, rye, corn, barley rice, sugar cane and bamboo belong to the Grass Family as well as all our rangeland, pasture and lawn grasses.

FOXTAIL BARLEY
Hordeum jubatum

Photo. p. 20
Perennial

FLOWERS:	Greenish to purple; minute, with awns 1 - 2 inches long; many in showy plume-like clusters; 3 stamens; 1 pistil.
FRUIT:	A small, seed-like grain.
LEAVES:	Narrow, clasping the stems at the joints.
HEIGHT:	9 - 24 inches.
HABITAT:	Fields, roadsides and waste places.
DISTRIBUTION:	Very common, throughout Alberta. June - August.

The foxtail-like plumes of this hardy perennial grass are familiar and are seen waving on moist and saline flats, low fields, roadsides and waste places. Each plume is made up of long, bristle-like appendages called awns and they range in colour from green to silver and from gold to bronze and are sometimes purple. It is edible before flowering but in hay, the long prickly awns cause a serious inflammation in the mouths of cattle and horses. Although the seeds are minute, this is the plant from which the agronomists have evolved the plump nutritious grains of our cultivated barley.

SEDGE FAMILY — *CYPERACEAE*

Members of this large and very diverse family of grass-like or rush-like plants grow in shallow water, low swampy ground and sometimes in very dry localities. They are mostly perennials with fibrous roots and a creeping underground stem that gives rise to aerial stems which are often three-sided. In some species, the leaves are long and narrow, in others they are small, and in still others they are absent. The flowers are small and arranged in spikes or spikelets, with the flowers having only three stamens, one pistil and a few bristles or scales. Together with reeds, rushes and swamp grasses, they constitute the vegetation along sloughs, lakes and sluggish streams and provide protective cover, nesting sites and food for many water and shore birds. No less than one hundred and fifty members of the Sedge Family occur in Alberta.

COTTON GRASS
Eriophorum angustifolium

Photo. p. 21
Perennial

FLOWERS:	Yellow-green; very small; several in the axils of scales arranged in spikelets in a terminal head of silky bristles; 1 - 3 stamens; 1 pistil.
FRUIT:	A head of white silky filamentous achenes, ¾ - 1¼ inches long.
LEAVES:	All basal, long, narrow, grass-like.
HEIGHT:	8 - 30 inches.
HABITAT:	Muskegs, wet ditches and boggy marshes.
DISTRIBUTION:	Fairly common throughout Alberta. June - August.

The Cotton Grass is a plant of the muskegs and boggy marshes where its snow-white cottony plume is one of the most striking features of the vegetation. The flowers are small and are arranged in spikelets at the end of the wand-like stem. Until pollination has occurred, this plant could be mistaken for almost any other sedge, but once the cotton-like seed heads are mature, it is easily recognized. It is a hardy perennial and one species of cotton grass extends northwards well into the Arctic tundra.

COMMON GREAT BULRUSH Photo. p. 21
Scirpus validus *Perennial*

FLOWERS: Reddish-yellow-green; numerous in showy, drooping clusters at or near the end of the long round coarse green stem.

FRUIT: A cluster of brownish achenes.

LEAVES: Absent.

HEIGHT: 2 - 8 feet.

HABITAT: Shallow water and margins of sloughs and lakes.

DISTRIBUTION: Common throughout Alberta. June - July.

Along the shoreline of lakes and sloughs, the waving whip-like stems of the Common Great Bulrush are a familiar sight. No other grass-like or rush-like plant has this distinguishing feature. Not only does a stem bear tight clusters of grass-like flowers near its end, but in the absence of leaves it takes over the duty of photosynthesis as well. The stem, if cut across, is made up of a white spongy porous tissue filled with air, which gives buoyancy to underwater parts, and supplies the roots with oxygen.

GOLDEN SEDGE Photo. p. 25
Carex aurea *Perennial*

FLOWERS: Greenish-yellow tinged with reddish brown; small; several in terminal and lateral spikes; both staminate and pistillate.

FRUIT: A plump, orange-yellow achene.

LEAVES: Basal, long, narrow, grass-like, overtopping the flower-spikes.

HEIGHT: 4 - 12 inches.

HABITAT: Moist banks and meadows.

DISTRIBUTION: Fairly common. June - July.

As well as the cotton grasses and the bulrushes, another large group of the Sedge Family simply goes by the name of sedge. In Alberta, there are about one hundred and twenty different kinds. One of these, the Golden Sedge, is one of the best known and is widely distributed. It grows on moist banks, in meadows and in open woods. It is a bunchy plant with both leaves and flower-stems forming soft cushion-like tufts. The flowers are pale green at first but turn a striking golden brown when the small, plump achenes are mature.

GOLDEN SEDGE
(Text p. 24)

WATER ARUM
(Text p. 26)

ARUM FAMILY — *ARACEAE*

This is a well known family of marsh or aquatic perennial herbs with long creeping rootstocks which give rise to several leaves and to prominent flowering stalks. The flowers are small and inconspicuous and are borne on a long, fleshy spike or spadix partially surrounded by a petal-like bract or spathe. Only two members of the Arum Family are found in Alberta.

WATER ARUM. WILD CALLA   Photo. p. 25
Calla palustris   *Perennial*

FLOWERS:	Inconspicuous; small; many at the end of the modified stem (scape) in a thickened spike (spadix) enclosed by a large oval bract (spathe); all flowers with stamens and pistils; no sepals or petals.
FRUIT:	A dense head of red berries.
LEAVES:	Basal, oval to round heart-shaped, 2 - 4 inches long, on stalks 3 - 8 inches long.
HEIGHT:	4 - 8 inches.
HABITAT:	Swamps and shallow water.
DISTRIBUTION:	Common along the margins of the forested regions of Alberta. June - July.

The Water Arum or Wild Calla is a well known plant, but because it makes its home in shallow pools and in swampy boggy places, it is usually viewed from a distance. The showy part or so-called flower, dull greenish-white above and darker green beneath, is actually a broad leaf-like bract or spathe. The true flowers are small and inconspicuous and are crowded on a centrally placed club-like spike or spadix. After fertilization, the spathe rots away and the spadix becomes a dense, fleshy head of orange-red berries.

SWEET FLAG. CALAMUS   Not Illustrated
Acorus calamus   *Perennial*

FLOWERS:	Yellow-brown; inconspicuous; small; many on a thickened, cylindrical spike (spadix) placed at the side of the leaf-like stem (scape) which terminates in the long, green bract (spathe); sepals and petals scale-like; both stamens and pistil present.
FRUIT:	Brown, few-seeded, dry, in a dense head.
LEAVES:	Long, narrow, sword-like, sheathing the base.
HEIGHT:	1½ - 3 feet.
HABITAT:	Swamps, shallow water and low wet ground.
DISTRIBUTION:	Fairly rare along the margins of the forested regions of Alberta. June - July.

The Sweet Flag is an odd-looking marsh plant with long, flat, sword-like leaves found growing among sedges and rushes along the sides of sloughs and sluggish streams. The flowering stem or scape resembles a leaf and leads into the long, narrow, tapering, green spathe. The point at which the scape ends and the spathe begins is marked by the long, cylindrical, flowering spike or spadix which grows out at an angle on one side. After fertilization, the spadix develops into a hard cluster of dry, berry-like fruits.

DUCKWEED FAMILY — *LEMNACEAE*

The Duckweed family is one of very small, submerged or floating water plants. The flowers are so minute they are seldom seen and reproduction is mainly by budding. They over-winter as small bulblets which sink to the bottom of the pond in the fall and rise and grow into new plants in the spring. They are common in quiet waters and form an important link in the food chains of many aquatic organisms.

COMMON DUCKWEED   Photo. p. 28
Lemna minor   *Perennial*

FLOWERS: Minute, seldom formed and rarely seen.

FRUIT: A tiny, 1-seeded capsule.

LEAVES: Absent.

HEIGHT: A floating, green, leaf-like body, 1/8 - 3/16 inch across.

HABITAT: Quiet waters of lakes, ponds and sloughs.

DISTRIBUTION: Common throughout Alberta. Midsummer.

The Common Duckweed is probably the smallest and simplest of all the flowering plants. In fact, it is so small and flowers so seldom that it is often mistaken for a kind of water moss. The plant consists of a very small, thickish, green body called a thallus which floats on the water and looks like a leaf. However, it is not a leaf but a plant that is leafless and stemless and has one or two very small roots. The interior is filled with air spaces that enables it to float on the water like a little green cork and the upper surface is coated with a film of wax. Reproduction is by budding, the new plants either separating immediately or hanging together in small colonies. This kind of reproduction is so effective that it soon forms a continuous green carpet over the whole surface of the pond.

RUSH FAMILY — *JUNCACEAE*

Rushes are a common component of our marshy vegetation, but sometimes they are found in sandy soil and in open woods. They, like the sedges, are grass-like plants that grow either from fibrous roots or creeping underground stems. The leaves are either slender and round or grass-like or sometimes even reduced to scales. The flowers are small and are borne in a loosely branched or tight cluster at or near the ends of the dark green aerial stems. The flowers have usually six stamens and a single pistil and six similar bracts that simulate a row of sepals and a row of petals. The fruit is a small, dry capsule. Rushes are difficult plants to identify without the aid of a botanical key. The rush in the accompanying photograph (p. 28) shows the general features of this kind of plant. About thirty members of the Rush Family grow in Alberta.

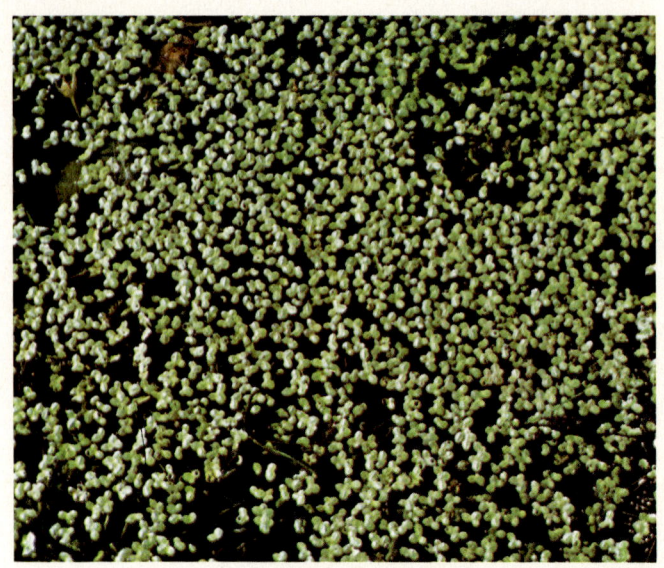

COMMON DUCKWEED
(Text p. 27)

RUSH
(Text p. 27)

28

COMMON
NODDING
ONION
(Text p. 30)

PURPLE WILD
ONION
(Text p. 30)

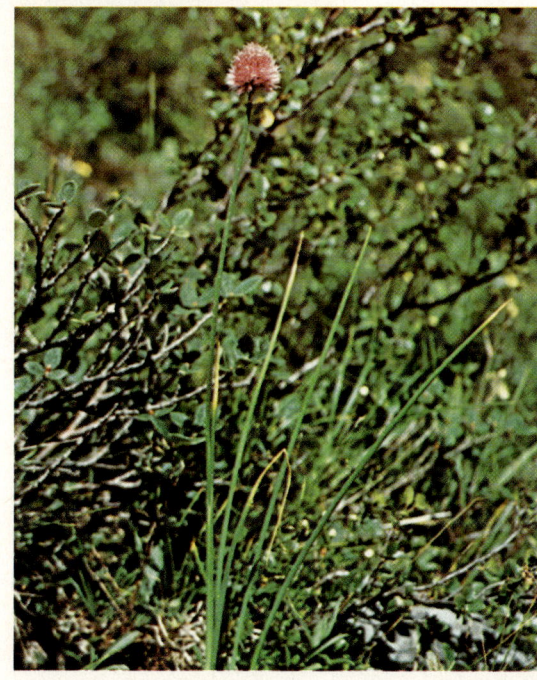

LILY FAMILY — *LILIACEAE*

A large family of perennial herbs of diverse form and habit of growth, springing from bulbs, fleshy rootstocks or rhizomes. The leaves which vary in number from few to many are shiny green and with few exceptions are noticeably parallel-veined. The conspicuous flowers are noteworthy for their simplicity and beauty. Each flower, whether borne singly or in clusters consists of 6 separate or united segments, the sepals and petals commonly alike. In most cases, there are 6 stamens and a single ovary consisting of 3 parts. The ovary matures into a dry, papery, many-seeded capsule or into a fleshy few-seeded berry. About 25 members from this large family are native to Alberta.

NODDING ONION   Photo. p. 29
Allium cernuum   *Perennial*

FLOWERS:	Pink-lavender or white; small; lily-shaped; several in a loose, nodding cluster at the end of a slender stem; each flower of 6 similar segments about ¼ inch long; 6 stamens, 3-loculed ovary; 1 style.
FRUIT:	A small, dry, few-seeded capsule.
LEAVES:	Several; narrow and not hollow.
HEIGHT:	5 - 20 inches.
HABITAT:	Open slopes, dry banks, rocky hillsides and thickets bordering open woods.
DISTRIBUTION:	Common in the parkland and prairie regions of Central and South-Central Alberta. June - August.

This gay and handsome herb, with a single, slender, flowering stem or scape and grass-like leaves, comes up every season from a coarse-necked bulb. The cluster of nodding, spreading flowers are placed so airily on the end of the leafless stem that it looks like a bursting sky-rocket. The general effect of this pretty cluster of flowers is rather like that of a single blossom, but individually each flower is like a small lavender lily. With maturity, the nodding flower-stalks or pedicels rise slowly until, by the time the seeds are ripe, the dry capsules stand stiffly erect.

PURPLE WILD ONION   Photo. p. 29
Allium schoenoprasum var. *sibiricum*   *Perennial*

FLOWERS:	Purple or pink; small; lily-shaped; several in a tight erect cluster at the top of a slender stem; each flower of 6 similar segments about ½ inch long; 6 stamens; 3-loculed ovary; 1 style.
FRUIT:	A small dry few-seeded capsule.
LEAVES:	Several, sheathing the base from an oblong-shaped bulb, long, nearly round, hollow.
HEIGHT:	8 - 20 inches.
HABITAT:	Low ground, depressions in prairie grassland, borders of open woods, stream banks and stony river bottoms.
DISTRIBUTION:	Occurs locally throughout Alberta. July - August.

Although the Purple Wild Onion is sometimes locally abundant in moist places, it is not nearly as common as the Nodding Wild Onion. It is a handsome plant with showy purple flowers, long round hollow leaves and underground, has a true onion bulb. What is sometimes mistaken for a single large purple blossom at first glance, is actually a collection of many small flowers crowded into a tight cluster at the end of the hollow flowering stem. Each individual small flower is fastened by a short stalk and is like an enlongated lily bell.

PRAIRIE ONION
Allium textile

Photo. p. 32
Perennial

FLOWERS:	White or pale pink; small; lily-shaped; several in a small cluster at the end of the slender stem; each flower of 6 similar segments about ¼ inch long; 6 stamens; 3-loculed pistil; 1 style.
FRUIT:	A small, dry, few-seeded capsule.
LEAVES:	Two, grooved, very narrow.
HEIGHT:	3 - 10 inches.
HABITAT:	Dry prairie hillsides.
DISTRIBUTION:	Common throughout the prairie region. May - June.

The Prairie Onion is widely distributed over dry plains and hillsides and is very abundant wherever it is found. Like all onions, it has a characteristic bulb, grass-like, fleshy leaves and a strong odour but is easily distinguished from the others by its small stature and white flowers. The flowers are borne in a small, erect cluster and each flower is a small, white lily. This plant appears early in the season when the prairie grasses are just beginning to show new signs of life.

MARIPOSA LILY
Calochortus apiculatus

Photo. p. 32
Perennial

FLOWERS:	Yellowish-white; 1 - 4 borne at the end of the rather weak stem; each flower of 3 broad, spreading petals, the upper surface hairy and sometimes tinged with purple; 3 sepals shorter than the petals and greenish at first; 6 stamens; 3-loculed ovary and 3-lobed stigma.
FRUIT:	A nodding, 3-angled, dry, papery, many-seeded capsule, about 1 inch long.
LEAVES:	1; basal, ¼ - ½ inch wide, shorter than the stem.
HEIGHT:	4 - 12 inches.
HABITAT:	Dry, open slopes, rocky ridges, and at the edge of woods.
DISTRIBUTION:	Foothills and mountain regions in Southwestern Alberta. June - July.

When found growing in small clumps, these rather delicate plants with their wide-spreading petals resemble a swarm of broad-winged yellow-white butterflies. Hence the name, Mariposa Lily which is Spanish for butterfly. The thick, fleshy bulb was relished by both the Plains Indians and early settlers as a food, rich in starch. Both its beauty and its practical use have caused Annora Brown to describe the Mariposa Lily as "one of those many plants that have everything".

31

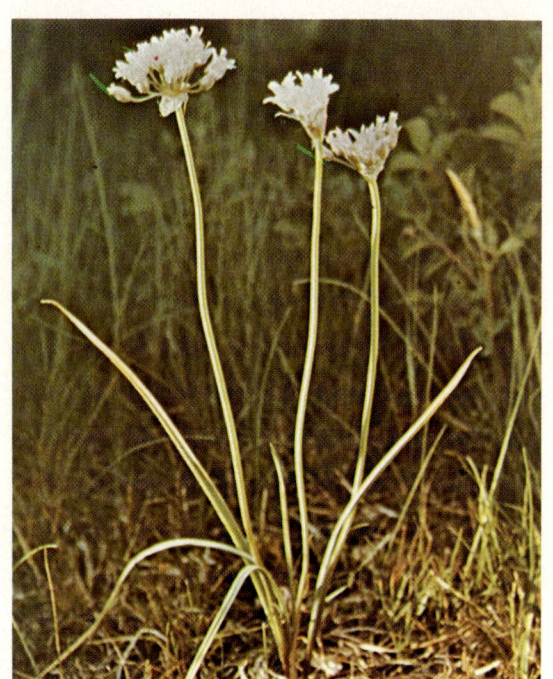

PRAIRIE ONION
(Text p. 31)

R. C. SWEET

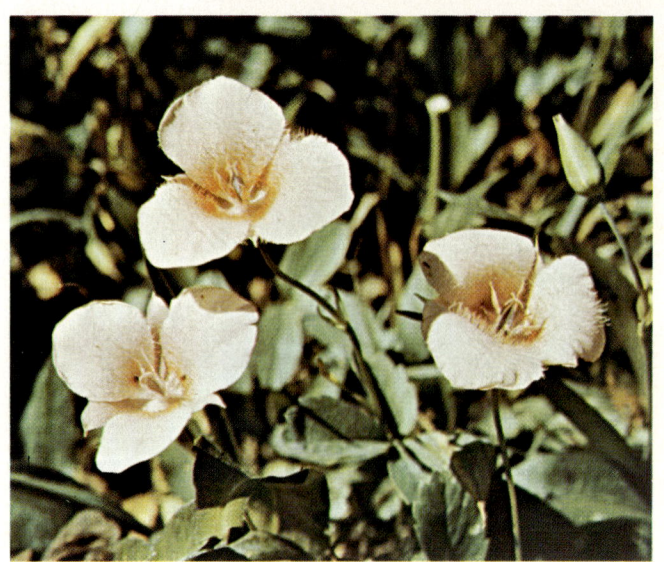

J. CLAESSEN

MARIPOSA LILY
(Text p. 31)

BLUE CAMAS
(Text p. 34)

ONE-FLOWERED CLINTONIA
(Text p. 34)

BLUE CAMAS
Camassia quamash

Photo. p. 33
Perennial

FLOWERS:	Blue or purple-blue; ½ - 1 inch long; borne in an open terminal raceme; each flower of 6 separate, similar, blue segments; 6 stamens; 3-loculed pistil; 3-lobed stigma.
FRUIT:	An ovoid, 3-angled capsule.
LEAVES:	Mostly basal, narrow, grass-like, 8 - 15 inches long.
HEIGHT:	1 - 2 feet.
HABITAT:	Moist depressions, marshy land near ponds and lakes, low grasslands and roadsides.
DISTRIBUTION:	Extreme southwestern corner of Alberta. June - July.

The Blue Camas is truly a western plant growing in wet meadows and moist bottomlands from June well into July. The completely separated purple-blue segments make the flowers appear ragged and somewhat uneven. Collectively, these plants form a sheet of startling blue which contrasts vividly with the drab gray-green of the waving grasses. Annora Brown describes some interesting anecdotes and Indian superstitions connected with the cooking of these thick, onion-like bulbs.

ONE-FLOWERED CLINTONIA. QUEEN CUP.
Clintonia uniflora

Photo. p. 33
Perennial

FLOWERS:	White, solitary, of 6 similar segments.
FRUIT:	A dark blue berry.
LEAVES:	2 - 4, basal, shiny green, 4 - 8 inches long by 1 - 2 inches broad.
HEIGHT:	Up to 6 inches.
HABITAT:	Moist shady coniferous woods.
DISTRIBUTION:	Common in the mountainous southwest corner of Alberta. June - July.

Whether it is known by the scientific name *Clintonia* or by the common name Queen Cup, this is one of our most beautiful mountain flowering plants. The former name honours De Witt Clinton, an early governor of the state of New York, while the latter calls attention to the snow-white chalice of its blossom. The plant with its sheath of basal leaves closely resembles the cultivated Lily-of-the-Valley. The Queen Cup commonly grows in clumps, the large glossy green leaves blanketing the solid mat of soft feathery mosses which hides the slender creeping perennial rootstock. By the end of August, the flower stalk bears a single, round, dark blue berry, just as beautiful in its own way as the flower it has replaced.

FAIRY BELLS   Photo. p. 36
Disporum trachycarpum   *Perennial*

FLOWERS:	Whitish or greenish-yellow; 1 - 4 drooping from slender stalks at the ends of the leafy stems; each miniature lily flower ½ - ¾ inch long; of 6 separate, similar segments.
FRUIT:	A large, soft, orange-red berry.
LEAVES:	Numerous on weak, spreading stalks, clasping; oval or lance-shaped.
HEIGHT:	12 - 30 inches.
HABITAT:	Moist, shady, poplar or mixed woods and thickets.
DISTRIBUTION:	Common throughout the wooded areas of Alberta. May - June.

Blooming well before the leaves on the trees are fully expanded, one has only to stray a few feet from the trail to spot this familiar woodland plant. At first glance, it can be mistaken for one of its close relatives, the Twisted Stalk or Solomon's Seal, but on closer inspection it can be distinguished by its flowers which hang down like greenish-white jewels at the ends of the leafy stalks. In the bud, they are closed and bell-shaped but once they begin to open the completely separated segments make them appear torn or ragged. Although the flowers last only a few days, the resulting soft, cushion-shaped, orange-red berries require the whole summer to ripen. By the autumn, the leafy stalks have died down to the thick underground stem and the berries are lying on the ground.

GLACIER LILY. DOG-TOOTH VIOLET   Photo. p. 36
Erythronium grandiflorum   *Perennial*

FLOWERS:	Bright yellow; pendant; one or two on a slender stalk; each lily flower about ¾ - 2 inches long; of 6 similar separate segments; recurved at the tips; 6 stamens; 3-lobed stigma.
FRUIT:	A dry, triangular-shaped, many-seeded capsule.
LEAVES:	Commonly 2 from the base of the stem, lance-shaped to oval lance-shaped, somewhat sharp pointed; 4 - 8 inches.
HEIGHT:	4 - 16 inches.
HABITAT:	Rich soil in moist coniferous woods, thinly wooded slopes and meadows, near banks of melting snow.
DISTRIBUTION:	From foothills to timberline in the Rocky Mountains. May - June.

Standing out like splashes of yellow gold against the dark green of pine and spruce and the white of melting snow, large colonies of this diminutive lily can be seen early in May. The name Dog-tooth Violet is a misnomer, for the flower of this plant with its six similar segments, six stamens and three-loculed pistil meets all the requirements for full membership in the Lily Family. As the flower matures, the showy segments bend sharply backwards exposing the stamens and pistil to full view. After the showy parts of the flower have withered, the ovary grows to several times its original size and develops within a few weeks into a dry, papery, many-seeded capsule.

FAIRY BELLS
(Text p. 35)

GLACIER LILY
(Text p. 35)

36

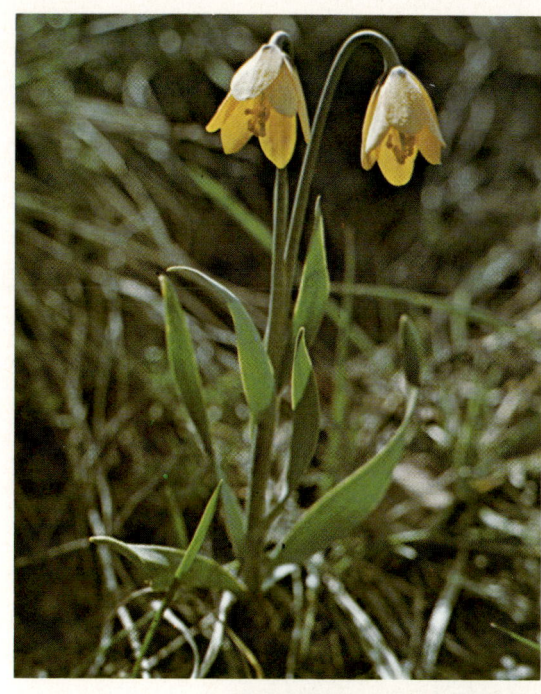

YELLOW BELL
(Text p. 38)

LUCILLE J. COSSINS

WILD-LILY-OF-
THE-VALLEY
(Text p. 38)

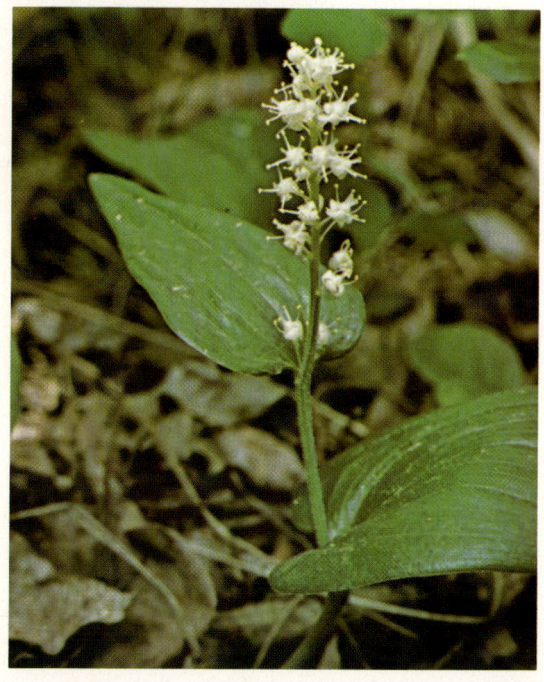

A. G. SAXBY

37

YELLOW BELL.   **FRITILLARIA**   Photo. p. 37
Fritillaria pudica   *Perennial*

FLOWERS: Pale greenish-yellow, faintly striped with purple,
                  turning orange to brown with age; usually 1; nodding;
                  somewhat cup-shaped of 6 similar, separate, segments
                  about ¾ inch long; 6 stamens; 3-loculed ovary;
                  3-cleft style.

FRUIT: A dry, papery, many-seeded capsule.

LEAVES: Few, narrowly oblong to lance-shaped.

HEIGHT: 4 - 12 inches.

HABITAT: Dry hillsides and stony mountain slopes.

DISTRIBUTION: Southwestern Alberta. May.

This small but showy member of the Lily Family has a single yellow
flower that hangs down like a bell at the end of a rather weak stem. The
fritillarias are native to both the New and the Old World and some of
the most popular species are under cultivation. A particularly beautiful
European species, the Chequered Lily, is renowned for its rose-pink bell,
chequered or mottled with maroon. The bell of our only Alberta species,
is not chequered but is etched faintly with fine purple lines.

WILD LILY-OF-THE-VALLEY   Photo. p. 37
Maianthemum canadense var. *interius*   *Perennial*

FLOWERS: White; small; numerous, in a short cluster at the end
                  of the leafy stem; each flower of 4 similar, spreading
                  segments and 4 stamens, 2-loculed ovary and stigma,
                  2-lobed.

FRUIT: A cluster of small, round, red berries.

LEAVES: 2 - 3 short-stalked, light green, upper leaves; 1 long-
                  stalked basal leaf, oval to lance-shaped, heart-shaped
                  at the base, ¾ - 3 inches long.

HEIGHT: 2 - 8 inches.

HABITAT: Moist, mixed woods and thickets.

DISTRIBUTION: Common and widely distributed in wooded regions
                  throughout the Province. May - June.

Growing through thick moss, through last year's leaves, and commonly
found under pine or aspen or shrubs, this small plant with its shiny leaves
and spire-like cluster of tiny flowers is familiar to every naturalist. Although
very small, each flower has the look of the lily about it, but when examined
under a hand lens, two of the customary six segments and two of the six
stamens are found to be missing. After fertilization, what was formerly a
tight cluster of minute flowers becomes an open bunch of pale red,
translucent berries.

FALSE SOLOMON'S SEAL   Photo. p. 40
Smilacina racemosa var. *amplexicaulis*   *Perennial*

FLOWERS:	White; minute; numerous in a dense cluster at the end of a leafy stem; each flower of 6 similar segments; 6 stamens; 3-loculed ovary; 1 style and 3-lobed stigma.
FRUIT:	A cluster of round, red berries.
LEAVES:	6 - 12 on a stem; oval to broadly lance-shaped; sharply pointed, 2 - 6 inches long; sessile or with very short petioles.
HEIGHT:	1 - 3 feet.
HABITAT:	Moist woods and thickets.
DISTRIBUTION:	Common throughout wooded areas of Alberta. June-July.

A beautiful woodland plant, with wand-like leafy branches, which comes up every spring from a thick, fleshy, underground stem. Although it resembles some of its close relatives in general appearance and in the luxuriance of its foliage, it can be distinguished by a dense cluster of minute white flowers at the ends of the leafy stems. Small as they are, each little flower has all the earmarks of a miniature lily. Each flower cluster develops into a bunch of pale red, purple-dotted berries.

THREE-LEAVED SOLOMON'S SEAL   Photo. p. 40
Smilacina trifolia   *Perennial*

FLOWERS:	White; small; few in number; borne in an open cluster; each flower of 6 separate, similar segments, 6 stamens, 3-loculed ovary.
FRUIT:	A cluster of dark red berries.
LEAVES:	Usually 3, shiny, dark green, clasping the stem, 1½ - 4 inches long.
HEIGHT:	Up to 8 inches.
HABITAT:	Bogs and wet woods, marshy or mossy borders of ponds and lakes.
DISTRIBUTION:	Common throughout parkland and mixed wooded regions of Alberta. May - June.

The smallest of the solomon seals, this plant is distinguished from the others by three shiny green leaves and an open spike of small white flowers. It superficially resembles the Wild Lily-of-the-Valley, but differs in the structure of the flowers which have the normal complement of six similar segments and six stamens. It is often found growing in great profusion in wet woods, bogs and marshy ground.

FALSE SOLOMON'S SEAL
(Text p. 39)

THREE-LEAVED SOLOMON'S SEAL
(Text p. 39)

STAR-
FLOWERED
SOLOMON'S
SEAL
(Text p. 42)

BRONZE BELLS
(Text p. 42)

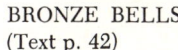

LILY FAMILY — *LILIACEAE*

STAR-FLOWERED SOLOMON'S SEAL   Photo. p. 41

Smilacina stellata   *Perennial*

FLOWERS: White; small; few to several borne at the ends of the leafy zigzag stems; each flower star-shaped of 6 separate, similar segments, 6 stamens; 3-loculed ovary.

FRUIT: A cluster of round, green berries with black stripes.

LEAVES: Many, with clasping bases, somewhat stiffly arranged along the whole length of the stem, often folded along the midrib, 1 - 5 inches long.

HEIGHT: 8 - 24 inches.

HABITAT: Moist river banks, open woods, thickets and fields.

DISTRIBUTION: Common and widely distributed in the wooded and parkland areas of Alberta. June - July.

This is a very familiar plant which we often brush against at the edge of thickets and along the sides of woodland paths and that often goes unnoticed. It is true the flowers are small and short-lived, but the stiff, zigzag stems with their abundance of blue-green leaves are worthy of notice. By the time they have died down in the fall, more than enough food has been manufactured and stored in the underground stem to insure the development of a new lot of leafy stems next spring.

BRONZE BELLS   Photo. p. 41

Stenanthium occidentale   *Perennial*

FLOWERS: Greenish-brown or greenish-purple; several, nodding on a slender stalk; each lily-shaped flower about ½ inch long, of six similar segments.

FRUIT: A small, dry, 3-beaked capsule.

LEAVES: Few, mainly basal, grass-like from a slender weak stem.

HEIGHT: 12 - 18 inches.

HABITAT: Moist, mossy coniferous woods.

DISTRIBUTION: Rocky Mountains and southern foothills. July.

This is not a rare plant, but like so many of our forest plants growing in remote foothill and mountainous regions, it is rarely seen. Once observed, it is a plant never-to-be-forgotten and one to be diligently looked for. The common name, Bronze Bells, refers to the unusual colour of the drooping bell-shaped flowers. However, close examination shows each flower with its six separate, similar segments and six stamens to be a diminutive lily. The elongated bulb buried in solid moss at the side of a mountain stream is another feature this plant has in common with many other members of the Lily Family.

42

TWISTED STALK
Streptopus amplexifolius

Photo. p. 44
Perennial

FLOWERS:	Greenish-white; pendant; borne singly or in pairs at the base of almost every leaf, their delicate stalks twisted or sharply bent; each flower of 6 similar lance-shaped segments; ¼ - ½ inch long.
FRUIT:	A drooping red berry, obscured by the leaves.
LEAVES:	Numerous, alternate, oval, clasping the forking stem, 2 - 5 inches long.
HEIGHT:	1 - 3 feet.
HABITAT:	Moist woods and shady streamsides.
DISTRIBUTION:	Foothills and Rocky Mountains. June - July.

The Twisted Stalk commonly grows along mossy streams in the deep shade of spruce and pine. It is a handsome plant with a short, fleshy, underground stem which gives rise each spring to a new lot of long, graceful, leafy stems. Looking down on this plant from above, it appears to be all leaves but on turning over the stems many, small, greenish-white flowers can be seen. Each lily-like flower dangles at the end of a fragile, sharply bent or twisted flower-stalk from which this plant derives its common name. After fertilization, the flowers are replaced by round or oval-shaped red berries which like the flowers are also invisible from above.

FALSE ASPHODEL
Tofieldia glutinosa

Photo. p. 44
Perennial

FLOWERS:	White or greenish-white; small; borne in a dense cluster or spike at the end of the sticky, scape-like stem; each flower of 6 separate, similar segments ⅛ - ¼ inch long; 6 stamens; 3-loculed ovary; 3 styles.
FRUIT:	A yellowish or orange, many-seeded capsule.
LEAVES:	Several, mainly basal, grass-like, 2 - 8 inches long.
HEIGHT:	4 - 20 inches.
HABITAT:	Mossy mounds, low ground at the edge of calcareous bogs and shores of forest ponds and lakes.
DISTRIBUTION:	Fairly common and widely spread throughout Alberta. July.

To the bird watcher, plant hunter or anyone who does not mind getting his feet wet at the edge of a forest pond or quaking bog, the False Asphodel is a well-known plant. The flowers, though small, are conspicuous, the purple anthers standing out like black dots against the white background of the expanded segments. The sticky nature of the upper portion of the flowering stem is distinctive. In another species, *Tofieldia pusilla*, occupying the same kind of habitat, the stems are thinner and not sticky.

TWISTED
STALK,
MATURE FRUIT
(Text p. 43)

DORTHEA CALVERLEY

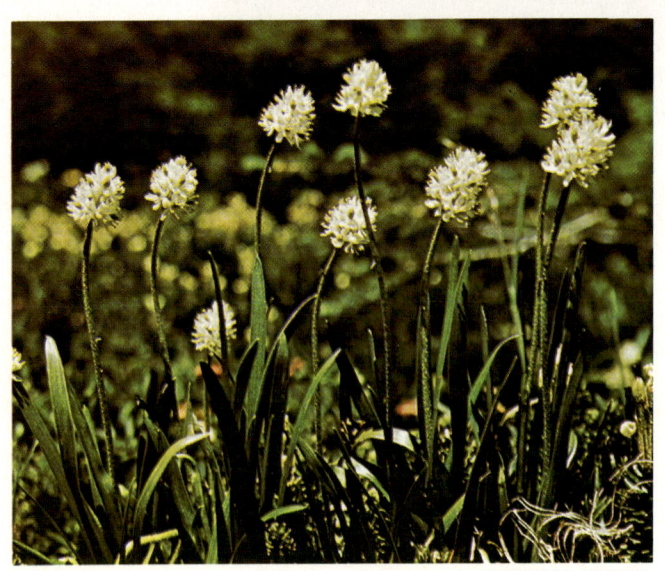

KATHLEEN HODGES

FALSE ASPHODEL
(Text p. 43)

44

FALSE
HELLEBORE
(Text p. 46)

JULIE HRAPKO

BEAR GRASS
(Text p. 46)

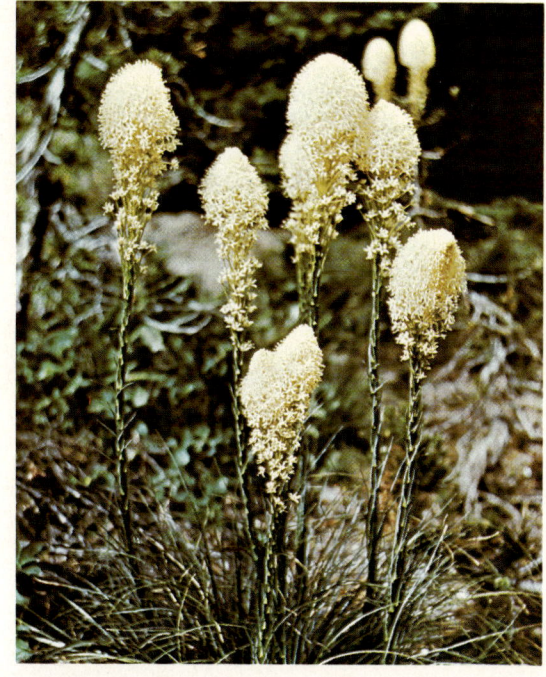

JULIE HRAPKO

FALSE HELLEBORE   Photo. p. 45
Veratrum eschscholtzii   *Perennial*

FLOWERS:	Greenish-yellow; numerous in a large, branched terminal stalk; each flower of 6 similar, separate segments about ⅜ inch long; 6 stamens; 3-lobed ovary and 3 short styles.
FRUIT:	An egg-shaped, dry, many seeded capsule; about 1 inch long.
LEAVES:	Many, over-lapping, yellowish-green, oval, prominently parallel-veined, clasping the stem at the base, 4 - 8 inches long.
HEIGHT:	3 - 6 feet.
HABITAT:	Rich soil, swamps, clearings in damp woods, moist meadows.
DISTRIBUTION:	Rocky Mountains. July - August.

This stout coarse plant grows from a thick rootstock with a single leafy stem topped by tassels of small greenish-yellow flowers. From a distance the False Hellebore looks like a stalk of Indian Corn and seems out of place in a mountain setting. If eaten, the leaves and rootstalks are extremely poisonous.

BEAR GRASS   Photo. p. 45
Xerophyllum tenax   *Perennial*

FLOWERS:	Creamy-white; small; very numerous in a large dense terminal cluster; each flower of 6 similar, separate segments about 5/16 inch long; 6 stamens; 3-loculed ovary; 1 thread-like style.
FRUIT:	A small, dry, oval capsule.
LEAVES:	Many, mainly in dense clumps at the base of the slender stalk, narrow, grass-like, strong and flexible, about 2 feet long.
HEIGHT:	2 - 4 feet.
HABITAT:	Open dry forests and mountain slopes.
DISTRIBUTION:	The mountainous southwest corner of Alberta. June-July.

A mountain species with a spectacular four-foot flower stalk growing out of a thatch of long, wiry leaves and capped by a torch-like cluster of hundreds of small cream-coloured flowers. Once seen, this "mop-topped" plant is never forgotten. The individual flowers are miniature lilies. After the return of the Lewis and Clark expedition, it was given the scientific name *Xerophyllum tenax*—the dry leaf that holds fast—because of its tough pliable leaves. The Rocky Mountain Indians used them to make watertight baskets.

SPANISH BAYONET. YUCCA

Yucca glauca

Photo. p. 48
Perennial

FLOWERS:	Greenish-white; large; 1 - 2 inches across; many, drooping, crowded in a long spike; each flower of six similar segments.
FRUIT:	An oblong many-seeded capsule.
LEAVES:	Many, basal, stiff, narrow, tapering to a sharp point, 8 - 16 inches long.
HEIGHT:	6 - 36 inches.
HABITAT:	Dry slopes.
DISTRIBUTION:	One locality in Southern Alberta. June - July.

The Yucca is a rare exotic growing locally in the extreme southern part of Alberta, south of Manyberries and close to the International Border. It is a strange looking plant with a brush of stiff grass-like leaves and a stout woody stem ending in a dense spike of lily-shaped flowers. Its dependency on one kind of insect, the Pronuba moth, for pollination is an interesting illustration of flower-insect relationship. Neither one can complete its life-history without the other.

WHITE CAMAS. GREEN LILY

Zygadenus elegans

Photo. p. 48
Perennial

FLOWERS:	Greenish or yellowish-white; small; lily-shaped in an open raceme; each flower of 6 similar widely-spreading segments, about ⅜ inch long; 6 stamens, 3-loculed ovary; 3 styles.
FRUIT:	A dry, 3-lobed many-seeded capsule.
LEAVES:	Several, grass-like, mainly basal, pale green with a whitish bloom and prominent keeled midrib.
HEIGHT:	1 - 2 feet.
HABITAT:	Moist meadows, grassy or open wooded slopes.
DISTRIBUTION:	Foothills and Rocky Mountains. July - August.

A graceful foothill and mountain plant found growing in many different places and at most elevations. The greenish-white, six-parted flowers grouped in an open cluster at the end of the slender stem, look like miniature lilies. The onion-like bulb is thought to be poisonous to livestock.

SPANISH BAYONET
(Text p. 47)

WHITE CAMAS
(Text p. 47)

48

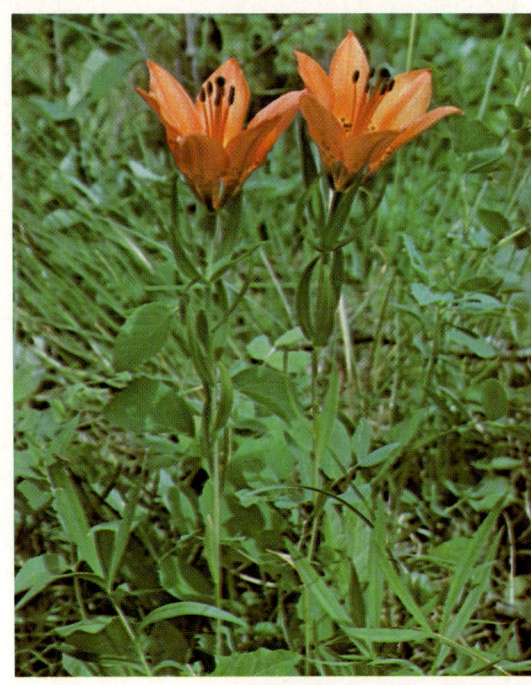

**WESTERN
WOOD LILY**
(Text p. 50)

A. KARVONEN

**BLUE EYED
GRASS**
(Text p. 51)

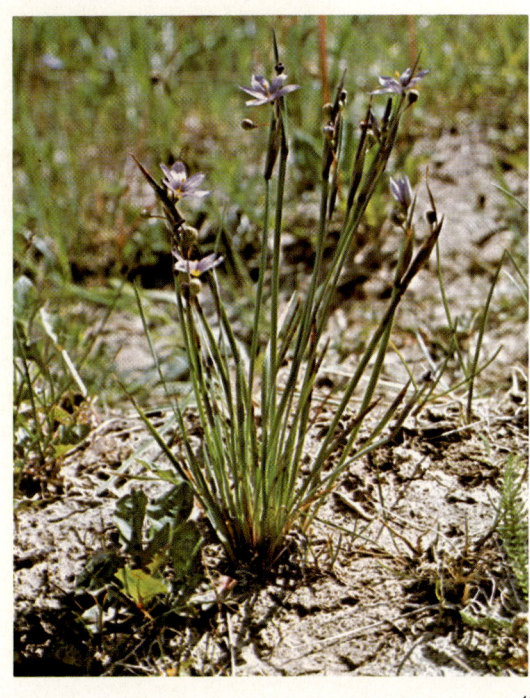

JULIE HRAPKO

49

DEATH CAMAS
Not Illustrated
Zygadenus gramineus

FLOWERS:	Pale yellow; small lily-shaped; numerous; arranged compactly in a raceme at the end of the slender stem; each flower of 6 similar, separate segments about 3/16 inch long; 6 stamens; 3-loculed ovary; 3 styles.
FRUIT:	A small, dry, many-seeded capsule.
LEAVES:	Several, grass-like, all sheathing at the base.
HEIGHT:	8 - 14 inches.
HABITAT:	Grassy slopes and fields, and around grassy sloughs.
DISTRIBUTION:	Common in South Central and Southwestern Alberta. May - June.

This fairly common rangeland plant is distinguished from its close relative, the White Camas, by its more compact spike of smaller flowers. If eaten, the onion-like bulb is very poisonous to children and to stock animals, especially sheep. This is one of the first rangeland plants to push up and turn green in the spring and consequently serious losses of stock animals occur at that time.

WESTERN WOOD LILY
Photo. p. 49
Lilium philadelphicum var. *andinum*
Perennial

FLOWERS:	Orange or orange-red with black spots; about 2½ inches long; commonly 1 - 3 erect on stem; sepals and petals, each 3, similar; 6 stamens and a 3-loculed ovary with a single style and 3-lobed stigma.
FRUIT:	A dry, egg-shaped capsule.
LEAVES:	Many, smooth, linear to lance-shaped, alternate except the uppermost which are whorled.
HEIGHT:	1 - 2 feet.
HABITAT:	Dry fields and hills, moist meadows, thickets, woodland borders, roadsides and railroad embankments.
DISTRIBUTION:	Common, widespread throughout Alberta. June - July.

The Western Wood Lily grows in so many different places that it is known to everyone. The simplicity of the flower with all the parts in threes or in multiples of three and the orange-red showy parts similar and separate, sets the pattern for membership in the Lily family. This lily was officially adopted as Saskatchewan's floral emblem in 1941 and appears now on a 5c Canadian commemorative stamp issued in 1966.

IRIS FAMILY — *IRIDACEAE*

Perennial herbs with tuberous, bulbous or creeping rootstocks and vertical sword-shaped leaves, commonly found in wet or moist places. The showy flowers consist of a perianth of 6 segments, all coloured and petal-like, in 2 series of 3 each; 3 stamens, a single 3-loculed ovary and 1 style ending in 3 stigmas. Only two members of the Iris Family are native to Alberta.

BLUE-EYED GRASS   Photo. p. 51
Sisyrinchium montanum   *Perennial*

FLOWERS: Blue-violet; produced one at a time in a small cluster; perianth of 6 nearly alike, spreading segments about ⅜ inch long; 3 stamens; 3-loculed ovary; 3-branched style.

FRUIT: A small, round capsule.

LEAVES: Mostly basal, grass-like.

HEIGHT: 4 - 16 inches.

HABITAT: Low, moist meadows and grassy margins of streams and ponds.

DISTRIBUTION: Common throughout Alberta. June.

Although this plant belongs to the Iris Family, the flower in no way resembles the well-known Flag or Fleur-de-lis of garden, ditch or pond. Indeed, this little plant with its stiff, narrow leaves looks like a grass with blue flowers and hence, its common name, Blue-Eyed Grass. Each small but showy flower is like a six-pointed blue star with a smaller six-pointed white star in its center, set off by an eye of golden yellow. Although a single flower lasts but a day, it can be truly said that it brightens every corner where it is found. In another species, *Sisyrinchium sarmentosum*, which is also found growing in moist, grassy places, the flowers are slightly smaller and are pale violet or almost white.

ORCHID FAMILY — *ORCHIDACEAE*

Perennial herbs springing from corms, bulbs or rootstocks and generally with fleshy roots. The leaves are simple, often basal and sheathing the stem. This family is remarkable for the beauty and structural diversity of the flowers. These are perfect and occur few to many on a spike, or solitary at the end of the stem. Each flower has 3 similar sepals, often petal-like, 3 petals, 2 of which are lateral and alike and the middle one (lip) variously modified with the basal portion sometimes contracted into a nectar-containing spur. With the exception of the lady slippers, the stamens are united with the style into a central column, the solitary anther facing the lip, directly above the sticky stigma with the pollen grains lumped into waxy masses (pollinia). The ovary which is inferior, 1-loculed, long and twisted, matures into a 3-valved papery capsule containing countless dust-like seeds. The roots are invested with a fungal growth which enables the plant to absorb water and minerals from the soil.

51

ONE-FLOWERED CLINTONIA—
BERRY

DORTHEA CALVERLEY

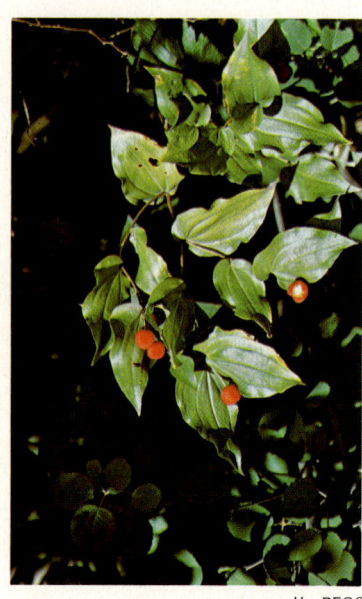

FAIRY BELLS — BERRY

H. PEGG

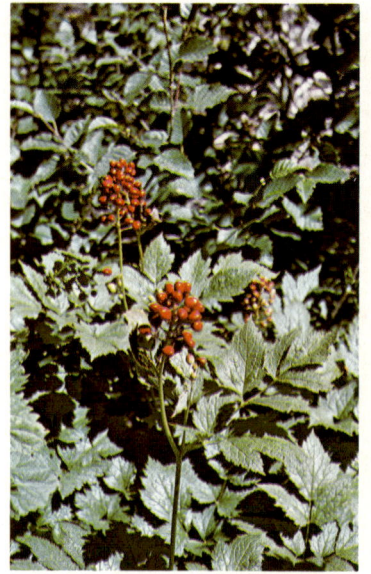

BANEBERRY (Red Variety)

R. W. SALT

BANEBERRY (White Variety)

B. R. SHANTZ

CALYPSO
(Text p. 54)

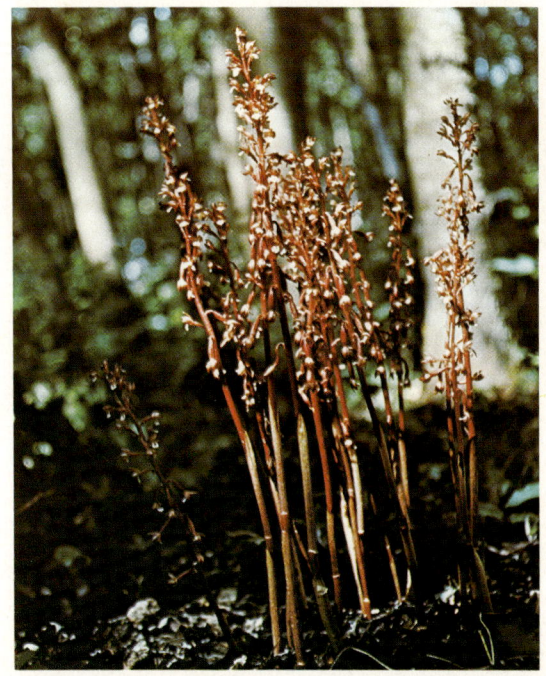

SPOTTED
CORAL
ROOT ORCHID
(Text p. 54)

53

CALYPSO. VENUS' SLIPPER

Calypso bulbosa

Photo. p. 53

Perennial

FLOWERS:	Variegated, purple, pink and yellow; sepals and lateral petals similar; lip large, sac-like, whitish with purple streaks, yellow hairy inside; about ¾ inch long.
FRUIT:	A brown, dry, many-seeded capsule.
LEAVES:	1, basal, dark green, round - oval, 1 - 1½ inches long.
HEIGHT:	3 - 7 inches.
HABITAT:	Moist to dry coniferous woods, commonly under pine.
DISTRIBUTION:	Northern and Western Alberta. Also in the Cypress Hills. June - July.

This little orchid, named after Homer's island nymph Calypso, has been described as the most beautiful of terrestrial orchids. The distinguishing feature of the flower is the unique construction of the lip, which is sometimes alluded to as a shoe. Unlike the pouch-shaped lip of the lady slippers, the overlapping edges of the lip fall down in a long, wide, whitish-rose coloured apron, spotted with purple and crowned with a plume of yellow hairs. In Alberta, Calypso is associated with mossy pine-spruce woods or sometimes with pine alone. Such is her true haunts, for as Mr. Morris in his enchanting book, "Our Wild Orchids", puts it, "To really see Calypso you must visit her secret bower of green and meet her enthroned, as she loves to be, on some mossy dias in the shadow of the evergreens".

SPOTTED CORAL-ROOT ORCHID

Corallorrhiza maculata

Photo. p. 53

Saprophyte

FLOWERS:	Purple and white; conspicuous; 10 - 40; sepals pale greenish-yellow trimmed with purple; lateral petals whitish with purple spots; lip white, spotted and blotched with purple, 3-lobed, ¼ inch long; spur yellowish, prominent.
FRUIT:	A dry, many-seeded capsule.
LEAVES:	Reduced to colourless scales and bracts sheathing the stout, purplish or yellow-brown flowering stalk.
HEIGHT:	8 - 20 inches.
HABITAT:	Dry soil, among pine and spruce needles in pine or spruce-pine woods.
DISTRIBUTION:	Not common but widely distributed throughout the wooded regions of Alberta. July - August.

Because it is dependent upon decaying plant material in the forest soil for nourishment, this bizarre orchid may be relatively abundant in one small corner of the forest floor one summer, and absent the next. Standing straight out or slightly downwards from the purple stem and with the lateral petals flung out like little arms, the flowers look all the world like midget acrobats on a pole. Besides colour differences, the flowers can be distinguished from those of other coral-root orchids by a conspicuous downward directed spur, united to the top of the ovary.

STRIPED CORAL-ROOT ORCHID   Photo. p. 56
Corallorrhiza striata   *Saprophyte*

FLOWERS:	Whitish, tinged and conspicuously striped with purple; drooping; conspicuous; 15 - 25; sepals and lateral petals somewhat similar, whitish, marked with 3 purple stripes; lip pure white, marked with 5 purple stripes; about ½ inch long; spurless.
FRUIT:	A dry, many-seeded capsule.
LEAVES:	Reduced to colourless scales sheathing the stout, purplish or yellow-brown flowering stalk.
HEIGHT:	8 - 20 inches.
HABITAT:	Dry soil, among pine and spruce needles in pine or mixed coniferous woods.
DISTRIBUTION:	Throughout the wooded regions of Alberta. Rare. July - August.

This orchid attracts immediate attention with its tall, stout, purple stems and large drooping flowers. As members of the Orchid Family, the flowers have the telltale lip marked in this case with broad stripes of deep purple. It is usually found growing in dry soil carpeted with needles, under the shade of pine and spruce. However, like all the other coral-root orchids, there is no predicting where or when it may be found.

PALE CORAL-ROOT ORCHID   Photo. p. 56
Corallorrhiza trifida   *Saprophyte*

FLOWERS:	Pale yellowish or yellow-green; small; 3 - 12; sepals and lateral petals greenish-yellow, similar; lip white, often spotted with purple, 3-lobed, about 1/5 inch long; spurless.
FRUIT:	A dry, many-seeded capsule.
LEAVES:	Reduced to colourless scales sheathing the yellowish flowering stalk.
HEIGHT:	3 - 11 inches.
HABITAT:	Low, moist, mossy places in thickets, coniferous and deciduous woods.
DISTRIBUTION:	Not common but widely distributed throughout the wooded regions of Alberta. June - August.

Lacking chlorophyll, this startlingly odd plant like some of our mushrooms and toadstools obtains its nourishment from decayed vegetable matter in the soil. The slender flower-stalk is pale yellow and the leaves are reduced to colourless sheathing scales. What is commonly taken to be a mass of coral-like roots is actually a cluster of short, fleshy, brittle, underground stems. The flowers, though small, have the typical orchid form. The plant itself can be distinguished from the other coral-root orchids by the pale yellow flower-stalk and by the flower with its small but conspicuously 3-lobed white or purple spotted lip. It seems relatively indifferent to soil conditions and may appear unexpectedly in the shade of coniferous trees, deciduous trees or both.

**STRIPED
CORAL ROOT
ORCHID**
(Text p. 55)

**PALE CORAL
ROOT ORCHID**
(Text p. 55)

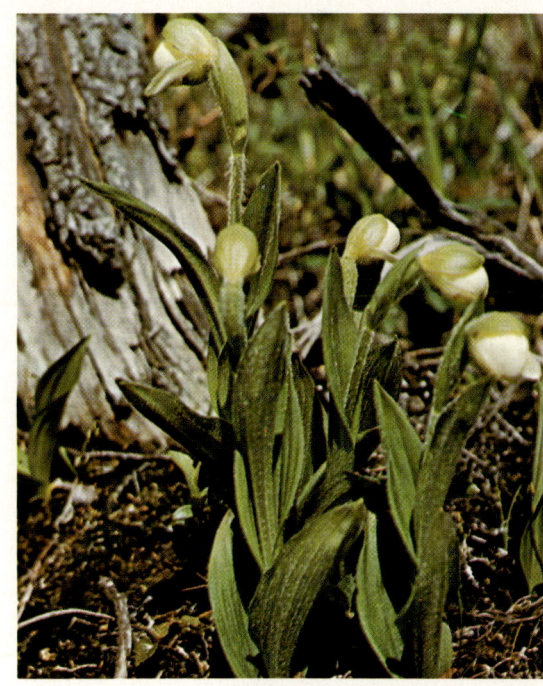

SPARROW'S EGG
LADY SLIPPER
(Text p. 58)

H. A. MacGREGOR

YELLOW LADY
SLIPPER
(Text p. 58)

G. W. MACHELL

57

ORCHID FAMILY — *ORCHIDACEAE*

YELLOW LADY SLIPPER Photo. p. 57

Cypripedium calceolus var. *pubescens* *Perennial*

FLOWERS: Yellow; 1 - 2; sepals yellowish or greenish, striped with purple, oval, lance-shaped; petals greenish-yellow to purplish-brown, spirally twisted; lip yellow, smooth, pouch-shaped, ⅔ - 1½ inches long.

FRUIT: A brown, dry, many-seeded capsule.

LEAVES: 3 - 4, oval to lance-shaped, prominently veined, 2 - 6 inches long.

HEIGHT: 4 - 16 inches.

HABITAT: Moist, rich woods and woodland bogs.

DISTRIBUTION: Wooded regions throughout Alberta. June - July.

The word orchid always brings to mind the lady slippers. For these plants with their wide leafy bases, their long graceful stems and their unique flowers are unsurpassed in elegance and charm. In Alberta, the Yellow Lady Slipper is by far the best known and most widely distributed. Like all the lady slippers, the distinctive feature of the flower is the lip inflated almost to the breaking point into a bladder-like pouch. The Yellow Lady Slipper grows in shady moist woods or moss-lined bogs. But, like all woodland plants, it enjoys fleeting moments in the sun when it shows off its gleaming slipper of pure gold to full advantage.

SPARROW'S EGG LADY SLIPPER. FRANKLIN'S LADY SLIPPER

Cypripedium passerinum *Perennial*

FLOWERS: White; 1 - 3; sepals green to olive; petals pure white, blunt oblong; lip soft white with purple dots inside, pouch-shaped, about 5/8 inch long.

FRUIT: A brown, dry, many-seeded capsule.

LEAVES: 4 - 5, oval to lance-shaped, prominently veined, somewhat soft-hairy, sheathing the stout, hairy stem, 2 - 6 inches long.

HEIGHT: 6 - 12 inches.

HABITAT: Borders of ponds and streams, deep mossy coniferous woods and bog forests.

DISTRIBUTION: Wooded regions extending west to the Rockies. June.

An exciting experience in June is to come upon a clump of stately, white lady slippers growing in the shade of tamarack and spruce. With their stems partially buried in sedgy mossy mounds, wet and cold from melted snow, these soft, pure-white slippers may remain firm and may last unfaded for several weeks in these cold-storage conditions. Another white-flowered and quite similar species, *Cypripedium montanum*, grows in the mountains of Southwestern Alberta.

RATTLESNAKE PLANTAIN
Goodyera oblongifolia

Photo. p. 60
Perennial

FLOWERS:	Greenish-white; small; numerous in a relatively long, single spiraled spike; sepals and lateral petals similar, united into a hood; lip spout-shaped; spurless.
FRUIT:	A dry, many-seeded capsule.
LEAVES:	Several in a basal rosette, dark green blotched with white, oblong, 1¼ - 2½ inches long.
HEIGHT:	Flower-stalk 6 - 16 inches.
HABITAT:	Dry coniferous woods.
DISTRIBUTION:	Not common, found occasionally in the Cypress Hills and in Western Alberta. August.

The Rattlesnake Plantain is an orchid found in coniferous woods and one which prefers conditions so dry that in August, the carpet of needles crackles under one's foot. It is easily recognized by its rosette of beautiful blue-green leaves which are variously streaked with white and have a crinkly appearance. The flowers are small and greenish-white and spiral around the upper one-third of the long, slender, leafless flower-stalk. The individual flowers have the same general shape and structure as those of the Hooded Ladies' Tresses. They have the same wide open mouth with over-hanging hood but the lip is short, grooved in the inside and shaped like a spout. Another very similar species, *Goodyera repens,* grows in the same open coniferous woods but differs slightly in leaf and flower.

TALL WHITE BOG ORCHID
Habenaria dilatata

Photo. p. 60
Perennial

FLOWERS:	White; small; sweet scented; numerous in a long dense bracted spike; sepals and lateral petals waxy white and similar; lip waxy white; lance-shaped, expanded at the base, 5/16 inch long; spur slender, sharp pointed, about as long as the lip.
FRUIT:	A dry, many-seeded capsule.
LEAVES:	Several, dark green, mostly lance-shaped, gradually reduced above to bracts, 2 - 8 inches long.
HEIGHT:	12 - 30 inches.
HABITAT:	Wet places in meadows, bogs and coniferous woods.
DISTRIBUTION:	Not common, but widely distributed mainly in foothill and mountain regions. June - August.

The Tall White Bog Orchid is one of our most attractive wild orchids. It so closely resembles the Northern Green Bog Orchid in general appearance that they can easily be taken for twins. That they are not identical twins is shown by the flowers which are of a pure waxy whiteness and have a heavy sweet perfume that is like a blending of mock orange and cloves. In mountain and foothill regions, they are found growing in bog forests, clearings, and bordering on the sedgy calcareous shores of ponds and muskeg lakes. To come upon a patch of these graceful "Tall Whites", standing by the score on the side of an abandoned forestry road, is a sight long to be remembered.

RATTLESNAKE
PLANTAIN
(Text p. 59)

JANETTE GOODWIN

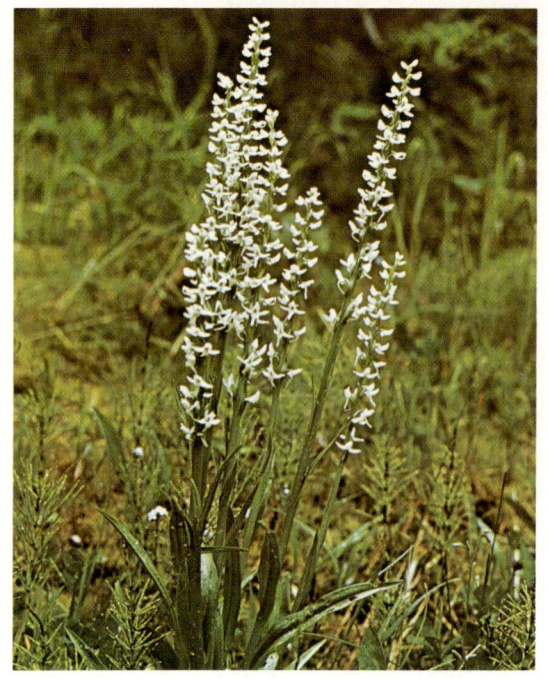

TALL WHITE
BOG ORCHID
(Text p. 59)

DORTHEA CALVERLEY

60

NORTHERN
GREEN BOG
ORCHID
(Text p. 62)

H. PEGG

BLUNT-LEAF
ORCHID
(Text p. 62)

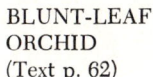

J. D. ERICKSON

61

NORTHERN GREEN BOG ORCHID

Habenaria hyperborea

Photo. p. 61

Perennial

FLOWERS:	Green or yellow-green; small; numerous in a long dense bracted spike; sepals and petals greenish and similar; lip pale green, tongue-shaped, ¼ inch long; spur club-shaped, about as long as the lip.
FRUIT:	A dry, many-seeded capsule.
LEAVES:	Several, dark green, narrow-oblong to lance-shaped, gradually reduced above to bracts, 2 - 12 inches long.
HEIGHT:	8 - 36 inches.
HABITAT:	Cool, wet woods and meadows, bog forests, borders of streams and ponds.
DISTRIBUTION:	Widely distributed in wet woods and meadows throughout Alberta. June - August.

The group of orchids called bog orchids is the largest and most varied of North American orchids. Seven species grow in Alberta and of these, the Northern Green Bog Orchid, or as it is sometimes called, the Tall Leafy Green Orchid is the most common and most widely distributed. However, it often goes unnoticed and is not always recognized as belonging to the Orchid Family. It is a tall, robust, leafy plant with a terminal spike of closely set, small, greenish flowers. Each flower is a typical little orchid and can be distinguished from those of other bog orchids by the small, green, tongue-shaped lip and club-shaped spur. With the exception of the Tall White Bog Orchid, our Alberta bog orchids are not distinguished for their beauty, but some of the eastern species with their tall, dense spikes of showy, white, yellow, orange or purple flowers, can vie with any other terrestrial orchid in the world.

BLUNT-LEAVED BOG ORCHID

Habenaria obtusata

Photo. p. 61

Perennial

FLOWERS:	Greenish-white; small; few in a relatively short, loose, bractless spike; sepals and lateral petals green, oblong lance-shaped, similar; lip pale greenish-white; narrow, lance-shaped, bent abruptly downward, about ⅜ inch long; spur slender, tapering, about as long as the lip.
FRUIT:	A dry, many-seeded capsule.
LEAVES:	1, basal, oval to spatula-shaped, blunt-tipped, tapering at the base, 2 - 5 inches long.
HEIGHT:	3 - 10 inches.
HABITAT:	Cool, mossy bogs, moist, coniferous woods, damp meadows and shaded, mossy stream banks.
DISTRIBUTION:	Fairly common locally in moist coniferous woods and in the mountains. June - August.

This small and dainty bog orchid is easily distinguished by the single, basal, blunt-tipped leaf. The otherwise bare flowering stalk causes the greenish-white flowers to appear larger than they actually are. The distinctive hood, formed by the sepals and two lateral petals, overhangs the narrow, pendent lip like a flat-topped porch. The Blunt-Leaved Bog Orchid prefers damp, shady places under spruce and spreads freely along the moss-covered sides of springs and streams.

ORCHID FAMILY — *ORCHIDACEAE*

BRACTED BOG ORCHID   Photo. p. 64
Habenaria viridis var. *bracteata*   *Perennial*

FLOWERS: Greenish; small; numerous in a long, loose, conspicu-
                  ously bracted spike; sepals green, lance-like; lateral
                  petals greenish-white, narrow, thread-like; lip greenish-
                  white, sometimes streaked with purple, spatula-shaped,
                  2 - 3 lobed at apex, about ⅜ inch long; spur sac-like,
                  very short, broad and blunt; floral bracts 2 - 4 times
                  the length of the flowers.

FRUIT: A dry, many-seeded capsule.

LEAVES: Several, dark green, oval to lance-shaped, rapidly
                  reduced above, about 2 - 5 inches long.

HEIGHT: 6 - 24 inches.

HABITAT: Damp meadows, deciduous and coniferous woods.

DISTRIBUTION: Not common but widely distributed throughout foothill
                  and mountain regions. June - July.

The Bracted Bog Orchid grows in open woods and on damp, grassy slopes. It is an erect plant with inconspicuous green flowers, separated from each other by long, tapering bracts. The bracts are much more prominent than the flowers and stand straight out from the flowering stalk. The flowers are similar in character to those of the Northern Green Bog Orchid but the lip is spatula-shaped and notched at the tip.

NORTHERN TWAYBLADE   Photo. p. 64
Listera borealis   *Perennial*

FLOWERS: Pale green; showy; several in a loose spike; sepals
                  and lateral petals green, awl-shaped; lip green, broadly
                  oblong, flat, 2-lobed, about ½ inch long; spurless.

FRUIT: A small, many-seeded capsule.

LEAVES: Opposite, simple, oval to elliptical, dark green, ½ - 2
                  inches long.

HEIGHT: 3 - 7 inches.

HABITAT: Moist, mossy woods.

DISTRIBUTION: Not common, in coniferous wooded regions of Alberta.
                  July - August.

At the edge of tiny springs and rushing mountain streams under the shade of spruce trees and always where the moss is thickest and least disturbed, one is most likely to find a twayblade orchid. As a group, they are easily recognized by their relatively small size, their two small opposite leaves and over-all unnatural green colour. The Northern Twayblade is the largest and the one most commonly found in Alberta. It is easily distinguished from the others by its broad, flat, platter-like lip. The tip of the lip is deeply cleft and at the base there are two small ear-like appendages. In colour, the lip is a transluscent pale green marked by a darker band of green down the centre. The Heart-Leaved Twayblade, *Listera cordata*, and the Broad-Leaved Twayblade, *Listera convallarioides*, grow in the same shady mossy places but are less common.

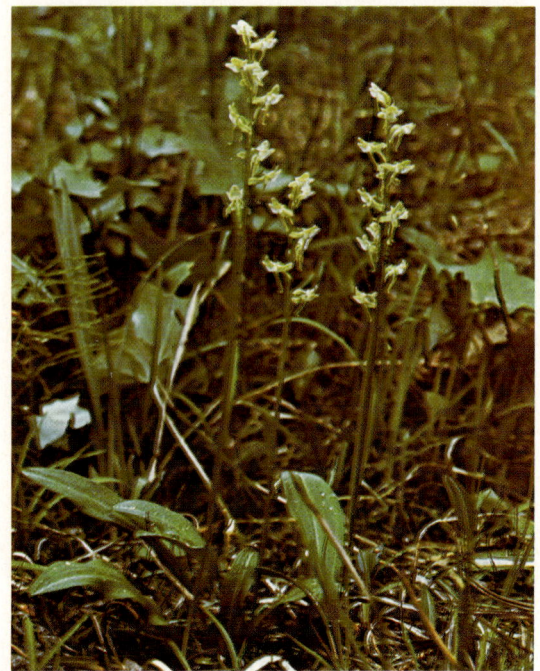

**BRACTED BOG
ORCHID**
(Text p. 63)

**NORTHERN
TWAYBLADE**
(Text p. 63)

64

ROUND-
LEAVED
ORCHID
(Text p. 66)

J. D. ERICKSON

HOODED
LADIES'
TRESSES
(Text p. 66)

A. KARVONEN

65

ORCHID FAMILY — *ORCHIDACEAE*

ROUND-LEAVED ORCHID   Photo. p. 65

Orchis rotundifolia   *Perennial*

FLOWERS:	Pink-mauve; several; bracted; sepals and lateral petals pale pinkish; lip white, spotted with purple, 3-lobed, the middle lobe large and notched at the apex, about ⅓ inch long; spur stoutish, slightly curved.
FRUIT:	A brown, dry, many-seeded capsule.
LEAVES:	1, basal, dull green, smooth, round to oval, 1½ - 3 inches long.
HEIGHT:	6 - 10 inches.
HABITAT:	Moist, coniferous woods or mixed woods under spruce.
DISTRIBUTION:	Widely distributed in wooded regions throughout Alberta. June.

This beautiful little plant extends from Newfoundland to British Columbia and even up to the Yukon. In Alberta, it can be found in boggy, mossy hollows and along stream sides in the shade of coniferous trees. Under a small, lavender-coloured hood formed by the sepals and the two lateral petals, is the white tongue-like lip, dotted with purple, which is the distinguishing feature of this flower. Occasionally, a plant with white flowers turns up while a rare variety of this plant with two broad maroon stripes on the lip instead of the usual spots has been found in the Cypress Hills.

HOODED LADIES' TRESSES   Photo. p. 65

Spiranthes romanzoffiana   *Perennial*

FLOWERS:	Creamy white; fragrant; small; numerous in a relatively short, dense, bracted, 3-ranked, twisted spike; sepals and lateral petals similar, united into a hood; lip fiddle-shaped, bent abruptly downward, about ⅜ inch long; spurless.
FRUIT:	A dry, many-seeded capsule.
LEAVES:	Several, oblong lance-shaped to linear, about 2 - 6 inches long.
HEIGHT:	3 - 16 inches.
HABITAT:	Bogs, open woods, wet meadows, wet clay banks and mossy depressions.
DISTRIBUTION:	Not common, but widely distributed throughout the Province. July - September.

Another large and widely spread group of orchids is the ladies' tresses. Only one member of this group, the Hooded Ladies' Tresses, is native to Alberta. It is by no means a common plant, but where it is found it usually occurs in abundance. The characteristic feature is the spiral arrangement of the cream-coloured flowers on the short flowering stalk. As the name suggests, the flowers are distinguished by the overhanging hood which when viewed from the side looks like the peak of an old-fashioned sunbonnet. It is found in the open woods and on damp grassy slopes and blooms well into September.

LARGE ROUND-LEAVED BOG ORCHID
Habenaria orbiculata

Photo. p. 68
Perennial

FLOWERS:	Whitish-green; conspicuous; numerous in a long, loose spike; sepals and petals lance-shaped; lip oblong and narrow, 2/3 - 4/5 inch long; spur club-shaped, up-curved at tip, 3/5 - 1½ inches long.
FRUIT:	A dry, many-seeded capsule.
LEAVES:	2, basal, flat, oval to round, dark green above, silvery beneath, 4 - 7 inches broad.
HEIGHT:	1 - 2 feet.
HABITAT:	Rich, cool, moist, mossy coniferous woods.
DISTRIBUTION:	Rare. Swan Hills and northwards. July.

One of the rarest of our Alberta orchids, the Large Round-Leaved Bog Orchid, is found only in Northern Alberta, where it grows in shady, mossy coniferous woods. It is a statuesque plant with two large, fleshy, dark green saucer-shaped leaves which lie flat on the mosses and between which rises one stout, fleshy, green flower-stalk. Besides the large leaves, this orchid is distinguished from the other bog orchids by its flowers. These are whitish-green and are beautifully and loosely arranged on a long terminal spike. The special feature of the flowers is the long, narrow, downward-pointing lip and the inch-long, club-shaped spur. It is so spectacular, so hard to find, it is the ambition of every orchid photographer to record it in his or her own collection.

NETTLE FAMILY — *URTICACEAE*

This is a family of herbaceous plants with erect, simple or branching stems, opposite leaves, inconspicuous, greenish flowers and stinging hairs. The Common Nettle exemplifies beautifully the chief features of the Nettle Family.

COMMON NETTLE
Urtica gracilis

Photo. p. 68
Perennial

FLOWERS:	Green; small; numerous in branched clusters; 4 sepals; no petals; both staminate and pistillate flowers on one plant or on separate plants.
FRUIT:	A small, flattened achene.
LEAVES:	Opposite, simple, petioled, narrowly lance-shaped, coarsely toothed, with stinging hairs.
HEIGHT:	2 - 6 feet.
HABITAT:	Damp soil, in thickets and waste places.
DISTRIBUTION:	Common and widely distributed throughout Alberta. June - July.

The Common Nettle is one plant that has nothing in its favour and like the Poison Ivy it should be given a wide berth. It grows in weedy, noisome places; its flowers are small, green and unattractive, and its stinging hairs make it most objectionable. Many plants have hairs but those of this nettle are unique. When examined with a hand lens, each hair looks like a minute glass vial with a swollen base and a needle-sharp point. On contact, the hairs break off like fine slivers of glass and discharge a chemical substance, which on penetrating the skin causes an irritating rash.

LARGE ROUND-
LEAVED
ORCHID
(Text p. 67)

DORTHEA CALVERLEY

D. S. S. CORMACK

COMMON NETTLE
(Text p. 67)

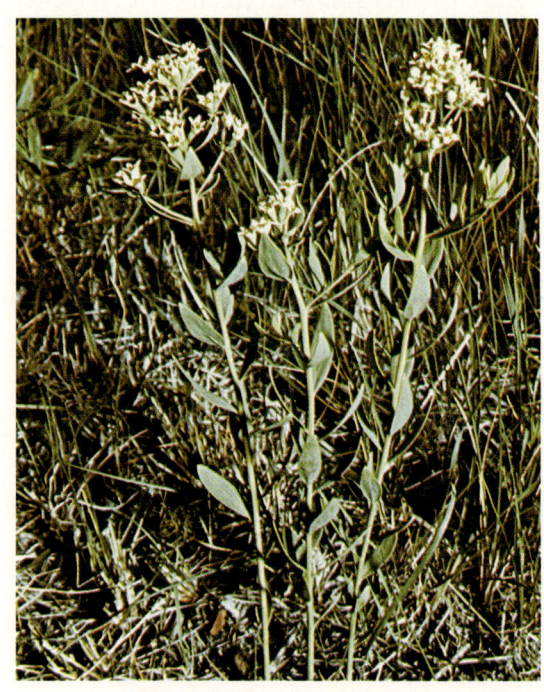

PALE
COMANDRA
(Text p. 70)

R. C. SWEET

JULIE HRAPKO

DWARF MISTLETOE
(Text p. 70)

69

SANDALWOOD FAMILY — *SANTALACEAE*

The two members of this family in Alberta are short-stemmed, perennial herbs with alternate, simple, smooth leaves, perfect or imperfect flowers and dry or fleshy, berry-like fruits. They are partially parasitic on the roots of other plants.

PALE COMANDRA
Photo. p. 69
Comandra pallida
Perennial

FLOWERS:	Whitish-green; small, 3/16 inch long; few in small clusters at the end of the leafy stem; calyx of 5 petal-like sepals; no petals; 5 stamens; 1 pistil.
FRUIT:	Olive green, dry, firm berry.
LEAVES:	Alternate, simple, numerous, small, smooth, pale green, narrow, ½ - 1 inch long.
HEIGHT:	6 - 16 inches.
HABITAT:	Dry, sandy soil, gravelly slopes and open pine woods.
DISTRIBUTION:	Very common throughout Alberta. June.

The Pale Comandra is very common on dry, sandy soil and on hillsides. It is parasitic on the roots of other plants and is frequently found growing in little clumps with short-stemmed sedges, with rushes and at the edge of open pine woods. It is a drab plant. Its leaves are small and are a pale green colour and hug an equally pale green stem at the top of which is a small cluster of whitish-green flowers. Even the small, round, berry-like fruits are green and do little to make the plant conspicuous. Another very similar and closely related species, *Geocaulon lividum*, is a less sombre plant with greener leaves and bright, orange-red berries.

MISTLETOE FAMILY — *LORANTHACEAE*

The Dwarf Mistletoe described below is the only representative in Alberta of this large family of parasitic or semi-parasitic plants. It grows on the branches of Jack and Lodgepole Pine and causes abnormal growths which are commonly called witches' brooms.

DWARF MISTLETOE
Photo. p. 69
Arceuthobium americanum
Parasite

FLOWERS:	Greenish-yellow; inconspicuous, clustered in the axils of the scales; staminate and pistillate.
FRUIT:	A one-seeded, gelatinous berry.
LEAVES:	Opposite, minute, scale-like.
HABITAT:	Parasitic on pine trees.
DISTRIBUTION:	Common in coniferous wooded areas throughout Alberta. June - July.

The Dwarf Mistletoe is a parasite on the branches of Jack and Lodgepole Pine and is as damaging to these trees as any parasitic fungus. It consists of a misshapen mass of swollen greenish-yellow stems, scale-like leaves and small flowers. It has no resemblance to the imported European mistletoe which hangs from the chandelier at Christmas time. Although the flowers are inconspicuous, they set normal fruits which when mature shoot out the seeds to a distance of thirty feet. If they lodge on the bark of a tree, and if germination is successful, a sucker-like growth penetrates to the young tissue of the bark and infection begins. The most striking symptom of the disease is the formation of a conspicuous cluster of abnormal branches commonly called witches' brooms.

70

BUCKWHEAT FAMILY — *POLYGONACEAE*

With a few exceptions, the Buckwheat Family is made up of un-interesting and unattractive plants, many of them troublesome weeds. Some of these are the docks, wild buckwheats, knotweeds and smartweeds. Two well known cultivated plants, rhubarb and buckwheat, belong to this family. The buckwheats are annuals or perennials with swollen joints marked by sheathing scale-like stipules. The flowers are small and incon-spicuous. Petals are absent but sometimes the sepals are petal-like.

YELLOW UMBRELLA PLANT
Eriogonum flavum

Photo. p. 72
Perennial

FLOWERS:	Yellowish or rose-tinged; small; many in a fluffy cluster, subtended by several large leaf-like bracts; 6 sepals, petal-like; no petals; 9 stamens; 1 pistil with 3 styles.
FRUIT:	A small, dry achene.
LEAVES:	Basal, oval, thick, greenish above, densely white woolly beneath, 1 - 2 inches long.
HEIGHT:	Flower-stalk 4 - 16 inches.
HABITAT:	Dry eroded slopes.
DISTRIBUTION:	Southern and Southwestern Alberta. June - August.

The Yellow Umbrella Plant is found only on the western foothills and in the Rocky Mountains. Here, firmly anchored by a stout woody root, it covers thin grassy ground, hard stony ground or eroded banks and gullies with thick spreading mats of prostrate leaves and slender white-hairy flower stalks. The leaves are greenish above and woolly white beneath and resemble some of the everlastings beside which they often grow. The tiny yellowish or rose-tinged flowers are borne in dense, fluffy, flat-topped clusters and like all the other buckwheats are minus petals. Several other members of this group grow in the Rockies. These include the Sulphur Plant, *Eriogonum piperi*, a densely hairy species with yellow flowers and *Eriogonum androsaceum*, a small species with yellowish-white flowers, which forms low thick mats at very high altitudes.

GREEN SMARTWEED
Polygonum scabrum

Photo. p. 72
Annual

FLOWERS:	Green or greenish-white; small; many in dense thick spikes; calyx 5-lobed, petal-like; no petals; usually 5 stamens; 1 pistil with 2 - 3 styles.
FRUIT:	A shiny black, flattened achene.
LEAVES:	Alternate, simple, oblong or lance-shaped, petioled, pale green with a dark blotch, 2 - 5 inches long.
HEIGHT:	1 - 3 feet.
HABITAT:	Fields and waste places.
DISTRIBUTION:	Common. Introduced weed. July - August.

The smartweeds and/or knotweeds make up a heterogenous mixture of native plants and introduced weeds. Most of them are extremely variable and several varieties and forms make their appearance in Alberta. They are found everywhere: thickets, ditches, roadsides, fields, farmyards and gardens. The Green Smartweed is a good example. It is a common, un-attractive roadside and garden weed with an abundance of pale green foliage and numerous spikes of small, greenish-white flowers. These flowers are characteristic of the whole group. Like most annuals, it has a weak root system and can be pulled out easily.

YELLOW UMBRELLA PLANT
(Text p. 71)

GREEN SMARTWEED
(Text p. 71)

WATER SMARTWEED
(Text p. 74)

BISTORT
(Text p. 74)

73

WATER SMARTWEED   Photo. p. 73
Polygonum amphibium   *Perennial*

FLOWERS: Rose-red; small; in a short, dense, terminal spike; calyx
                    5-parted; no petals; several stamens; 1 pistil.

FRUIT: A small, lens-shaped achene.

LEAVES: Alternate, simple, oblong, two kinds: aerial and
                    floating.

HEIGHT: Stems sometimes aerial, floating or submerged.

HABITAT: On the muddy shores of ponds, sloughs and ditches
                    and in the water.

DISTRIBUTION: Common throughout Alberta. July - August.

The Water Smartweed, as its specific name *amphibium,* suggests, is
found growing either in the water or on land at the water's edge. It grows
from a creeping perennial root-stock and sends up either on land or in the
water long, branching, leafy stems, bearing at their ends, short spikes of
rose-red flowers. If the plant is growing on land, the leaves are narrow and
have very short petioles; if growing in water, the leaves are much broader
and float on the surface of the water at the end of long floating petioles.
The leaves are kept afloat by an abundance of air spaces within and kept
dry by a coating of wax without. The Water Smartweed is the most spectacular of all our native buckwheats. It is a most variable species and
many varieties and forms have been described.

BISTORT   Photo. p. 73
Polygonum viviparum   *Perennial*

FLOWERS: Pink or white in a short dense terminal spike, calyx
                    coloured, no petals, 5 stamens, 3 styles.

FRUIT: A 3-angled achene.

LEAVES: Basal leaves long petioled, narrow, glossy dark green,
                    2-4 inches long. Upper leaves, firm and short petioled.

HEIGHT: 4-10 inches.

HABITAT: Cool moist meadows and woods.

DISTRIBUTION: Common in Western Alberta. June - July.

This small plant, only a few inches tall, grows in clumps in alpine
meadows and at the margins of mountain lakes and streams. The flowers
are a beautiful pink or sometimes white and, as the scientific name *viviparum*
implies, are capable of forming little bulblets which, when they fall to the
ground, grow into new plants. Another somewhat larger species, *Polygonum
bistortoides,* that goes by the same common name and that grows in the
same moist places, has red stems, glossy dark green leaves and tufts of
tightly packed white flowers.

SHEEP SORREL. DOCK   Photo. p. 76
Rumex acetosella   *Annual*

FLOWERS:	Greenish to yellowish; small; many in a branched flower cluster; 6 sepals; no petals; 6 stamens; 1 pistil with 3 styles.
FRUIT:	A three-angled, winged, reddish-brown achene.
LEAVES:	Alternate, simple, mainly basal, narrowly spear-shaped, long-petioled, acid-tasting, 1 - 4 inches long.
HEIGHT:	8 - 12 inches.
HABITAT:	In dry or sandy places and on acid soils.
DISTRIBUTION:	Common. An introduced weed. June - July.

Although one may not know them by name, the docks or sorrels are so familiar that they are seldom given a second glance. One of the most common is the Sheep Sorrel, a weed of fields, grazed poplar woods and waste places. It is a vigorous-growing perennial that spreads by seed and by a creeping rootstock. The small, inconspicuous flowers are densely crowded on a long, branched, slender stalk. Like all the buckwheats, the flowers have no petals but consist of six greenish, yellowish or orange sepals. The outer three are leaf-like while the inner three after fertilization form a protective sheath around the small achene. By the end of August, the plant is much more spectacular when the fruits turn a rich golden brown.

WESTERN DOCK   Photo. p. 76
Rumex occidentalis var *fenestratus*   *Perennial*

FLOWERS:	Greenish; very small; densely numerous in a long flower-cluster; 6 sepals; no petals; 1 pistil with 3 styles.
FRUIT:	A small, 3-sided achene enclosed in the dry, papery, reddish-brown sepals.
LEAVES:	Lower leaves alternate, simple, oblong or lance-shaped, heart-shaped at the base, up to 12 inches long; upper leaves smaller.
HEIGHT:	2 - 5 feet.
HABITAT:	Wet open ground, roadsides and thickets.
DISTRIBUTION:	Common throughout Alberta. July.

The coarse Western Dock is as familiar in moist fields and roadside ditches as the garden rhubarb to which it is closely related. Like all the docks, the small green flowers lack petals and are borne in a long, dense flower-cluster. The plant is much more conspicuous in fruit than in flower because then the three inner, wing-like sepals enclosing the small achene turn a rich reddish-brown. Two other native docks are also common in wet open ground or thickets; the Narrow-Leaved Dock, *Rumex mexicanus,* with long, narrow, bluish-green leaves and the Golden Dock, *Rumex maritimus* var. *fueginus,* a low bushy species whose flower-stalks turn a beautiful golden brown at maturity. The Plains Indian used the thick yellow roots of the dock for a dye.

SHEEP SORREL
(Text p. 75)

WESTERN
DOCK
(Text p. 75)

WILD BEGONIA
(Text p. 78)

MOUNTAIN
SORREL
(Text p. 78)

WILD BEGONIA. VEINED DOCK   Photo. p. 77

Rumex venosus   *Perennial*

FLOWERS: Greenish; small; many in a terminal cluster; 6 sepals in 2 circles of 3; no petals; 6 stamens; 1 pistil with 3 styles.

FRUIT: A 3-angled achene invested by the bright rose-red inner 3 sepals, about 1½ inches broad.

LEAVES: Simple, alternate with sheathing stipules, short-petioled, 2 - 5 inches long.

HEIGHT: 4 - 18 inches.

HABITAT: Dry sandy soil.

DISTRIBUTION: Southern Alberta. July - August.

Almost as brilliantly coloured as the Scarlet Mallow with which it often grows, the Wild Begonia or Veined Dock is found along the sides of roads and railway embankments. Here, it spreads freely by running woody rootstocks and sends up at intervals stout, branching, leafy stems. The leaves are pale green and are sheathed at the point of attachment to the stem by large, white, papery stipules. The flowers are small and greenish and are borne in numerous, short, dense clusters at the ends of the stems. These flowers are replaced by masses of rose-red, strongly veined, papery fruits.

MOUNTAIN SORREL   Photo. p. 77

Oxyria digyna   *Perennial*

FLOWERS: Greenish; small; several, whorled in a dense cluster; 4 sepals; no petals; 6 stamens; 1 pistil.

FRUIT: A lens-shaped, broadly-winged achene.

LEAVES: Mostly basal, alternate, simple, long-petioled, round kidney-shaped, smooth, stipuled, 1 - 2 inches broad.

HEIGHT: Flower stalk 2 - 12 inches.

HABITAT: Alpine meadows and stony ground.

DISTRIBUTION: At the higher levels in the Rocky Mountains. June-July.

The Mountain Sorrel is a dwarf perennial that grows in moist rock crevices and on the sheltered side of rocky ledges usually at high elevations. It has a thick root, a stout rootstock, a low cluster of bright green kidney-shaped leaves and several, smooth, short flower-stalks. These branch at their ends and bear short sprays of small green flowers. The flowers are succeeded by almost spherical, bright red fruits. The colour of the fruits is due to the persistent and enlarged sepals which form a thin papery envelope around the single achene. These quiver in the faintest breeze and add a bright touch of red to the alpine scene.

GOOSEFOOT FAMILY — *CHENOPODIACEAE*

The Goosefoot Family has few members that attract attention. Most are obnoxious weeds, Lamb's Quarters being a prime example and whose leaves, shaped like a goose's foot, give the name to the whole family. The flowers are small, green and lack petals but are produced in great numbers which in turn produce vast numbers of seed. In this family, only spinach, swiss chard and beet are economically important.

LAMB'S QUARTERS
Chenopodium album

Photo. p. 80
Annual

FLOWERS:	Bluish-green; very small; many in dense clusters; calyx white-mealy, 5-lobed, persistent; no petals; 1 - 5 stamens; 1 pistil with 1 - 5 styles.
FRUIT:	A one-seeded achene.
LEAVES:	Alternate, simple, mealy-coated beneath, oval or lance-shaped, irregularly toothed, up to 3 inches long.
HEIGHT:	1 - 4 feet.
HABITAT:	Waste places and gardens.
DISTRIBUTION:	Common as an introduced weed throughout Alberta. June - August.

Lamb's Quarters is a familiar troublesome world-wide weed as well known in Alberta as anywhere else. It is a short-lived annual without one attractive feature. It is easily recognized by its longitudinally grooved stem, profusion of branches, leaves and flower clusters. The leaves are green above and whitish-mealy beneath while the flowers have a bluish-green tinge. Although the flowers are small and inconspicuous, a single plant will produce a large quantity of fruits. These are small and one-seeded and are enclosed within the dry, papery calyx. It looks like spinach, is related to spinach and in dire need is used as spinach.

STRAWBERRY BLITE
Chenopodium capitatum

Photo. p. 80
Annual

FLOWERS:	Green; small; many in dense round clusters; calyx 5-lobed; no petals; 1 - 5 stamens; 1 pistil with 1 - 5 styles.
FRUIT:	A small, thin, 1-seeded achene, enclosed by the red, fleshy calyx.
LEAVES:	Alternate, simple, broadly spear-shaped, coarsely toothed, petioled, 1 - 2½ inches long.
HEIGHT:	8 - 16 inches.
HABITAT:	In thin, stony soil, in clearings, waste places and margins of woods.
DISTRIBUTION:	Fairly common throughout Alberta. June - August.

The goosefoots are all annuals of a somewhat weedy nature and when in flower there is nothing to distinguish the Strawberry Blite from any other member of this group. However, when in fruit, it is easily recognized. The leaves have the typical spear or goosefoot shape and the small green flowers are crowded into small, round clusters strung at intervals along the leafy stems. These flowers have no petals and their most conspicuous feature is the small green calyx. This enlarges after fertilization to become red and soft and collectively they turn the round flower cluster into a crimson ball resembling a ripe strawberry. The intensely red fruits were used by the Indians as the source of a red dye.

LAMB'S QUARTERS
(Text p. 79)

D. S. S. CORMACK

JANETTE GOODWIN

STRAWBERRY BLITE
(Text. p. 79)

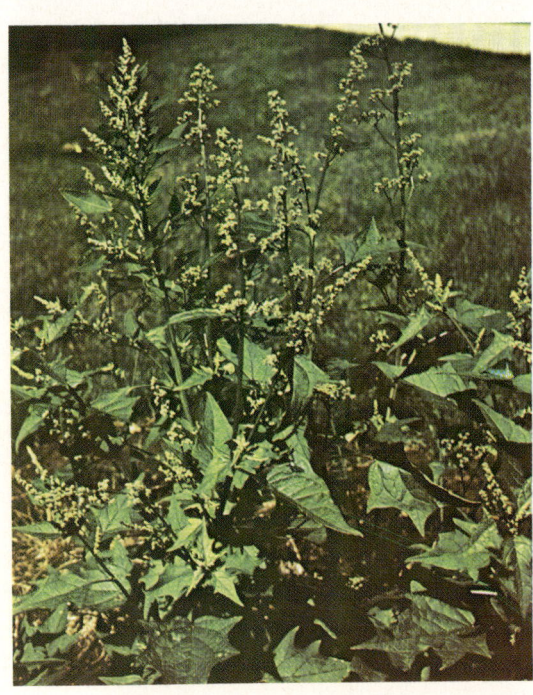

MAPLE-LEAVED
GOOSEFOOT
(Text p. 82)

A. J. WHYTE

W. H. VANDEN BORN

RUSSIAN THISTLE
(Text p. 82)

MAPLE-LEAVED GOOSEFOOT
Chenopodium hybridum var. *gigantospermum*

Photo. p. 81
Annual

FLOWERS:	Greenish; small; many in small round clusters arranged in a loose spike-like cluster; calyx 5-lobed; no corolla; 1 - 5 stamens; 1 pistil.
FRUIT:	A small achene.
LEAVES:	Alternate, simple, petioled, spear-shaped, sharp-pointed, shiny green, 1½ - 6 inches long.
HEIGHT:	1 - 4 feet.
HABITAT:	Thickets and waste places.
DISTRIBUTION:	Common throughout Alberta. July - August.

The Maple-Leaved Goosefoot has the same general form and appearance as the Lamb's Quarters and it often grows side by side with it in the same waste places. It is a tall annual with a freely-branching, grooved stem and it has dense, shining green foliage. The leaf blades are more halberd-shaped than maple-shaped, with one to four large sharp teeth on each side. In common with all the goosefoots, the flowers are small, green and inconspicuous and are produced in small rounded clusters on long terminal spikes. It spreads rapidly by seed and is often a troublesome weed in fields and gardens. However, because of its weak root system it is easily eradicated.

RUSSIAN THISTLE
Salsola kali var. *tenuifolia*

Photo. p. 81
Annual

FLOWERS:	Greenish; small; many in the axils of the leaves; 2-bracted; calyx 5-parted, winged in fruit; no petals; 5 stamens; 1 pistil with 2 styles.
FRUIT:	A small, hard, flattened achene.
LEAVES:	Early leaves, thread-like; later leaves shorter and broader, sharp-pointed.
HEIGHT:	1 - 2½ feet.
HABITAT:	Fields, waste places, dry ditches.
DISTRIBUTION:	Very common, particularly in the dry prairies. June-July.

The Russian Thistle was introduced into South Dakota in a carload of grain from Asia in 1874. Since that time it has spread westward and northwestward into the Rocky Mountains. It is a somewhat round, much-branched annual with dark green, succulent leaves which come to a sharp hard point. Each small, green, inconspicuous flower is borne in the axil of a leaf and has a pair of sharp-pointed bracts at the base. At maturity, the sharp tips of both leaves and bracts become hard, making the whole plant prickly, and the dry, reddish-coloured stem breaks off close to the ground. The whole plant blows away, scattering hundreds of small, winged fruits as it goes. As the "tumbling tumbleweed" of song and story, the Russian Thistle is as characteristic of the great western plains as the cactus and sagebrush.

GOOSEFOOT FAMILY — *CHENOPODIACEAE*

GREASEWOOD   Photo. p. 84
Sarcobatus vermiculatus   *Perennial*

FLOWERS: Yellowish-green; very small; staminate and pistillate in dense cylindical spikes; calyx 5-parted, winged; no petals; 3 stamens; 1 pistil with 2 styles.

FRUIT: A small, dry achene.

LEAVES: Alternate, simple, narrow, fleshy, pale green, 1 - 1½ inches long.

HEIGHT: 1 - 6 feet.

HABITAT: Saline sloughs and flats.

DISTRIBUTION: Common. Southern Alberta. June.

The goosefoots or pigweeds are not noted for their attractiveness and the Greasewood is no exception. The flowers are small and inconspicuous and its many leafy, spiny, whitish stems give it a rough bushy appearance. The flowers are either staminate or pistillate and are borne in terminal spikes or in the axils of the yellowish-green leaves. After fertilization, the flowers develop into small achenes which are protected by the persistent calyx and by a broad, paper-thin wing. It grows in company with other goosefoots and pigweeds in alkaline sloughs and flats. During the spring and summer, it absorbs enough potassium and sodium salts to make it rather poisonous to livestock, particularly new born lambs.

PURSLANE FAMILY — *PORTULACACEAE*

Native members of this family of annual or perennial herbs number only a very few species and most of them grow in the mountains. They are characterized by unusually low growth, succulent leaves and stems and perfect, regular, star-shaped flowers. The Western Spring Beauty is our best known Alberta species and is an excellent example of the whole group.

WESTERN SPRING BEAUTY   Photo. p. 84
Claytonia lanceolata   *Perennial*

FLOWERS: White or pinkish with purple lines; showy; star-shaped; about ½ inch across; several in a short cluster; 2 sepals, falling early; 5 petals; several stamens; 1 pistil.

FRUIT: A dry, papery, many-seeded capsule.

LEAVES: Opposite, one pair, succulent, narrow to oval, ¾ - 2 inches long.

HEIGHT: 3 - 8 inches.

HABITAT: Moist rich soil, bordering woods and clearings.

DISTRIBUTION: Rocky Mountains and Cypress Hills. May - July.

The Western Spring Beauty is an exceedingly pretty and delicate plant found growing in early spring in the borders of woods and in shady banks. Here it forms dense low mounds of dark green leaves and pale pink flowers until concealed by the vigorous new growth of herbs and grasses. The reddish, weak stem grows from a round corm or tuber-like root and bears a pair of succulent lance-shaped leaves half-way up, and a small cluster of star-shaped blossoms at the top. The exquisite delicacy of the pale pink petals, streaked with fine purple lines has been praised in verse by many poets.

GREASEWOOD
(Text p. 83)

WESTERN SPRING BEAUTY
(Text p. 83)

PURSLANE
(Text p. 86)

SANDWORT
(Text p. 86)

PURSLANE
Portulaca oleracea

Photo. p. 85
Annual

FLOWERS:	Yellow; small, about ¼ inch across; borne singly in the axils of the leaves; 2 sepals; 5 petals; 7 - 12 stamens; 1 pistil with 4 - 6 parted style.
FRUIT:	A small, cone-shaped capsule.
LEAVES:	Alternate, simple, dark shiny green, wedge-shaped, thick and fleshy, ¼ - 1 inch long.
HEIGHT:	Prostrate, mat-forming.
HABITAT:	Waste places and neglected gardens.
DISTRIBUTION:	An introduced weed. Very common. July - August.

The Purslane is a familiar wayside and garden weed and is so common that few of us bother to know its name. It grows in mats, sometimes a foot or more across, its reddish-coloured, greatly-branched stems and dark green leaves spreading out flat on the ground. Although it blooms most of the summer, its small yellow flowers are open only in the morning sunshine. It is sometimes confused with the Common Yard Knotweed with which it often grows but the stems and leaves of the Purslane are smooth and succulent and feel rubbery to the touch.

PINK FAMILY — *CARYOPHYLLACEAE*

Some forty members of the Pink Family grow in Alberta. They are all soft-stemmed plants with swollen joints and opposite, simple leaves. The flowers are usually showy with a calyx of four or five separate or united sepals and a corolla of the same number of petals and ten stamens. This family includes such well known cultivated plants as pinks, sweet williams and carnations, famed for their beauty and fragrance.

SANDWORT
Arenaria lithophila

Photo. p. 85
Perennial

FLOWERS:	White; small, 3/16 - 1/4 inch long; few in a loose terminal cluster; 5 sepals; 4 - 6 petals; 10 stamens; 1 pistil with 3 styles.
FRUIT:	A small, dry capsule.
LEAVES:	Opposite, simple, very narrow, not petioled, ½ - 2 inches long.
HEIGHT:	4 - 10 inches high.
HABITAT:	Dry banks and rocky slopes.
DISTRIBUTION:	Widespread. June - July.

There are ten native Alberta species of sandwort, some growing in the prairie, some in moist boggy places, and others in rock crevices and on open mountain slopes. They grow in tufts or mats, have opposite, narrow leaves and all have tiny, white, star-shaped flowers. The species photographed, *Arenaria lithophila,* abounds on dry banks and slopes and serves as a good example of the whole group.

MOUSE-EAR CHICKWEED
Cerastium arvense

Photo. p. 88
Perennial

FLOWERS:	White; showy; small, about 3/8 inch across; many in loose clusters; 5 sepals; 5 petals, deeply cleft; 10 stamens; 1 pistil with 5 styles.
FRUIT:	A dry, cylindrical capsule.
LEAVES:	Many, opposite, simple, small, no petiole, densely hairy to smooth, 3/8 - 3/4 inch long.
HEIGHT:	3 - 6 inches.
HABITAT:	Dry, stony ground or thin, grassy slopes.
DISTRIBUTION:	Common in the prairie-parkland region and in the foothills and mountains. May - July.

This particular plant is one of half-a-dozen similar plants which go by the name of Mouse-Ear Chickweed, because the upper part of the leaf resembles a mouse's ear and is covered with long silky hairs. It is the most common species and is the one with the largest and showiest flowers. The leafy, straggling stems grow in tufts, but all combine to form wide patches of snow-white bloom. The five petals are deeply cleft and when fully expanded the flowers look like ten-rayed stars. It grows everywhere on dry or stony ground but is most conspicuous in the foothills and on the lower levels of mountain slopes. Another very similar species but with much smaller flowers, *Cerastium beeringianum,* grows on dry, rocky slopes and in crevices at very high elevations.

ALPINE CAMPION. NODDING PINK
Lychnis apetala

Photo. p. 88
Perennial

FLOWERS:	Greenish-purple; showy; about ½ inch long; usually solitary, nodding at the end of the leafy stem; calyx 5-toothed, hairy, inflated, purple-lined; corolla purple; 10 stamens; 1 pistil.
FRUIT:	A dry capsule.
LEAVES:	Opposite, simple, narrowly oblong.
HEIGHT:	2 - 6 inches.
HABITAT:	Stony ground at high elevations.
DISTRIBUTION:	Rocky Mountains. Western Alberta. June.

It is a strange thing that some of our most unusual and interesting wild flowers grow in the most inaccessible places and it is in the screes and moraines of the mountain tops that we must look for this quaint little Nodding Pink or Alpine Campion. The distinguishing feature of this dwarf perennial is the flowers which droop at the end of the short, leafy stems and which look more like green gooseberries than flowers. What seems to be the corolla is actually the calyx-tube, which is inflated, densely-hairy, greenish-coloured with purple stripes and narrowed at the mouth. The beautiful purple petals scarcely extend beyond the mouth of the calyx-tube and soon wither, while the calyx-tube remains the same and at maturity encloses the seed capsule.

MOUSE EAR CHICKWEED
(Text p. 87)

ALPINE CAMPION
(Text p. 87)

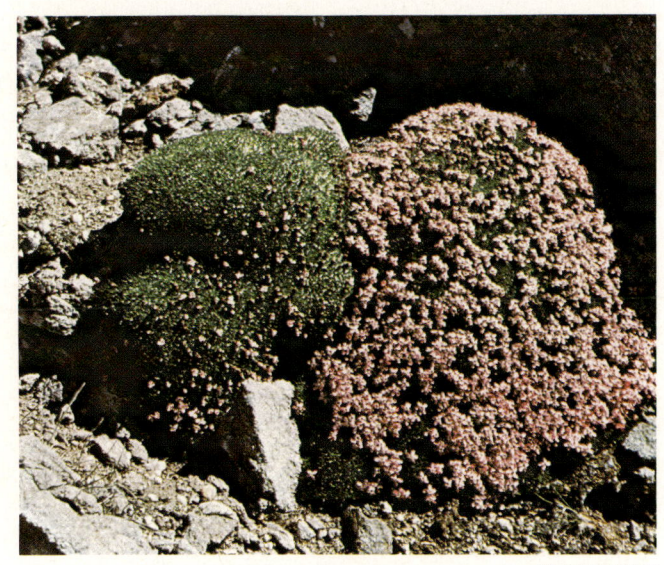

MOSS CAMPION
(Text. p. 90)

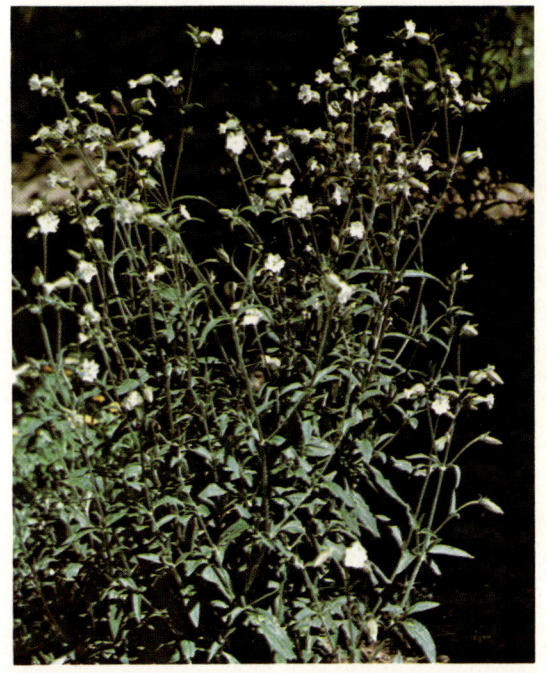

NIGHT-
FLOWERING
CATCHFLY
(Text p. 90)

89

PINK FAMILY — *CARYOPHYLLACEAE*

MOSS CAMPION   Photo p. 89
Silene acaulis var. *exscapa*   *Perennial*

FLOWERS:	Pink or lavender; small, about ¼ inch across; many in a dense low mat; calyx cup-shaped; 5 widely-spread petals; 10 stamens; 1 pistil with 3 styles.
FRUIT:	A small, dry capsule.
LEAVES:	Opposite, simple, smooth, narrow to lance-shaped, ¼ - ½ inch long.
HEIGHT:	1 - 2 inches.
HABITAT:	Alpine meadows, stony ground.
DISTRIBUTION:	Rocky Mountains. June - August.

The Moss Campion is a dwarf, arctic-alpine plant that grows at high elevations in the Rockies on stony ground, in alpine meadows and on treeless rocky slopes. The plant is composed of tufts of dwarfed branches which grow from a deep stout root and which pile up one upon another to form a thick, springy, cushion-like mound. From this mound the short, narrow leaves make a velvety mat. Beginning in June, the plant breaks into a solid carpet of small, bright pink flowers with only the wheel-shaped, five-lobed corollas showing above the even level of the leaves. In spite of their delicacy, the flowers are surprisingly resistant to the icy winds and harsh climate of the mountains and after fertilization give rise to small, dry capsules.

NIGHT-FLOWERING CATCHFLY   Photo. p. 89
Silene noctiflora   *Annual*

FLOWERS:	White or pinkish; large, about ¾ inch across; fragrant; several in spreading cluster; calyx tubular, sticky, 5-toothed; 5 petals, deeply-lobed; 10 stamens; 1 pistil with 3 styles.
FRUIT:	An acorn-shaped, many-seeded capsule.
LEAVES:	Opposite, simple, oval to lance-shaped, hairy and slightly sticky, 2 - 5 inches long.
HEIGHT:	1 - 3 feet.
HABITAT:	Gardens, roadsides and waste places.
DISTRIBUTION:	An introduced weed, becoming widely spread. July-August.

The Night-Flowering Catchfly, a native of Europe, is now a common and troublesome roadside and garden weed in Alberta. It is an annual and is easily recognized by the stickiness of its stems, leaves and flowers. The flowers have a sweet scent and open during the evening and close again in the morning. The distinguishing feature is the conspicuous swollen calyx which looks like a miniature citron melon and is beautifully marked with alternating dark green and greenish-white stripes. The five petals are deeply cleft and when fully open present a conspicuous jagged wheel of fluorescent white that attracts moths and other night-flying insects.

BLADDER CAMPION
Silene cucubalus

Photo. p. 92
Perennial

FLOWERS:	White; showy; ½ - ¾ inch across; several in a loose cluster; calyx-tube round, bladder-like, 5-lobed; 5 petals, 2-cleft; 10 stamens; 1 pistil.
FRUIT:	A dry, many-seeded capsule.
LEAVES:	Opposite, simple, lance-shaped, smooth, 1 - 3 inches long.
HEIGHT:	6 - 24 inches.
HABITAT:	Fields, lanes and waste places.
DISTRIBUTION:	An introduced weed. Fairly common. July - August.

Spreading westwards from Eastern Canada, the Bladder Campion is now well established in Eastern and Central Alberta as a noxious weed. Its deep-seated perennial root enables it to compete successfully with short-lived annuals and biennials in the same area and the production of large quantities of seed enables it to invade new territory. It is a smooth, leafy plant with many showy white flowers. The distinguishing feature of the flower is the smooth, pale green calyx-tube, which is inflated until it is almost round. The corolla is made up of five deeply-lobed petals which spread out like a wheel just beyond the rim of the calyx-tube.

LONG-LEAVED CHICKWEED
Stellaria longifolia

Photo. p. 92
Perennial

FLOWERS:	White; small; ¼ - ⅜ inch across; numerous at the end of the leafy stems; 5 sepals; 5 petals, deeply cleft; 10 stamens; 1 pistil with 3 styles.
FRUIT:	A small, dry capsule.
LEAVES:	Many, opposite, simple, narrow, ½ - 2½ inches long.
HEIGHT:	6 - 18 inches.
HABITAT:	Moist places and shady woodlands.
DISTRIBUTION:	Common. May - July.

All the species of the genus *Stellaria* are characterized by their growing in mats, their weak leafy stems and their small, star-shaped flowers. However, they are difficult to identify and most of us are content to give the name "Chickweed" to any plant that bears any resemblance to the common garden weed. They are found in ditches, fields and shady woods where the soil is moist. The plant shown in the photograph is possibly the Long-Leaved Chickweed whose petals are so deeply cleft they look like ten rather than five.

**BLADDER
CAMPION**
(Text p. 91)

R. C. SWEET

G. J. MITCHELL

LONG-LEAVED CHICKWEED
(Text p. 91)

MONKSHOOD
(Text p. 95)

A. M. REVELL

R. J. SCHRAA

YELLOW POND LILY
(Text p. 94)

WATER LILY FAMILY — *NYMPHAEACEAE*

The Water Lily Family is a well known family of aquatic perennial herbs with broad, floating leaves and solitary flowers borne at the end of long, buoyant stalks which spring from a thick creeping rootstock. The flowers are large and showy with 5 - 6 petal-like sepals and numerous, small, stamen-like petals. The Yellow Pond Lily is the only member of this family native to Alberta.

YELLOW POND LILY   Photo. p. 93
Nuphar variegatum   *Perennial*

FLOWERS: Greenish-yellow; solitary; about 2 inches across; long-stalked; sepals 6 petal-like; petals numerous, small, stamen-like; numerous stamens; ovary 8 - 30 loculed; stigmas on a circular disk.

FRUIT: Many-seeded with a hard rind.

LEAVES: Floating, borne singly on long petioles, heart-shaped, 3 - 6 inches broad.

HABITAT: Quiet, sheltered bays, ponds and slow-moving streams.

DISTRIBUTION: Common throughout the wooded regions of Alberta. June - July.

No water plant is better known or more easily recognizable than the Yellow Pond Lily. The large, floating leaves have a lustrous waxy surface and, as every boy knows, it is impossible to hold them under the water with a paddle or an oar. The flowers, which protrude above the water on long, buoyant stalks, are pollinated by insects. The long-living part of the plant is the stout, creeping rootstock, as thick as a man's wrist, which lies buried in the mud at the bottom of the pond. The rootstock is hard and rind-like on the outside, but soft and spongy inside. Every summer, it gives rise to new leaf and flower stalks and to new roots.

BUTTERCUP OR CROWFOOT FAMILY — *RANUNCULACEAE*

This large family of early blooming perennial or annual herbs is characterized by the density of its foliage and by the simplicity and diversity of its flowers. The flowers are usually showy, regular or irregular, perfect or imperfect, with both petals and sepals or with only sepals. When only the sepals are present, they are coloured and petal-like. Stamens and pistils are usually numerous, the latter developing into small, one-seeded fruits (achenes) or into many-seeded pods (follicles). Nearly sixty members of this family are found in Alberta and of this number about twenty-five are buttercups.

MONKSHOOD. ACONITE
Aconitum delphinifolium

Photo. p. 93
Perennial

FLOWERS:	Blue; showy; large, 1 - 1½ inches long; numerous in a short terminal spike; 5 blue petal-like sepals, the upper one forming a hood; 2 blue and 3 abortive petals; spurless; numerous stamens; several pistils.
FRUIT:	Several short pods. Seeds poisonous.
LEAVES:	Simple, 5-parted and deeply lobed.
HEIGHT:	1 - 2½ feet.
HABITAT:	Moist meadows and mixed coniferous woods.
DISTRIBUTION:	Rocky Mountains. Western Alberta. June - August.

The Monkshood is a true Rocky Mountain plant found growing in mountain meadows and in thin scrubby woods. The royal blue flowers are airily arranged on a short spike at the end of the leafy, flower-stalk. Like the columbines and the larkspurs, the Monkshood is an unorthodox member of the Buttercup Family with irregular, oddly-shaped blossoms. The five showy sepals are blue and petal-like; the uppermost forms the characteristic hood while the lower four hang downward like wings. Unlike the columbines and the larkspurs, there is no nectar-collecting spur, but ample nectar and pollen are provided for the bumblebee which alone is powerful enough to pollinate the flowers. The seeds and tuber-like roots contain a deadly ingredient which is extremely poisonous to cattle.

RED AND WHITE BANEBERRY
Actaea rubra

Photo. p. 96
Perennial

FLOWERS:	White; small; numerous in a dense terminal cluster; 3 - 5 white, petal-like sepals; 4 - 10 white petals; numerous white stamens; 1 pistil; 2-lobed stigma.
FRUIT:	A large cluster of waxy red or white berries. Poisonous.
LEAVES:	Compound, divided into several sharp-toothed, oval leaflets.
HEIGHT:	1 - 2½ feet.
HABITAT:	Rich, shady, poplar woods and mixed woods and thickets.
DISTRIBUTION:	Common and widely distributed throughout the forested regions of Alberta. May - June.

Growing with violets, Solomon's Seal, Wild Sarsaparilla, Fairy Bells and Wild Lily-of-the-Valley in rich woods and thickets, the Baneberry is better known for its berries than for its flowers. It is a perennial herb with large, attractive, compound leaves and with scores of very small flowers forming a cone-shaped cluster at the end of each leafy stem. As soon as a single flower bud opens, the small, white, petal-like sepals fall away, making each small flower look even smaller. Despite the small size of the flowers, pollination by tiny insects is effective as evidenced by the thick clusters of waxy red or white poisonous berries that replace them at the close of the summer. Both red and white berry-producing plants are thought to be the same species.

BANEBERRY
(Text p. 95)

DORTHEA CALVERLEY

G. W. MACHELL

CANADA ANEMONE
(Text p. 98)

96

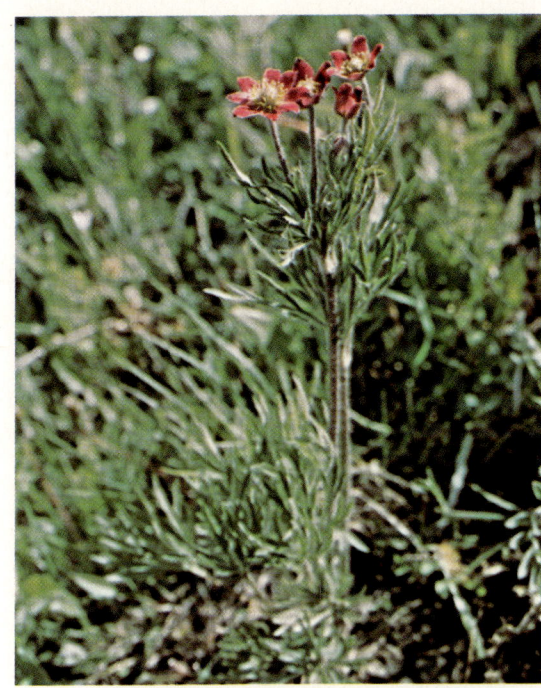

WIND FLOWER
(Text p. 98)

B. R. SHANTZ

EVA HACKETT

PRAIRIE ANEMONE
(Text p. 99)

97

BUTTERCUP OR CROWFOOT FAMILY — *RANUNCULACEAE*

CANADA ANEMONE   Photo. p. 96
Anemone canadensis   *Perennial*

FLOWERS:	Pure white; large; 1 - 1¼ inches across; solitary at the ends of coarse, hairy stems; 5 white, petal-like sepals; no petals; numerous stamens; numerous pistils.
FRUIT:	A spherical head of achenes.
LEAVES:	A whorl of stem leaves or leaf-like bracts and several, 3 - 5 deeply parted, basal leaves.
HEIGHT:	8 - 24 inches.
HABITAT:	Damp fields, low wet ground and in thickets and borders of woods.
DISTRIBUTION:	Common and locally abundant throughout Alberta. June - July.

The anemones constitute one of the largest and most attractive groups of plants belonging to the Buttercup Family. About a dozen different kinds of anemones are found in Alberta and they all have solitary, cup-shaped or salver-shaped, showy flowers, a whorl of leaf-like bracts beneath the flower, long-stalked, dissected basal leaves and a conspicuous fruiting head of closely-packed achenes. The Canada Anemone is one of the best known and is found growing in large patches in the shaded edge of thickets and woods, in low moist fields and in damp depressions. It is distinguished from the other Anemones by its dense, rich green foliage and pure white, star-shaped flowers.

WIND FLOWER. CUT-LEAVED ANEMONE   Photo. p. 97
Anemone multifida   *Perennial*

FLOWERS:	White, yellow, blue, maroon; showy; ½ - ¾ inch across, 5 - 8 petal-like sepals; no petals; numerous stamens and pistils.
FRUIT:	A rounded head of soft hairy achenes.
LEAVES:	Stem and basal leaves 3-parted, deeply and finely segmented.
HEIGHT:	3 - 18 inches.
HABITAT:	Dry, open sandhills, native grasslands, dry thin woods, mountain valleys and slopes.
DISTRIBUTION:	Common and widely distributed throughout mountain, foothill and prairie regions of Alberta. June - July.

The Wind Flower or Cut-Leaved Anemone is a dainty little cosmopolitan species, at home on prairie grasslands, wooded or grassy hillsides and on high wind-swept mountain slopes. The silky-hairy stems possess the customary collar of stem leaves a few inches below the solitary flowers, which range in colour from greenish-white to blue, from purple to maroon. However, it is the finely-divided or deeply-cut stem and basal leaves that are the distinguishing feature and which give to this anemone one of its common names. The other common name, Wind Flower, refers to the fact that the wind blows open the flowers, shakes them and blows them away. After the flowers, a thimble-shaped head of white, woolly, one-seeded achenes takes their place.

BUTTERCUP OR CROWFOOT FAMILY — *RANUNCULACEAE*

PRAIRIE ANEMONE. PRAIRIE CROCUS   Photo. p. 97
Anemone patens var. *wolfgangiana*   *Perennial*

FLOWERS:	Bluish-purple; large; 1½ - 2½ inches across; solitary on silky, hairy stalks; 5 - 7 blue, silky, petal-like sepals; petals absent; numerous stamens; numerous pistils; styles long and feathery.
FRUIT:	A dense head of hairy achenes with persistent feathery styles about 1 inch long.
LEAVES:	Several, mainly basal, long-petioled, divided into narrow lobes.
HEIGHT:	3 - 8 inches.
HABITAT:	Dry prairie grassland and dry open woods and thickets.
DISTRIBUTION:	Very common throughout the Parkland and Prairie regions of Alberta. April - May.

The Prairie Anemone or Prairie Crocus is the conspicuous anemone found on hills, open fields, grasslands and railway embankments throughout the Prairie Provinces. The large, soft, showy blooms push up above the cold earth even before the snow has melted and long before the woolly leaves appear. It is not until after the blue-purple of the flowers has turned ashen gray that the leaves become fully expanded and show the typical anemone form and shape. In early summer, the sepals fall away and the flowers are replaced by a cluster of long, silvery, feathery fruits. The Prairie Crocus was chosen as the official floral emblem of Manitoba in 1906 and appears now on a 5¢ Canadian commemorative stamp issued in 1965.

WESTERN ANEMONE   Photo. p. 100
Anemone occidentalis   *Perennial*

FLOWERS:	White or sometimes tinged with purple; large; 2 - 2½ inches across; solitary on long, silky, hairy stems, 5 - 6 white, petal-like sepals; no petals; numerous stamens and pistils.
FRUIT:	An elongated head of achenes with persistent feathery styles.
LEAVES:	Purplish, finely dissected stem leaves; few, 3-parted, finely dissected basal leaves.
HEIGHT:	6 - 18 inches.
HABITAT:	Alpine meadows and grassy slopes.
DISTRIBUTION:	At high altitudes in the Rocky Mountains. June.

The Western Anemone or Chalice Flower, as it is sometimes called, is a Rocky Mountain species found blooming soon after the snow melts in alpine meadows and in grassy slopes. With the exception of the Prairie Crocus, its beautiful waxy white or sometimes mauve flowers are the largest and most beautiful of our Alberta anemones. The only other mountain plant it might be mistaken for is the Globe Flower, which has the same general form and appearance and whose flowers are much the same colour and are almost as large. However, it can be distinguished easily by its soft, silky, hairy stems and by its greatly-divided stem leaves and basal leaves. After the sepals have blown away and the fruits begin to form, the flowering stalk elongates to two to three times its original length and supports a tousled head of plumed-topped fruits.

WESTERN ANEMONE
(Text p. 99)

ALPINE ANEMONE
(Text p. 102)

TALL BLUE COLUMBINE
(Text p. 102)

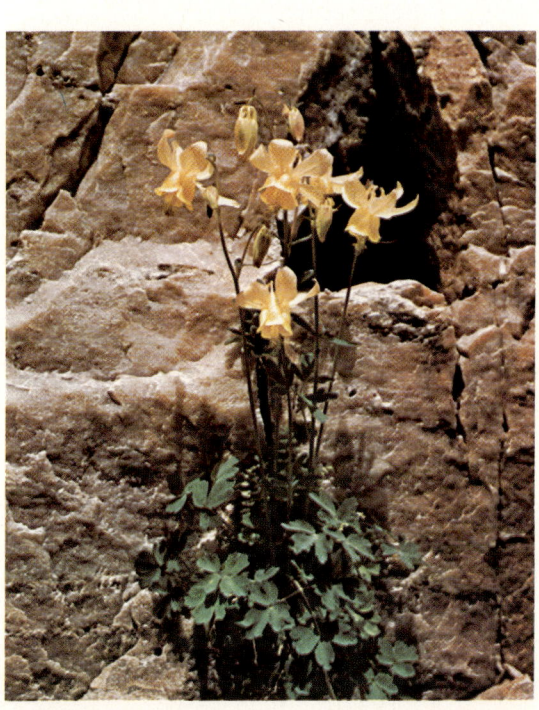

**YELLOW
COLUMBINE**
(Text p. 103)

BUTTERCUP OR CROWFOOT FAMILY — *RANUNCULACEAE*

ALPINE ANEMONE
Anemone parviflora

Photo. p. 100
Perennial

FLOWERS:	White or tinged with blue or pink; solitary; 5-6 petal-like sepals; no petals; numerous stamens and pistils.
FRUIT:	A round head of woolly achenes.
LEAVES:	Leaf blades thick, deeply 3-parted into broadly wedge-shaped segments.
HEIGHT:	4-12 inches.
HABITAT:	Common in open woods and slopes from gravelly lowlands to timberline and above.
DISTRIBUTION:	Rocky Mountains. June - July.

Low and frequently growing in clumps, this species of Anemone, as its common name suggests, grows in high mountain regions. The flower-stem, with its beautiful terminal flower and three-parted shining leathery leaves, is its chief distinguishing feature. After pollination, the showy but short-lived flowers are replaced by a round head of woolly achenes. Another very similar alpine species, *Anemone drummondii,* bears flowers that have the added distinction of being pale blue outside and white within.

TALL BLUE COLUMBINE
Aquilegia brevistyla

Photo. p. 101
Perennial

FLOWERS:	Blue and cream; large; 5/8 - 1 inch long; solitary on long, wand-like stalks; 5 blue, wing-shaped, petal-like sepals; 5 tube-shaped, cream-coloured petals ending in a spur; numerous stamens; 5 pistils.
FRUIT:	A head of 5 many-seeded pods.
LEAVES:	Several, mainly basal, compound and divided into 3 leaflets.
HEIGHT:	1 - 2 feet.
HABITAT:	Meadows, open woods, thickets and rock crevices.
DISTRIBUTION:	Widely distributed but sporadic throughout the forested areas of Alberta. May - July.

Our native columbines resemble the cultivated varieties so closely that there is no mistaking them. Of the three species, the Tall Blue Columbine is the most widely spread and occurs in thickets and open deciduous woods. Its wiry graceful stems are skirted at the base by a growth of compound leaves and end in a loose cluster of drooping blue-cream coloured flowers. The flower has a distinctive structure and consists of five blue, wing-like sepals and five cream-coloured petals situated between the sepals. Each petal is modified to form a wide-mouthed tube which ends in a hooked spur. The nectar is concentrated in the spur and can only be reached by long-mouthed insects. The other Blue Columbine, *Aquilegia jonesii,* a dwarfed alpine species found growing on rocky exposed slopes, has but a single flower.

BUTTERCUP OR CROWFOOT FAMILY — *RANUNCULACEAE*

YELLOW COLUMBINE   Photo. p. 101
Aquilegia flavescens   *Perennial*

FLOWERS:	Yellow, tinged with pink; showy; large; 1 - 1½ inches across; solitary, drooping at the ends of long, slender stems; 5 yellow, wing-shaped, petal-like sepals; 5 tube-shaped, yellow petals ending in a spur; numerous stamens; 5 pistils.
FRUIT:	A head of 5 many-seeded pods.
LEAVES:	Several, mostly basal, compound, much divided into broad blunt lobes.
HEIGHT:	1 - 2 feet.
HABITAT:	Thin open woods, rock slides and talus slopes at high altitudes.
DISTRIBUTION:	Occasional in the Rocky Mountains. May - July.

Similar to the Tall Blue Columbine in almost every respect, except in the colour of its flowers, the Yellow Columbine is strictly a Rocky Mountain species. The beautiful canary yellow flowers are sometimes tinged with pink or orange.

MARSH MARIGOLD   Photo. p. 104
Caltha palustris   *Perennial*

FLOWERS:	Bright yellow; large; 1 - 1½ inches across; several at the ends of smooth hollow stems; 5 - 9 yellow, petal-like sepals; no petals; numerous stamens; numerous pistils.
FRUIT:	A dense head of small many-seeded pods.
LEAVES:	Mostly basal, large, kidney-shaped and heart-shaped at the base, margin round-toothed.
HEIGHT:	6 - 20 inches.
HABITAT:	Marshy, wet ground, swampy fields, sides of sluggish streams, roadside ditches and wet, boggy woods.
DISTRIBUTION:	Common in the forested regions of Alberta. April-May.

The Marsh Marigold is indeed the first harbinger of spring. This thick, hollow-stemmed marsh plant produces round or kidney-shaped, deep green leaves and then beautiful sprays of brilliant golden-yellow flowers. These marigolds are found in wet meadows or damp ditches and en masse are indeed a sight to behold.

MOUNTAIN MARSH MARIGOLD   Photo. p. 104
Caltha leptosepala   *Perennial*

FLOWERS:	White tinged with blue or mauve; large; about 1 inch across; 1 - 2 at the ends of smooth hollow stems; 5 - 15 whitish petal-like sepals; no petals; numerous stamens; numerous pistils.
FRUIT:	A dense head of small many-seeded pods.
LEAVES:	Mostly basal, large, oval, heart-shaped at the base, margin round-toothed.
HEIGHT:	4 - 16 inches.
HABITAT:	Wet ground in alpine meadows, near timber-line.
DISTRIBUTION:	Rocky Mountains. June - August.

This is a Rocky Mountain species which blooms early in the season in high sunny alpine meadows and sheltered grassy slopes. Here, either by itself or in company with the Globe Flower, Alpine Anemone and Alpine Buttercup, it may be found growing in wet ground or in tiny trickles of icy water left by the melting snow. It is very similar to the Common Marsh Marigold with the exception of its flowers which are white and tinged with blue or mauve on the outside.

MARSH MARIGOLD
(Text p. 103)

MOUNTAIN MARSH MARIGOLD
(Text p. 103)

DORTHEA CALVERLEY

WESTERN CLEMATIS
(Text p. 106)

R. W. SALT

BLUE CLEMATIS
(Text p. 106)

BUTTERCUP OR CROWFOOT FAMILY — *RANUNCULACEAE*

WESTERN CLEMATIS   Photo. p. 105
Clematis ligusticifolia   *Perennial*

FLOWERS: White; showy; about ½ inch across; numerous in large clusters; 4 white petal-like sepals; no petals; numerous stamens and pistils.

FRUIT: A dense head of hairy achenes with persistent feathery styles, about 2 inches long.

LEAVES: Alternate, compound of 3 long-stalked leaflets.

HEIGHT: A climbing or trailing vine of variable length.

HABITAT: Coulees and river banks.

DISTRIBUTION: Common in Southern Alberta. July - August.

As the Western Clematis is the only white-flowered vine native to Alberta, it is easily recognized. In its native habitat, it trails and scrambles over low bushes and shrubs and is found in coulees and on scrubby river banks. The stem is somewhat woody and it clings to other plants by a twist or a kink of its leaf-stalks. The flowers are borne in dense clusters and resemble those of the Blue Clematis in every respect except size and colour. There are no petals but the four sepals are petal-like and white. When fertilized, each flower turns into a plume-like head of hairy achenes.

BLUE CLEMATIS   Photo. p. 105
Clematis verticellaris var. *columbiana*   *Perennial*

FLOWERS: Blue; showy; 2 - 4 inches across; solitary on long stalks; 4 - 5 blue petal-like sepals; petals absent or stamen-like; numerous stamens; numerous pistils; styles long and thread-like.

FRUIT: A dense head of hairy achenes with persistent feathery styles about 2 inches long.

LEAVES: Alternate, compound of 3 long-stalked leaflets, each 1 - 3 inches long.

HEIGHT: A climbing or trailing vine of variable length.

HABITAT: Woods and thickets.

DISTRIBUTION: Widely distributed but sporadic in Alberta. May - June.

The Blue Clematis that sprawls over the underbrush and drapes itself around the trunks of the trees resembles the cultivated member of this family so closely that it is unmistakable. The large, showy flowers add a splash of blue that breaks the pale green monotony of an aspen grove early in spring. What seems at first to be the corolla is actually the calyx which is four-pointed, star-shaped and pale blue. In midsummer, the flowers are replaced by clusters of silvery plumes that prolong the beauty of the Blue Clematis.

BUTTERCUP OR CROWFOOT FAMILY — *RANUNCULACEAE*

LOW LARKSPUR Photo. p. 108
Delphinium bicolor *Perennial*

FLOWERS:	Blue and white; showy; large; ¾ - 1¼ inches across; numerous in a long, loose spike; 5 dark blue petal-like sepals; 4 blue or cream-coloured petals; spur conspicuous; numerous stamens; few pistils.
FRUIT:	A head of a few many-seeded pods.
LEAVES:	Many, cleft and dissected, long-stalked.
HEIGHT:	8 - 20 inches.
HABITAT:	Rich black soil, in sheltered places and open woods.
DISTRIBUTION:	Not common, but frequently locally abundant. Widely distributed in prairie grassland, mountain slopes and wooded regions of Southern Alberta. May - June.

The Low Larkspur is an extremely variable species found growing on mountain slopes, thin open woods and prairie grasslands. The flowers have the same general structure and appearance as the Tall Larkspur but differ from it in that the uppermost pair of petals are often whitish. These two petals, together with the upper sepal, form the conspicuous, long spur. A somewhat similar but dwarfed species, *Delphinium nuttallianum,* found in high forested slopes and in alpine meadows, has smaller, fewer and more loosely arranged blue-purple flowers.

TALL LARKSPUR Photo. p. 108
Delphinium glaucum *Perennial*

FLOWERS:	Blue-purple; showy; large, about 1 inch across; numerous in a long, dense spike; 5 blue, petal-like sepals; 4 blue petals; spur conspicuous; numerous stamens; few pistils.
FRUIT:	A head of usually 3 many-seeded pods.
LEAVES:	Several to many, narrowly lobed and parted.
HEIGHT:	1 - 6 feet.
HABITAT:	In and at the edge of moist deciduous woods and willow thickets, wet meadows and river bottoms.
DISTRIBUTION:	Common and widespread throughout the foothill and forested regions of Alberta. June - July.

Our native larkspurs look so much like the garden varieties that they are easy to recognize. The two species most commonly found in Alberta are the Tall Larkspur and the Low Larkspur. The flowers of both have the same irregular shape and are formed of five petal-like sepals and four petals. The characteristic feature of the Larkspur flower is its long, conspicuous spur, which is formed by the upper sepal and the uppermost pair of petals. The Tall Larkspur cannot only be distinguished by its greater height but by its long spike of numerous, closely-set, blue-purple flowers. All the larkspurs are extremely poisonous to cattle.

LOW
LARKSPUR
(Text p. 107)

B. R. SHANTZ

TALL
LARKSPUR
(Text p. 107)

JANETTE GOODWIN

SMALL FLOWERED BUTTERCUP
(Text p. 110)

TALL BUTTERCUP
(Text p. 110)

SMALL-FLOWERED BUTTERCUP
Ranunculus abortivus

Photo. p. 109
Perennial

FLOWERS: Yellow; small; ¼ - 3/8 inch across; numerous in wide spreading clusters; 5 sepals, bent downwards; 5 petals; numerous stamens and pistils.

FRUIT: A round to oval head of small achenes.

LEAVES: Basal leaves long-stalked; simple or divided, rounded to kidney-shaped, round-toothed; upper leaves usually stalkless, usually divided into 3 narrow segments, often toothed.

HEIGHT: 6 - 24 inches.

HABITAT: Open woodlands, margins of sloughs and streams, wet places.

DISTRIBUTION: Fairly plentiful in moist places throughout Alberta. June - July.

The Small-Flowered Buttercup because of its small flowers and its partiality for slough margins, lake shores and other damp places is often mistaken for the Celery-Leaved Buttercup. However, a close look at the two plants shows that the leaves and mature fruiting heads are quite different. A special distinguishing feature is the peculiar habit of the sepals of the Small-Flowered Buttercup of bending downwards until they almost touch the slender flower stalk. Individual plants vary greatly in their different habitats. If growing in wet places, the plant is shorter, the flowering stalks are widely spread and are many branched with numerous small flowers. If growing in drier places, it is usually taller, less branched and has fewer flowers.

TALL BUTTERCUP
Ranunculus acris

Photo. p. 109
Perennial

FLOWERS: Bright yellow or cream; large; ¾ - 1 inch across; numerous on long stalks; 5 green sepals; 5 yellow petals; numerous stamens and pistils.

FRUIT: A rounded head of smooth flattish achenes.

LEAVES: Basal leaves long-stalked, much cleft and divided; upper leaves short-stalked, 3-divided.

HEIGHT: 1 - 3 feet.

HABITAT: Roadside ditches, moist fields and pastures.

DISTRIBUTION: Common. Becoming more and more abundant. June-July.

There are two dozen different kinds of buttercups in Alberta. Some of them are so confusingly similar that it is necessary to consult a botanical key to run them down. The best known is the Tall Buttercup, an introduced species from Europe, but now so widely distributed in Canada that it is one of our most common pasture and roadside plants. Shunned by cattle and horses because of their acrid taste, they are usually found growing in isolated clumps in moist fields and pastures. With its showy flowers, consisting of five green sepals, five yellow petals, numerous stamens and pistils and with both stem and basal leaves deeply parted, the Tall Buttercup could well stand as the example of the whole group.

BUTTERCUP OR CROWFOOT FAMILY — *RANUNCULACEAE*

WHITE WATER CROWFOOT
Ranunculus circinatus var. *subrigidus*

Photo. p. 112
Perennial

FLOWERS:	White; showy; ½ inch across; floating on the surface of the water; 5 sepals; 5 petals; numerous stamens and pistils.
FRUIT:	An oval-shaped head of small achenes.
LEAVES:	Submerged, finely dissected.
HEIGHT:	Submerged, long, branching.
HABITAT:	Ponds, lakes, ditches, slow-moving streams.
DISTRIBUTION:	Common and widespread throughout Alberta. July-August.

The White Water Crowfoot grows in ponds, lakes, ditches and slow-moving streams. The whole plant is submerged except the flowers which are buoyed above the surface on short stalks. The white, showy flowers have the typical crowfoot form and are pollinated by insects. The leaves are the distinguishing feature of this plant and these are divided into numerous thread-like filaments. They are rich in chlorophyll and carry on photosynthesis like leaves of land plants, absorbing the carbon dioxide essential for this process from the water, instead of from the air. The interior of the stem is riddled with a branching system of air spaces which enables the plant to maintain its shape and form in the water. When removed from the water, the whole plant collapses in a shapeless heap. Several other species of water crowfoot occur in Alberta.

YELLOW WATER CROWFOOT
Ranunculus gmelinii

Photo. p. 112
Perennial

FLOWERS:	Yellow; showy; about ½ inch across; 1 - 4 on long stalks well above the water; 5 sepals; 5 petals; numerous stamens and pistils.
FRUIT:	A short head of small achenes.
LEAVES:	Submerged leaves finely divided; aerial or floating leaves having wider lobes.
HEIGHT:	Partially submerged, long, branching.
HABITAT:	Ponds, sloughs and ditches.
DISTRIBUTION:	Fairly common in wooded and semi-wooded regions throughout Alberta. June - July.

The scientific name of the buttercups, *Ranunculus,* derived from the Latin name, *Rana* a frog, refers to marshy and watery places where both frogs and some species of buttercups abound. One of these is the Yellow Water Crowfoot. This plant grows beside or in shallow water, often forming half-submerged, half-floating mats of stems and leaves. The leaves of both are circular or kidney-shaped, but the underwater leaves are finely lobed, while those above water are smaller, thicker and have much wider lobes. The flowers are typical bright yellow buttercups and are carried well above the surface of the water on long slender stalks. Two varieties, differing in minor details of leaf and flower, are prevalent in ponds, ditches and slow-moving streams.

WHITE WATER CROWFOOT
(Text p. 111)

YELLOW WATER CROWFOOT
(Text p. 111)

CREEPING BUTTERCUP
(Text p. 114)

PRAIRIE
BUTTERCUP
(Text p. 114)

113

CREEPING BUTTERCUP   Photo. p. 113
Ranunculus cymbalaria   *Perennial*

FLOWERS:	Yellow; small; about 3/8 inch across; few on leafless stalks; 5 sepals; 5 petals; numerous stamens and pistils.
FRUIT:	A cylindrical head of small achenes.
LEAVES:	Simple, long-petioled, small, spoon-shaped with round-toothed margins, ½ - 1 inch across.
HEIGHT:	2 - 8 inches.
HABITAT:	Wet ground bordering ponds and sloughs, muddy sides of stream banks.
DISTRIBUTION:	Common throughout Alberta. June - July.

This buttercup grows at the edge of saline lakes, sloughs, ponds and streams, where it spreads over the ground by means of slender creeping stems or runners. These weak stems root at the nodes and give rise to little clusters of leaves and flowering stalks. It is a small plant with small yellow flowers and can be distinguished from other buttercups with the same creeping habit by its leaves. These are shiny green with long petioles and small, spoon-shaped, round-toothed blades. In another species, *Ranunculus flammula*, the leaf blades are small and extremely narrow.

PRAIRIE BUTTERCUP   Photo. p. 113
Ranunculus rhomboideus   *Perennial*

FLOWERS:	Light yellow; showy; ½ - ¾ inch across; numerous in several spreading clusters; 5 yellow, lavender tinged sepals; 5 narrow yellow petals; numerous stamens and pistils.
FRUIT:	A round head of small achenes.
LEAVES:	Basal leaves, long-petioled, spoon-shaped, apical portion wavy-margined; stem leaves, 3 - 5 deeply divided.
HEIGHT:	6 - 18 inches.
HABITAT:	Sandy, light soils in fields and meadows.
DISTRIBUTION:	Common throughout the prairie regions of Alberta. May - June.

Most of our Alberta buttercups grow in wet or moist places but the Prairie Buttercup as its common name suggests grows in the open plains. It flowers very early in the spring and is found everywhere. It can be distinguished from the Tall Buttercup by its shorter stem, its rounded or oval, wavy-margined basal leaves and by its much narrower petals.

BUTTERCUP OR CROWFOOT FAMILY — *RANUNCULACEAE*

CELERY-LEAVED BUTTERCUP
Ranunculus sceleratus

Photo. p. 116

Annual

FLOWERS:	Light-yellow; small; ¼ - ⅓ inch across; numerous in spreading clusters; 5 sepals; 5 petals; numerous stamens and pistils.
FRUIT:	A short cylindrical head of plump achenes.
LEAVES:	Basal leaves long-stalked, succulent, kidney-shaped, deeply 3-parted and lobed; upper leaves 3-parted or undivided.
HEIGHT:	½ - 2 feet.
HABITAT:	Moist rich soil, in ditches and bordering ponds and sloughs.
DISTRIBUTION:	Common in low places and marshy land throughout Alberta. June - August.

The Celery-Leaved Buttercup grows in wet ditches, marshy ground and on the hummocky borders of ponds and sloughs. With its small but bright yellow, open-faced flowers and luxuriant dark green foliage it is easily recognized as a member of the Buttercup Family. It is distinguished from other marshland buttercups by its smooth hollow stem and succulent, deeply-lobed, celery-like leaves. This plant sometimes goes by the name of Cursed Buttercup because of a very bitter juice that causes severe intestinal inflammation when eaten by grazing animals. In another common and small-flowered species, *Ranunculus abortivus,* that grows in the same moist places, the sepals bend downwards until they touch the stalk.

ALPINE OR SNOW BUTTERCUP
Ranunculus eschscholtzii

Photo. p. 116

Perennial

FLOWERS:	Yellow; large; ¾ - 1 inch across; few on a stem; 5 lavender-tinged sepals; 5 yellow petals; numerous stamens and pistils.
FRUIT:	An oval head of small achenes.
LEAVES:	Mainly basal from a stout, woody stem-base, 3 - 5 parted, deeply toothed.
HEIGHT:	2 - 6 inches.
HABITAT:	Alpine tundra, moist mossy meadows and thin alpine fir woods.
DISTRIBUTION:	Rocky Mountains. Above timberline. July - August.

The Alpine or Snow Buttercup is only seen by those who venture above timberline. It is only a few inches tall but it is very hardy and is often found growing in tiny pools of water which have been left by the melting snow. It has bright yellow flowers which have the typical buttercup form and shape and which appear incongruously large for such a small plant. At this height, the season for growing flowers and producing seed is short but the Snow Buttercup has a stout perennial stem-base which sends up new leaves and flowering stalks each year.

CELERY-LEAVED BUTTERCUP
(Text p. 115)

ALPINE BUTTERCUP
(Text p. 115)

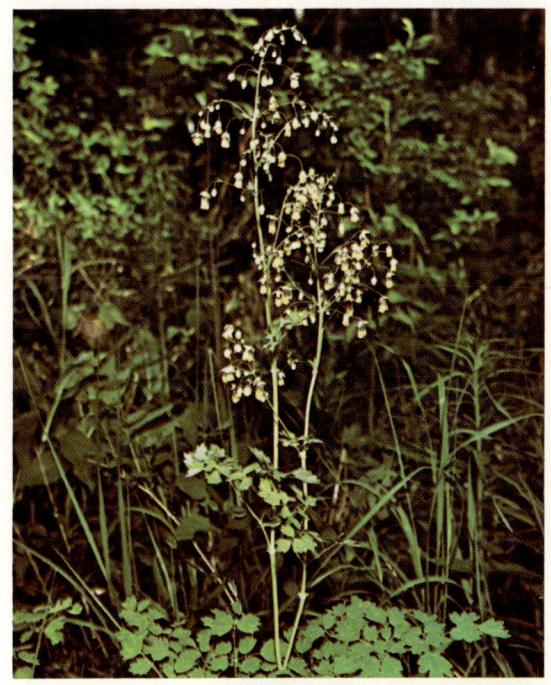

VEINY
MEADOW RUE
(Text p. 118)

H. PEGG

GLOBE
FLOWER
(Text p. 118)

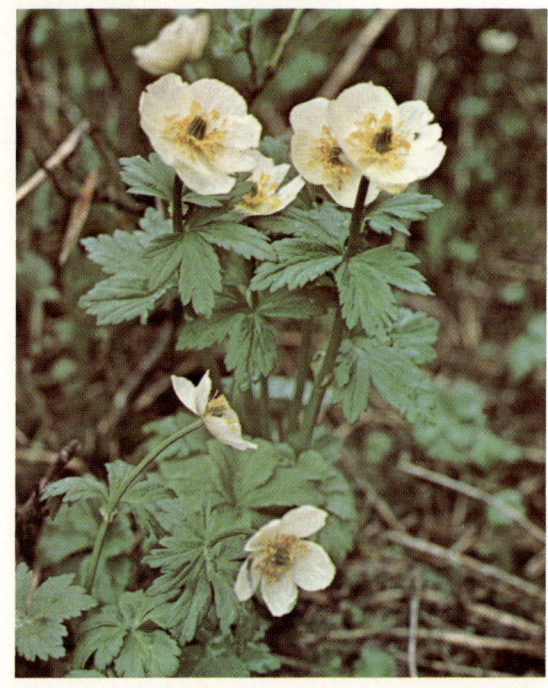

A. KARVONEN

117

VEINY MEADOW RUE
Thalictrum venulosum

Photo. p. 117
Perennial

FLOWERS:	Greenish or greenish-purple; small; numerous in large clusters; 4 - 5 petal-like sepals; no petals; some with stamens only, some with pistils only, some with both stamens and pistils.
FRUIT:	A head of small, ribbed, green achenes.
LEAVES:	Several, bluish-green, prominently veined, compound, divided several times into many 3-lobed, fan-shaped leaflets.
HEIGHT:	1 - 3 feet.
HABITAT:	Rich soil, damp meadows, woods and thickets.
DISTRIBUTION:	Very common throughout the wooded regions of Alberta. June - July.

The Veiny Meadow Rue grows among grasses and shrubs and is at home beside streams and the moist borders of woods and thickets. With its beautiful lacy, dark green leaves and fragile clusters of greenish or greenish-purple flowers, it is one of the most delicately formed and graceful of our woodland plants. The flowers are not always the same; some have only a shower of yellow stamens, others have only a few bristle-like pistils and still others have both stamens and pistils. The Western Meadow Rue, *Thalictrum occidentale*, with staminate and pistillate flowers on separate plants and the Tall Meadow Rue *Thalictrum dasycarpum*, with few but large leaves are also common in moist woods, thickets and meadows throughout Alberta.

GLOBE FLOWER
Trollius albiflorus

Photo. p. 117
Perennial

FLOWERS:	Grayish-white; large; 1 - 1½ inches across; 1 to few on long, smooth stems; 5 - 7 whitish, petal-like sepals; 5 - 8 inconspicuous petals; numerous stamens; 10 - 20 pistils.
FRUIT:	A head of several, ½ inch long, erect, many-seeded pods.
LEAVES:	All except the uppermost petioled, ½ - 3 inches broad, deeply 5 - 7 parted, the segments somewhat 4-sided and variously toothed.
HEIGHT:	6 - 12 inches.
HABITAT:	At the edge of pools and low wet ground in alpine scrubby forests and meadows.
DISTRIBUTION:	Rocky Mountains. July - August.

This Rocky Mountain member of the Buttercup Family is found along marshy borders of alpine streams and in alpine scrub forests and in damp meadows. The Globe Flower, blooming as soon as the snow melts, derives its name from the appearance of the partially-opened flowers which look like small balls or globes. Once fully opened, the flowers have the star-shaped anemone form, centered with puffs of yellow stamens, and resemble the Western Anemone. The foliage is thick and luxuriant. Later on, the flowering stem supports a head of numerous, stiffly erect, brown-coloured pods.

BARBERRY FAMILY — *BERBERIDACEAE*

This small family of herbs and shrubs has only one Alberta species—a low, evergreen shrub. The flowers are small and the various parts of the flower are in multiples of two or three with the sepals coloured like the petals. In most cases, there are as many stamens as petals and there is one pistil. The latter develops into a berry-like fruit. Many members of this family have been introduced into the garden as ornamentals.

CREEPING MAHONIA. ROCKY MOUNTAIN GRAPE   Photo. p. 120

Berberis repens   *Perennial*

FLOWERS:	Yellow; small; numerous in short, tight clusters; 6 yellow sepals; 6 yellow petals; 6 stamens; 1 pistil.
FRUIT:	A blue, juicy, sour berry.
LEAVES:	Compound of 3 - 7 leathery, oval, dark glossy green, leaflets with prickly margins.
HEIGHT:	4 - 12 inches long, trailing.
HABITAT:	Rocky slopes and open mountain woods.
DISTRIBUTION:	In the mountainous, extreme Southwest corner of Alberta. May - June.

The Creeping Mahonia or Rocky Mountain Grape is a true mountain species growing on rocky ledges and in moss in thin coniferous woods. It is a low-growing evergreen shrub which looks like Holly and which has waxy, leathery, prickly leaves. Both leaves and flowers spring from a perennial rootstock and though the yellow flowers soon give way to bunches of blue berries, the leaves, after turning red in the fall, last through the winter. This shrub was greatly prized by the Mountain Indians, who ate the berries, extracted dyes from the yellow woody stems and used the bitter bark as medicine.

POPPY FAMILY — *PAPAVERACEAE*

This is a well known family of herbaceous plants with milky juice, dissected leaves, and showy, perfect and regular flowers. The characteristic feature of them all is the union of the several stigmas into a flattened crown surmounting the ovary and the development of the ovary into the familiar dry poppy-head or capsule. Our only native representatives are two very similar dwarfed species that grow on exposed rocky slopes and crevices at high elevations in the Rocky Mountains.

CREEPING MAHONIA
(Text p. 119)

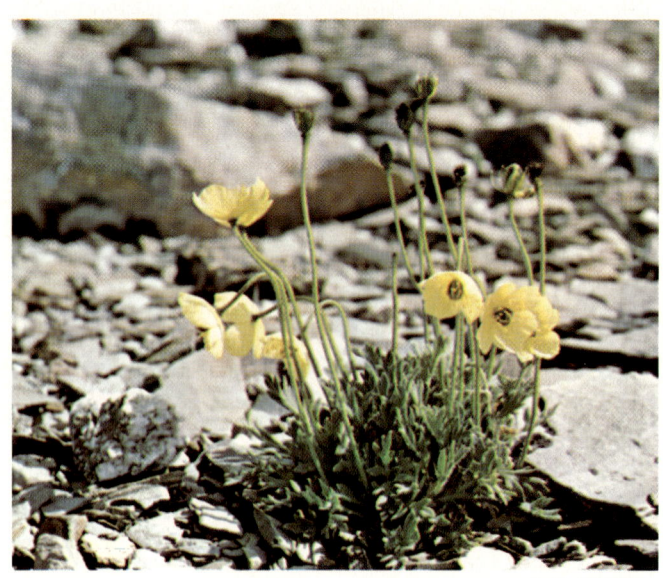

ALPINE POPPY
(Text p. 122)

H. PEGG

GOLDEN CORYDALIS
(Text p. 122)

G. J. MITCHELL

PINK CORYDALIS
(Text p. 123)

ALPINE POPPY
Papaver kluanensis

Photo. p. 120
Perennial

FLOWERS:	Yellow; large, about 1 inch across; solitary at the end of a long hairy stalk; 2 sepals, falling early; 4 petals; numerous stamens; 1 pistil with several stigmas united into a flat crown.
FRUIT:	A dry papery many-seeded capsule opening by small pores at the top.
LEAVES:	Numerous, all basal, small, lobed, hairy, with milky juice.
HEIGHT:	3 - 6 inches.
HABITAT:	Rocky slopes and ledges.
DISTRIBUTION:	At high altitudes in the Rocky Mountains. July-August.

The Alpine Poppy is a dwarfed replica of our garden poppy, whose canary yellow flowers welcome the intrepid climber on the highest crags and peaks. It grows in dense tufts from a perennial rootstock and is found in cracks and crannies. A single plant consists of a cluster of small basal leaves and several short hairy flower-stalks each ending in a fat nodding bud. After the buds open, the crumpled petals spread out and the flower-stalk straightens up and turns to face the sun. At the base of the petals a ring of golden stamens surrounds the green flat-topped ovary which after pollination grows into the familiar seed capsule. There is a ring of small holes at the top of the capsule and when the wind blows the seeds are shaken out and scattered in all directions.

FUMITORY FAMILY — *FUMARIACEAE*

A family of soft-stemmed herbaceous plants, usually perennials with finely divided leaves and irregular flowers. Like the Mustard Family, to which it is closely related, the flowers have four petals and six stamens. However, these are sack-shaped with a spur, rather than cross-shaped and the stamens are in two equal sets. There are only two Alberta species, both of which differ in habit of growth and in the colour of the flowers.

GOLDEN CORYDALIS
Corydalis aurea

Photo. p. 121
Biennial

FLOWERS:	Golden yellow; showy; about ½ inch long; numerous in clusters; sack-like; 2 sepals; soon falling; 4 petals, one ending in a spur; 6 stamens in 2 sets; 1 pistil.
FRUIT:	A long, slender, many-seeded capsule, ¾ - 1 inch long.
LEAVES:	Alternate, compound of many fine divisions, pale green.
HEIGHT:	4 - 12 inches, somewhat prostrate.
HABITAT:	Disturbed soil, railway grades, roadsides, open woods.
DISTRIBUTION:	Common throughout Alberta. May - July.

The Golden Corydalis is one of our most beautiful wild flowers. It grows along railroad embankments, roadsides and along the edge of woods, but because this weak-stemmed plant sprawls along the ground it is often missed. It has pale green, lacey leaves and clusters of golden yellow flowers which are sack-like, have a swollen tip and a conspicuous spur, this formed by one of the four united petals. After pollination, the flowers are replaced by long, slender seed pods which resemble mustards.

FUMITORY FAMILY — *FUMARIACEAE*

PINK CORYDALIS   Photo. p. 121
Corydalis sempervirens   *Biennial*

FLOWERS:	Pink or magenta with yellow tips; showy; ½ - ¾ inch long; several in loose clusters; sack-like; 2 sepals; soon falling; 4 petals, one ending in a spur; 6 stamens in 2 sets; 1 pistil.
FRUIT:	A long, narrow, round, many-seeded capsule, about 1 inch long.
LEAVES:	Alternate, compound of many fine divisions, pale bluish-green.
HEIGHT:	12 - 30 inches.
HABITAT:	Rocky woodlands, open woods, clearings and roadsides.
DISTRIBUTION:	Common throughout Alberta. May - July.

The Pink Corydalis has the same pale green, lacey foliage and the same sack-shaped flowers as the Golden Corydalis. In contrast, however, its stems are erect and its flowers are pale pink or magenta with a bright yellow tip and these appear at the ends of thread-like stalks. Although not as common as the Golden Corydalis, it may turn up almost anywhere in open woods, clearings and along sides of roads.

MUSTARD FAMILY — *CRUCIFERAE*

A large family of annual, biennial and perennial herbaceous plants which includes such well known cultivated plants as stocks, wallflowers, radishes, cabbages, mustards and many others. Of the seventy or more representatives of this family in Alberta, at least half of them are introduced weeds. The distinctive feature of the family is the perfect symmetry of the flowers. Each flower has four sepals, four petals, six stamens and a centrally-placed pistil. The sepals and petals are arranged in pairs in the shape of a Maltese Cross, from which the scientific name of the family is derived. The fruit is a pod-like capsule (silique or silicle) that splits along two sides or sometimes a nut-like pod that does not open.

WILD MUSTARD   Photo. p. 124
Brassica kaber var. *pinnatifida*   *Annual*

FLOWERS:	Yellow; small; about ¼ inch across; numerous in dense clusters; 4 sepals; 4 petals; 6 stamens; 1 pistil.
FRUIT:	A long, usually smooth, seed pod with an equally long angular beak.
LEAVES:	Lower leaves, variable in size, deeply divided; upper leaves, small, deeply toothed.
HEIGHT:	1 - 2½ feet.
HABITAT:	Fields and waste places.
DISTRIBUTION:	An introduced weed, common throughout Alberta. June.

The Wild Mustard is one of about twenty plants commonly found in Alberta that go by the name of mustard. They all have cross-shaped flowers and pod-like seed capsules characteristic of the whole Mustard Family but differ one from the other in details of leaf, flower and capsule. This particular species is very common and may be found growing in waste places, roadsides and fields. It has an erect leafy stem, an elongated cluster of yellow flowers and long, sausage-like seed pods.

**WILD
MUSTARD**
(Text p. 123)

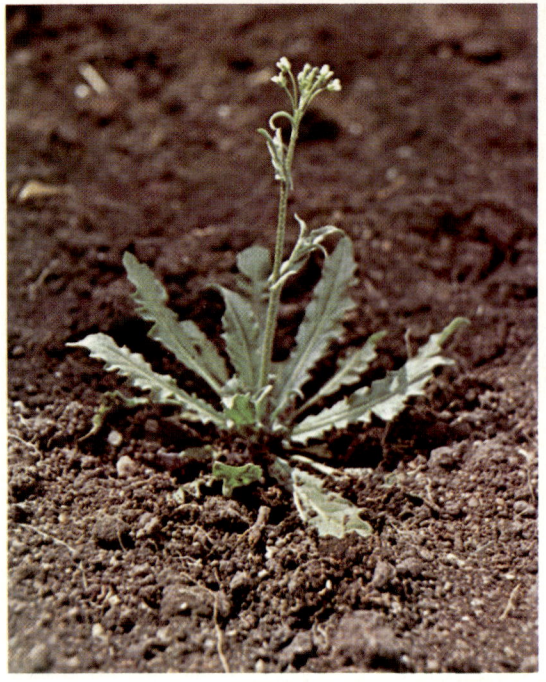

**SHEPHERD'S
PURSE**
(Text p. 126)

TANSY
MUSTARD
(Text p. 126)

H. A. MacGREGOR

E. GUSHUL

DRABA
(Text p. 127)

125

SHEPHERD'S PURSE

Photo. p. 124

Capsella bursa-pastoris   *Annual*

FLOWERS:	White; very small; numerous in a long terminal cluster; 4 sepals; 4 petals; 6 stamens; 1 pistil.
FRUIT:	A small heart-shaped seed capsule.
LEAVES:	Basal leaves, simple, deeply cleft or toothed, 1¼ - 3 inches long; stem leaves, small, lance-shaped, faintly toothed, clasping.
HEIGHT:	6 - 20 inches.
HABITAT:	Gardens, waste places.
DISTRIBUTION:	An introduced weed. Common throughout Alberta. May - June.

The Shepherd's Purse is a very common annual weed of roadsides, gardens, fields and waste places. The slender stem rises from a rosette of deeply-toothed basal leaves and bears at the top a small tight cluster of tiny white flowers. As the stem elongates the flowers are replaced by a succession of small green seed pods. The resemblance of the seed pods to the small purse carried by shepherds accounts for its long Latin name.

TANSY MUSTARD. FLIXWEED

Photo. p. 125

Descurainia sophia   *Annual*

FLOWERS:	Yellow; very small; numerous in clusters at the end of the stems; 4 sepals; 4 petals; 6 stamens; 1 pistil.
FRUIT:	A narrow cylindrical pod (silique) 5/8 - 7/8 inch long.
LEAVES:	Alternate, compound of numerous finely divided segments, grayish-green, fine hairy.
HEIGHT:	1 - 3 feet.
HABITAT:	Fields, waste places, roadsides.
DISTRIBUTION:	Very common throughout Alberta. June - July.

This unattractive branching grayish-green herb is one of Alberta's most common weeds. It is easily recognized by its feathery leaves which resemble those of the Common Tansy, a member of the Daisy Family, and which gives this Mustard one of its common names. The tiny, yellow, cross-shaped flowers grow in dense clusters at the ends of the leafy branches. The individual short-lived flowers open a few at a time and are succeeded in turn by slender cylindrical seed pods. By the time all the flowers have matured into seed pods, the flowering stalk has grown nearly two feet and the lowest pods have shed their seeds. There are two other very similar species of Tansy Mustard.

MUSTARD FAMILY — *CRUCIFERAE*

DRABA. WHITLOW GRASS
Draba paysonii var. *treleasii*

Photo. p. 125
Perennial

FLOWERS:	Yellow; small, about 3/16 inch long; numerous in a terminal cluster; 4 sepals; 4 petals; 6 stamens; 1 pistil.
FRUIT:	A small, flattened, hairy pod.
LEAVES:	All basal, crowded, narrow with marginal hairs, ¼ - ½ inch long.
HEIGHT:	1 - 2 inches.
HABITAT:	Rocky slopes and crevices.
DISTRIBUTION:	Rocky Mountains. June - July.

The drabas or whitlow grasses constitute a small but distinctive group of the Mustard Family which, because they are restricted to the Western Foothills and Rocky Mountains, are not very well known. Most of them are low-growing, tufted plants and they all have small, cross-shaped flowers and tiny, flat seed pods. This particular species is a dwarfed, matted plant scarcely two inches high. It has numerous, small, hairy leaves and clusters of tiny, lemon-yellow flowers are set on top of short, leafless, flowering stems.

WORMSEED MUSTARD
Erysimum cheiranthoides

Photo. p. 128
Annual

FLOWERS:	Yellow; small, about 1/5 inch across; numerous in dense terminal clusters; 4 sepals; 4 petals; 6 stamens; 1 pistil.
FRUIT:	A long, narrow, 4-angled seed pod.
LEAVES:	Alternate, simple, narrowly lance-shaped, dark green, 1 - 4 inches long.
HEIGHT:	8 - 24 inches.
HABITAT:	Moist places, fields and gardens.
DISTRIBUTION:	Widely distributed throughout Alberta. June - August.

The Wormseed Mustard is a fairly tall, somewhat hairy native species that is usually an annual but sometimes lives through the winter. Like most mustards, it can be recognized at a glance by its small, yellow, closely-clustered, cross-shaped flowers. However, to distinguish it from other mustards, it is necessary to examine the leaves and seed pods. The leaves are not dissected but are simple, narrow and very faintly toothed, while the seed pods are narrow, four-angled and stand stiffly erect. It grows in moist river flats and other moist places and is becoming more and more common as a troublesome weed in fields and gardens.

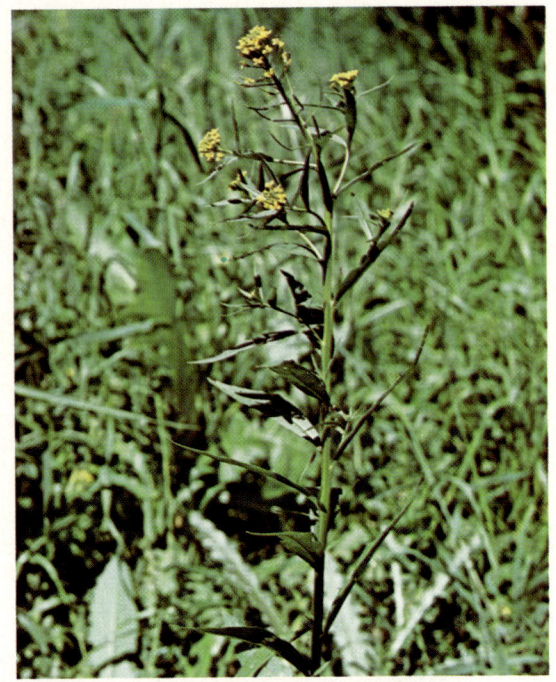

**WORMSEED
MUSTARD**
(Text p. 127)

H. PEGG

P. D. SEYMOUR

DOUBLE BLADDER POD
(Text p. 130)

ALPINE WALLFLOWER
(Text p. 130)

PENNY CRESS
(Text p. 131)

ALPINE WALLFLOWER

Erysimum pallasii

Photo. p. 129

Biennial

FLOWERS:	Bright purple; showy; about 3/8 inch across; numerous in a compressed cluster; 4 sepals; 4 petals; 6 stamens; 1 pistil.
FRUIT:	An erect, long, narrow, purple seed pod, 1½ - 4 inches long.
LEAVES:	Many in a rosette, simple, narrow, tapering into a narrow petiole; 2 - 3 inches long.
HEIGHT:	1½ - 5 inches.
HABITAT:	Rocky slopes.
DISTRIBUTION:	Occasionally, locally abundant. Rocky Mountains at high altitudes. June - July.

Mountain climbers, above timberline, are rewarded by often seeing scattered, low clumps of flowers called Alpine Wallflowers. These short-lived perennials have a dense rosette of narrow leaves which grow from a long, thick root which in turn is anchored securely to the rocks. The flowers, which are relatively large for the size of the plant, are characteristically cross-shaped and are a beautiful rich purple. The flower-stem is usually so stunted and the flower-cluster is so flattened that an individual flower scarcely shows above the rosette of leaves. However, after fertilization the flower-stem elongates and carries the stiffly erect, long narrow seed pods well above the top of the leaves.

DOUBLE BLADDER-POD

Physaria didymocarpa

Photo. p. 128

Perennial

FLOWERS:	Yellow; small; several in a short terminal cluster; 4 sepals; 4 petals; 6 stamens; 1 pistil.
FRUIT:	A hairy inflated bladder-like capsule.
LEAVES:	Basal leaves, numerous, small, spatula-shaped, densely silvery hairy; stem leaves, small.
HEIGHT:	3 - 6 inches.
HABITAT:	Stony ground, dry slopes.
DISTRIBUTION:	Foothills and Rocky Mountains. June - July.

The Double Bladder-Pod is a squat little perennial that grows in tufts on dry clay cut-banks and hard stony ground. A deep tap root anchors it to the soil while several short densely hairy weak stems sprawl out in an irregular circle around a rosette of small mealy-white leaves. Its small cross-shaped yellow flowers clearly mark it as a member of the Mustard Family and it can be distinguished from other members by its inflated bladder-like gray-green seed pods. These are borne in pairs and when they are mature the slender weak stems lie trailing on the ground.

PENNY CRESS.   STINKWEED   Photo. p. 129
Thlaspi arvense   *Annual*

FLOWERS:	White; small; about 1/8 inch across; numerous in clusters at the end of the stem; 4 sepals; 4 petals; 6 stamens; 1 pistil.
FRUIT:	A flat, deeply notched at the top, broadly winged capsule (silicle) ½ - ¾ inch long.
LEAVES:	Lowest leaves petioled, narrowly oval, falling early; upper leaves clasping, sometimes toothed.
HEIGHT:	2 - 18 inches.
HABITAT:	Fields and waste places.
DISTRIBUTION:	Very common as an introduced weed. May - June.

The Penny Cress or Stinkweed is a gregarious little plant found growing in fields, roadsides and waste places. A short-lived annual, it spreads rapidly by seed and may dominate newly-made lawns until choked out by the grass. It is an erect plant with smooth stem and leaves, clusters of small white flowers and a strong disagreeable odour. As the flower-clusters lengthen, the lower flowers wither and grow into flat seed capsules, while above them more flowers open while still others are in bud. Its pure white blossoms, if not praised by poets, are favourites of children. Like the Dandelion, they can be picked with wild abandon and discarded without regret. It is a rare day in May that a bouquet of Penny Cress does not grace some Grade I teacher's desk.

SUNDEW FAMILY — *DROSERACEAE*

The Sundews comprise a small family of curious and unusual plants found growing in deep moss in cool moist muskegs and boggy coniferous woods. They are all insectivorous or carnivorous plants whose small leaves are modified to trap insects. Three sundews are found in Alberta but only the Round-Leaved Sundew is common.

ROUND-LEAVED SUNDEW   Photo. p. 132
Drosera rotundifolia   *Perennial*

FLOWERS:	White; small, about 1/16 inch across; few near the end of a leafless flower-stem; 4 - 8 each of sepals; petals and stamens; 1 pistil.
FRUIT:	A small many-seeded capsule.
LEAVES:	Simple with long petioles, small rounded blades densely glandular and fringed with long reddish glandular hairs, ½ - 1½ inches long.
HEIGHT:	Flower stem 4 - 10 inches.
HABITAT:	In sphagnum bogs.
DISTRIBUTION:	Fairly common in coniferous wooded regions of Alberta. July - August.

This very small plant is the most common of the sundews and grows in wet boggy black spruce woods. It is a weak plant with a rosette of red-coloured leaves that spread out sideways half-buried in mounds of Sphagnum Moss. The long narrow petioles end in small roundish thick blades about the size of a dime and both are covered with long fine hairs or tentacles that drip clear drops of sticky fluid. When an insect is caught in the fluid all the tentacles slowly fold over it and digest it. In this way the plant compensates for the deficiency of nitrogen in muskeg soil. In July, a slender leafless red-coloured flower-stem grows up from the centre of the rosette. This is made up of several small white or pinkish flowers on a short terminal spike. After fertilization, the flowers are replaced by small many-seeded capsules. Another less common species, the Long-Leaved Sundew, *Drosera longifolia*, which grows in the same boggy places, has erect leaves with long narrow blades.

131

ROUND-LEAVED SUNDEW
(Text p. 131)

COMMON STONECROP
(Text p. 134)

GOLDEN SAXIFRAGE
(Text p. 134)

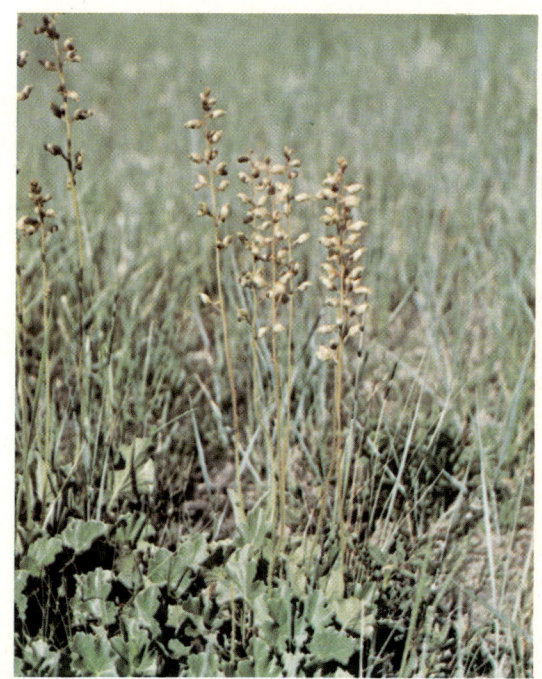

ALUM ROOT
(Text p. 135)

133

ORPINE FAMILY – *CRASSULACEAE*

The Sedums or Stonecrops constitute a well known family of low herbaceous perennials. They have small, yellow or purple flowers which form dense terminal clusters. Three species are found in Western and Southwestern Alberta.

COMMON STONECROP. SEDUM Photo. p. 132
Sedum stenopetalum *Perennial*

FLOWERS: Yellow; showy; about ½ inch across; several in a compact cluster; 4 - 5 sepals; 4 - 5 petals; 8 - 10 stamens; 1 pistil.
FRUIT: A group of small pods.
LEAVES: Alternate, simple, short, narrow, thick, succulent, about ½ inch long.
HEIGHT: 3 - 7 inches.
HABITAT: Gravelly soil and rocky slopes.
DISTRIBUTION: Common in Western Alberta and in the Cypress Hills. June - July.

All species of stonecrop or sedum grow in clumps, have short, fleshy, succulent stems and leaves and at the end of the stems have clusters of bright, star-shaped flowers. Like the cultivated sedums of the rock garden, the Common Stonecrop is found in cracks and crevices in rocky places where the soil is thin and dry. Its succulent stems and leaves store enough water for the plant to endure long periods of drought due to frozen soil and to the rapid run-off of surface water. In the Rose Root *Sedum rosea,* the flowers are dark purple, otherwise it is very similar to the Common Stonecrop.

SAXIFRAGE FAMILY – *SAXIFRAGACEAE*

A large family of perennial herbs and shrubs of diverse size, shape, form and habit of growth, this family has such well known cultivated plants as the gooseberries, currants, Mock Orange and many rock garden plants. With few exceptions, the flowers are small, regular, perfect with four to five sepals, four to five petals, several stamens and a single pistil. The fruits are of various kinds: pods, capsules and berries. Of the fifty species native to Alberta, one-quarter are shrubs and the rest are mainly plants of rocky ledges and the foothills.

GOLDEN SAXIFRAGE Photo. p. 133
Chrysosplenium iowense *Perennial*

FLOWERS: Yellowish-green; small; in small terminal clusters; 4 petal-like sepals; petals absent; several ·stamens; 1 pistil.
FRUIT: A dry, 2-lobed capsule.
LEAVES: Alternate, thick, round or kidney-shaped, round-toothed, dark green, ¼ - ¾ inch wide.
HEIGHT: 2 - 6 inches.
HABITAT: Shady damp places, boggy woods and ditches.
DISTRIBUTION: Not common, but locally abundant. June.

The Golden Saxifrage grows in low wet places in shady woods and along streamsides. Here, because of its weak stems and sprawling appearance, dark green leaves and small, yellowish-green flowers, it is often difficult to see among the grasses and leaves of other plants. It pulls up easily from the wet soil and when examined it is seen to be an attractive little plant and one well worthwhile looking for. Each tiny, saucer-shaped flower consists of four, broad, spreading sepals, yellowish inside and greenish outside, several orange-coloured stamens and a solitary pistil which ripens into a two-lobed capsule. There are no petals, although the sepals are often mistaken for them.

ALUM ROOT
Heuchera richardsonii

Photo. p. 133
Perennial

FLOWERS:	Purplish; small, about 3/8 inch long; numerous in a dense spike at the end of the leafless flower-stalk; 5 sepals; 5 petals; 5 stamens; 1 pistil with 2 styles.
FRUIT:	A 2-beaked capsule.
LEAVES:	All basal, long petioled, glandular-hairy; leaf blades dark green, leathery, rounded heart-shaped, toothed, 1 - 2½ inches across.
HEIGHT:	Flower-stem 12 - 18 inches.
HABITAT:	Rocky ground, gravelly slopes.
DISTRIBUTION:	Common and widely spread on prairie foothills and low mountain slopes. June - July.

This species is the most common and most widely spread of all our native Alum Roots. In the mountains it grows in crevices and ledges and on dry rocky slopes. In the foothills and eastward in the prairie and open parkland regions it grows in dry, hard soil and on gravelly hillsides. It is a plant that is easily recognized by its beautiful leaves and by its tall, slender, leafless flower-stems. The leaves are particularly noticeable as they all grow close to the ground from the thick, scaly rootstock and have long, somewhat bristly-glandular petioles and rounded, scalloped leaf blades. In addition, they are leathery and extremely drought-resistant, turning russet brown in the fall or remaining green under the snow. The odd-shaped flowers are arranged in a fairly close spiral around the upper half of the glandular-hairy flower-stem. There are two similar species, *Heuchera cylindrica* and *Heuchera flabellifolia*; the former grows in the mountains and has greenish flowers, while the latter grows in the foothill grasslands and has yellowish or white flowers.

LEATHER-LEAVED SAXIFRAGE
Leptarrhena pyrolifolia

Photo. p. 136
Perennial

FLOWERS:	White or pinkish; small; numerous in a tight terminal cluster; 5 sepals; 5 petals; 10 stamens; 1 pistil.
FRUIT:	A dry, many-seeded capsule.
LEAVES:	Mainly basal, alternate, simple, spoon-shaped, leathery, shiny green above, brownish beneath, 1½ - 3 inches long.
HEIGHT:	Flowering stalk, 6 - 15 inches.
HABITAT:	Mossy streamsides.
DISTRIBUTION:	Rocky Mountains. July - August.

The Leather-Leaved Saxifrage is one of the prettiest of our Rocky Mountain wild flowers. It is found most often growing along a shady streamside with its roots in water and the leaves at the bottom surrounded by moss. The flowers are small, white and star-shaped and form a dense cluster at the top of the reddish-purple, rigid flower-stalk. Along the flower-stalk are two small, widely-separated leaves. However, it is the handsome foliage, leathery, glossy and dark green, rather than the flowers that is its most attractive feature. Later on, after the flowers have faded, the red-purple seed capsules attract attention.

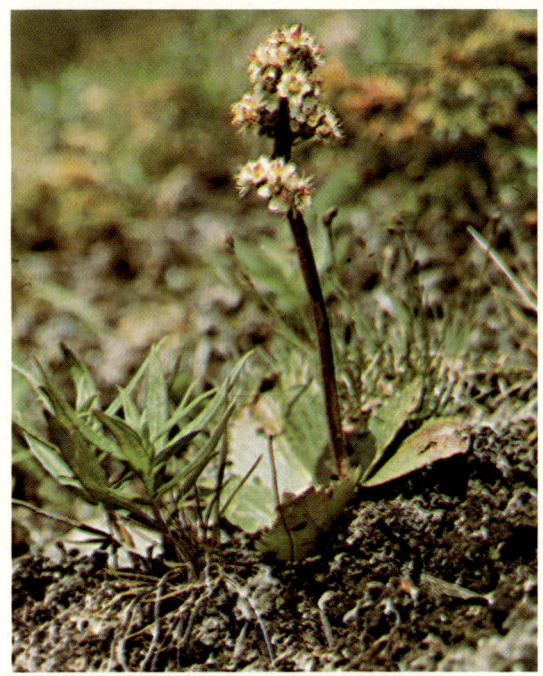

**LEATHER-
LEAVED
SAXIFRAGE**
(Text p. 135)

R. N. SMITH

DORTHEA CALVERLEY

BISHOP'S CAP
(Text p. 138)

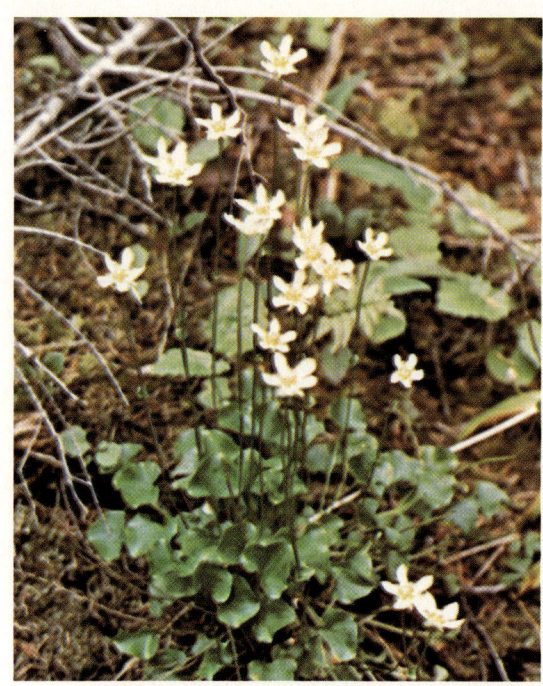

GRASS-OF-
PARNASSUS
(Text p. 138)

P. D. SEYMOUR

B. R. SHANTZ

WILD GOOSEBERRY
(Text p. 139)

BISHOP'S CAP. MITREWORT
Mitella nuda

Photo. p. 136
Perennial

FLOWERS:
Yellowish-green; delicate; small, about ¼ inch across; several on a short leafless hairy flowering stem; 5 greenish sepals; 5 yellowish-green finely divided petals; 10 stamens; 1 pistil.

FRUIT:
A greenish, 2-valved, few-seeded capsule.

LEAVES:
Simple, mostly basal, long-petioled, rounded, kidney-shaped, heart-shaped at base, sparsely hairy, margins round-toothed, dark green, ¾ - 2 inches across.

HEIGHT:
Flowering stalk, 2 - 8 inches.

HABITAT:
Moist shady woods.

DISTRIBUTION:
Common and widely spread throughout the wooded regions of Alberta. May - June.

The Bishop's Cap or Mitrewort is one of our smallest and daintiest woodland plants. It is easily recognized by its mat of small dark green leaves which often stay green under the snow. The small yellowish-green flowers are almost stalkless and are arranged in a loose spiral around the upper part of the short leafless hairy flowering stem, like little pin-wheels. The most striking feature of the flower is the five small petals. These are delicately fringed and look like fine antennae strung between the smaller unbranched sepals. The Latin name *Mitella* means "Bishop's Cap" and refers to the unopened capsule. However, once this breaks open it looks like a miniature bird's nest with a clutch of tiny black eggs. Two much rarer species, *Mitella breweri* and *Mitella pentandra,* occur in the mountainous Southwestern corner of Alberta.

GRASS OF PARNASSUS
Parnassia palustris var. *neogaea*

Photo. p. 137
Perennial

FLOWERS:
White, veined with green; large, ½ - 1 inch across; solitary at the end of the long flower-stem; 5 sepals; 5 petals; 5 fertile stamens; 1 pistil.

FRUIT:
A many-seeded capsule.

LEAVES:
Almost all basal, long-petioled with smooth, broadly oval, glossy green blades; 1 small heart-shaped leaf clasping the middle of the stem.

HEIGHT:
4 - 12 inches.

HABITAT:
Wet shady places in woods.

DISTRIBUTION:
Common and widely spread throughout the wooded regions of Alberta. July - August.

This delicate and beautiful Grass of Parnassus must be looked for in wet shady places and on boggy ground. A favourite haunt is the mossy banks of springs under the shade of pine and spruce trees. The whole plant has a glossy, waxy sheen, especially the leaves. These have long petioles and heart-shaped cup-like blades and lie curled up among the mosses at the base of the plant. The distinguishing feature of this plant is the single small leaf that clasps the flower-stem half way up. The solitary white flower delicately lined with green is at the very top. In a Rocky Mountain species, *Parnassia fimbriata,* occupying the same moist mossy places, the petals are fringed at the base and the leaves are kidney-shaped.

WILD GOOSEBERRY

Photo. p. 137

Ribes oxyacanthoides

Perennial

FLOWERS:	Greenish-purple or white; small; in small clusters; 5 sepals; 5 petals; 5 stamens; 1 pistil with 2 styles.
FRUIT:	A dark red edible berry when ripe.
LEAVES:	Alternate, simple, 3 - 5 lobed, somewhat hairy, often glandular-dotted beneath, ¾ - 1½ inches broad.
HEIGHT:	1 - 3 feet.
HABITAT:	Moist woodlands.
DISTRIBUTION:	Common throughout the wooded regions of Alberta. May.

Our native gooseberries resemble our garden gooseberries but have a wilder look. There are three species and all are difficult to identify without the aid of a botanical key. The species photographed, *Ribes oxyacanthoides*, is a low bristly and spiny shrub and is common in open woodlands. It has typical gooseberry leaves, flowers and fruits. The fruits are yellowish-green at first but turn reddish-purple when ripe.

WILD BLACK CURRANT

Photo. p. 140

Ribes hudsonianum

Perennial

FLOWERS:	Whitish; small; numerous in erect loose clusters; 5 sepals; 5 petals; 5 stamens; 1 pistil with 2 styles.
FRUIT:	A black edible berry.
LEAVES:	Alternate, simple, 3 - 5 lobed, somewhat hairy, glandular-dotted beneath, 1 - 4 inches broad.
HEIGHT:	3 - 5 feet.
HABITAT:	Swamps and shady woods.
DISTRIBUTION:	Common throughout the wooded regions of Alberta. May.

The Wild Black Currant is one of seven species native to Alberta and like all of them, it resembles closely the garden currant. It has smooth, erect stems, three to five-lobed leaves and tassels of small, whitish flowers. The latter soon give way to clusters of juicy black berries. Two other common species of wild currant, the Bristly Black Currant, *Ribes lacustre*, with prickly stems and bristly, jet-black fruits and the Skunk Currant, *Ribes glandulosum*, with dark red, ill-smelling fruits, are also found in swamps and wet woods.

WILD BLACK CURRANT

WILD BLACK CURRANT

WILD GOOSEBERRY

WILD RED CURRANT

COMMON SAXIFRAGE
(Text p. 142)

PURPLE SAXIFRAGE
(Text p. 142)

COMMON SAXIFRAGE

Saxifraga bronchialis

Photo. p. 141

Perennial

FLOWERS:	White, spotted with maroon or orange; small, 3/16 inch long; several in a flat-topped flower cluster; 5 sepals; 5 petals; 10 stamens; 1 pistil.
FRUIT:	A small dry capsule.
LEAVES:	Densely developed, narrowly lance-shaped, sharp-pointed, ¼ - ½ inch long.
HEIGHT:	Stems creeping.
HABITAT:	On rocks, thin soil.
DISTRIBUTION:	Common in foothills and Rocky Mountains. June - July.

The Common Saxifrage is one of our best known foothill and mountain plants. Its tufts of dark green needle-like leaves and short flower-stems often fill cracks and crannies on bare rock surfaces at high levels in the Rockies and also form thick mats on thin mossy soil at lower elevations. The tiny leathery sharp-pointed leaves overlap each other. The flowers always have a fresh newly-starched look about them, the five white petals speckled with maroon or orange dots. Though small in stature, it is far from frail and the whole plant assumes a stiff erect appearance.

PURPLE SAXIFRAGE

Saxifraga oppositifolia

Photo. p. 141

Perennial

FLOWERS:	Purple; small; showy; solitary on short stalks at the ends of the leafy stems; 5 sepals; 5 petals; 10 stamens; 1 pistil with 2 styles.
FRUIT:	A small, dry capsule.
LEAVES:	Very small, fleshy, in 4 rows, completely covering the short stems.
HEIGHT:	1 - 2 inches.
HABITAT:	Alpine meadows, rocky slopes and moist ledges.
DISTRIBUTION:	High altitudes in the Rocky Mountains. July.

The Purple Saxifrage grows on mountain tops and is found in rock crevices or clinging to a rocky shelf, where its stout, stem-base and densely-matted, leafy stems allow it to withstand the never-ending, swirling, icy winds. Like all the members of the genus *Saxifraga*, the Purple Saxifrage has many, small, star-shaped flowers, but where the flowers of other alpine saxifrages are coloured white or yellow, its flowers are a beautiful royal purple. Its tiny, fleshy, swollen, overlapping leaves with hairy margins distinguish it from the Moss Campion.

FALSE MITREWORT. FOAM FLOWER Photo. p. 144
Tiarella unifoliata *Perennial*

FLOWERS:	White; small; many in a loose feathery cluster; 5 pinkish-white sepals; 5 white petals; 10 stamens protruding; 1 pistil with 2 long styles.
FRUIT:	A small crown-shaped capsule.
LEAVES:	Mainly basal, simple, long-petioled, broadly heart-shaped, 3 - 5 lobed, margins double-toothed, ½ - 4 inches broad.
HEIGHT:	6 - 15 inches.
HABITAT:	Rich moist woods.
DISTRIBUTION:	Not common, Rocky Mountains and foothills. Western Alberta. June - July.

The False Mitrewort or Foam Flower is another attractive member of the Saxifrage Family and is found growing in cool, moist coniferous forests. The maple-like leaves and delicate sprays of lacey, star-shaped, white flowers are the characteristic features of this saxifrage. These plants usually grow in large clumps along streams or winding trails and their white masses of feathery bloom show up in sharp contrast to the dark evergreens. This saxifrage derives its scientific name of *Tiarella* or "little tiara" from the coronet-like shape of the seed capsule, while *unifoliata* points to the single leaf on the flower-stem. A similar but much rarer species, *Tiarella trifoliata*, with compound leaves of three leaflets has been found in the Swan Hills.

ROSE FAMILY — *ROSACEAE*

A large family of herbs, woody shrubs or small trees, famed for its beautiful showy flowers and for its sweet edible fruits. From this family come our roses, plums, cherries, apples, raspberries, strawberries and many other cultivated plants. The leaves are alternate, stipulate and either simple or compound. The flowers are usually in clusters and are regular and perfect with a saucer-shaped to tube-shaped floral tube *(hypanthium)* surrounding or enclosing the ovaries. Each flower consists of a 5-sepaled calyx, a 5-petalled corolla, numerous stamens and a superior or inferior ovary of 1 to many carpels. The fruits are of various kinds; achenes, pods, drupes and pomes. Some fifty members of the Rose Family occur in Alberta.

AGRIMONY Photo. p. 144
Agrimonia striata *Perennial*

FLOWERS:	Bright yellow; very small; numerous in a long slender spike; 5 sepals forming a short tube; 5 yellow petals; numerous stamens; 1 pistil.
FRUIT:	A small, dry, cup-shaped bur.
LEAVES:	Alternate, compound of 7 - 9 coarsely-toothed leaflets, smooth above, hairy beneath.
HEIGHT:	1 - 2½ feet.
HABITAT:	Open poplar woods and thickets.
DISTRIBUTION:	Common throughout the wooded regions of Alberta. June - July.

Agrimony is a plant of the open woods, commonly found growing in thickets, clearings and along the sides of woodland paths. It is often mistaken for the Yellow Avens, the resemblance of leaves, and yellow, rose-shaped flowers being very close. However, the flowers of Agrimony are very tiny and are closely set in a long slender terminal spike. After the petals fade the flowering stem continues to lengthen, seperating the flowers which develop into small, hooked, cup-shaped, dry fruits. These bur-like fruits adhere to one's clothing and to the fur of animals.

FALSE MITREWORT
(Text p. 143)

AGRIMONY
(Text p. 143)

SASKATOON
BERRY
(Text p. 146)

ROUND-
LEAVED
HAWTHORN
(Text p. 146)

145

ROSE FAMILY — *ROSACEAE*

SASKATOON BERRY Photo. p. 145
Amelanchier alnifolia *Perennial*

FLOWERS: White; small; showy; numerous in dense clusters; 3/8 - ½ inch across; 5 sepals; 5 white petals; about 20 stamens; 1 ovary inferior; 5 styles.

FRUIT: A blue-purple berry-like pome with a bloom, juicy, sweet.

LEAVES: Alternate, simple, rounded at both ends, coarsely toothed at the apex, ½ - 2 inches long.

HEIGHT: 4 - 12 feet.

HABITAT: Bluffs, coulees, thickets in and around open woods.

DISTRIBUTION: Common and widespread throughout the Province. May - June.

The Indians called this familiar western shrub Misaskutum, shortened today to Saskatoon, which means, "the tree with much wood". The strong, pliable wood was prized for arrow-making, the beautiful, white, somewhat ragged flowers were used in ceremonies to symbolize spring and the plump, purple berries were a favourite sweet. Cooked in huge, spruce-bark tubs, between layers of red hot stones, the berries were cooled, broken up by hand, sprinkled with the juices obtained in cooking and were finally dried over a slow fire. The berries with their sweet, nutty flavour are just as delectable today in preserves and pies as they were in the days of the Indians and early settlers.

ROUND-LEAVED HAWTHORN Photo. p. 145
Crataegus chrysocarpa *Perennial*

FLOWERS: White; showy; about ½ inch across; in small clusters; 5 sepals; 5 petals; numerous stamens; ovary inferior, of several carpels.

FRUIT: A round, red, berry-like pome.

LEAVES: Alternate, simple, rounded, doubly toothed, sometimes lobed, 1 - 2 inches across.

HEIGHT: 5 - 10 feet. Thorny.

HABITAT: Coulees, streambanks and open woods.

DISTRIBUTION: Common throughout Alberta. May.

The name hawthorn, praised often in song and verse, suggests at once the hedgerows of England. In Alberta, there are two native hawthorns just as beautiful as their English cousins. The most common one is the Round-Leaved Hawthorn, a round-topped shrub found growing on the slopes of coulees, streambanks and thickets. The white flowers are charming little apple blossoms produced in showy clusters at the ends of thorny branches. The fruits that follow look like small round red apples. The other Alberta hawthorn (*Crataegus douglasii*) has leaves which are oval and fruits which are purplish-black.

ROSE FAMILY — *ROSACEAE*

YELLOW MOUNTAIN AVENS. DRUMMOND'S MOUNTAIN AVENS

Photo. p. 148

Dryas drummondii

Perennial

FLOWERS:	Yellow; showy; about ¾ inch across; solitary on slender hairy stalks; 8 - 10 sepals; 8 - 10 petals; numerous stamens and pistils.
FRUIT:	A dense head of long-plumed achenes.
LEAVES:	Simple, small, leathery, oval with round-toothed margins, dark green and crinkly above, hoary-white beneath.
HEIGHT:	Prostrate stems; flower stalks 6 - 12 inches.
HABITAT:	Gravel banks and river bars and flats.
DISTRIBUTION:	Rocky Mountains and foothills. June - August.

One of our best-loved and best-known mountain and foothill plants is the Yellow Mountain Avens. It forms a thin to dense mat of green and silver in low-lying meadows, river bars and gravelly flood plains. The variable colour pattern is produced by the prostrate, small leaves which are dark green and shining on top and silver and woolly underneath. The nodding flowers and the erect feathery seed-heads which follow grow a few inches above the foliage on slender, woolly stalks. The flowers are funnel-shaped in the bud but when open are typical little roses. The dark green sepals are covered on the back with a velvety coat of black, gland-tipped hairs and stand out in sharp contrast to the small yellow petals. After pollination both petals and sepals persist and form a dry papery cup for the long silvery plumed achenes.

WHITE MOUNTAIN AVENS

Photo. p. 148

Dryas hookeriana

Perennial

FLOWERS:	Creamy white; showy; about ¾ inch across; solitary on slender hairy stalks; 8 - 10 sepals; 8 - 10 petals; numerous stamens and pistils.
FRUIT:	A dense head of long plumed achenes.
LEAVES:	Simple, small, oblong, leathery, coarsely round-toothed, somewhat rolled under along the margins, upper surface dark green and strongly wrinkled, lower surface white-woolly.
HEIGHT:	Prostrate stems. Flower stalks densely hairy, 2 - 6 inches.
HABITAT:	Dry stony or gravelly ground.
DISTRIBUTION:	Rocky Mountains. At timberline and higher. June-August.

The White Mountain Avens is very like its yellow namesake, only it has creamy white flowers and grows in dry sandy or stony ground mostly above timberline. It is one of the earliest alpine plants to bloom and from June through August it may be found in flower close to banks of melting snow and at higher elevations. Like the yellow species, it also forms mats of beautiful foliage close to the ground and has showy rose-shaped flowers.

YELLOW MOUNTAIN AVENS
(Text p. 147)

WHITE MOUNTAIN AVENS
(Text p. 147)

WILD STRAWBERRY
(Text p. 150)

YELLOW AVENS
(Text p. 150)

WILD STRAWBERRY Photo. p. 149
Fragaria glauca *Perennial*

FLOWERS: White; about ¾ inch across; several in a loose cluster; 5 sepals; 5 petals; many stamens and pistils.

FRUIT: A red juicy edible berry with numerous small seed-like achenes.

LEAVES: Basal from a short perennial rootstock, long-petioled, compound with 3 pale green, coarsely toothed leaflets.

HEIGHT: 3 - 6 inches.

HABITAT: Borders of moist woods and thickets, shady banks, trail sides, clearings and open fields.

DISTRIBUTION: Common and widespread throughout Alberta. May-June.

The Wild Strawberry resembles the cultivated variety so closely that it is unmistakable. Each spring the thick perennial rootstock develops new pale green, three-parted leaves, flowering stalks and long creeping runners or stolons which root at the nodes and produce new plants. When the stolon eventually rots away the tiny new plants are left on their own. The snow white flowers with their golden centres gladden stream banks, woodland paths and dusty roadsides, while the luscious, sweet berries give pleasure to small and large animals, birds and berry-pickers.

YELLOW AVENS Photo. p. 149
Geum allepicum var. *strictum*

FLOWERS: Bright-yellow; showy; ½ - 1 inch across; several in widely-branched clusters; 5 lance-shaped green sepals; 5 yellow petals; numerous stamens and pistils.

FRUIT: A bur-like head of barbed achenes.

LEAVES: Mostly basal, hairy, long-petioled, with large stipules, lyre-shaped, compound of 5 - 7 coarsely-toothed leaflets.

HEIGHT: 1½ - 4 feet.

HABITAT: Wet or moist ground.

DISTRIBUTION: Common in grassland and open woodland regions of Alberta. June - July.

The Yellow Avens is a coarse, hairy, erect perennial with dense dark green foliage. It is common in open woods, damp meadows and shady river banks. It attracts attention only when in flower and in seed. The flowers resemble small yellow roses, with the five yellow petals spread out flat between the long dark green sepals. After pollination the flowers are replaced by bur-like balls of barbed achenes which stick to fur and clothing. The large, basal, lyre-shaped leaves are the distinguishing feature of the plant. These are long-stalked and are divided into several coarsely toothed leaflets, with the terminal one much the largest. In another woodland, yellow-flowered species, *Geum macrophyllum*, the leaves are even larger and coarser.

ROSE FAMILY — *ROSACEAE*

PURPLE OR WATER AVENS   Photo. p. 152
Geum rivale   *Perennial*

FLOWERS:	Brownish-yellowish-purple conspicuous; about ¾ inch across; few; nodding; 5 purple or yellowish sepals; 5 yellow, purple-streaked petals; numerous stamens and petals.
FRUIT:	A bur-like head of achenes.
LEAVES:	Basal leaves; petioled, lyre-shaped, compound of 3 coarsely toothed leaflets; stem leaves, small, variously divided.
HEIGHT:	1 - 3 feet.
HABITAT:	Wet swampy ground.
DISTRIBUTION:	Occasional in boggy land throughout Alberta. June-July.

The Purple or Water Avens as the common name suggests is a plant of boggy swamps and wet places. It has the same lyre-shaped leaves and nodding flowers as the Three-Flowered Avens but the flowers are an odd mixture of yellow, brown and purple and open wide when mature. The only other plant it might be mistaken for is the Purple Cinquefoil for both share a partiality for marshy places. However, the flowers of the latter plant are definitely purple and the leaves have the five to seven leaflets characteristic of the cinquefoils.

THREE-FLOWERED AVENS.   OLD MAN'S WHISKERS Photo. p. 152
Geum triflorum   *Perennial*

FLOWERS:	Purplish-pink; large; ½ - ¾ inch across; in 3's; each flower at the end of a slender nodding stalk; 5 purplish-pink, petal-like, bracted sepals; 5 yellowish petals; numerous stamens and pistils.
FRUIT:	A dense head of achenes with long, feathery, persistent styles.
LEAVES:	Mostly basal, compound of 9 - 19 leaflets.
HEIGHT:	6 - 18 inches.
HABITAT:	Dry grasslands.
DISTRIBUTION:	Abundant everywhere on open prairie and in the foothills and mountains. May - June.

The Three-Flowered Avens is a common but attractive perennial whose bright green, fern-like leaves are among the first new foliage to appear in spring. In early summer, its rosy stems and rose-purple flowers add a touch of pink to the variegated carpet of herbs and grasses which covers hundreds of miles of prairie and foothill grasslands. The single flowering stem bears a tuft of leaves half-way up and at the very top, three odd urn-shaped flowers, each one on a separate drooping stalk. During pollination, the five rose-coloured sepals open just wide enough to expose an inner lining of five cream-coloured petals and a tuft of stamens. After pollination, the flowers are replaced by heads of long, plume-like achenes which give to the plant the common name of Old Man's Whiskers. By the time the achenes are ripe, the three nodding flower stalks have grown erect and the plant looks like a three-branched candlestick.

DORTHEA CALVERLEY

PURPLE or WATER AVENS
(Text p. 151)

H. J. BRODIE

THREE-FLOWERED AVENS
(Text p. 151)

SILVERWEED
(Text. p. 154)

EARLY
CINQUEFOIL
(Text p. 154)

SILVERWEED
Potentilla anserina

Photo. p. 153
Perennial

FLOWERS:	Yellow; showy; ¾ - 1 inch across; borne singly; long stalked; 5 sepals; 5 petals; numerous stamens and pistils.
FRUIT:	A head of small achenes.
LEAVES:	Basal, in tufts, 3 - 18 inches long, compound of 7 - 21 toothed leaflets, smooth and green above, silky-silvery hairy beneath.
HEIGHT:	Prostrate, creeping.
HABITAT:	Low, wet places and slough margins.
DISTRIBUTION:	Common throughout Alberta. June - September.

The Silverweed is one of the best known of the cinquefoils, even though its leaves often have many more leaflets than the customary five. It grows in dense tufts or mats in low meadows, mudflats and along the margins of lakes and sloughs, sending out long leafy runners which root at the nodes and eventually give rise to a series of new plants. The leaves are the most noticeable feature of this plant, for they are usually green and smooth on top and silvery-hairy underneath. Although sometimes mistaken for a buttercup, the bright yellow flowers are not cup-shaped but are like a rose and bloom from early spring right through September.

EARLY CINQUEFOIL
Potentilla concinna

Photo. p. 153
Perennial

FLOWERS:	Yellow; showy; ¼ - ½ inch across; solitary; 5 hairy sepals; 5 petals; numerous stamens and pistils.
FRUIT:	A head of small achenes.
LEAVES:	Mostly basal, compound of usually 5 oblong, toothed leaflets, greenish-silky hairy above, densely white-woolly beneath, each leaflet ½ - 1 inch long.
HEIGHT:	Up to 4 inches.
HABITAT:	Dry prairie and hillsides.
DISTRIBUTION:	Common throughout Southern Alberta. April - July.

About twenty-five different species of cinquefoils are found in Alberta. They all have leaves made up of several leaflets and have rose-shaped flowers, but they differ in detail. The Early Cinquefoil begins blooming in April and is distinguished by a dense cluster of basal leaves and several leafy stems which spread out from the deeply rooted stem-base. The leaves consist of five small leaflets arranged like fingers on the end of the petiole. These are dull green silky-hairy on top and densely white-woolly beneath. In the wind, the leaves appear white more often than they do green. The pretty yellow flowers like shiny gold pieces add a touch of colour to the dry hillsides and grassy slopes.

SHRUBBY CINQUEFOIL

Potentilla fruticosa

Photo. p. 156

Perennial

FLOWERS:	Yellow; large; ¾ - 1 inch across; numerous, usually in small clusters; 5 sepals; 5 petals; numerous stamens and pistils.
FRUIT:	A head of densely hairy achenes.
LEAVES:	Numerous, compound of 5 toothed, hairy leaflets, about ½ inch long.
HEIGHT:	1 - 3 feet.
HABITAT:	Moist meadows and dry slopes.
DISTRIBUTION:	Common throughout the prairie and foothill regions of Southern Alberta, grassy areas in the Rocky Mountains and boggy thickets of Northern Alberta. June - August.

The Shrubby Cinquefoil, as its name suggests, has woody stems and a shrubby form. It is widely distributed throughout the ranchland regions of Alberta. When growing in abundance its presence indicates overgrazing by cattle and horses. When grazing is restricted or controlled, these low growing woody shrubs are soon overtopped and eventually smothered out by the taller and more vigorously growing grasses. It has the beautiful rose-shaped flowers characteristic of the cinquefoils and is frequently grown in the garden as an ornamental shrub.

ROUGH CINQUEFOIL

Potentilla norvegica

Photo. p. 156

FLOWERS:	Yellow; showy; ¼ - ½ inch across; numerous in a fairly dense leafy cluster; 5 sepals with 5 bractlets; 5 petals; numerous stamens and pistils.
FRUIT:	A head of small, brown achenes.
LEAVES:	Lower leaves long-petioled, compound of 3 hairy, coarsely toothed leaflets; upper leaves compound of 3 hairy leaflets, no petioles.
HEIGHT:	6 - 24 inches.
HABITAT:	Wet meadows, roadsides and waste places.
DISTRIBUTION:	Common throughout Alberta. June - August.

The Rough Cinquefoil grows almost anywhere: on stream banks, in moist fields, in waste places and in gardens. It is a very leafy plant with erect, somewhat spreading stems. These are densely covered with rough hairs and are often green on one side and red on the other. It has the yellow, rose-shaped flowers typical of most of the cinquefoils but differs from them in having leaves of three leaflets instead of the usual five. The lower leaves are long-stalked and resemble those of the strawberry plant while the fruit, with the enlarged green calyx enclosing a head of small achenes, looks like a strawberry that has failed to enlarge and to ripen.

155

SHRUBBY CINQUEFOIL
(Text p. 155)

ROUGH CINQUEFOIL
(Text p. 155)

ALPINE CINQUEFOIL
(Text p. 158)

PIN CHERRY
(Text p. 158)

ALPINE CINQUEFOIL
Potentilla nivea

Photo. p. 157
Perennial

FLOWERS:	Yellow; small; 3/16 - ½ inch across; few on long stalks in a terminal cluster; 5 sepals; 5 petals; numerous stamens and pistils.
FRUIT:	A head of small achenes.
LEAVES:	Mostly basal, compound of usually 3 rounded-oblong, toothed leaflets, green above, white-hairy beneath.
HEIGHT:	4 - 8 inches.
HABITAT:	Rocky slopes.
DISTRIBUTION:	High altitudes in the Rocky Mountains. June - July.

The Alpine Cinquefoil grows on exposed slopes and in rocky crevices well above timberline and comes into bloom early in June, often through banks of snow which are still to be seen in sheltered places. It is a dwarfed but sturdy plant with a stout stem-base and numerous small three-parted leaves that hug the ground in a dense silvery-green mat. The flowering stems are usually short and bear a few tiny leaflets at the joints while several small, yellow, rose-shaped flowers appear at the top.

PIN CHERRY
Prunus pennsylvanica

Perennial
Photo. p. 157

FLOWERS:	White; small; about 1/4 - 3/8 inch across; numerous in a round-topped cluster; floral tube cup-shaped; 5 sepals, soon falling off; 5 petals, white; stamens about 20 extending beyond the petals; 1 ovary; 1 style.
FRUIT:	A small, round, fleshy, sour, bright red, 1 seeded-stone fruit (drupe).
LEAVES:	Alternate, simple, lance-shaped, finely toothed, shiny green above, smooth, 3 - 7 inches long.
HEIGHT:	12 - 30 feet.
HABITAT:	Dry woods and thickets, bluffs, ravines and hillsides.
DISTRIBUTION:	Common and widespread throughout the Province. April - May.

Only two cherries, the Pin Cherry and the Choke Cherry, are native to Alberta. Both are tall shrubs rather than trees. The Pin Cherry is found in bluffs, ravines, sandy hillsides, fence rows and in clearings. In the spring it is easily distinguishable from the Choke Cherry by its flowers which grow in long-stemmed, small, lateral clusters. In the fall the fruits are small, bright red cherries each hanging on a separate long stalk. They are greedily devoured by the birds. For humans these cherries make delicious jelly and preserves.

CHOKE CHERRY   Photo. p. 160
Prunus virginiana var. *melanocarpa*   *Perennial*

FLOWERS: White; small; numerous in dense cylindrical clusters; floral tube cup-shaped, about 3/8 inch across; 5 sepals soon falling away; 5 white petals; about 20 stamens extending beyond the petals; 1 ovary; 1 style.

FRUIT: A small, round, black, fleshy drupe, juicy and astringent.

LEAVES: Alternate, simple, egg-shaped or broadly oval, thickish, sharply toothed, smooth on both sides, 1 - 3 inches long.

HEIGHT: 6 - 25 feet.

HABITAT: Bluffs, ravines, sand hills, thickets and open woodlands.

DISTRIBUTION: Common and widespread throughout Alberta. May-June.

The most conspicuous white-flowering tall shrub or small tree of spring in Alberta is the Choke Cherry. It is common in thickets and along the borders of open woods, roadsides and streams. The flowers appear in May and June in thick cylindrical clusters up to six inches long. It is in this respect that it differs from the Pin Cherry with which it is sometimes confused. The Choke Cherry is just as conspicuous in the fall when its branches are bent down by the weight of the black juicy berries. The cherries have a bitter astringent quality that puckers up the mouth but they make a feast for the birds.

PRICKLY ROSE   Photo. p. 160
Rosa acicularis   *Perennial*

FLOWERS: Pink; large; showy; singly or in clusters; 2 - 3 inches across; 5 green leaf-like sepals, 5 pink widely-spreading petals; numerous stamens; ovary inferior, of many carpels.

FRUIT: Commonly called a rose hip, orange-red and composed of the fleshy, floral tube and enclosed hairy achenes.

LEAVES: Alternate, compound with 5 - 7 coarsely toothed leaflets. Stipules broad and hairy.

HEIGHT: 1 - 3 feet.

HABITAT: In and around open woods, thickets, clearings, burns, fields, bluffs, roadsides, railroad embankments and riverbanks.

DISTRIBUTION: Common and widespread throughout the Province. June - August.

The Prickly Rose is a bushy shrub with dark green foliage, prickly stems and large, showy, open-faced flowers, the pink petals of which rim a shower of yellow-gold stamens in the centre. It can be found growing almost anywhere and it is Alberta's best known and best loved wild flower. It hybridizes freely with another common and confusingly similar species, the Common Wild Rose, *Rosa woodsii*. The orange-red fruits or hips, though dry and fibrous, are rich in vitamins. It became Alberta's floral emblem in 1930 after it was voted on by Alberta's school children. It also appears on a 5c Canadian Commemorative Stamp issued in 1966.

CHOKE CHERRIES
(Text p. 159)

PRICKLY ROSE
(Text p. 159)

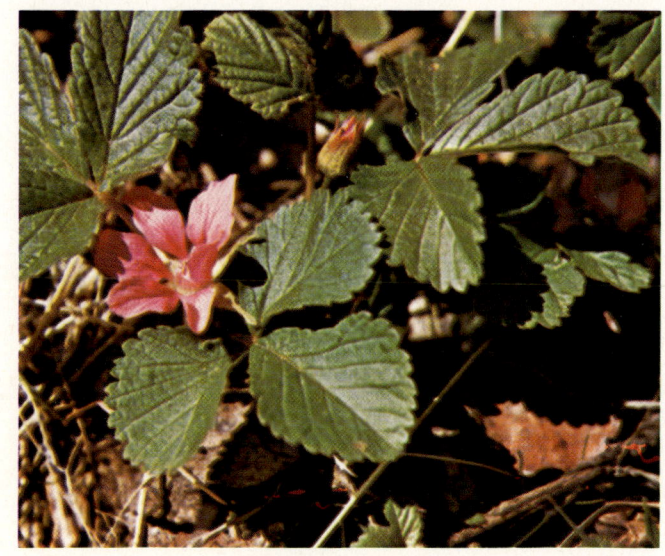

J. H. WHYTE

DWARF RASPBERRY
(Text. p. 162)

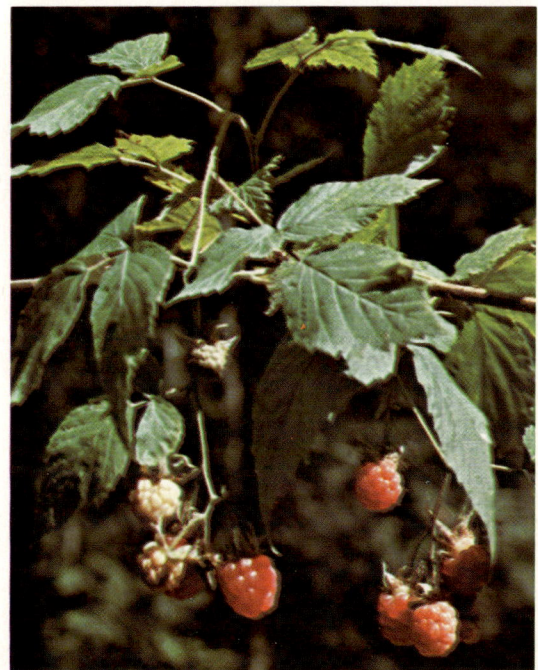

WILD RED
RASPBERRY
(Text p. 162)

J. CLAESSEN

161

DWARF OR ARCTIC RASPBERRY
Rubus acaulis

Photo. p. 161
Perennial

FLOWERS:
Rose or red-purple; large; ¾ - 1 inch across; solitary; 5 sepals; 5 petals; numerous stamens and pistils.

FRUIT:
A large red juicy berry.

LEAVES:
Several in tufts from a perennial rootstock; compound of 3 leaflets, margins unevenly toothed.

HEIGHT:
3 - 10 inches.

HABITAT:
In Sphagnum Moss, damp boggy woods and muskegs.

DISTRIBUTION:
Widely distributed throughout the wooded regions of Alberta. May - July.

Almost anywhere in muskeg country or boggy woods, the Dwarf or Arctic Raspberry is sure to be found pushing up through a damp mantle of spruce needles and Sphagnum Moss. Like the Labrador Tea, among which it grows, it is one of the most characteristic plants of the muskeg vegetation. It grows close to the ground and its leaves, flowers and red juicy fruits correspond to the typical raspberry pattern. However, it can be distinguished easily from other raspberries by its red-purple flowers.

WILD RED RASPBERRY
Rubus strigosus

Photo. p. 161
Perennial

FLOWERS:
White; showy; about ½ inch across; several in small clusters; 5 sepals; 5 petals; numerous stamens and pistils.

FRUIT:
A large, red, juicy berry.

LEAVES:
Alternate, compound of 3 - 5 oval leaflets, dark green above and white-woolly beneath.

HEIGHT:
3 - 6 feet.

HABITAT:
In shady borders of woods, cleared or burned-over woodlands, bluffs and river banks.

DISTRIBUTION:
Common and widely spread throughout the wooded regions of Alberta. June - July.

The Wild Raspberry is abundant on the borders of woods, thickets, clearings and roadsides. Its stems or so-called canes, leaves, flowers and fruits are all so similar to the cultivated variety that it is easily recognized. The stout more or less bristly stems may reach a height of six feet and have the habit of bending over until the tips reach the earth. Once in the ground, buds and roots develop and when the canes either break or rot away the rooted stem tips grow into new raspberry bushes. The same thing occurs when the canes are bent down under the weight of a fallen tree or heavy snow. The round, light red berries with a sweetness all their own have been the constant food of Indians and early settlers and have helped many an explorer and trapper to stave off starvation.

DEWBERRY. TRAILING RASPBERRY

Photo. p. 164

Rubus pubescens   *Perennial*

FLOWERS: White or pinkish; showy; about ½ inch across; several in small clusters; 5 sepals, bent backwards; 5 petals; numerous stamens and pistils.

FRUIT: A round red berry.

LEAVES: Alternate, compound of 3 or occasionally 5 oval, sharply-toothed leaflets, green on both sides.

HEIGHT: Trailing.

HABITAT: Damp woods and thickets.

DISTRIBUTION: Common throughout the parkland region of Alberta. June - July.

The Dewberry looks like the Wild Red Raspberry, but instead of growing upright it sprawls on the ground in a tangle of trailing stems and leaves. The flowers are typical of the raspberries and give rise to round, red, juicy fruits. Another trailing species, *Rubus pedatus,* grows in shady coniferous woods and is one of our prettiest mountain and foothill plants. It creeps over the mossy forest floor by means of slender strawberry-like runners which at the nodes, send up one long thread-like stalk with a single flower and two or three five-cleft leaves and send down several roots into the moss. These strings of small, white, star-shaped flowers and dainty leaves may be two or three feet long.

THIMBLEBERRY. SALMON BERRY

Photo. p. 164

Rubus parviflorus   *Perennial*

FLOWERS: White; large; 1 - 2 inches across; few in a long cluster; 5 sepals; 5 petals; numerous stamens and pistils.

FRUIT: A half spherical red juicy edible berry.

LEAVES: Simple, large, velvety, maple-like, 3 - 5 lobed, coarsely toothed margins, 4 - 10 inches broad.

HEIGHT: 2 - 6 feet.

HABITAT: Moist shady borders of woods and thickets, clearings, mountain and foothill slopes and valleys.

DISTRIBUTION: Common in Southwestern Alberta. June - July.

A shrubby mountain species found growing along the moist borders of woods and thickets, the Thimbleberry is notable for its large, velvety leaves which form a dark green background for the large white flowers and bright red fruits. The flower resembles the Wild Rose and the berry, about the size of a quarter, looks like a flat raspberry. The berries have a tart taste and are very seedy and do not make as good preserves as the raspberries and brambles to which group, the Thimbleberry is closely related.

DEWBERRY
(Text p. 163)

THIMBLEBERRY
(Text p. 163)

CLOUDBERRY
(Text p. 166)

CLOUDBERRY FRUIT
(Text p. 166)

CLOUDBERRY. BAKED APPLE BERRY
Rubus chamaemorus

Photo. p. 165
Perennial

FLOWERS:	White; large; ½ - 1 inch across; solitary; long-stalked; 5 sepals; 5 petals; both staminate and pistillate flowers.
FRUIT:	A large, soft, yellowish berry.
LEAVES:	1 - 3, long-petioled, leathery, round, 5 - 7 lobed, toothed margins, 1 - 3 inches broad.
HEIGHT:	4 - 10 inches.
HABITAT:	In Sphagnum Moss, muskegs, bogs and bog forests.
DISTRIBUTION:	Common in boggy wooded areas throughout Alberta. June.

It is hard to believe that this common muskeg and bog forest plant derives its name from its home-base in the clouds of the high White Mountains of New Hampshire. A low plant, it grows in mounds of Sphagnum Moss, that softest and most absorbent of all mosses that "squishes" like a sponge when it is tread upon. Although flowers and fruits resemble those of its close relatives, the raspberries, it can be distinguished by its leaves. These are few in number and spring from a perennial creeping rootstock. The thick, leathery leaf blades are relatively broad, almost round with five to seven coarsely toothed rounded lobes. The large, juicy, amber-coloured berries are enjoyed by birds, chipmunks and berry-pickers.

WESTERN MOUNTAIN ASH. ROWAN TREE
Sorbus scopulina

Photo. p. 168
Perennial

FLOWERS:	White; small, ¼ - 3/8 inch across; urn-shaped; numerous in a dense, slightly rounded cluster, 3 - 6 inches across; 5 sepals; 5 petals; many stamens; 1 pistil with several styles.
FRUIT:	A small, orange-red berry.
LEAVES:	Alternate, compound of 11 - 13 elliptical to lance-shaped, toothed leaflets.
HEIGHT:	3 - 12 feet.
HABITAT:	Woods, ravines and moist, open hillsides.
DISTRIBUTION:	Occasionally found in Western Alberta, Swan Hills and Cypress Hills. June.

The Western Mountain Ash grows in woods and moist, open slopes and resembles the cultivated species so closely that it is easily recognized. It is most conspicuous in early fall when both leaves and berries turn a bright red. It is easily transplanted and makes an attractive ornamental. Another very similar but somewhat shrubbier species, *Sorbus sitchensis*, grows in the mountains of the southwestern corner of Alberta.

SIBBALDIA   Photo. p. 168
Sibbaldia procumbens   *Perennial*

.FLOWERS:	Yellow; small; about ¼ inch across; numerous in dense clusters; 5 sepals with alternating bracts; 5 petals; 5 stamens; numerous carpels.
FRUIT:	A head of small achenes.
LEAVES:	Compound of 3 leaflets, each leaflet toothed at the apex and ½ - 1¼ inches long.
HEIGHT:	2 - 4 inches.
HABITAT:	Alpine meadows, stony ground.
DISTRIBUTION:	High altitudes in the Rocky Mountains. June - July.

Sibbaldia is a wee creeping alpine plant found in the Rocky Mountains among rocks and shaly slopes at high elevations. Here it forms dense tufts of matted stems and dark green leaves. Its scientific name, Sibbaldia, is after the Scottish botanist. The three-parted leaves resemble those of the Wild Strawberry but the flowers are yellow and smaller and instead of developing into juicy berries, they form dry heads of small achenes. Each flower resembles a small cart wheel, the short yellow petals, like yellow spokes, alternating with the larger dark green sepals.

WHITE MEADOWSWEET. SPIRAEA   Not Illustrated
Spiraea lucida   *Perennial*

FLOWERS:	White; minute; numerous in a dense flat-topped cluster; 5 sepals; 5 petals; many stamens; 1 pistil.
FRUIT:	A small dry papery pod.
LEAVES:	Alternate, simple, short-petioled, green above, pale beneath, coarsely toothed towards the apex, ¾ - 2½ inches long.
HEIGHT:	1 - 2 feet.
HABITAT:	Open coniferous woods, clearings.
DISTRIBUTION:	Western Alberta, mainly in the foothills and Rocky Mountains. July - August.

The White Meadowsweet is a low mountain and foothill shrub found growing at the edge of pine and poplar woods in clearings and on rocky thinly wooded slopes. It grows from a creeping perennial rootstock and although it is called a shrub, it often consists of only one erect leafy stem. The tiny white flowers appear at the end of the stem in a flat-topped cluster. Although minute, each flower has the usual rose-type shape and gives way after fertilization to a small dry pod-like fruit.

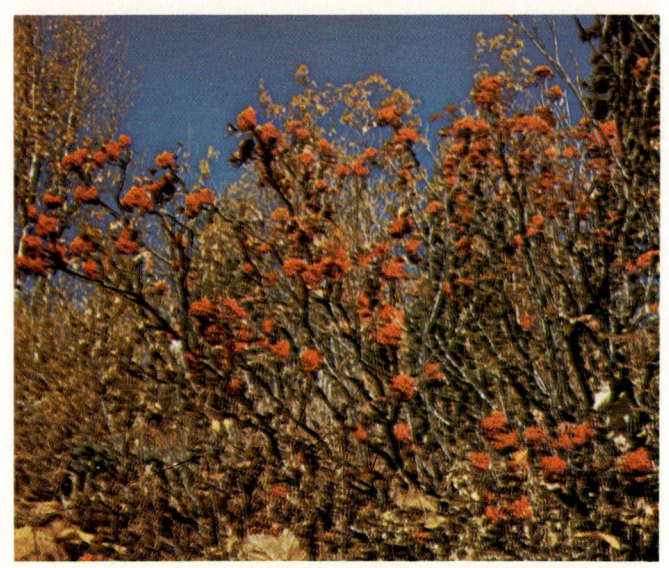

WESTERN MOUNTAIN ASH
(Text p. 166)

SIBBALDIA
(Text p. 167)

GROUND PLUM
(Text p. 170)

J. A. CAMPBELL

NARROW-LEAVED MILK VETCH
(Text p. 170)

PEA FAMILY — *LEGUMINOSAE*

The Alberta representatives of this large and well known family number well over sixty species. A few are annuals but most of them are low-growing, herbaceous perennials with stipulate, compound leaves and distinctive butterfly-shaped flowers. Each flower consists of 5 sepals, 5 petals, 10 stamens and 1 pistil. The uppermost and largest petal is called the standard, the two at the sides are called wings and the lower two are fused to form the characteristic keel which houses the stamens and pistil. When a bee pushes down on the wings of the flower, the keel opens suddenly and the stigma and stamens are pressed against the bee's hairy body. The single pistil ripens into a dry pod called a legume. Many important crop plants belong to this family and are commonly classed as legumes.

GROUND PLUM Photo. p. 169
Astragalus crassicarpus *Perennial*

FLOWERS: Yellowish-white with purple tinged keel; showy; about 3/4 inch long; numerous in a loose cluster; 5 sepals; 5 petals; 10 stamens; 1 pistil.

FRUIT: A reddish, fleshy, round pod, about ¾ inches in diameter.

LEAVES: Numerous, compound of 17 - 25 narrowly oblong leaflets, smooth above, hairy beneath.

HEIGHT: Stems prostrate, mat-forming.

HABITAT: Open prairie and dry grassy hillsides.

DISTRIBUTION: Southern Alberta. May - June.

The Ground Plum is one of about two dozen plants belonging to the Pea Family and which form a distinct group called the milk vetches. This hardy perennial grows in the open prairie, grassy hillsides and along the edges of the cut-banks, and blooms most of the summer. The leafy stems which end in small tufts of yellowish-white, purple-tipped flowers, sprawl over the ground from a stout stem-base and sometimes form a dense mat two to three feet across. The flowers, although long and narrow, are typical pea-shaped blossoms. The rounded flower-keel distinguishes it from the loco weeds. Its red round seed pods attract more attention that its flowers as they look like red plums spread out over the dry leaves. Some Milk Vetches are poisonous to cattle but the Ground Plum is harmless.

NARROW-LEAVED MILK VETCH Photo. p. 169
Astragalus pectinatus *Perennial*

FLOWERS: Yellowish-white; showy; about 3/4 inch long; in loose clusters; 5 sepals; 5 petals; 10 stamens; 1 pistil.

FRUIT: A broad, oblong, dry, hard pod.

LEAVES: Compound of 9 - 17 long and very narrow leaflets.

HEIGHT: ½ - 2 feet.

HABITAT: Lighter soils of prairie and foothill regions.

DISTRIBUTION: Southern Alberta. May - June.

The Narrow-Leaved Milk Vetch is another widely-spread species found on the lighter soils of Southern Alberta. It forms a clump of erect or spreading leafy stems ending in conspicuous clusters of narrowly elongated, yellowish-white, pea-shaped flowers. Its distinguishing feature is its numerous and very narrow leaflets. This plant has the bad reputation of absorbing the poisonous chemical selenium from the soil and storing it in large enough amounts to be injurious to cattle. However, it is generally avoided by grazing stock animals.

TWO-GROOVED MILK VETCH
Astragalus bisulcatus

Photo. p. 172
Perennial

FLOWERS:	Reddish-purple; showy; about ½ inch long; borne in long dense clusters; 5 sepals; 5 petals; 10 stamens; 1 pistil.
FRUIT:	A narrowly-oblong, dry pod with two deep grooves.
LEAVES:	Compound of 17 - 27 elliptical leaflets.
HEIGHT:	1 - 3 feet.
HABITAT:	Shallow light soils on coulee slopes and valleys.
DISTRIBUTION:	Common throughout Southern Alberta. June - July.

Growing often in large clumps, on dry hillsides and in coulees, the Two-Grooved Milk Vetch is the most spectacular of all the milk vetches. The pea-shaped flowers are a beautiful deep purple and are borne in the customary vetch fashion in a long dense spike at the end of the erect leafy stalks. Both flowers and pods point downwards and the latter, when dry and papery, are clearly marked by two deep grooves on the upper side. Like the Narrow-Leaved Milk Vetch, this plant has a bad name for gathering selenium from the soil in large enough quantities to make it poisonous to cattle and sheep.

DRUMMOND'S MILK VETCH
Astragalus drummondii

Photo. p. 172
Perennial

FLOWERS:	Yellowish-white; showy; about ¾ inch long; borne in long dense clusters; 5 sepals; 5 petals; 10 stamens; 1 pistil.
FRUIT:	A narrow, dry, smooth, drooping pod.
LEAVES:	Compound of 15 - 33 oblong elliptical leaflets, hairy above.
HEIGHT:	1 - 2 feet.
HABITAT:	Dry hillsides.
DISTRIBUTION:	Southern and Central Alberta. June - July.

Drummond's Milk Vetch, like most of the two dozen Alberta milk vetches, is a plant of the open prairie and rolling foothills. It is a handsome plant with several stems which end in long clusters of yellowish-white pea-shaped flowers. Both stems and the upper surfaces of the leaves are loosely covered with fine soft hairs. The flower keel is sometimes tinged with purple and ends in a blunt tip which is characteristic of the milk vetches and which distinguishes them from the loco weeds. After fertilization, the flower clusters turn to clusters of downward-pointing smooth narrow pods. This plant is not poisonous to cattle and sheep.

171

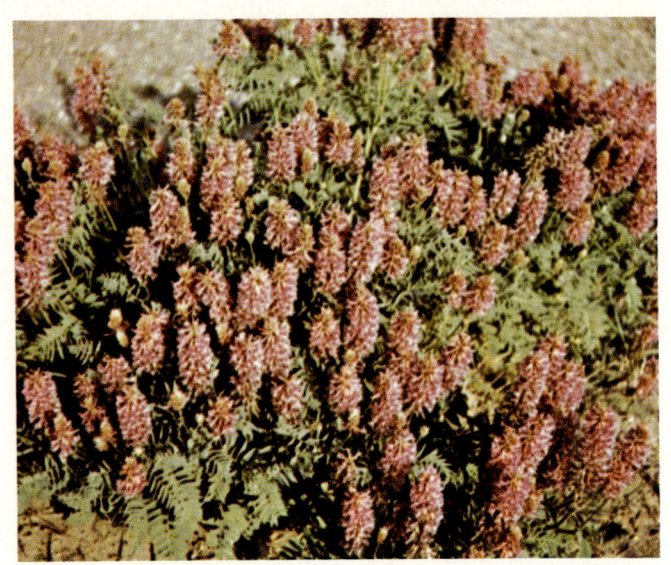

TWO-GROOVED MILK VETCH
(Text p. 171)

DRUMMOND'S MILK VETCH
(Text p. 171)

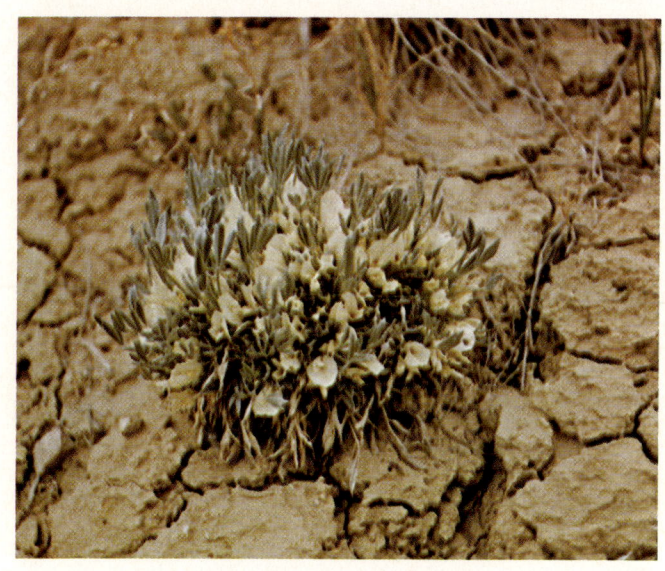

E. GUSHUL

CUSHION MILK VETCH
(Text. p. 174)

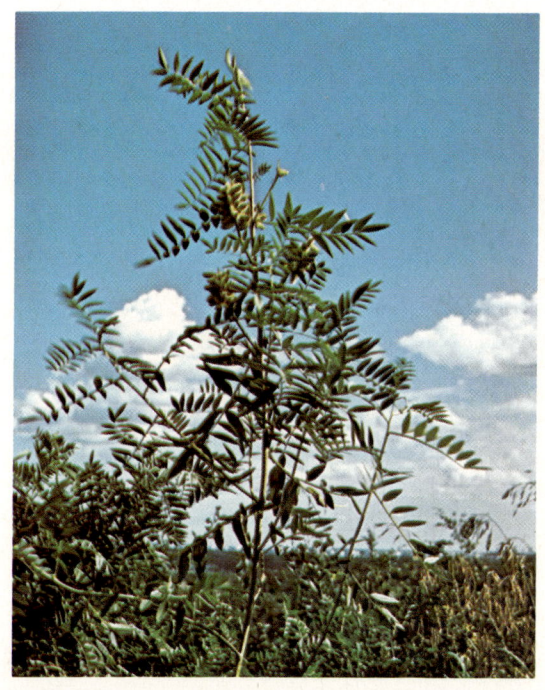

WILD
LICORICE
(Text p. 174)

H. A. MacGREGOR

173

CUSHION MILK VETCH
Astragalus triphyllus

Photo. p. 173
Perennial

FLOWERS: Yellowish-white; showy; ½ - ¾ inch long; numerous in short clusters; 5 sepals; 5 petals; 10 stamens; 1 pistil.

FRUIT: A short, oval, silvery hairy pod.

LEAVES: Compound of 3 elliptical leaflets, silvery hairy.

HEIGHT: 2 - 4 inches.

HABITAT: Open prairie and dry hillsides.

DISTRIBUTION: Fairly common. Southern Alberta. May - June.

The Cushion Milk Vetch is a low-growing species which forms dense mats of leaves and flower stems on the eroded sides of coulees and gullies and on dry hillsides. The distinguishing feature of this milk vetch is its three-parted clover-like leaves. These are densely covered with soft silvery hairs and they are so thickly clustered around the base of the stunted stem that they partially hide the short-stemmed clusters of cream-coloured flowers. The pods, too, are covered with the same silvery hairs as the leaves. Several other mat-forming milk vetches grow in the dry prairie region, differing mainly in the details of leaves and in the colour of the flowers.

WILD LICORICE
Glycyrrhiza lepidota

Photo. p. 173
Perennial

FLOWERS: Yellowish-white; showy; about ½ inch long; numerous in short dense clusters; 5 sepals; 5 petals; 10 stamens; 1 pistil.

FRUIT: An oblong, reddish-brown pod, ½ - ¾ inch long, covered with hooked prickles.

LEAVES: Several, compound of 11 - 19 oblong, pale green glandular-dotted leaflets.

HEIGHT: 1 - 3 feet.

HABITAT: Moist prairie slopes, coulees and stream banks.

DISTRIBUTION: Common throughout Southern and Central Alberta. July.

The Wild Licorice is a coarse perennial and is conspicuous in moist depressions on the prairie, river banks and coulees. Its compound leaves and pea-shaped flowers mark it at once as a member of the Pea Family, but is most easily recognized by its fruits. These are oblong, reddish-brown pods densely covered with long-hooked barbs. Although related to the European plant that provides the black extract used for making licorice candy, the tough rootstocks of the Alberta species have only a slight licorice flavour. The Indians, however, after roasting the roots in embers to remove the fibrous cores, used them as a vegetable to balance their customary diet of fish and berries.

MACKENZIE'S HEDYSARUM
Hedysarum mackenzii

Photo. p. 176
Perennial

FLOWERS: Reddish-purple; showy; about ¾ inch long; numerous in densely crowded, long, spike-like clusters; 5 sepals; 5 petals; 10 stamens; 1 ovary.

FRUIT: A flat, jointed, seed pod.

LEAVES: Compound with numerous, smallish leaflets.

HEIGHT: 8 - 16 inches.

HABITAT: River banks and grassy hillsides.

DISTRIBUTION: Not common, but widely distributed eastward from the Rocky Mountains. May - July.

The hedysarums belong to a group of the Pea Family which is noted for its jointed seed pods and for the colour of its flowers. Mackenzie's Hedysarum is a low, somewhat bushy, perennial with long, crowded flower-clusters terminating each leafy stem. The individual pea-shaped flowers are a reddish-purple and the plant in full bloom looks as though it were on fire. This gorgeous plant enhances many a river bank, grassy slope and open mountain wood. Three other species of hedysarum grow in Alberta; two with lighter purple or pinkish flowers and one with sulphur yellow or cream-coloured flowers.

WILD SWEET PEA. VETCHLING
Lathyrus ochroleucus

Photo. p. 176
Perennial

FLOWERS: Yellowish-white; showy; about ⅝ inch long; several in a cluster; 5 sepals; 5 petals; 10 stamens; 1 pistil.

FRUIT: A somewhat flattened pod, about 1½ inches long.

LEAVES: Alternate, compound, with broad stipules and terminal tendril.

HEIGHT: Long and twining.

HABITAT: In bluffs, open woods and thickets.

DISTRIBUTION: Common throughout wooded areas of Alberta. May-July.

The Wild Sweet Pea or Vetchling is the native counterpart of the cultivated sweet pea. A climbing plant with a smooth, slender, somewhat angled stem, the Wild Sweet Pea twines about any shrubbery which borders open woods and thickets and grows along the sides of roads and streams. Although the cream-coloured flowers are smaller than the cultivated sweet pea and lack fragrance, they add charm and colour to the sombre green of a poplar wood in early summer. The flower has the conventional pea family structure; one upright petal or standard, two lateral petals or wings and the boat-shaped keel.

MACKENZIE'S HEDYSARUM
(Text p. 175)

WILD SWEET
PEA
(Text p. 175)

176

PURPLE WILD PEA VINE
(Text p. 178)

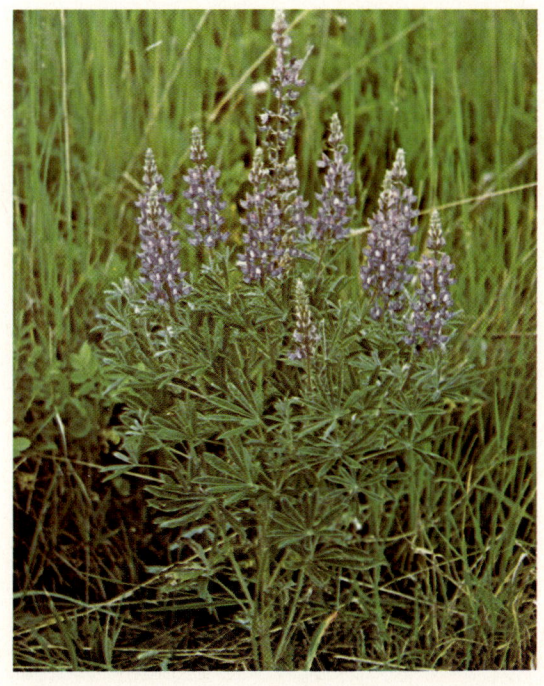

WILD LUPINE
(Text p. 178)

PURPLE WILD PEA VINE Photo. p. 177

Lathyrus venosus var. *intonsus* *Perennial*

FLOWERS:	Purple; showy; ½ - ⅝ inch long; 12 - 20 in dense clusters; 5 sepals; 5 petals; 10 stamens; 1 pistil.
FRUIT:	A dry, veiny pod, about 2 inches long.
LEAVES:	Alternate, compound, with small stipules and terminal tendril.
HEIGHT:	Climbing; stem stout and 4-angled.
HABITAT:	Open woods and thickets.
DISTRIBUTION:	Common throughout the wooded areas of Alberta. July.

Dense clusters of beautiful, purple, pea-shaped blossoms growing erect along a leafy climbing stem explain the popular name of the Purple Wild Pea Vine. Many short papery pods which hang in clusters follow the flowers. Like many of our native legumes, it is a valuable source of wild hay in scrubby wooded regions of the province.

WILD LUPINE Photo. p. 177

Lupinus argenteus *Perennial*

FLOWERS:	Blue or violet; showy; about 3/8 inch long; numerous in a long spike; 5 sepals; 5 petals; 10 stamens; 1 pistil.
FRUIT:	A slightly flattened, silky-hairy pod, ¾ - 1 inch long.
LEAVES:	Alternate, compound of 6 - 9 leaflets, silvery hairy beneath.
HEIGHT:	1 - 2 feet.
HABITAT:	Fields, grasslands and roadsides.
DISTRIBUTION:	Common in prairie and foothill regions throughout Southern Alberta. July - August.

This Wild Lupine is the most common and most widely spread of several species which are very similar in appearance and it turns fields and roadsides throughout the prairie and foothill regions a glorious blue. During midsummer, there is probably no more beautiful sight in nature than the olive green of waving grasses tinged with the blue of lupines and the pink of the Three Flowered Avens. Their showy spikes of sky-blue flowers and silky, rich green, shapely leaves endear the lupines to rancher and motorist alike. This particular species is a sturdy perennial and grows in dense colourful clumps. The individual flowers are built on the typical pea-blossom pattern, the broad upright standard bending backwards at the sides away from the sickle-shaped keel. Although some of the lupines are considered poisonous to sheep, all three Alberta species are held in good repute as forage. Occasionally Wild Lupines with white flowers are found but these are not considered to be a separate species.

ALFALFA. LUCERNE
Medicago sativa

Photo. p. 180
Annual or Perennial

FLOWERS: Blue, mauve or whitish; showy; ¼ - 3/8 inch long; numerous in dense short clusters; 5 sepals; 5 petals; 10 stamens; 1 pistil.

FRUIT: A spirally twisted hairy pod.

LEAVES: Compound of 3 oval, toothed leaflets, ½ - 1¼ inches long.

HEIGHT: 1 - 3 feet.

HABITAT: Roadsides and waste places.

DISTRIBUTION: Common throughout most of Alberta. June - July.

Alfalfa is another valuable introduced fodder plant that has become commonly established in dry fields, ditches and along roadsides. It grows in a bunchy, spreading way: its trefoil leaves, corkscrew-shaped pods and absence of tendrils helps to distinguish it from the vetches with which it is sometimes confused. Its roots, like those of most legumes, bear countless numbers of small swellings produced by bacteria. Protected and nourished by the root tissue, the bacteria convert gaseous nitrogen into soluble nitrates. The Alfalfa plant uses some of this stored nitrogen for growth, but the bulk is returned to the soil after the plant is turned under by the plough.

WHITE SWEET CLOVER
Melilotus alba

Photo. p. 180
Annual or Biennial

FLOWERS: White; small; about 3/16 inch long; numerous, densely crowded in long, narrow, tapering clusters; 5 sepals; 5 petals; 10 stamens; 1 pistil.

FRUIT: A short, thick, straight 1 - 2 seeded pod.

LEAVES: Compound of 3 leaflets, each ½ - 1 inch long; toothed.

HEIGHT: 2 - 6 feet.

HABITAT: Roadside and waste places.

DISTRIBUTION: Common throughout Alberta. June - July.

The White Sweet Clover is not a native plant, but has reverted from cultivation and is so common in waste places, clearings and along roadsides that it is often classed as a weed. The extremely small, elongated, pea-shaped flowers are strung on a long, delicate, tapering spike. The plant is a tall, much-branched, bushy perennial and by early summer the flowers are in such profusion that the small trefoil leaves are scarcely visible. The leaves become more conspicuous when the flowers are replaced by small yellowish pods. The seeds are minute beans with extremely hard seed coats. Another similar species, *Melilotus officinalis,* has yellow flowers. Both plants are excellent nectar producers and are extensively grown for fodder and fertilizing the soil.

179

ALFALFA
(Text p. 179)

WHITE SWEET
CLOVER
(Text p. 179)

A. H. DICKSON

PURPLE PRAIRIE CLOVER
(Text p. 182)

SHOWY LOCO WEED
(Text p. 182)

PURPLE PRAIRIE CLOVER
Petalostemon purpureum

Photo. p. 181
Perennial

FLOWERS:	Rose or purple; small; numerous in a densely packed, cylindrical head from ½ - 2 inches long; 5 sepals; 5 petals; 5 stamens; 1 pistil.
FRUIT:	A cylindrical head of many small dry pods.
LEAVES:	Alternate, compound of 3 - 5 narrow, small leaflets.
HEIGHT:	½ - 2 feet.
HABITAT:	Dry slopes and banks, and gravel flats.
DISTRIBUTION:	Common in prairie grasslands throughout Southern Alberta. July - September.

The Purple Prairie Clover is one of the most ornamental of all the wild flowers that weave a coat of many colours over wide tracts of prairie grassland in midsummer. It is a drought resistant perennial with several slender leafy stems about two feet in length. Whether the stems grow erect or lie flat on the ground, they end in cylindrical heads of many small rose-purple flowers. Each individual flower, although of basic pea-structure, has its five petals of almost the same shape and size and there is no keel. The plant has everlasting qualities, the mature flowering heads retaining their natural colour and form. A variety of this purple species with densely woolly stems occurs in certain places, while another species, *Petalostemon candidum*, with white flowers is also common.

SHOWY LOCO WEED
Oxytropis splendens

Photo. p. 181
Perennial

FLOWERS:	Blue or purple; showy; about ½ inch long; numerous in a dense spike; 5 sepals; 5 petals; 10 stamens; 1 pistil.
FRUIT:	A densely hairy, short pod.
LEAVES:	Many, all basal, compound of numerous leaflets in whorls, densely silky-hairy.
HEIGHT:	4 - 16 inches.
HABITAT:	Grassy slopes, dry gravelly banks and open woods.
DISTRIBUTION:	Common in prairie and foothill regions throughout Southern Alberta. June - August.

Second to the lupines, the loco weeds form one of the most attractive groups of prairie plants of the Pea Family. They are called loco weeds because some of them contain a habit-forming chemical often poisonous to cattle. The Showy Loco Weed is an innocent member of this group and is widely distributed throughout the prairie and foothill regions of Alberta. It grows with a bushy luxuriance and the whole plant including the stalks, leaves and flower clusters are covered with silvery-silky hairs. Its flower keel, ending in a sharply upcurved beak, distinguishes it from the milk vetches and the densely-packed heads of blue-purple flowers and the silvery-gray cast of the whole plant separates it from other loco weeds. One of the most brilliant of our mid-summer flowers, it is found growing in isolated clumps or in such profusion that the waving grasses are tinged with blue as far as the eye can see.

EARLY YELLOW LOCO WEED   Photo. p. 184
Oxytropis sericea var. *spicata*   *Perennial*

FLOWERS:	Pale yellow; showy; about ¾ inch long; numerous in a dense spike; 5 sepals; 5 petals; 10 stamens; 1 pistil.
FRUIT:	A hairy, short pod.
LEAVES:	Many, all basal, compound of 11 - 15 leaflets, silvery-hairy, poisonous.
HEIGHT:	8 - 20 inches.
HABITAT:	Dry hillsides.
DISTRIBUTION:	Common in prairie and foothill regions throughout Southern Alberta. May - June.

A species very similar to the Showy Loco Weed in general appearance and distribution, its distinguishing feature is its yellow flowers. This plant contains a harmful habit-forming chemical that causes a serious mental disturbance in cattle and as the common name suggests, it blooms early in the season at the time the range grasses are just beginning to send up fresh green shoots.

COMMON RED CLOVER   Photo. p. 184
Trifolium pratense   *Biennial*

FLOWERS:	Red-purple; ½ - ¾ inch long; numerous in a densely crowded, rounded head, about 1 inch across; 5 sepals; 5 petals; 10 stamens; 1 pistil.
FRUIT:	A rounded head of many, small, dry pods.
LEAVES:	Alternate, long-petioled, compound of 3 oval, slightly hairy leaflets.
HEIGHT:	6 - 18 inches.
HABITAT:	Roadsides and waste places.
DISTRIBUTION:	Common throughout most of Alberta. June - August.

The Common Red Clover was introduced into Alberta as a hay crop and is used in long term rotation with grain crops. In June and July, the fields are coloured with red-purple blossoms and a sweet scent fills the air. However, it has become so common in waste places, roadsides and at the edge of woods and thickets that it is often regarded as a wild flower. Like all the clovers, it has typical pea-shaped flowers, with standard, wings and keel, but these are small and narrow and are crowded into a dense head at the end of the flower-stem. Not only is the Red Clover a valuable forage plant, but its roots return large amounts of nitrogen to the soil and its flowers produce greater quantities of nectar. In 1965, Alberta led all other provinces in the production of honey, producing over sixteen million pounds, the bulk of which came from the clovers.

JULIE HRAPKO

EARLY YELLOW LOCO WEED
(Text p. 183)

D. S. S. CORMACK

COMMON RED CLOVER
(Text p. 183)

WHITE CLOVER
(Text p. 186)

WILD VETCH
(Text p. 186)

WHITE CLOVER. DUTCH CLOVER   Photo. p. 185
Trifolium repens   *Perennial*

FLOWERS: White or pinkish; about 5/16 inch long; numerous in
                  a densely crowded rounded head; ½ - ¾ inch across;
                  5 sepals; 5 petals; 10 stamens; 1 pistil.

FRUIT: A rounded head of many small dry pods.

LEAVES: Alternate, long-petioled, compound of 3 oval to ellipti-
                  cal leaflets.

HEIGHT: Creeping.

HABITAT: Lawns, roadsides, waste places.

DISTRIBUTION: Common throughout most of Alberta. June - August.

The White Clover is another well known cultivated plant that grows wild in lawns, waste places and along roadsides. It is a smaller, lower-growing plant than the Red Clover but has the same dense rounded flower-heads. The white or pinkish pea-shaped flowers stand almost erect at first but become almost horizontal as they mature and begin to set seeds. Like most of the clovers, when the seeds are ripe the petals do not fall off but turn brown and enfold the pod. This sweet-scented clover is a favourite bee-flower and has been grown in Alberta as a green pasture plant.

WILD VETCH   Photo. p. 185
Vicia americana   *Perennial*

FLOWERS: Bluish-purple; showy; about 1 inch long; usually 5 - 7
                  in a cluster; 5 sepals; 5 petals; 10 stamens; 1 pistil.

FRUIT: A flat, smooth pod slightly over 1 inch long.

LEAVES: Alternate, compound of 8 - 14 leaflets, with small
                  arrow-shaped stipules and ending in a branched tendril.

HEIGHT: 1 - 3 feet. Twining.

HABITAT: In open woods, thickets and low grassland.

DISTRIBUTION: Common throughout parkland regions of Alberta. June-
                  July.

The Wild Vetch resembles the Wild Sweet Pea in most ways except that it has more and narrower leaflets and narrower petals. The plant is fairly common. It grows along shrubby fence rows, grassy river banks and in fields and thickets, where it forms a tangle of dark green leaves and twining stems. Here, it is quite indistinguishable until the flowers open and sprinkle the shrubs and grasses with spots of bluish-purple. In another very similar but introduced species *Vicia cracca*, the flowers are also bluish-purple but they are far more numerous and are arranged in an elongated one-sided cluster. All the vetches make good hay and enrich the soil by building up nitrates in their roots.

PEA FAMILY — *LEGUMINOSAE*

BUFFALO BEAN   Photo. p. 188
Thermopsis rhombifolia   *Perennial*

FLOWERS:	Golden yellow; showy; about ½ inch long; many in a dense spike; 5 sepals; 5 petals; 10 stamens; 1 pistil.
FRUIT:	A grayish-hairy curved pod, about 2 inches long. Very poisonous.
LEAVES:	Compound of 3 oval-shaped leaflets, silky-hairy, with leaf-like stipules.
HEIGHT:	6 - 20 inches.
HABITAT:	Sandy soils, railroad embankments, roadsides.
DISTRIBUTION:	Very common in the prairie and parkland regions. May - June.

The Buffalo Bean is a plant of the prairies, but for some time it has been spreading northwards into the sandy areas of the parkland region via railroad embankments and roadsides. It is a hardy perennial and grows from a running rootstock. It is a plant that is easily recognizable by its short but stout leafy stalks, bearing numerous bright yellow blossoms fashioned on the pea family plan. An early blooming plant, it with the dandelion help to keep fields and sunny slopes of roads and cut-banks predominantly yellow until buttercups and the mustards take over in June. The flowers are succeeded by grayish-hairy curved pods which are extremely poisonous. They look like small bean pods and children should be repeatedly warned not to eat them.

INDIAN BREAD-ROOT   Photo. p. 188
Psoralea esculenta

FLOWERS:	Bluish-purple; showy; about ½ inch long; numerous in a short thick spike; 5 sepals; 5 petals; 10 stamens; 1 pistil.
FRUIT:	A dry, papery, long-beaked pod.
LEAVES:	Alternate, compound of 5 leaflets, hairy beneath.
HEIGHT:	4 - 12 inches.
HABITAT:	Prairie and dry banks.
DISTRIBUTION:	Fairly common throughout Southern Alberta. June-July.

The Indian Bread-Root is a low, short-stemmed legume that grows from a large tuberous root or cluster of thick tuberous roots about two inches long. It looks like a stunted lupine and the bluish-purple, pea-shaped flowers are crowded onto a short, stout spike which is covered with loose, white hairs. It grows in sheltered coulees and on sandy cut-banks on the rolling plains. The roots are rich in starch and sugar and the plant was frequently called "prairie potato" or "prairie turnip". The tuberous roots were a staple diet of the Plains Indians and the mainstay of explorers, trappers and the early settlers when game was scarce. The Silver Leaf, *Psoralea argophylla,* is another species fairly common on the prairies. It has much smaller, blue or purple flowers and the whole plant, including the seed pods, is densely covered with silky, silvery hairs.

187

BUFFALO BEAN
(Text p. 187)

M. OSTAFICHUK

KATHLEEN HODGES

INDIAN BREAD ROOT
(Text p. 187)

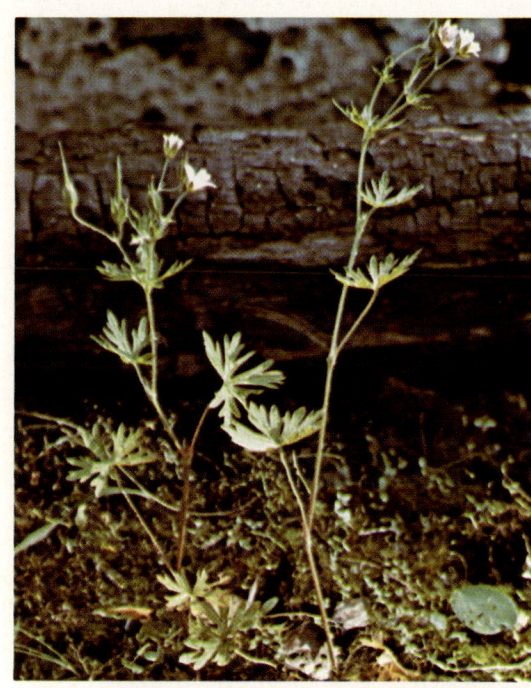

BICKNELL'S
GERANIUM
(Text p. 190)

J. CLAESSEN

DORTHEA CALVERLEY

WILD WHITE GERANIUM
(Text p. 190)

GERANIUM FAMILY — *GERANIACEAE*

There are six members of this family in Alberta. They are either herbaceous annuals or perennials with deeply divided or cleft leaves, usually with stipules and symmetrical, regular and perfect flowers. The parts of each flower are in fives or multiples of five. The ovary develops into a long-beaked dry capsule which at maturity splits from below upwards into five divisions, ejecting the seeds. The common house or garden geranium belongs to another group of the Geranium Family called the Pelargoniums.

BICKNELL'S GERANIUM
Geranium bicknellii

Photo. p. 189

Annual

FLOWERS:	Rose-purple; showy; 3/8 - ½ inch across; borne in pairs on short hairy stalks; 5 sepals; 5 petals; 10 stamens; 1 pistil of 5 carpels.
FRUIT:	A long-beaked dry capsule splitting lengthwise into 5 divisions.
LEAVES:	Opposite, deeply dissected into narrow segments, 3/4 - 2½ inches broad.
HEIGHT:	6 - 18 inches.
HABITAT:	Clearings, open woods, disturbed soil.
DISTRIBUTION:	Fairly common in wooded and semi-wooded areas. May - August.

Bicknell's Geranium is a familiar woodland plant and is particularly common in clearings and along logging roads in logged and burned over areas. When growing in sunny open places the leafy stems are short and bunched with numerous flowers. When growing in the shade the stems are longer and more straggly and have fewer flowers. In many respects, it is a small replica of the Sticky Purple Geranium as the flowers are the same shape and are the same beautiful purple, but they are not sticky and they are only one-third as large. It blooms continuously all summer and by fall the stems are covered with characteristic crane's bill-shaped seed capsules.

WILD WHITE GERANIUM
Geranium richardsonii

Photo. p. 189

Perennial

FLOWERS:	White or pinkish; showy; large; 1 - 1½ inches across; 2 on a stalk; 5 sepals; 5 petals; 10 stamens; 1 pistil.
FRUIT:	A long-beaked dry capsule, splitting lengthways into 5 divisions.
LEAVES:	Opposite, long-petioled, somewhat hairy, divided into 3 - 7 toothed divisions.
HEIGHT:	1½ - 3 feet.
HABITAT:	Moist thickets and open woods.
DISTRIBUTION:	Common and widely spread throughout the forested areas of the Foothills, Rocky Mountains and Cypress Hills. June - July.

The Wild White Geranium is very similar to the Sticky Purple Geranium but grows more frequently in moist thickets and in open woods. In contrast to the latter plant, it is only sparsely hairy and not sticky and its petals are white with purple veins.

STICKY PURPLE GERANIUM
Photo. p. 192

Geranium viscosissimum
Perennial

FLOWERS:	Rose-purple; showy; large; 1¼ - 1½ inches across; several on densely glandular hairy stalks in a flat-topped cluster; 5 sepals; 5 petals; 10 stamens; 1 pistil of 5 carpels.
FRUIT:	A long-beaked dry capsule, splitting lengthways into 5 divisions.
LEAVES:	Opposite, long-petioled, densely glandular hairy, deeply divided into 5 - 7 sharply toothed divisions.
HEIGHT:	1 - 2 feet.
HABITAT:	Moist places in prairie grassland, thickets and open woods.
DISTRIBUTION:	Common throughout Southern Alberta. June - July.

The Sticky Purple Geranium is a well known herbaceous plant that adds a splash of magenta to the dark green of aspen groves and to the light green of prairie grasslands in early summer. The whole plant is densely hairy and somewhat sticky. It blooms prolifically all summer and the salver-shaped flowers with their rose-purple petals strongly veined with purple, are most attractive. Its sticky surface and purple flowers distinguish it at once from the Wild White Geranium with which it frequently grows.

FLAX FAMILY — *LINACEAE*

The well known and economically important Flax Family is represented in Alberta by two native species and by one cultivated species. This latter species is often found growing along dry roadsides and in waste places. The showy, saucer-shaped, brightly coloured, delicate flowers are characteristic of them all, and, all the parts of these flowers are in fives.

WILD BLUE FLAX
Photo. p. 192

Linum lewisii
Perennial

FLOWERS:	Pale blue; large, 3/4 - 1½ inches across; several in a loose terminal cluster; 5 sepals; 5 petals; 5 stamens; 1 pistil with 5 styles.
FRUIT:	A dry, rounded capsule.
LEAVES:	Alternate, simple, numerous, narrow, 3/8 - 3/4 inch long.
HEIGHT:	8 - 24 inches.
HABITAT:	Plains, mountain slopes and hillsides.
DISTRIBUTION:	Common. June - July.

Whether it is the native species growing wild on mountain slopes and prairie hillsides, or whether it is the cultivated growing in the fields, the Wild Blue Flax can easily be identified. Both plants are almost identical and the flowers are coloured the same heavenly blue. The Wild Blue Flax is one of the most difficult plants to photograph as its delicate salver-shaped flowers poised at the top of the slender wiry stem, quiver in ceaseless motion. The flowers are borne in loose clusters and all bloom one at a time. Each flower in turn opens in the morning, closes in the afternoon and blows away the following day. Another common prairie species, the Yellow Flax, *Linum rigidum*, is a much shorter plant and has yellow flowers.

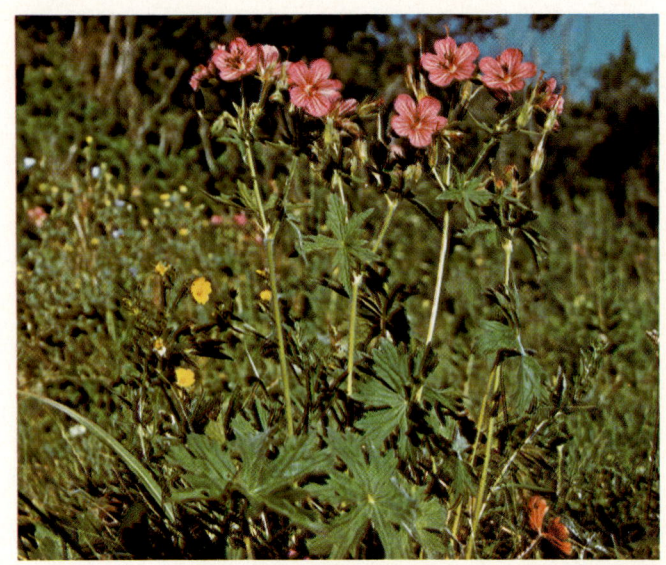

STICKY PURPLE GERANIUM
(Text p. 191)

WILD BLUE FLAX
(Text p. 191)

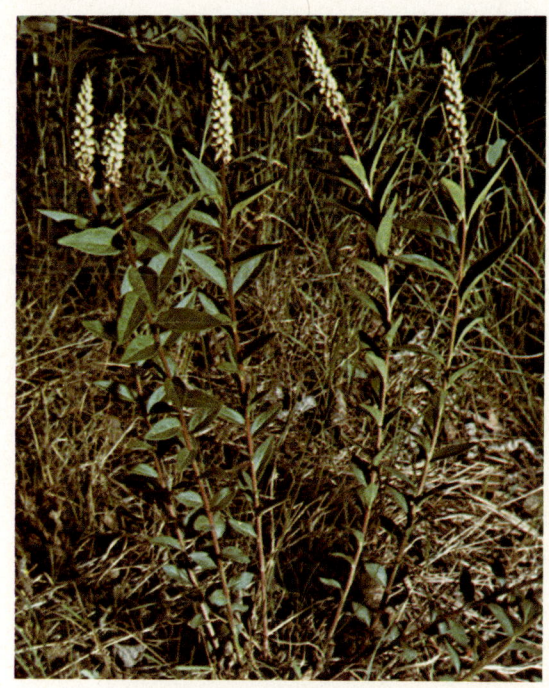

SENECA ROOT
(Text p. 194)

R. C. SWEET

J. J. SEXSMITH

LEAFY SPURGE
(Text p. 194)

MILKWORT FAMILY — *POLYGALACEAE*

The Milkwort Family is made up of small perennial herbs. It is represented in Eastern Canada by several species but in Alberta by only one, the Seneca Root. A brief description of this plant follows below.

SENECA ROOT   Photo. p. 193
Polygala senega   *Perennial*

FLOWERS:	Greenish-white; small, about 3/16 inch across; many in a short terminal spike; 5 sepals, free, petal-like, winged; 3 petals; 8 stamens; 1 pistil.
FRUIT:	A small, 2-seeded capsule.
LEAVES:	Alternate, simple, numerous, narrowly lance-shaped, 1 - 2 inches long.
HEIGHT:	4 - 20 inches.
HABITAT:	Open woods and moist prairies.
DISTRIBUTION:	Fairly common throughout prairie-parkland region. June.

Seneca Root is a perennial and has several, erect, leafy stems, each having a terminal spike of small, greenish-white flowers. Its leaves are lance-shaped. It is rather an inconspicuous plant and is sometimes mistaken for one of the bistorts as both plants grow in the same moist places. However, the flowers of the Seneca Root have three petals while the bistorts have none. It has the distinction of being the only member of this family in Alberta, although there are several in Eastern Canada.

SPURGE FAMILY — *EUPHORBIACEAE*

The family *Euphorbiaceae* is mainly a tropical family but in Alberta is represented by a single genus, *Euphorbia*. In it, there are only four species. Two of these are native to Alberta and the other two are introduced weeds. All have a milky juice and a unique floral arrangement. This consists of two leaf-like bracts which are joined to form a platform for a collection of small staminate and pistillate flowers. The whole structure looks like a single flower.

LEAFY SPURGE   Photo. p. 193
Euphorbia esula   *Perennial*

FLOWERS:	Yellowish-green; umbel-like; a collection of staminate and pistillate flowers on a pair of leaf-like bracts; no sepals; no petals.
FRUIT:	A dry, 3-seeded capsule.
LEAVES:	Alternate, narrowly-oblong, scattered along the stem and whorled at the top.
HEIGHT:	½ - 2 feet.
HABITAT:	Fields and waste places.
DISTRIBUTION:	An introduced weed, becoming very plentiful in many localities. May - June.

A native of Europe, Leafy Spurge is now one of our most objectionable and persistent weeds. It grows in waste places, roadsides and river flats and is taken notice of in this book because it is often thought to be a native wild flower. It is a perennial herb with deep tough roots, smooth hard stems, pale green foliage and small greenish-yellow flowers. The coloured portion of the flower is a bract-like structure which bears a few stamens and pistils. There are no sepals or petals. Although it produces large amounts of seed, it also spreads by means of creeping roots. Another prominent feature is its milky juice.

CROWBERRY FAMILY — *EMPETRACEAE*

The Crowberry is the only representative of this family in Alberta. It is a low, heath-like shrub with coal black berries and its chief features are described below.

CROWBERRY   Photo. p. 196
Empetrum nigrum   *Perennial*

FLOWERS: Purplish; very small; crowded in the axils of the leaves; perfect, or both staminate and pistillate; 3 sepals; 3 petals; 3 stamens; 1 pistil.

FRUIT: A round, black berry.

LEAVES: Densely crowded on the stems, narrow, evergreen, margins rolled under, about ⅓ inch long.

HEIGHT: Trailing, 1 - 10 inches.

HABITAT: Muskegs and mossy coniferous woods.

DISTRIBUTION: Western Alberta and north of Lesser Slave Lake and the Swan Hills. May - June.

Growing in the wet moss of muskeg and boggy pine-spruce woods and in the company of Creeping Snowberry, blueberries, Small Bog Cranberries, wintergreens and club mosses, the Crowberry is another heath-like evergreen. It is low-growing with trailing leafy stems which form thick mats over the mosses. The leaves are very heath-like: they are thick, narrow and only one-third of an inch long; they are shiny green above and downy and grooved underneath; they are rolled under along the margins. The flowers are not heath-like: they are extremely small and grow in the axils of the leaves; they form little purplish tufts near the ends of the stems very early in spring. The fruits are plump, black berries and these provide food for migrant birds.

SUMACH FAMILY — *ANACARDIACEAE*

This is a family of small trees and very small shrubs. It has compound leaves, small perfect or imperfect flowers and acrid sap. In Alberta, there are only two species, Poison Ivy and Skunk Bush.

POISON IVY   Photo. p. 196
Rhus radicans var. *rydbergii*   *Perennial*

FLOWERS: Yellowish-green; small; in dense clusters; 5 united sepals; 5 petals; 5 stamens; 1 pistil with 3 styles.

FRUIT: A round, smooth, hard, yellowish-white berry.

LEAVES: Alternate, compound of 3 light green, drooping, strongly veined leaflets, often toothed, 1½ - 4 inches long.

HEIGHT: 4 - 12 inches.

HABITAT: Shady, moist woods, stream banks and coulees.

DISTRIBUTION: Not common but locally abundant throughout Alberta. July.

Poison Ivy is a low, somewhat sprawling, shrub that spreads rapidly by a creeping rootstalk and grows in moist ravines, shady woods and along river flats and streamsides. It is easily recognized by its compound leaves of three green drooping leaflets, tight clusters of small yellowish-green flowers which are followed by showy bunches of dull white, round, hard berries. The slightest contact with any part of the plant will cause a vexatious and painful skin rash. Immediate washing of the affected part with warm water and strong soap will often produce a cure or bring relief. However, in the case of serious poisoning or if the victim is a child, it is wise to call a physician.

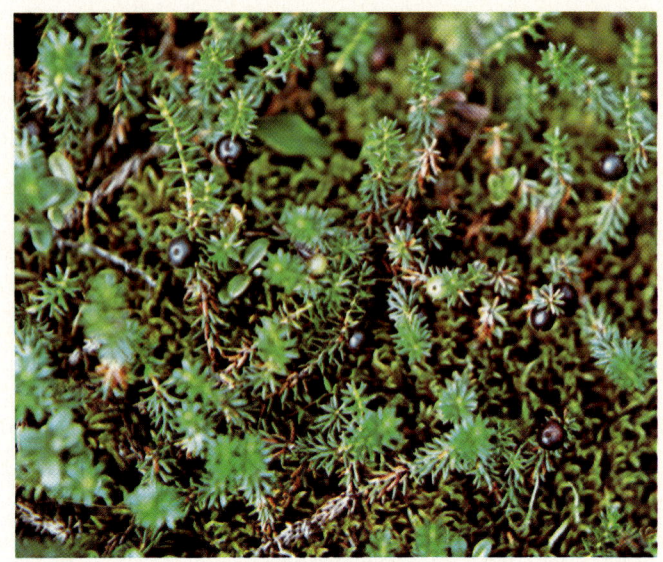

H. PEGG

CROWBERRY
(Text p. 195)

B. R. SHANTZ

POISON IVY
(Text p. 195)

SKUNK BUSH
(Text p. 198)

TOUCH-ME-NOT
(Text p. 198)

SUMACH FAMILY — *ANACARDIACEAE*

SKUNK BUSH   Photo. p. 197
Rhus trilobata   *Perennial*

FLOWERS:	Yellowish-green; small; in dense terminal clusters; 5 united sepals; 5 petals; 5 stamens; 1 pistil with 3 styles.
FRUIT:	A red, round berry.
LEAVES:	Alternate, compound of 3 elliptical leaflets with scalloped or lobed margins, each leaflet ½ - 1¼ inches long.
HEIGHT:	3 - 6 feet.
HABITAT:	Coulees and dry hillsides.
DISTRIBUTION:	Found occasionally in Southern Alberta. May.

The Skunk Bush is a small, many-branched, somewhat straggling shrub found only in Southern Alberta, where it grows on the denuded, rocky sides of coulees and dry hillsides. It is easily distinguished from other shrubs in this region by its leaves of three leaflets and its cluster of minute, yellowish-green flowers which have an unpleasant odour. The flowers appear before the leaves begin to expand and give rise to bunches of red, round berries. Although many members of the Sumach Family have poisonous qualities, there is no evidence that this shrub is poisonous.

TOUCH-ME-NOT FAMILY — *BALSAMINACEAE*

A family of herbaceous plants, represented in Alberta by only two species. The chief characteristics are soft, juicy stems and irregular perfect flowers. The Jewelweed or Touch-Me-Not described below is a good example.

TOUCH-ME-NOT.   JEWELWEED   Photo. p. 197
Impatiens capensis   *Annual*

FLOWERS:	Reddish-orange to yellow; spotted with purple dots; large, 3/4 - 1 inch long; 2 small greenish sepals, 1 orange sepal forming the long-spurred pouch; 3 lobed orange petals; 5 stamens; 1 pistil, 5-divisioned.
FRUIT:	A green pod splitting along 5 valves when mature.
LEAVES:	Alternate, simple, petioled, thin, oval, coarsely toothed, 3/4 - 4 inches long.
HEIGHT:	2 - 4 feet.
HABITAT:	Shady river banks, lake margins and moist woods.
DISTRIBUTION:	Locally abundant in wooded regions of Alberta. July-August.

The Touch-Me-Not or Jewelweed has all the appearance of a rank-growing weed and is common in the moist places of shady poplar woods and thickets. It would go unnoticed in the underbrush were it not for its transluscent, succulent stems, pendant, orange-yellow, purple-spotted flowers which hang down like earrings and explosive seed capsules. A striking feature of this plant is the explosive bursting at the slightest touch of the ripe but still green seed capsules and the scattering of the seeds in all directions. In addition to the showy flowers, the Jewelweed produces a number of very small, inconspicuous flowers which do not open but do produce normal seeds. Another very similar species, *Impatiens noli-tangere*, grows in the same kind of moist places but has yellow flowers and a less curved spur.

MALLOW FAMILY — *MALVACEAE*

This is a well known family of herbs or shrubs and two native species grow in Alberta. All of them have more or less lobed leaves and showy crepe paper-like flowers. In this family are our hollyhocks, exotic hibiscus and many other garden ornamentals. Each saucer-shaped flower consists of five petals twisted in the bud, five sepals and numerous stamens joined by their stalks forming a tube around the ovary.

WILD OR MOUNTAIN HOLLYHOCK   Photo. p. 200
Iliamna rivularis   *Perennial*

FLOWERS:	Mauve or pink; showy; large, about 2 inches across; 5 united sepals; 5 partially joined petals; numerous stamens in a tube surrounding the style; 1 pistil of many carpels.
FRUIT:	A collection of dry, few-seeded segments.
LEAVES:	Alternate, simple, maple-shaped, 4 - 7 lobed, coarsely-toothed, 2 - 6 inches broad.
HEIGHT:	2 - 6 feet.
HABITAT:	Mountain slopes and meadows.
DISTRIBUTION:	Rocky Mountains, Southwestern Alberta. July - August.

The Wild or Mountain Hollyhock is the native form of our garden hollyhock and it closely resembles its cultivated cousin in most points except size and colour of the flowers. The upright, leafy stalk may reach a height of six feet and carries at its very end numerous, large, mauve-coloured, saucer-shaped flowers, these separated by smaller leaves. A good spotting feature is the joining together of the numerous stamens to form a tube around the centrally placed style. It is found in flower during late July and early August in mountain meadows and along the sides of streams and trails.

SCARLET MALLOW   Photo. p. 200
Sphaeralcea coccinea   *Perennial*

FLOWERS:	Orange-red; showy; ½ - ¾ inch across; numerous in short, dense, leafy spikes; 5 sepals; 5 petals, numerous stamens in a tube surrounding the style; 1 pistil of many carpels.
FRUIT:	A collection of dry, few-seeded segments.
LEAVES:	Alternate, simple, deeply 3 - 5 divisioned, the divisions lobed or forked, covered with soft hairs, ½ - ¾ inch across.
HEIGHT:	Stems prostrate, mat-forming.
HABITAT:	On dry prairie in light sandy soil.
DISTRIBUTION:	Common throughout the prairie grassland region of Southern Alberta. July.

The Scarlet Mallow is definitely a prairie species and grows in a sprawling, mat-forming way in dry ground and in the disturbed soil of cut-banks and roadsides. Its several leafy stems spread out from a stout woody base and end in dense clusters of brilliant brick-red flowers. Both stems and leaves are covered with fine white hairs which give the plant a grayish-green appearance. The flowers are of the typical hollyhock shape and form. In areas where the soil is not only disturbed but sandy, the Scarlet Mallow blooms beside the Sand Dock in great profusion. Here, orange-red blossoms of the former combine with the pink-red fruits of the latter to set the countryside aflame with colour.

MOUNTAIN HOLLYHOCK
(Text p. 199)

SCARLET
MALLOW
(Text p. 199)

R. W. SALT

ST. JOHN'S WORT
(Text p. 202)

H. PEGG

EARLY BLUE VIOLET
(Text p. 202)

ST. JOHN'S WORT FAMILY — *HYPERICACEAE*

The St. John's Wort Family is represented in Alberta by a single species, the St. John's Wort. It is a soft-stemmed perennial and its chief features are described below.

ST. JOHN'S WORT   Photo. p. 201
Hypericum formosum var. *scouleri*   *Perennial*

FLOWERS:	Yellow; showy; about ½ inch across; several in a loose cluster; 5 sepals; 5 petals, black dotted; numerous stamens; 1 pistil.
FRUIT:	A small, dry capsule.
LEAVES:	Opposite, simple, no petioles, oblong to oval, margins black dotted, ½ - 1¼ inches long.
HEIGHT:	8 - 16 inches.
HABITAT:	Open spruce woods, streamsides and boggy lake shores.
DISTRIBUTION:	Rocky Mountains at high altitudes. July - August.

This small Rocky Mountain plant, St. John's Wort, appears on moist slopes along the margins of streams and wet boggy places right up to the timberline. Although many mountain plants have five yellow petals, once recognized the St. John's Wort will seldom be confused with any other plant. Its opposite, simple leaves separate it from the buttercups and cinquefoils. Its most distinguishing feature is its closed buds which are tinged with red. The black glandular dots on the margins of both leaves and petals are another distinguishing feature. When fully open, the wide-spread petals expose a brush of golden yellow stamens and a prominent cone-shaped pistil.

VIOLET FAMILY — *VIOLACEAE*

In Alberta, there are fifteen species of violets, all of them renowned for the beauty and charm of their flowers. The singular feature of them all is the beautiful irregular-shaped corolla, composed of five petals, of which the lowest and largest is prolonged into a swollen sac or spur. This feature is so constant that the family can always be recognized, though it is sometimes difficult to distinguish one species from another. Besides the five petals, there are five sepals, five stamens and one pistil. In addition to the showy flowers, some species possess flowers which lack normal petals and do not open, but which produce fertile seeds.

EARLY BLUE VIOLET   Photo. p. 201
Viola adunca   *Perennial*

FLOWERS:	Blue or violet; showy; several from the axils of the leaves; 5 sepals; 5 petals, spur often hooked; 5 stamens; 1 pistil.
FRUIT:	A dry, 3-valved, many-seeded capsule.
LEAVES:	Mainly from the stem, simple, oval to rounded oval, heart-shaped at base, long-petioled, sometimes hairy, margins round-toothed, ½ - 1 inch wide.
HEIGHT:	1½ - 12 inches.
HABITAT:	Moist places on the prairie, open woods.
DISTRIBUTION:	Common throughout Alberta. May - June.

The Early Blue Violet is one of the loveliest and one of the earliest of our wild flowering plants. Besides coming in May, it differs from the Bog Violet and some of the other blue-flowered species by its leafy stem. The beautiful blue-purple flowers are fashioned on the violet pattern, the lowermost and largest petal continuing backwards into a conspicuous and somewhat hooked spur. It transplants readily into gardens but tends to produce smaller flowers and to go mainly to leaves.

VIOLET FAMILY — *VIOLACEAE*

BOG VIOLET Photo. p. 204
Viola nephrophila *Perennial*

FLOWERS:	Blue-purple or violet; showy; several from a thick-set rootstock; 5 sepals; 5 petals; somewhat hairy, spur conspicuous; 5 stamens; 1 pistil.
FRUIT:	A dry, 3-valved, many-seeded capsule.
LEAVES:	All basal, simple, oval to kidney-shaped, heart-shaped at base, bluntly pointed, smooth, margins round-toothed, 1½ - 2½ inches across.
HEIGHT:	2 - 4 inches.
HABITAT:	Boggy meadows and open woods, and mossy banks of streams.
DISTRIBUTION:	Common in boggy places throughout Alberta. May-June.

The Bog Violet has all the qualities one could ask of any wild flower: beauty, fragrance, grace and charm. It is one of several stemless violets, the leaves and flower stalks growing directly from the stout, erect rootstock. The flowers are large for violets and are of a blue-purple colour. As its common name suggests, this violet must be looked for in moist places, particularly around the margins of sloughs and bogs and shady streamsides. It is probably the most common of the blue violets and is one of the most prized of all our spring flowers.

YELLOW PRAIRIE VIOLET Photo. p. 204
Viola nuttallii *Perennial*

FLOWERS:	Bright yellow; showy; several from the axils of the upper leaves; 5 sepals; 5 petals, spur short; 5 stamens; 1 pistil.
FRUIT:	A dry, 3-valved, many-seeded capsule.
LEAVES:	Alternate, simple, narrow, lance-shaped, tapering to stem, hairy. 1 - 2¾ inches long.
HEIGHT:	2 - 4 inches.
HABITAT:	Open grassland and hillsides.
DISTRIBUTION:	Common throughout the prairie grassland region of Southern Alberta. May - June.

The Yellow Prairie Violet grows in open grassland, frequently in very dry places. With the exception of two Rocky Mountain species which grow in moist woods at timberline, it is the only native yellow-flowered violet. Besides its yellow flowers, it can be distinguished by its narrow, lance-shaped and somewhat hairy leaves. This pretty little violet is a great favourite because it is one of the first wild flowers to bloom in the spring.

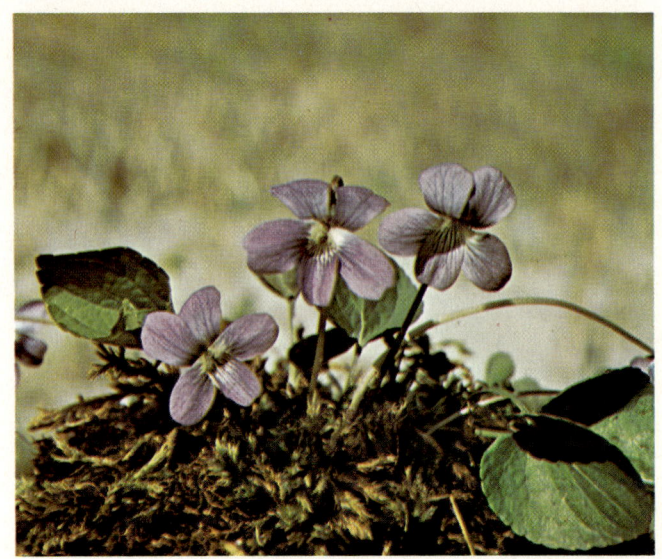

BOG VIOLET
(Text p. 203)

YELLOW PRAIRIE VIOLET
(Text p. 203)

WESTERN
CANADA
VIOLET
(Text p. 206)

J. CLAESSEN

M. OSTAFICHUK

EVERGREEN VIOLET
(Text p. 206)

WESTERN CANADA VIOLET

Viola rugulosa

Photo. p. 205

Perennial

FLOWERS:	White or sometimes pinkish with purplish veins and yellow center; showy; several from the axils of the upper leaves; 5 sepals; 5 petals, spur stout; 5 stamens; 1 pistil.
FRUIT:	A dry, 3-valved, many-seeded capsule.
LEAVES:	Alternate, simple, long-petioled, oval or kidney-shaped, heart-shaped at the base and sharply pointed, margins coarsely round-toothed, 2 - 4 inches broad.
HEIGHT:	8 - 24 inches.
HABITAT:	Rich soil in shady woods and thickets.
DISTRIBUTION:	Common throughout the wooded regions of Alberta. May - August.

The Western Canada Violet is the commonest of all our Alberta violets and may be found growing in shady woodlands everywhere. It is much taller than most violets and spreads through the rich leaf mold by means of underground stems. It is easily distinguished by its flowers which are white with purplish veins and yellowish towards the center. These charming and much beloved little flowers are known to everyone and give pleasure the moment they unfold in early spring.

EVERGREEN VIOLET

Viola orbiculata

Photo. p. 205

Perennial

FLOWERS:	Yellow, veined with purple; showy; several from the rootstock; 5 sepals; 5 petals, spur short; 5 stamens; 1 pistil.
FRUIT:	A dry, 3-valved, many-seeded capsule.
LEAVES:	Basal, simple, circular or broadly egg-shaped, petioled, margins round-toothed.
HEIGHT:	1½ - 3 inches.
HABITAT:	Moist, mossy coniferous woods.
DISTRIBUTION:	Rocky Mountains. Southwestern Alberta. June - July.

The Evergreen Violet is one of two mountain violets which have yellow flowers. Both species grow in moist shady spruce or pine woods and the bright yellow flowers streaked with violet are quite similar. However, they are easily distinguished one from the other by their stems and leaves. The Evergreen Violet is a small plant and grows close to the ground among the mosses and needles. It has no stem. Both the short-stalked flowers and short-petioled leaves grow from the top of the thick perennial rootstock. The beautiful dark green, circular blades of the leaves spread out flat on the ground where they stay green under the snow.

YELLOW MOUNTAIN VIOLET   Photo. p. 208
Viola glabella   *Perennial*

FLOWERS: Yellow, veined with purple; showy; several from the
                    rootstock; 5 sepals; 5 petals, spur very short; 5 stamens;
                    1 pistil.
FRUIT: A dry, 3-valved, many-seeded capsule.
LEAVES: Both basal and stem leaves, simple, long petioled,
                    margins round-toothed, kidney-shaped to oval, short-
                    pointed, heart-shaped at base.
HEIGHT: 2 - 12 inches.
HABITAT: Moist, mossy coniferous woods.
DISTRIBUTION: Rocky Mountains. Southwestern Alberta. June - July.

Although the flowers of the Evergreen Violet and the Yellow Mountain
Violet are very similar, the latter is a much larger plant and has a long
straggling stem. The conspicuous, long-stalked, yellow flowers are borne
on the upper half of the stem, while several, long-petioled, kidney-shaped,
dark green leaves grow from its base and along its entire length.

CACTUS FAMILY — *CACTACEAE*

This is a large family of long-living perennials with fleshy, succulent
stems. They grow in dry, often stony, ground on open prairie and hillsides
and are famous for the beauty of their flowers and for their ability to
endure long periods of drought. The stems are characteristically covered
with long spines or prickles which are modified leaves. In the absence of
normal leaves, the stem takes over the role of photosynthesis, the deep-
seated location of the green tissue accounting for its usual gray-green
colour. The flowers are large and showy with many sepals, petals and
numerous stamens and one pistil, the latter growing into a fleshy or dry
berry-like fruit.

CUSHION OR BALL CACTUS   Photo. p. 208
Mamillaria vivipara   *Perennial*

FLOWERS: Purplish-red; showy; large, 1½ - 2 inches across; many
                    sepals, petals and stamens; 1 pistil, of several united
                    carpels.
FRUIT: A soft, sweet, edible berry.
LEAVES: None, represented by clusters of 3 - 8 brownish spines,
                    ½ - ¾ inch long.
HEIGHT: 1 - 3 inches.
HABITAT: Dry open prairie and hillsides.
DISTRIBUTION: Very common throughout Southern Alberta. June-
                    August.

The Cushion or Ball Cactus, characteristic of the dry prairie of
Southern Alberta, is a good example of the cushion type, a small pin
cushion-like stem rising only a few inches above the surface of the ground.
The whole surface of the stem is covered with evenly-spaced, spine-tipped
projections. The flowers grow between the projections and are a beautiful
shade of purple or red with a shower of golden yellow stamens in the
centre. Protected by a barrier of spines, they grow into round, soft, edible
berries which are eaten by antelope and sheep and sometimes made into
jam.

YELLOW MOUNTAIN VIOLET
(Text p. 207)

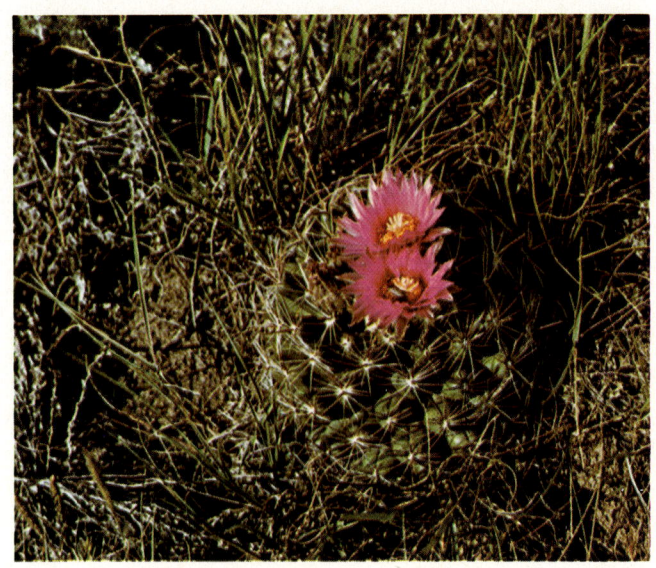

CUSHION or BALL CACTUS
(Text p. 207)

PRICKLY PEAR CACTUS
(Text. p. 210)

SILVER BERRY
(Text p. 210)

PRICKLY PEAR CACTUS
Opuntia polyacantha

Photo. p. 209
Perennial

FLOWERS: Bright yellow or orange; showy; large, 2 - 3 inches across; many sepals, petals and stamens; 1 pistil, of several united carpels.
FRUIT: A soft, spiny, sweet, edible berry.
LEAVES: None, represented by clusters of 5 - 9 straight spines, ½ - 2 inches long.
HEIGHT: Prostrate, forming mats.
HABITAT: Light soils and dry prairie.
DISTRIBUTION: Very common throughout Southern Alberta. July-August.

Belonging to a group of the Cactus Family that sometimes reaches gigantic size in other parts of the world, the Alberta species of Prickly Pear Cactus is a comparatively small plant. Its prostrate gray-green stems grow in irregular mound-like clumps and are made up of several segments. These are flattened and covered with clusters of hard, sharp spines and the joints between the segments are clearly marked. The beautiful yellow or orange flowers give brilliance to the drab green of the grasses and to the gray-blue green of the Sage. Both sagebrush and cactus are indicators of poor rangeland, intensified by over-grazing. A very similar species, *Opuntia fragilis,* but with somewhat rounder stems grows on warm, dry, south-facing slopes in the Peace River region.

OLEASTER FAMILY — *ELAEAGNACEAE*

Shrubs and small trees make up this family. They have silvery or brown scurfy branches, simple leaves dotted with silvery or brown scales and have berry-like fruit. The flowers may be perfect, staminate or pistillate. Sometimes both staminate and pistillate flowers are on the same shrub (monoecious); sometimes they are on separate shrubs (dioecious). This latter condition explains why one shrub may be loaded with fruit and a neighbouring one have none at all.

SILVER BERRY. WOLF WILLOW
Elaeagnus commutata

Photo. p. 209
Perennial

FLOWERS: Silvery yellow; small; fragrant; in clusters of 2 - 3; calyx tube of 4 sepals enclosing the 4 - 8 stamens and 1-loculed ovary; about ½ inch long.
FRUIT: A silvery-coloured, dry, mealy berry containing a large, stony seed.
LEAVES: Alternate, simple, oblong, silvery-scaly on both sides, 1 - 4 inches long.
HEIGHT: 2 - 12 feet.
HABITAT: In lighter soils, deep coulees, cutbanks and stream-banks and valley slopes.
DISTRIBUTION: Common and widespread throughout the Parkland region of Alberta. June.

Growing on dry hillsides, sandy banks and open fields throughout the Parkland region of Alberta, the Silver Berry is one of our best known shrubs. Although this shrub derives its common name from the grayish-white colour of its berries, every part of it, stems, leaves, branches and flowers, is covered with the same lustrous coating of silvery scales. The small tubular flowers are lemon yellow within and have an overpowering heavy scent. The berries are dry and mealy and contain a single stony seed marked with light yellow striped grooves. The Silver Berry is frequently grown in the garden as an ornamental shrub.

THORNY BUFFALO BERRY
Shepherdia argentea

Photo. p. 212
Perennial

FLOWERS:	Brownish; inconspicuous; in small clusters; staminate and pistillate flowers on separate shrubs.
FRUIT:	An orange, sour, edible berry.
LEAVES:	Alternate, simple, oblong, silvery on both sides, 1 - 2 inches long.
HEIGHT:	4 - 15 feet.
HABITAT:	Coulees and river valleys.
DISTRIBUTION:	Common throughout the southern part of Alberta. May.

Whereas the Canadian Buffalo Berry grows in the foothills, mountains and other wooded areas of Alberta, the Thorny Buffalo Berry grows in coulees and river valleys of the prairie regions. The Thorny Buffalo Berry can be distinguished by its thorny, silvery branches and by its leaves which are silvery on both sides. The branches have a twisted or broken appearance and in the fall the whole branch is covered with red or amber yellow berries. The berries have a sharp, sour taste when eaten raw but make a delicious jelly when cooked. The Plains Indians, explorers and early settlers served Buffalo Berry jelly with their buffalo steaks and made thongs and laces out of the tough, pliable Buffalo Berry bark.

CANADIAN BUFFALO BERRY
Shepherdia canadensis

Photo. p. 212
Perennial

FLOWERS:	Yellowish; inconspicuous; in small clusters; 4 sepals; spreading; staminate and pistillate flowers on separate shrubs.
FRUIT:	A red or orange, inedible berry.
LEAVES:	Alternate, simple, oval to elliptical, smooth and green above, whitish brown-scaly beneath, 1 - 1½ inches long.
HEIGHT:	1 - 8 feet.
HABITAT:	Open coniferous or mixed woods.
DISTRIBUTION:	Fairly common throughout the wooded regions of Alberta. May - June.

A shrub that is characteristic of open pine or pine-spruce woods, the Canadian Buffalo Berry is easily recognizable by its somewhat sprawling appearance, its brown scurfy branches, its luxuriant foliage and orange-red berries. Like its near relative, the Silver Berry, every part of the shrub—branches, tiny twigs, buds, leaves, flowers and fruit—is covered with thin shiny scales, which in this case are rust-coloured. The leaves are particularly distinctive as they are olive green and smooth on the upper surface and whitish and sprinkled with brownish scales on the lower surface. There are both staminate-flowering and pistillate-flowering shrubs and in the fall the latter are covered with small juicy berries. These have a nauseating taste when eaten raw and feel soapy when crushed between the fingers but make a delightful feast for the birds.

THORNY BUFFALO BERRY
(Text p. 211)

CANADIAN
BUFFALO
BERRY
(Text p. 211)

COMMON
FIREWEED
(Text p. 214)

MARY & ALAN
ROBERTS

P. H. POHLMAN

MOUNTAIN FIREWEED
(Text p. 214)

EVENING PRIMROSE FAMILY — *ONAGRACEAE*

A well known and distinctive family of herbaceous plants, some of which live as annuals, others as biennials and still others as perennials. There are twenty-five members of this family in Alberta. Most of them are familiar and include the evening primroses, fireweeds and the Scarlet Butterfly Weed. The family as a whole is characterized by erect stems, opposite or alternate leaves and perfect flowers. The parts of each flower are mostly in fours; four sepals, four petals, eight stamens and a single pistil with an inferior ovary, a prominent style and four-lobed stigma.

COMMON FIREWEED. GREAT WILLOW HERB   Photo. p. 213
Epilobium angustifolium   *Perennial*

FLOWERS:	Magenta; large, ⅔ - 1¼ inches across; many in a long terminal spike; 4 sepals; 4 petals; 8 stamens; 1 pistil.
FRUIT:	A long, narrow capsule containing many seeds, each with a tuft of hairs.
LEAVES:	Alternate, simple, no petiole, narrow, conspicuously veined, 2 - 6 inches long.
HEIGHT:	2 - 5 feet.
HABITAT:	Dry banks and slopes, open woodlands, burned forest land.
DISTRIBUTION:	Very common throughout Alberta. June - September.

In summer, aspen thickets, forest clearings, the sides of trails and roads are bright with the Common Fireweed. In burned-over forest areas it spreads like wild-fire through the dead but still standing trees, over windfalls up to the edge of unburned pine and spruce where the shade of the trees hinders its further advance. It heals over the scars of the fire until replaced by willow and aspen and finally by pine and spruce. The distinguishing feature of the plant is the dull red or magenta colour of the flowers, which appears also in the stems, buds, calyx-tubes and eventually in the pod-like fruits. Another distinguishing feature and one that gives the plant its other common name, Great Willow Herb, is the long, narrow, dark green, willow-like leaves. The flowers have the habit of opening from below upwards to the top of the spike, so that buds, mature flowers and pod-like capsules may appear on the same spike at the same time. Another common species, *Epilobium palustre,* grows in bogs and mossy streamsides.

MOUNTAIN FIREWEED. BROAD-LEAVED WILLOW HERB
                                                                  Photo. p. 213
Epilobium latifolium   *Perennial*

FLOWERS:	Red-purple; large, 1 - 2 inches across; many in a short leafy spike.
FRUIT:	A long, narrow capsule containing many seeds, each with a tuft of hairs.
LEAVES:	Both alternate and opposite, simple, thick, oblong, conspicuously veined, 1 - 2 inches long.
HEIGHT:	6 - 18 inches.
HABITAT:	Stony streamsides and moist rocky places.
DISTRIBUTION:	Fairly common. Rocky Mountains. July - August.

Out of a dozen native species, the Mountain Fireweed or Broad-Leaved Willow Herb is the most conspicuous. It resembles the Common Fireweed in general appearance but it has shorter stems and larger and more brilliantly coloured flowers. The red-purple of the widely spread petals gives this mountain species a beauty that no other fireweed possesses. It grows along mountain streams and dried-up water courses where its dense blue-green foliage covers up the stony ground and its short steeple-like flower clusters form a low carpet of brilliant colour.

214

ALPINE WILLOW HERB

Photo. p. 216

Epilobium alpinum — *Perennial*

FLOWERS:	Pink or purplish; small, about ¼ inch long; few near the top of the stem; 4 sepals; 4 petals; 8 stamens; 1 pistil.
FRUIT:	A long slender capsule.
LEAVES:	Alternate, simple, oblong-oval, scarcely petioled, 3/8 - ¾ inch long.
HEIGHT:	2 - 6 inches.
HABITAT:	Meadows and wet rocky slopes.
DISTRIBUTION:	Rocky Mountains at high altitudes. July - August.

Sheltering behind stones and wet rocky outcrops at fairly high altitudes, the Alpine Willow Herb forms low clumps of bent leafy stems from which grow several small pink or purplish flowers. Although the corolla lobes are short and not widely spread like the Common Fireweed and the Broad-Leaved Willow Herb, the flowers conform to the willow herb pattern and after the petals wither give rise to the characteristic long slender seed pods.

SCARLET BUTTERFLY WEED

Photo. p. 216

Gaura coccinea — *Perennial*

FLOWERS:	Orange-red; small, about 3/8 inch across; several in a terminal cluster; 4 sepals, bent downwards; 4 petals; 8 stamens; 1 pistil.
FRUIT:	A small, few-seeded, nut-like capsule.
LEAVES:	Numerous, alternate, simple, without petioles, narrow, wavy-margined, 3/8 - 1¼ inch long.
HEIGHT:	4 - 12 inches.
HABITAT:	Dry prairies and hillsides.
DISTRIBUTION:	Common on the prairie of Southern Alberta and on south-facing slopes northward. July - August.

Growing on dry hillsides and open south-facing slopes the Scarlet Butterfly Weed is a true prairie plant. It is a perennial with a short, weak, reclining, grey hairy stem, numerous small grey hairy leaves and a terminal spike of small butterfly-shaped flowers. The flowers are white when they first open but within a few hours they change to red-orange or brick red. When they are fully expanded they have a somewhat bedraggled appearance which is accentuated by the long drooping red-tipped stamens. The flowers open only one or two at a time and although the plant blooms for several weeks it never presents a solid cone of colour as does its close relative the Common Fireweed.

215

J. CLAESSEN

ALPINE WILLOW HERB
(Text p. 215)

SCARLET
BUTTERFLY
WEED
(Text p. 215)

R. C. SWEET

216

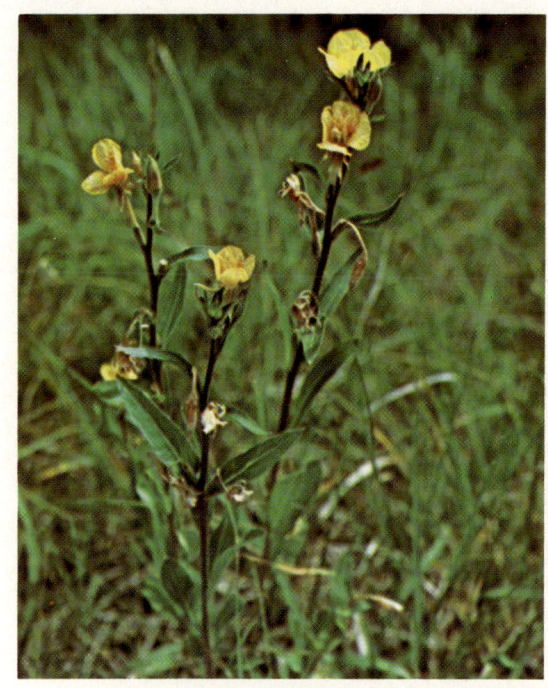

YELLOW
EVENING
PRIMROSE
(Text p. 218)

BUTTE PRIMROSE
(Text p. 218)

217

YELLOW EVENING PRIMROSE
Photo. p. 217

Oenothera biennis   *Biennial*

FLOWERS:	Bright yellow; large, about 1 - 2 inches across; numerous in a leafy terminal cluster; 4 sepals, bent downwards; 4 petals, 8 stamens; 1 pistil, inferior.
FRUIT:	A dry, many-seeded capsule.
LEAVES:	Alternate, simple, narrow, hairy, mostly without petioles, 1 - 6 inches long.
HEIGHT:	1 - 6 feet.
HABITAT:	Roadsides, banks and waste places.
DISTRIBUTION:	Very common on lighter soils throughout Alberta. July-August.

The Evening Primrose is one of our best known wild flowers and is found everywhere on roadsides, fields and waste places. Like many biennial plants, it forms a rosette of leaves in the first year and a tall leafy stem with flowers and fruits in the second year. The flowers are yellow, large and showy with all the parts in fours or multiples of four. However, they are seldom seen at their best for they open just before sundown and fade early the following morning. During the brief time that they are open, they attract bees and several kinds of moths. It is a most variable species and several varieties have been described.

BUTTE PRIMROSE. ROCK ROSE
Photo. p. 217

Oenothera caespitosa   *Perennial*

FLOWERS:	White to pinkish; large, 1½ - 3 inches across; several on short stalks; 4 sepals, bent downwards; 4 petals; 8 stamens; 1 pistil.
FRUIT:	A dry, woody, stalkless capsule.
LEAVES:	Simple, clustered, oblong to lance-shaped, wavy-margined, no petioles, 3 - 8 inches long.
HEIGHT:	Stemless.
HABITAT:	Dry slopes and gumbo soil.
DISTRIBUTION:	Locally abundant throughout Southern Alberta. June-August.

The Butte Primrose or Rock Rose is a stemless perennial that grows on clay banks and dry gumbo flats from a thick woody tap root. The flowers are the showiest of all our evening primroses and grow from the root-crown on very short stalks together with the dark green widely spread leaves. The beautiful white sweet-scented flowers open early in the morning and because of the glaring sun fade to a brownish-pink colour in a few hours. It is sometimes called the Rock Rose but any resemblance to the Wild Rose is superficial for the petals are four in number, not five, and the fruit is a dry, short, woody capsule.

MARE'S TAIL FAMILY — *HIPPURIDACEAE*

This is a family of smooth, soft-stemmed marsh plants with leaves in whorls and inconspicuous flowers. One species only is found in Alberta, the Mare's Tail.

MARE'S TAIL   Photo. p. 220
Hippuris vulgaris   *Perennial*

FLOWERS:	Green; tiny; numerous; inserted between the leaves on the slender stem; no sepals; no petals; 1 stamen; 1 pistil.
FRUIT:	Nut-like.
LEAVES:	In close dense whorls, of 6 - 12 in each whorl, smooth, firm, ½ - 1 inch long.
HEIGHT:	8 - 20 inches above the water.
HABITAT:	In shallow water and mud of streams and sloughs.
DISTRIBUTION:	Common throughout Alberta. July.

The Mare's Tail is a common marshy plant characterized by a spongy, creeping rootstock, several simple leafy unbranched stems that grow one foot or more above the water and inconspicuous flowers. A single flower consists of only one stamen and one pistil and develops into an equally small fruit. The leaves grow out in dense whorls around the closely set joints of the rounded stem and the tiny green flowers are interspersed between them. The Mare's Tail has the peculiarity of producing two kinds of leaves: aerial and submerged. Those formed in the air are short and firm while those formed under the water are narrow, thin, flaccid and much longer. Only one kind of leaf is produced at a time depending upon the level of the water and each kind of leaf is structurally adapted to carry on photosynthesis in its own particular environment.

GINSENG FAMILY — *ARALIACEAE*

The Ginseng Family is a small but well known family of herbaceous and woody perennials. Only two members occur in Alberta. The flowers are small and are borne in crowded clusters and give rise to bunches of berry-like fruits. Unlike many members of this family, the two Alberta plants do not possess medicinal properties.

WILD SARSAPARILLA   Photo. p. 220
Aralia nudicaulis   *Perennial*

FLOWERS:	Whitish or greenish; small; in usually 3 dense clusters on a single, leafless stalk; 5 minute sepals; 5 petals; 5 stamens; 1 pistil of 2 - 5 carpels, 5 styles.
FRUIT:	A round, purplish-black berry.
LEAVES:	1 compound of 3 divisions, each division of 3 - 5 oval, toothed leaflets, each leaflet 2 - 5 inches long.
HEIGHT:	About 1 foot.
HABITAT:	Moist poplar woods and thickets.
DISTRIBUTION:	Common throughout the wooded regions of Alberta. June.

The Wild Sarsaparilla is a familiar plant in poplar woods and thickets and it grows in rich leaf mold in the company of Fairy Bells, Star-Flowered Solomon's Seal, Baneberry and the Western Canada Violet. It is most conspicuous in early June, when its single, spreading, compound leaf is a beautiful bronze. Once the foliage turns dark green, the plant is likely to go unnoticed. The distinctive feature of this woodland plant is not the flowers or the leaves but the long, creeping rootstock and stout stem-base which lie just beneath the surface of the ground. Although held by some to have medicinal properties, none have actually been proven.

MARE'S TAIL
(Text p. 219)

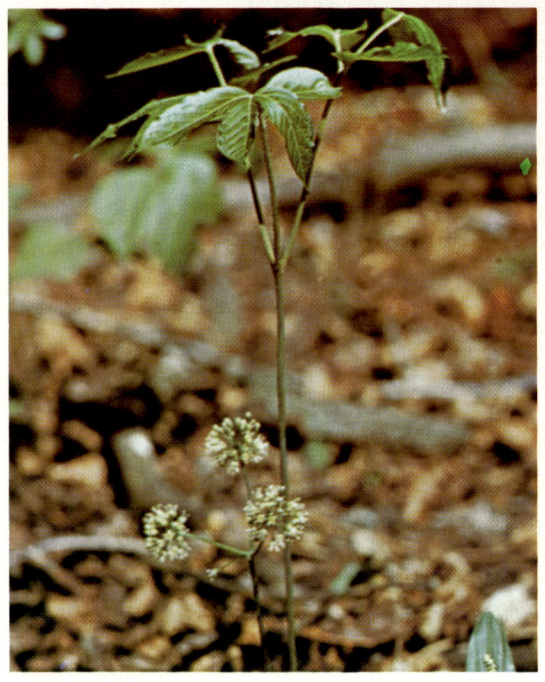

WILD
SARSAPARILLA
(Text p. 219)

DEVIL'S CLUB
(Text p. 222)

WHITE ANGELICA
(Text p. 222)

DEVIL'S CLUB   Photo. p. 221
Oplopanax horridum   *Perennial*

FLOWERS: Greenish-white; small; a great many in a dense
                terminal cluster, 4 - 12 inches long; no sepals; 5 petals;
                5 stamens; 1 pistil with 2 styles.
FRUIT: A scarlet inedible berry.
LEAVES: Alternate, simple, long-petioled, deeply-lobed, spiny
                on the underside, 6 - 24 inches long.
HEIGHT: 3 - 8 feet.
HABITAT: Stony soil in woods.
DISTRIBUTION: In scattered places in wooded regions of Western
                Alberta. July.

The Devil's Club is a local, coarse, perennial shrub occurring at
scattered points along the east slope of the Rocky Mountains and also
in the region of Lesser Slave Lake. Wherever it is found it grows very
abundantly. It is distinguished by a single, thick stem armed with long,
sharp, poisonous spines and by an abundance of large maple-like leaves,
covered with equally sharp spines along the prominent veins on the
underside. The minute greenish-white flowers are crowded in a dense
cluster at the end of the stem and soon give way to a cluster of inedible
bright red berries. As its scientific name implies, it is indeed a horrible
plant; its trailing, thorny stems added greatly to the hardships of the early
explorers and even today makes many a mountain trail impassable.

CARROT FAMILY — *UMBELLIFERAE*

This is a large family of herbaceous plants, mainly perennials, which
includes the carrot, dill, parsnip, celery, parsley, Poison Hemlock and
many others. In general, they have hollow stems, much-divided compound
leaves with sheathing bases and have small flowers arranged in a broad
flat-topped cluster called an umbel from which the family derives its
scientific name. In this kind of flower-cluster, all the branches always
meet at one point on the flower-stem and they always have a symmetrical
arrangement. Umbels may sometimes be compound, that is, each umbel is
made up of smaller ones. Each tiny flower consists of 5 petals, 5 stamens,
1 pistil with 2 styles and usually no sepals. The fruit is nut-like. About two
dozen members of this family occur in Alberta.

WHITE ANGELICA   Photo. p. 221
Angelica arguta   *Perennial*

FLOWERS: White; small; very numerous in a large flat compound
                umbel.
FRUIT: Dry and nut-like.
LEAVES: Alternate, compound of several lance-shaped, sharp-
                toothed leaflets, with very broad sheathing bases which
                clasp the stem.
HEIGHT: 2 - 5 feet.
HABITAT: Moist woods, thickets and stream banks.
DISTRIBUTION: Mountains. Southwestern Alberta. July.

White Angelica is one of three Alberta species of this genus and may
be found in moist meadows and along the sides of mountain streams.
Although it is closely related to the Cow Parsnip it is a much more
attractive plant. The conspicuous umbel, though just as large as the Cow
Parsnip, is much more delicate and consists of many smaller umbels, all
borne at the same level. The flowers when newly open are pure white and
have a misty softness and a delicate fragrance. After fertilization, the
flat-topped umbel turns into a dense cluster of reddish or purplish dry
oval fruits.

WATER HEMLOCK
Cicuta maculata

Photo. p. 224
Perennial

FLOWERS:	White; tiny; many in a flat-topped compound umbel.
FRUIT:	Dry and nut-like.
LEAVES:	Alternate, large, compound of numerous sharp-toothed, rather broad leaflets.
HEIGHT:	2 - 6 feet.
HABITAT:	Slough margins, streamsides and wet pastures.
DISTRIBUTION:	Common in wet places throughout Alberta. June - July.

The genus *Cicuta* contains the most deadly poisonous plants of the North American continent. There are three species of Water Hemlock native to Alberta; all three are poisonous but *Cicuta maculata* is the most frequently encountered. The poison is concentrated in the cluster of dahlia-like roots, and a piece of root the size of a walnut will kill a cow. There is no known antidote for stock animals. The only safety measure is to eradicate all suspicious looking plants from pastures and watering places. This should be done in the spring when the young green shoots are attractive to hungry cattle and when the roots have been churned up in the soft earth. Children are often poisoned, but if free-vomiting is promptly produced by an emetic the victim is likely to recover. The large compound leaves, the tuberous roots and the chambered appearance of the thick root-base when cut lengthwise are the chief characteristics of Water Hemlock.

COW PARSNIP
Heracleum lanatum

Photo. p. 224
Perennial

FLOWERS:	White; tiny; hundreds in a large, flat, compound umbel, 6 - 12 inches broad.
FRUIT:	Dry and nut-like.
LEAVES:	Alternate, large, hairy, dark green, 4 - 12 inches across, compound of 3 toothed and deeply lobed leaflets.
HEIGHT:	4 - 8 feet.
HABITAT:	Rich moist soil in shady woods and thickets.
DISTRIBUTION:	Common throughout the wooded regions of Alberta. June - July.

Standing erect, four to eight feet tall, with corrugated, coarse, hollow stems, huge rough three-parted leaves and large white flat-topped flower clusters, the Cow Parsnip is one of the most common sights in moist fields, open grazed poplar woods and along roadsides. Considered a rank weed by the passer-by and shunned by cattle because of its bitter juice and strong odour, it is often seen standing alone in solitary splendor. Its only redeeming feature lies in the perfect symmetry of the compound umbel which when the flowers are mature serves as a landing strip for many winged insects and when in seed as a banquet table for many birds.

WATER
HEMLOCK
(Text p. 223)

B. GODWIN

COW PARSNIP
(Text p. 223)

JANETTE GOODWIN

224

LONG-FRUITED PRAIRIE PARSLEY
(Text. p. 226)

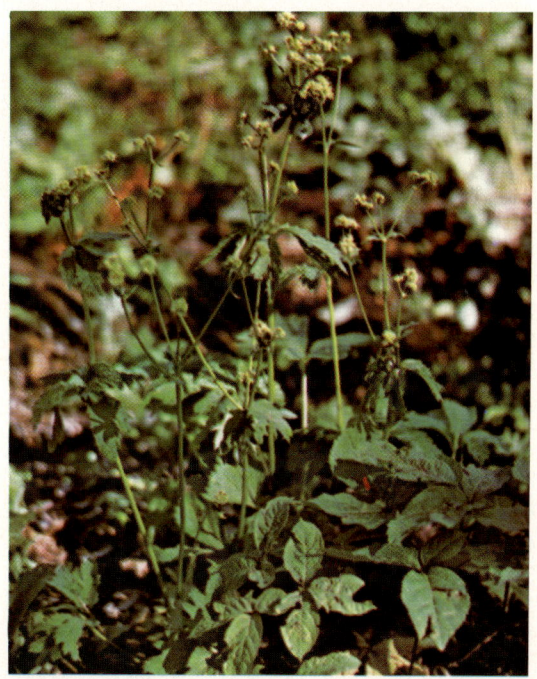

SNAKE-ROOT
(Text p. 226)

225

LONG-FRUITED PRAIRIE PARSLEY

Lomatium macrocarpum

Photo. p. 225

Perennial

FLOWERS:	Yellow; tiny; numerous in a compound umbel.
FRUIT:	Dry and nut-like.
LEAVES:	Alternate, very finely dissected, fine hairy, blue-green.
HEIGHT:	4 - 20 inches.
HABITAT:	Dry often rocky hillsides.
DISTRIBUTION:	Fairly common in Southern Alberta. May - June.

The Long-Fruited Prairie Parsley is one of a half a dozen species of the Carrot Family characterized by thick tuberous roots, very short stems, finely dissected parsley-like leaves and dense umbels of yellow, white or purplish flowers. This particular species is a low squat plant and grows on dry open hillsides. It has bright yellow flowers and a thin covering of grayish hairs which give a blue-gray tinge to the leaves and to the flowering stems. After fertilization the flowers are replaced by dense clusters of flat, papery, creamy-white fruits and when these are mature the dried-out flower stalks lie flat on the ground. The exceptional length of the fruits gives this plant its common name.

SNAKE ROOT

Sanicula marilandica

Photo. p. 225

Perennial

FLOWERS:	Whitish-green; small; several, borne in small head-like umbels, each from ¼ - ½ inch across.
FRUIT:	Dry, densely covered with hooked prickles.
LEAVES:	Lower leaves, alternate, long-petioled, compound of 5 - 7 segments; upper leaves, no petioles.
HEIGHT:	1 - 3 feet.
HABITAT:	Moist woods and thickets.
DISTRIBUTION:	Common in moist rich woodlands throughout Alberta. June.

The Snake Root is a common woodland plant whose green leaves and stems and small whitish-green flowers allow it to grow unobtrusively among the grasses and underbrush. The flowers are borne in umbels characteristic of the family but they are round and unusually small. It may attract attention toward the end of summer, when the umbels turn into round heads of prickly burs which stick to one's clothing or to the fur of animals.

WATER PARSNIP   Photo. p. 228
Sium suave   *Perennial*

FLOWERS:	White; small; numerous in a compound umbel, 2 - 3 inches across.
FRUIT:	Dry and nut-like.
LEAVES:	Alternate, compound of 3 - 8 pairs of narrow, lance-shaped leaflets, 1½ - 4 inches long.
HEIGHT:	2 - 6 feet.
HABITAT:	At the edge of sloughs, and in wet ground.
DISTRIBUTION:	Common. June - July.

The Water Parsnip is often found growing with the Cow Parsnip and sometimes with the Water Hemlock and, as its name suggests, is found in sloughs and wet ditches. The Water Parsnip can be distinguished at a glance from the more robust Cow Parsnip, but it can only be distinguished from the Water Hemlock by a careful study of the leaves and roots. The leaves of both plants are compound but each leaf of the Water Parsnip has three to eight pairs of long, narrow leaflets while each leaf of the Water Hemlock has numerous, rather broad, sharply-toothed leaflets. As for the roots, those of the Water Parsnip are fibrous while those of the Water Hemlock are thick and tuberous. Although the poisonous nature of this plant is not clearly understood, all pastures should be rid of it as a precautionary measure.

HEART-LEAVED ALEXANDERS   Photo. p. 228
Zizia cordata   *Perennial*

FLOWERS:	Yellow; small; numerous, in a flat-topped compound umbel.
FRUIT:	Dry and nut-like.
LEAVES:	Basal leaves, simple, oval and heart-shaped, long-petioled; stem leaves, short-petioled, compound of 3 oval toothed leaflets.
HEIGHT:	1 - 2 feet.
HABITAT:	Moist meadows.
DISTRIBUTION:	Common. May - June.

The Heart-Leaved Alexanders is an Alberta member of the Carrot Family and has yellow flower clusters shaped like small umbrellas. But the leaves are its distinguishing feature. These are of two kinds: leaves which grow from the base of the stem to near the top and those which appear a short distance below the clusters of flowers. The former are long-petioled, heart-shaped and simple, the latter are smaller, short-petioled and divided into three small leaflets. It blooms early in the spring in moist fields and in marshy places which are dry in summer.

WATER
PARSNIP
(Text p. 227)

DORTHEA CALVERLEY

HEART-LEAVED
ALEXANDERS
(Text p. 227)

G. W. MACHELL

BUNCHBERRY
(Text p. 230)

RED OSIER DOGWOOD
(Text p. 230)

DOGWOOD FAMILY — *CORNACEAE*

The Dogwood Family is a well known family of perennial herbs and shrubs. Only two species, one a low herbaceous plant and the other a medium-sized woody shrub are found in Alberta. The flowers are very small and are borne in a dense terminal cluster surrounded by several conspicuous white bracts or leaflets which look like petals. The shrubby Dogwoods are prized for their decorative stems, luxuriant foliage, colourful berries and hard wood.

BUNCHBERRY. DWARF DOGWOOD   Photo. p. 229
Cornus canadensis   *Perennial*

FLOWERS:	Greenish; tiny; several in a tight cluster surrounded by 4 white, petal-like bracts, about 1 inch across.
FRUIT:	An orange-red, insipid berry.
LEAVES:	4 - 6 in an apparent whorl, simple, oval-shaped, dark green, prominently veined, 1 - 3 inches long.
HEIGHT:	3 - 6 inches.
HABITAT:	Shady, moist woods.
DISTRIBUTION:	Very common throughout the wooded regions of Alberta. June - July.

The Bunchberry is one of our best known wild flowers and is widely distributed in the Northern Forest Zone across the whole breadth of Canada. It grows in cool, shady woods, principally those of spruce or of spruce and pine. Here, it forms thin to dense patches among the mosses and fallen needles. A single plant is three to six inches in height but its whorl of dark green leaves, its showy so-called flower and its bright red berries more than make up in prominence for its low stature. What seems to be a single flower of four white petals is actually a whorl of four white petal-like bracts which surround a small central cluster of true flowers. As the bracts fade they become a brownish colour, while the cluster of inconspicuous flowers develops into a bunch of red, tasteless berries.

RED OSIER DOGWOOD   Photo. p. 229
Cornus stolonifera   *Perennial*

FLOWERS:	Greenish-white; small; several borne in flat-topped clusters.
FRUIT:	A round, grayish-white, juicy, insipid berry.
LEAVES:	Opposite, simple, generally oval-shaped, green on top, paler beneath, 1 - 3 inches long.
HEIGHT:	3 - 6 feet.
HABITAT:	Moist woods, shady ravines and stream banks.
DISTRIBUTION:	Common throughout the wooded regions of Alberta. June - July.

The Red Osier Dogwood is a straggling, medium-sized shrub found growing along streamsides and in moist meadows and low marshy ground. Along the sides of streams, it spreads by subterranean shoots forming dense clumps or broad impenetrable thickets. Here, its leafy branches provide protection and some shade for the stream, while in the water, under the overhanging banks, the roots give shelter to lurking trout. Although the small, greenish-white flowers offer little attraction, the bright red stems and branches are beautiful in form and colour. These make the shrub conspicuous in all seasons but particularly in winter when they stand out in sharp contrast against the snow. By autumn, clusters of grayish-white berries replace the flowers and the leaves turn a glorious red.

230

WINTERGREEN FAMILY — *PYROLACEAE*

An unmistakable family of low herbaceous perennial plants, with scaly rootstocks and simple, petioled, shiny green leaves. The Wintergreens are prized for the beauty and fragrance of the flowers, arranged daintily in a loose raceme on the leafless flower-stalk or scape. Each flower consists of a 4 - 5-lobed calyx, a deeply 5-parted or 5-petalled corolla, 8 - 10 stamens, a single 4 - 5-lobed ovary, a stoutish style and a 5-lobed stigma. They are all woodland plants and are closely related to the heaths. Ten members of this family can be found within the boundaries of Alberta.

PRINCE'S PINE. PIPSISSEWA   Photo. p. 232
Chimaphila umbellata var. *occidentalis*   *Perennial*

FLOWERS:	Pink, purple or white; fragrant; small; nodding; several in a loose cluster; corolla salver-shaped of 5 waxy petals about ½ inch across; 10 stamens; ovary green and prominent; style short and stout ending in a broad, 5-lobed stigma.
FRUIT:	A globular, dry, brown, many-seeded capsule.
LEAVES:	In whorls or scattered along the somewhat woody stem; shiny, dark green, leathery, finely toothed; 1 - 2½ inches long.
HEIGHT:	4 - 12 inches.
HABITAT:	Dry coniferous woods.
DISTRIBUTION:	Foothill and mountain regions throughout Southwestern Alberta. July - August.

A beautiful evergreen plant commonly found growing under pine trees and in company with other wintergreens and with some of its close relatives the heaths. The fragrant, waxy, pink flowers grow in a small loose cluster at the end of the leafless flower-stalk. Individual flowers are shaped like small shallow saucers; the five deeply divided petals arching backward at maturity expose the stamens and broad, sticky stigma to insect visitors. The ring of delicate magenta around the base of the ovary is characteristic. The waxy nature of the petals, which is true for all the wintergreens, is so pronounced that the flowers are often thought to be artificial.

COMMON PINK WINTERGREEN. PYROLA   Photo. p. 232
Pyrola asarifolia   *Perennial*

FLOWERS:	Pale to deep pink; small; nodding; several; arranged in a loose raceme; corolla of 5 waxy petals about ½ inch across; 10 stamens; ovary prominent; style protruding and conspicuous; 5-lobed stigma.
FRUIT:	A small, round, dry, many-seeded capsule.
LEAVES:	Several, basal, leathery, dark green and shining, rounded at the apex, petioled, 1 - 2 inches wide.
HEIGHT:	6 - 15 inches.
HABITAT:	Moist coniferous or mixed woods.
DISTRIBUTION:	Fairly common in wooded regions throughout Alberta. June - July.

As the common name suggests, this is the most widely distributed of all the wintergreens of the genus *Pyrola*, and possibly the best known. Each small flower has the typical wintergreen cup or bell shape with five, pink, waxen petals and a prominent pistil, the style of which bends downward and then curves upward like an elephant's trunk. Although it is sometimes taken for an orchid, this beautiful little plant does not have to take second place to any orchid, for the flowers have a delicate fragrance which most orchids lack. There are several varieties of this pink-flowered wintergreen.

DORTHEA CALVERLEY

PRINCE'S PINE
(Text p. 231)

COMMON
PINK
WINTERGREEN
(Text p. 231)

H. PEGG

ONE-FLOWERED WINTERGREEN
(Text. p. 234)

WHITE
WINTERGREEN
(Text p. 234)

ONE-FLOWERED WINTERGREEN Photo. p. 233
Moneses uniflora *Perennial*

FLOWERS:	White; fragrant; solitary; nodding; corolla of 5 waxy, widely spreading petals about ¾ inch across; 10 stamens; ovary green and conspicuous; style straight and stout; stigma 5-lobed.
FRUIT:	A globular, dry, brown, many-seeded capsule.
LEAVES:	Several, basal, bright green, rounded, finely-toothed.
HEIGHT:	2 - 6 inches.
HABITAT:	Moist, shady fir-spruce woods and poplar-spruce woods, mossy stream sides and bog forests.
DISTRIBUTION:	Widely distributed throughout the wooded regions of Alberta, including the Cypress Hills. July.

The smallest and perhaps the most beautiful of all the wintergreens, this quaint little plant is restricted to moist, mossy places under the shade of pine or spruce. The solitary nodding flower has the typical wintergreen form, five united but widely spreading, waxy, ivory white petals and conspicuous pistil. The pure whiteness of the flowers and their faint but delightful fragrance make it appear as though they were molded out of wax and impart an almost ethereal quality to the little plant. Although the flower stalk nods in flower, it elongates and straightens up in fruit, the mature capsules looking like little brown coloured chimney pots.

WHITE WINTERGREEN. PYROLA Photo. p. 233
Pyrola elliptica *Perennial*

FLOWERS:	White; fragrant; small; nodding; several in a long loose spike; calyx 5-parted; corolla of 5 waxy petals about ½ inch across; 10 stamens; ovary prominent with a stout protruding up-curved style and 5-lobed stigma.
FRUIT:	A small, round, dry, many-seeded capsule.
LEAVES:	Several, basal, thick, elliptical, petioled, 1½ - 3 inches long.
HEIGHT:	4 - 10 inches.
HABITAT:	Mossy pine-spruce woods.
DISTRIBUTION:	Fairly common throughout the wooded regions of Alberta. July - August.

The White Wintergreen is a species generally distributed in mossy mixed coniferous woods, usually found in the northern part of the Province. It resembles the Greenish-Flowered Wintergreen in general appearance and has the same delicate fragrance. The flowers are white with a prominent downward-directed and then up-curved style. The leaf blades are oval and pointed at the apex and longer than the petioles while those of the Greenish-Flowered Wintergreen are almost round and shorter than the slender petioles. All the wintergreens are beautiful and give pleasure to everyone who sees them.

ARCTIC WINTERGREEN. PYROLA
Pyrola grandiflora

Photo. p. 236
Perennial

FLOWERS:	Creamy white or pale pink; large, fragrant; several, crowded at the tip of the leafless flower stalk; corolla of 5 large spreading petals, 10 yellow stamens, style slightly curved.
FRUIT:	A small, round, dry, many-seeded capsule.
LEAVES:	Several, rounded at both ends, thick, leathery, shiny; ¾-1½ inches long.
HEIGHT:	2-6 inches.
HABITAT:	Moist ground at high altitudes.
DISTRIBUTION:	Uncommon. Northern Alberta and Rocky Mountains.

The Arctic Wintergreen is a small alpine species sparingly found in moist mossy ground and at the edge of stunted trees. However, the faint fragrance and beauty of the large, creamy white or pink flowers more than make up for its small size. The short leafless flower-stalk is surrounded at the base by a cluster of small evergreen leaves which in this case are particularly thick and leathery and shiny green. Another small species, *Pyrola minor* is much more common and occurs throughout the wooded regions of Alberta. It has small greenish-white flowers.

ONE-SIDED WINTERGREEN. PYROLA
Pyrola secunda

Photo. p. 236
Perennial

FLOWERS:	Greenish-white; small; nodding; many; crowded on to one side of the short, arching, flowering stalk; corolla bell-shaped, of 5 waxy petals about ¼ inch across; 10 stamens; style long, straight, protruding beyond the petals.
FRUIT:	A small, round, dry, many-seeded capsule.
LEAVES:	Many, mainly near or at the base of the stem, thin, oval to lanceolate, pointed at either end, margins nearly smooth, petioled, 1 - 2½ inches long.
HEIGHT:	3 - 10 inches.
HABITAT:	Dry pine woods, boggy spruce woods and mixed coniferous woods.
DISTRIBUTION:	Common throughout the wooded regions of Alberta. July.

This common but lovely member of the Wintergreen Family grows in dense, leafy colonies from a much-branched rootstock and is found among a scattering of dead pine needles. When in full bloom, the slender stem bends gracefully downwards as though the weight of the many, small flowers, all on the lower side, were too much for it to bear. Commonly described as miniature bells or lanterns, the greenish-white flowers do not correspond exactly to the typical wintergreen pattern, but the waxy petals, the long protruding style and the evergreen leaves clearly identify this plant as one of the *Pyrolas*.

ARCTIC WINTERGREEN
(Text p. 235)

ONE-SIDED WINTERGREEN
(Text p. 235)

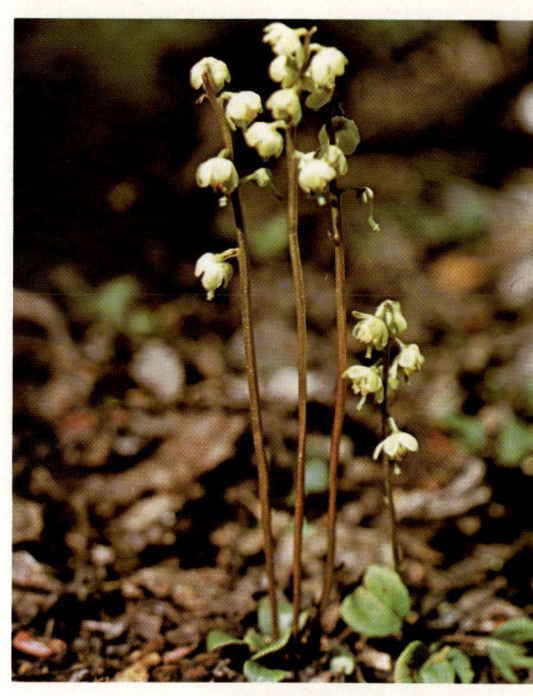

GREENISH-
FLOWERED
WINTERGREEN
(Text p. 238)

DORTHEA CALVERLEY

INDIAN PIPE
(Text p. 238)

A. M. REVELL

WINTERGREEN FAMILY — *PYROLACEAE*

GREENISH-FLOWERED WINTERGREEN. PYROLA Photo. p. 237
Pyrola virens *Perennial*

FLOWERS:	Greenish-white; small; nodding; several; arranged in a loose raceme; corolla of 5 waxy petals about ½ inch across; 10 stamens; ovary prominent; style protruding, stout, curved upward at apex; stigma 5-lobed.
FRUIT:	A small, round, dry, many-seeded capsule.
LEAVES:	Several, basal, thick, dull green, rounded at both ends, very finely toothed, petioled.
HEIGHT:	4 - 10 inches.
HABITAT:	Mossy, pine-spruce woods.
DISTRIBUTION:	More frequently found in the foothill and mountainous regions of Alberta. July.

The Greenish-flowered Wintergreen is similar in appearance to the Common Pink Wintergreen except that the olive green leaves are somewhat smaller, thicker and more rounded, and, the flowers are a greenish-white. Both species are found in mossy, mixed, coniferous woods but the Greenish-flowered Wintergreen is much less common. In the deep shade of pine and spruce, the flowers appear fluorescent and diffuse into the moist air a delicate fragrance. When the petals wither, the conspicuous ovary develops into a small, round capsule.

INDIAN PIPE FAMILY — *MONOTROPACEAE*

The Indian Pipe Family is made up of a small number of fleshy herbaceous flowering plants characterized by a rounded mat of malformed roots, scale-like leaves and the absence of chlorophyll. Lacking chlorophyll, they are unable to manufacture their own food by photosynthesis and are, therefore, obliged to obtain it from an outside source. This they do from partially decayed vegetable matter in the soil by the aid of a fungus. Once supplied with the basic organic nutrients, they can live as any other green plant and produce normal flowers and seeds. They are commonly called saprophytes. This mode of life is common among the fungi and the bacteria but is rare among flowering plants. The Indian Pipe Family is closely related to the wintergreens and heaths and their flowers are very similar. Three members of this family are found in Alberta.

INDIAN PIPE Photo. p. 237
Monotropa uniflora *Saprophyte*

FLOWERS:	Waxy white, sometimes pinkish; showy; about ¾ inch long; solitary; drooping at the end of the clammy white transluscent stem; 2 - 4 sepals; 5 petals; 10 - 12 stamens; 1 pistil.
FRUIT:	An erect many-seeded capsule.
LEAVES:	Colourless scales.
HEIGHT:	4 - 8 inches.
HABITAT:	Rich moist forest soil.
DISTRIBUTION:	Occasional throughout the wooded regions of Alberta. July.

The Indian Pipe is the best known member of this peculiar group of flowering plants and once recognized is not easily forgotten. It appears almost overnight, like a mushroom, in dimly-lighted coniferous woods and grows in clumps. The stem pushes up through the rich forest soil completely doubled up, and although it is not long in straightening up, the solitary bell-shaped flower remains in a nodding position. From its appearance at this stage, it has gotten its name. The stem is thick and dead white and the leaves are reduced to colourless scales. The white or sometimes delicately pink flower is normal in every way and after fertilization becomes erect and develops into a salmon-coloured, many-seeded capsule.

INDIAN PIPE FAMILY — *MONOTROPACEAE*

PINE SAP   Photo. p. 240
Monotropa hypopithys   *Saprophyte*

FLOWERS:	Yellow, pink or reddish; showy; about ½ inch long; urn-shaped; numerous in a terminal cluster; 4 - 5 sepals; 4 - 5 petals; 10 stamens; 1 pistil.
FRUIT:	A many-seeded capsule.
LEAVES:	Scale-like.
HEIGHT:	6 - 12 inches.
HABITAT:	Rich coniferous woods.
DISTRIBUTION:	Rare. Reported from Cypress Hills and Peace River district. July.

Pine Sap is similar to the Indian Pipe in many respects but it is a much rarer plant. Like the Indian Pipe, it has fleshy, clammy stems, scale-like leaves and urn-shaped flowers. However, the flowers are numerous and both they and the stems are either yellow, pink or reddish-brown.

PINE DROPS   Photo. p. 240
Pterospora andromedea   *Saprophyte*

FLOWERS:	Whitish; small, ¼ - 3/8 inch across; urn-shaped; numerous in a long densely glandular hairy spike; calyx 5-parted; corolla 5-lobed; 10 stamens; 1 pistil.
FRUIT:	A yellowish-pink many-seeded capsule.
LEAVES:	Thick, brownish, scale-like, crowded near the base of the sticky glandular hairy stem.
HEIGHT:	8 - 30 inches.
HABITAT:	Rich soil in shady pine woods.
DISTRIBUTION:	Occasional in coniferous wooded areas in Southwestern Alberta. July.

Pine Drops is a somewhat saprophytic plant that grows on the needle-strewn floor of shady pine woods. It is easily recognized by its reddish-brown sticky stems which end above in long spikes of many small urn-shaped yellowish-white flowers and end below the ground in a mass of deformed roots. Leaves are represented by thick colourless scales which clasp the base of the stem.

PINE SAP
(Text p. 239)

DORTHEA CALVERLEY

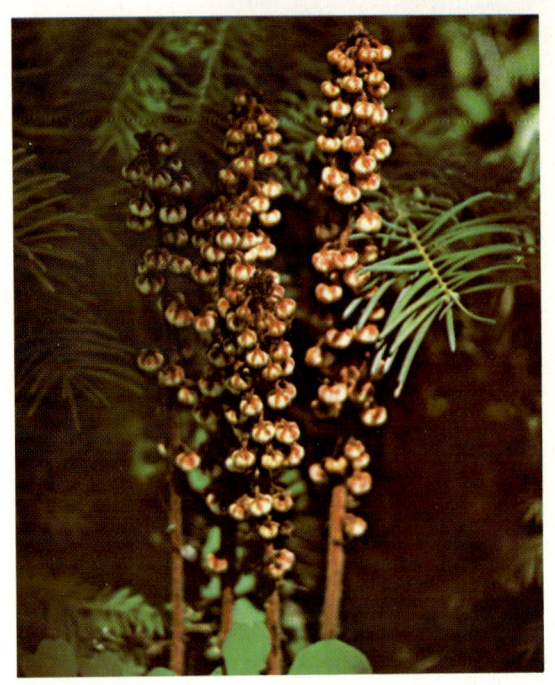

PINE DROPS
(Text p. 239)

ALISON JACKSON

BOG ROSEMARY
(Text p. 242)

ALPINE BEARBERRY
(Text p. 242)

The Heaths are famed for their smallish, shiny green leathery leaves, for their small but dainty cup, urn or bell-shaped flowers and for their edible fruits. All the Alberta members of this family are woody, perennial shrubs and most of them are evergreen in habit. The calyx consists of 4 - 5 sepals, the corolla of 4 - 5 pointed lobes or occasionally with distinct petals and the stamens are usually twice as many as the corolla lobes. The ovary is 4 - 5 celled with a single style and a simple or lobed stigma and matures into a capsule, drupe or berry.

BOG ROSEMARY
Andromeda polifolia

Photo. p. 241
Perennial

FLOWERS:	Pinkish; small; few; nodding at the ends of the branches; calyx small, 5-lobed; corolla urn-shaped; 5-lobed, about ¼ inch long; 10 stamens.
FRUIT:	A small, round, dry, many-seeded capsule, with persistent style.
LEAVES:	Alternate, simple, almost sessile, narrow, sharp pointed, evergreen, margins rolled under, 3/8 - 1¼ inches long.
HEIGHT:	4 - 12 inches.
HABITAT:	Wet, mossy muskegs and open bog forests.
DISTRIBUTION:	Widespread throughout wet forestlands of Alberta. June.

The Bog Rosemary is a low, heathy shrub found in wet, mossy bog forests and at the margins of muskeg pools and lakes. In such places, the tough, woody stems, thickly set with glossy green leaves, form thin to dense evergreen patches at the water's edge. Like those of many other heaths, the leaves have a leathery texture and are distinctly rolled under along the margins. The small, pink flowers, produced in small nodding clusters at the ends of the leafy branches, have the characteristic urn shape and give way in August to small, dry capsules.

ALPINE BEARBERRY
Arctostaphylos rubra

Photo. p. 241
Perennial

FLOWERS:	White; small; few in a terminal cluster; urn-shaped; calyx deeply 5-parted; corolla 5-lobed; about 3/16 inch long; 10 stamens.
FRUIT:	A round, red, juicy berry.
LEAVES:	Alternate, simple, margins round-toothed, conspicuously veined, bright green turning deep red, ¾ - 1½ inches long.
HEIGHT:	2 - 8 inches.
HABITAT:	Rocky ridges and open scrub forests at high altitudes.
DISTRIBUTION:	Rocky Mountains and Northern Alberta. July.

In the Rocky Mountains, the Alpine Bearberry is associated with exposed rocky ledges and ridges at elevations well above the tree line. Here, the low, creeping, leafy stems take advantage of every nook and cranny to protect it from the strong winds and the harsh alpine climate. Under the shelter of a rocky ledge, it sometimes forms a thick layer of living and dead branches with Alpine Willow and Creeping Juniper. Although its flowers and fruits are similar to those of the Common Bearberry, it can be distinguished by its strongly veined, lighter green and much larger leaves which turn bright scarlet in the fall.

COMMON BEARBERRY. KINNIKINIK
Arctostaphylos uva-ursi

Photo. p. 244
Perennial

FLOWERS:	Pinkish-white; several; drooping; in dense clusters; corolla urn-shaped, 4 - 5-lobed, about 3/16 inches long.
FRUIT:	A bright red, mealy, insipid berry.
LEAVES:	Alternate, simple, paddle-shaped, thick, shiny evergreen, ½ - 1 inch long.
HEIGHT:	Stems and branches mat forming, 6 - 24 inches long.
HABITAT:	Dry, often sandy - gravelly slopes and hillsides, rocky ledges, old burns and dry pine woods.
DISTRIBUTION:	Common throughout the Province. May - July.

This tough, prostrate evergreen shrub forms thick matted growths in dry pine woods on exposed hillsides and rocky slopes. Here, it is often found growing among the thicker stems of Creeping Juniper. The small, pinkish or white urn-shaped flowers and the waxy, bright red berries that follow are half hidden by the small, leathery, dark green leaves. The mealy berries are relished by bears and birds. The Indians called this tough little trailing shrub Kinnikinik and used the berries to make a kind of pemmican and the dried leaves to smoke in their pipes.

WHITE MOUNTAIN HEATHER
Cassiope tetragona

Photo. p. 244
Perennial

FLOWERS:	White; small; solitary; nodding on slender stalks; calyx 4 - 5-parted; corolla open, bell-shaped, 5-lobed, about ¼ inch long; 8 or 10 stamens.
FRUIT:	A small, dry capsule.
LEAVES:	Minute, scale-like, dense in 4 ranks, evergreen, very thick, about 1/16 inch long.
HEIGHT:	4 - 12 inches.
HABITAT:	Moist alpine meadows and open scrub forests at or above timberline.
DISTRIBUTION:	Common in the Rocky Mountains. Western Alberta. June - July.

This dwarfed, evergreen shrub with its dark green, tufted branches sprayed with myriads of snow-white, waxy flowers is the most beautiful of the Rocky Mountain heathers and is a prime favourite of all mountain climbers. Each dainty flower is a perfect little bell, fully expanded with the five-parted petals slightly rolled back from the rim. A unique feature of this heather and one that distinguishes it from the others, is the four-sided appearance of the stems, caused by the four-ranked arrangement of the minute leaves that over-lap each other like fish scales.

P. H. POHLMAN

COMMON BEARBERRY
(Text p. 243)

A. KARVONEN

WHITE MOUNTAIN HEATHER
(Text p. 243)

CREEPING WINTERGREEN
(Text. p. 246)

MOUNTAIN
LAUREL
(Text p. 246)

HEATH FAMILY — *ERICACEAE*

CREEPING WINTERGREEN. CREEPING SNOWBERRY

Photo. p. 245

Gaultheria hispidula   *Perennial*

FLOWERS: White; tiny, less than 1/8 inch long; borne singly in the axils of the leaves; calyx 4-parted; corolla 4-lobed; cup-shaped; 8 stamens; 1 pistil.

FRUIT: A small white mealy berry.

LEAVES: Alternate, simple, oval, dark green above, pale and dotted with brown hairs beneath, margins rolled under, about ¼ inch long.

HEIGHT: Creeping, 4 - 12 inches long.

HABITAT: Moist, mossy, coniferous woods.

DISTRIBUTION: Widespread but not common. June.

The daintiest of all the Alberta Heaths, the Creeping Snowberry, forms mats of tough wiry stems and tiny evergreen leaves on the mossy floor of black spruce bogs or pine-spruce forests. It is a typical heath with cup-shaped flowers which are so tiny that they can scarcely be seen among the leaves. The plant owes its common name to the small white waxen berries which spread out like a broken chain of beads. These are edible and have a faint flavour of wintergreen. A trailing alpine species, *Gaultheria humifusa*, which grows at timberline has round leathery leaves about the size of a dime and small red berries.

MOUNTAIN LAUREL

Photo. p. 245

Kalmia polifolia var. *microphylla*   *Perennial*

FLOWERS: Deep pink; large; showy; in terminal clusters; calyx deeply 5-lobed; corolla saucer-shaped, 5-lobed, 3/8 - 5/8 inches across; 10 stamens; style elongated.

FRUIT: A dry, many-seeded capsule, persistent style.

LEAVES: Opposite, simple, nearly sessile, evergreen, elliptical, margins rolled under, darker green above than beneath, 3/8 - 1 inch long.

HEIGHT: 3 - 8 inches.

HABITAT: Swampy places, wet meadows and boggy scrub forests.

DISTRIBUTION: Northern Alberta and in the Alpine Zone in the Rocky Mountains. June - July.

The Mountain Laurel is a well known bogland plant found growing in Northern Alberta and in the Rocky Mountains. Here it forms thin to dense patches of evergreen growth in marshy meadows and in low ground bordering muskeg pools surrounded usually by coniferous trees. It is a typical low-growing heath with small, leathery, evergreen leaves, rolled under along the margins, and with clusters of showy, pink flowers. Each flower is shaped like a small saucer with five symmetrical lobes, each of which bears two pouch-like creases. Each crease contains a short-stalked stamen which, when the flower is touched, springs upwards releasing a shower of golden pollen. Although the flowers are beautiful, the leaves like those of most Laurels contain substances which are extremely poisonous to livestock, particularly to sheep.

COMMON LABRADOR TEA
Ledum groenlandicum

Photo. p. 248
Perennial

FLOWERS:	White; small; numerous in dense, terminal, round-topped clusters; about ⅓ inch across; 5 small, tooth-like sepals; 5 white, spreading petals; 5 - 10 stamens; 5-loculed ovary.
FRUIT:	An oblong, dry, many-seeded capsule with persistent style.
LEAVES:	Alternate, simple, almost sessile, oblong, green above, rusty-woolly beneath, margins rolled under, ½ - 2 inches long.
HEIGHT:	1 - 4 feet.
HABITAT:	Muskegs and moist coniferous woods.
DISTRIBUTION:	Common, widely distributed throughout moist wooded areas of Alberta. June - July.

The Common Labrador Tea is a bogland shrub with light brown, ascending branches and extremely velvety, hairy twigs. The flowers are white and grow in showy clusters at the ends of the woolly stems, but the leaves of this shrub are its distinguishing feature. These are leathery, narrowly oblong, dark green above and light rusty-woolly beneath, and strongly rolled under along the margins. It is the one shrub we expect to find first in any muskeg or moist coniferous wood.

FALSE HUCKLEBERRY. MENZIESIA
Menziesia glabella

Photo. p. 248
Perennial

FLOWERS:	Salmon-coloured or greenish-orange; small; several drooping in loose clusters on short stalks; corolla urn-shaped, 4-lobed, ¼ inch long; 8 stamens.
FRUIT:	A small, hard, dry capsule.
LEAVES:	Alternate, simple, in whorls, oblong to obovate, pale green, margins wavy, 1 - 2 inches long.
HEIGHT:	2 - 6 feet.
HABITAT:	Moist, shady, coniferous woods.
DISTRIBUTION:	Fairly common and widely spread in the Rocky Mountains. Western Alberta. June - July.

This mountain shrub is characteristic of cool, moist spruce woods where it is often found in company with the Tall Bilberry or Huckleberry and with which it is often confused. In fact, these two shrubs resemble each other so closely that it would be difficult to tell them apart were it not for the colour of the urn-shaped flowers. Those of Menziesia are a unique blending of green and pink while those of the Tall Bilberry are pinkish-white. These two shrubs are somewhat easier to tell apart in early fall, by which time the flowers of Menziesia have developed into small, round capsules while those of the Tall Bilberry have produced large, black, luscious berries.

COMMON LABRADOR TEA
(Text p. 247)

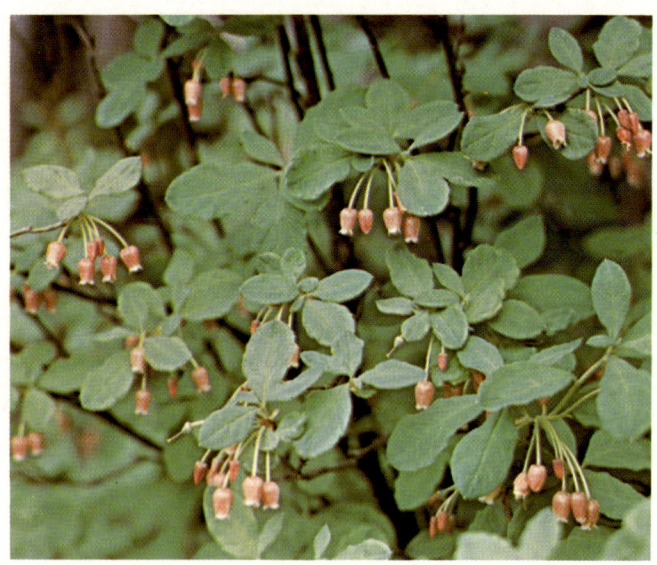

FALSE HUCKLEBERRY
(Text p. 247)

RED HEATHER
(Text p. 250)

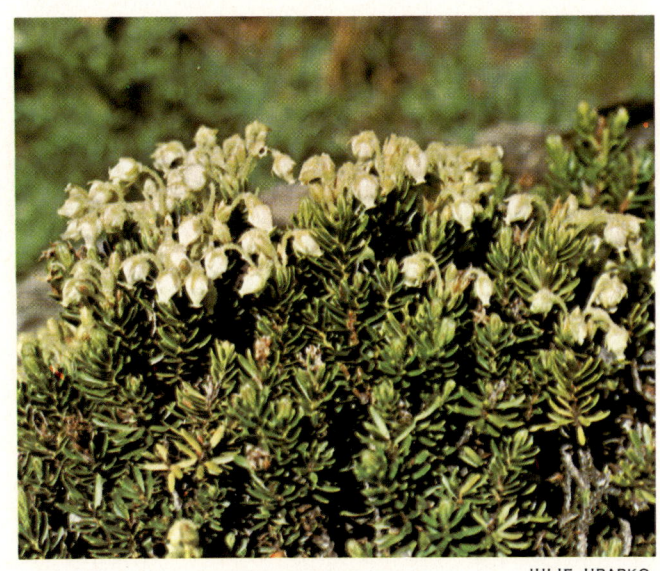

YELLOW HEATHER
(Text p. 250)

RED OR PURPLE HEATHER

Phyllodoce empetriformis

Photo. p. 249

Perennial

FLOWERS:	Rose-coloured; fragrant; small; slender-stalked; numerous in dense, terminal clusters; calyx small, 5 parted; corolla open, cup-shaped, about ⅓ inch long; 10 stamens; style slender.
FRUIT:	A small, round, dry capsule.
LEAVES:	Alternate, simple, evergreen, short, narrow, densely crowded, about 3/8 inches long.
HEIGHT:	6 - 12 inches.
HABITAT:	Alpine meadows and open coniferous forests near timberline.
DISTRIBUTION:	Abundant in the Rocky Mountains. Western Alberta. June - July.

Our Rocky Mountain Heathers are not the true heathers that cover wide tracts of moorland in Scotland, England and Northern Europe, but are nevertheless hardy evergreens with showy clusters of red, yellow and white flowers. To see all three of them at their best, one must climb to the tree line in late June or early July, when they are in full bloom. The most abundant is the Red Heather which forms a thick, almost continuous, dark-green and deep-rose carpet over the ground of alpine meadows and thinly forested slopes. At times, however, it grows in such close proximity with the Yellow and White Heathers that it looks as if all three differently coloured blossoms were growing on the same small shrub.

YELLOW HEATHER

Phyllodoce glanduliflora

Photo. p. 249

Perennial

FLOWERS:	Yellowish or greenish-white; small; on slender, glandular stalks in dense, terminal clusters; calyx small, glandular, 5 parted; corolla urn-shaped, about 5/16 inch long; 10 stamens; style slender.
FRUIT:	A small, round, dry capsule.
LEAVES:	Alternate, simple, evergreen, short, narrow, densely crowded, about 3/8 inch long.
HEIGHT:	3 - 12 inches.
HABITAT:	Alpine meadows and open coniferous forests near timberline.
DISTRIBUTION:	Abundant in the Rocky Mountains. Western Alberta. June - July.

The Yellow Heather is a well-known evergreen shrub characteristic of windswept meadows and scrubby open woods. With the Red Heather and other heathy shrubs, it fills in the gaps between the stunted, twisted trunks of spruce and pine. It resembles the Red Heather so closely that were it not for the flowers, it would be impossible to tell them apart. The flowers of the former are pale yellow or greenish-white and look like miniature vases, while those of the latter are rose-red and resemble tiny, open-mouthed bells. During June and July, the timberline changes from a drab desolate place to one of enchantment because of the glorious blooming of the heathers.

HEATH FAMILY — *ERICACEAE*

WHITE-FLOWERED RHODODENDRON Photo. p. 252
Rhododendron albiflorum *Perennial*

FLOWERS:	White or greenish-white; large; nodding; 1 - 3 in groups along the stems; calyx saucer-shaped, 5-lobed; corolla open cup-shaped with 5 rounded lobes; ¾ inch across; 10 pale yellow stamens; ovary 5-loculed; style long.
FRUIT:	An oval, dry, hard capsule.
LEAVES:	Alternate, simple, in whorls, oblong, tapered at both ends, thin, shiny green above, paler beneath, not evergreen, 1 - 2 inches long.
HEIGHT:	2 - 6 feet.
HABITAT:	Cool, moist spruce-fir forests.
DISTRIBUTION:	Rocky Mountains. Western Alberta. July.

In July, cup-shaped flowers of snow-white protruding beneath leaves of shining green make this probably our most beautiful mountain shrub. In the thin underbrush of a mature spruce forest and frequently at the side of a mountain stream, the White-Flowered Rhododendron finds the shade and cool, moist conditions it requires. Once the tall tree canopy is removed by fire and logging, it disappears and it may take scores of years before forest conditions become suitable for its return. If, as is often the case, the burned or logged area is opened up to grazing stock animals, its eventual return is even more remote.

TALL HUCKLEBERRY Photo. p. 252
Vaccinium membranaceum *Perennial*

FLOWERS:	Pinkish-white or yellowish-green; small; solitary on short stalks; calyx 5-parted; corolla bell-shaped, 5-lobed, about 3/16 inch long; 8 or 10 stamens.
FRUIT:	A large, black-purple, sweet, juicy berry.
LEAVES:	Alternate, simple, margins finely toothed, turning red in the fall, ½ - 2 inches long.
HEIGHT:	1 - 5 feet.
HABITAT:	Coniferous forests.
DISTRIBUTION:	Rocky Mountains. Western Alberta. June.

The Tall Huckleberry is a mountain shrub that grows up to five feet in height in the shade of spruce and fir. Despite its large size, it has the blueberry look about it and the small, round, bell-shaped flowers clearly mark it as a member of the Heath Family. Sombre green in the summer, the leaves turn bright scarlet in the fall. The big, black-purple, juicy berries are renowned for their fine flavour and make the best homemade huckleberry pies.

WHITE-FLOWERED RHODODENDRON
(Text p. 251)

TALL HUCKLEBERRY
(Text p. 251)

BLUEBERRY
(Text p. 254)

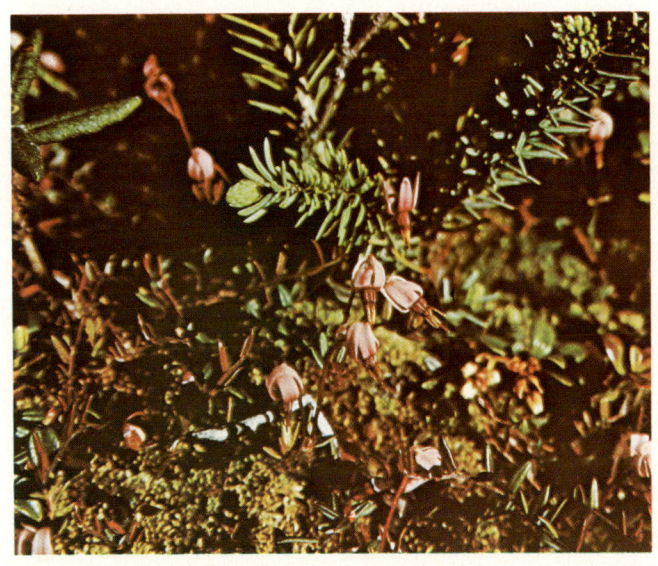

SMALL BOG CRANBERRY
(Text p. 254)

BLUEBERRY. DWARF BILBERRY
Vaccinium caespitosum

Photo. p. 253
Perennial

FLOWERS:	Pink or white; small; numerous; in clusters; calyx 5-parted; corolla bell-shaped, 5-lobed, about 3/16 inch long; 10 stamens; ovary inferior; style slender.
FRUIT:	A light blue, sweet berry with a pale bloom.
LEAVES:	Alternate, simple, nearly sessile, thin, oval, green and shiny on both sides, ½ - 1 inch long.
HEIGHT:	2 - 10 inches.
HABITAT:	Coniferous woods and open slopes.
DISTRIBUTION:	Widespread throughout Alberta. June.

About five very similar, low, healthy shrubs found in Alberta go by the common name of Blueberry, Huckleberry or Bilberry. In fact, they are all so much alike that it is necessary to consult a flora or botanical key to tell them apart. The most widely distributed species is the Blueberry or Dwarf Bilberry which grows on the dry, needle-littered floor of pine woods and on open or thinly wooded hillsides and on mountain slopes. The finely branched stems grow close to the ground and are thickly covered with small, shiny green leaves which in June, hide clusters of small, bell-shaped, pinkish flowers and in August, handfuls of luscious, light blue berries. The berries of all five Alberta species are famed for their delicious flavour and are used in making homemade preserves and blueberry pies.

SMALL BOG CRANBERRY
Vaccinium oxycoccus

Photo. p. 253
Perennial

FLOWERS:	Rose pink; small; about ¼ inch across; 1 - 4, nodding at the ends of delicate flower stalks; calyx 4-parted; corolla deeply 4-parted; 8 stamens; ovary inferior.
FRUIT:	A small, red, often spotted, acid berry.
LEAVES:	Alternate, simple, evergreen, thick, oval, dark shiny green above, margins strongly rolled under, about ¼ inch long.
HEIGHT:	Trailing, 4 - 16 inches long.
HABITAT:	In Sphagnum Moss, muskegs, bogs and bog forests.
DISTRIBUTION:	Common in boggy wooded areas throughout Alberta. June.

Growing in wet mounds of Sphagnum Moss and Labrador Tea, the Small Bog Cranberry is another heathy evergreen characteristic of muskegs and boggy woods. It is a dwarf, creeping plant with weak slender stems, bearing tiny, dark green shiny leaves and a few small but showy flowers on a slender flower stalk. The four deeply-parted pink petals are closed in the bud but soon bend sharply backwards exposing bright yellow anthers to a visiting insect. The bright red berries are true cranberries and may be found lying on the mosses still attached to the leafy stem by the thread-like flower-stalks.

GROUSE BERRY

Vaccinium scoparium

Not Illustrated

Perennial

FLOWERS: Pink or white; small; numerous; scattered; nodding; calyx small, 4 - 5-lobed; corolla urn-shaped, 5-lobed, ⅛ inch long; 8 or 10 stamens; ovary inferior; style slender.

FRUIT: A small, bright red berry.

LEAVES: Alternate, simple, thin, oval, about ½ inch long on green stems.

HEIGHT: 3 - 18 inches.

HABITAT: Mountain slopes, alpine meadows and open coniferous forests, commonly at timber line.

DISTRIBUTION: Rocky Mountains. Western Alberta. June - July.

A low, bushy shrub with erect green branches, small, shiny green leaves and small, pink, urn-shaped flowers. It is a common and characteristic shrub of alpine meadows and thinly forested mountain slopes. Together with juniper and other healthy shrubs, it often forms a low, dense cover for small animals while its bright red berries are relished by grouse and other birds.

BOG CRANBERRY

Vaccinium vitis-idaea var. *minus*

Photo. p. 256

Perennial

FLOWERS: Rose-pink; small; few, in terminal, nodding clusters; calyx 4-parted; corolla bell-shaped, 4-lobed, about ¼ inch long; 8 stamens; ovary inferior, style slender.

FRUIT: A small, dark red, acid berry.

LEAVES: Alternate, simple, evergreen, leathery, oval, dark shiny green above, pale and dotted with black hairs beneath, margins slightly rolled under, 1/4 - 5/8 inches long.

HEIGHT: 4 - 8 inches.

HABITAT: Dry, open coniferous woods and in dry places in bog forests.

DISTRIBUTION: Common and fairly widespread throughout Alberta. June.

This dwarf shrub forms scattered to dense patches of evergreen, mat-forming growth in rather dry bogs and on the mossy needle-sprinkled floor of open pine woods. It is a typical heath with clusters of small, pinkish, open, bell-shaped flowers and small, leathery leaves. The leaves, which are shiny dark green above and paler and dotted with dark hairs beneath, distinguish this small shrub from its low-growing relatives, the Common Bearberry and the Grouse Berry. The Bog Cranberry, the Small Bog Cranberry and the cultivated cranberry of commerce are true cranberries and are not to be confused with the High Bush and Low Bush Cranberries which belong to the Honeysuckle Family—an altogether different family of plants.

BOG CRANBERRY
(Text p. 255)

SWEET-
FLOWERED
ANDROSACE
(Text p. 258)

PIGMY FLOWER
(Text p. 258)

SHOOTING
STAR
(Text p. 259)

257

The Primrose Family contains several old-fashioned favourites of field and garden, two of which are cowslips and primroses. As a family of annual or perennial herbs with simple opposite or whorled leaves, it has showy flowers that have wheel-shaped, bell-shaped or funnel-shaped corollas. About eighteen species of this family grow in Alberta.

SWEET-FLOWERED ANDROSACE   Photo. p. 256
Androsace chamaejasme   *Perennial*

FLOWERS:	Creamy-white with yellow centre; showy; fragrant; 3/8 - 1/4 inch across; several in a terminal flower cluster; calyx 5-parted; corolla salver-shaped; 5 stamens; 1 pistil.
FRUIT:	A small, few-seeded capsule.
LEAVES:	Small, many in a dense rosette, narrow, hairy, 3/8 - 5/8 inch long.
HEIGHT:	1 - 4 inches.
HABITAT:	Open slopes, meadows and thin woods.
DISTRIBUTION:	Rocky Mountains. June - August.

This small, dainty plant with its beautiful and fragrant flowers is a favourite of those who look for wild flowers in the Rocky Mountains. It may be found in bloom from June to August, depending on the elevation, in grassy open places, in open pine woods and along the wooded sides of rushing streams. The flowers are creamy-white with an orange centre and are crowded at the top of a very short stem. In dry, windy, treeless places, the flower clusters hug the ground so closely that the stem and rosette of tiny leaves are completely covered. The individual flowers have tubular corollas, the tube spreading out into five flat lobes at the mouth. The flowers on withering give place to small, dry capsules.

PIGMY FLOWER.   FAIRY CANDELABRA   Photo. p. 257
Androsace septentrionalis   *Annual*

FLOWERS:	White or pinkish; tiny; several in a small much-branched terminal cluster; calyx 5-parted; corolla salver-shaped, 5-lobed; 5 stamens; 1 pistil.
FRUIT:	A small many-seeded capsule.
LEAVES:	Small, many in a dense rosette, hairy, ¼ - ½ inch long.
HEIGHT:	1 - 8 inches.
HABITAT:	Dry sandy soil.
DISTRIBUTION:	Very common in Southern Alberta. May.

The Pigmy Flower is such a small plant and the flowers are so tiny that it usually goes unnoticed but if it is seen, it is seldom recognized as a member of the showy and beautiful Primrose Family. It is a very variable species and grows on dry sandy soil on the open prairie. The whole plant consists of several slender spreading stems which grow from a tight rosette of small hairy leaves. Each short leafless stem gives rise to a terminal cluster of very small leaf-like bracts and a candelabra-like cluster of very small white flowers. On close inspection each flower is found to be a tiny saucer-shaped primrose.

SHOOTING STAR

Photo. p. 257

Dodecatheon radicatum   *Perennial*

FLOWERS:	Red-purple to lavender; showy; ½ - ¾ inch long; 1 - 12 in a terminal cluster; calyx 5-parted; corolla 5-lobed, bent backwards; 5 stamens, prominent; 1 pistil.
FRUIT:	A many-seeded capsule.
LEAVES:	Basal, simple, lance-shaped or spoon-shaped, tapered into petioles, 1½ - 7 inches long.
HEIGHT:	4 - 12 inches.
HABITAT:	Damp open ground.
DISTRIBUTION:	Common and widespread. June - July.

The Shooting Star is one of the best known flowers of the countryside and is familiar in moist fields, shaded woodland borders and along the edge of boggy ponds and lakes. It shows to greatest advantage when it is seen growing by the thousands in an open field where its red-purple flowers form a sea of brilliant colour. The plant is made up of one or several smooth, slender flower stalks which rise from a cluster of dark green, smooth leaves and end in a loose cluster of several flowers. These flowers have the typical primrose form. But, instead of flattening out, the five corolla lobes bend straight back to expose bright bands of yellow and red around the protruding stamens. The flowers look like miniature cyclamens which is not surprising as both plants belong to the same family. Another very similar species, *Dodecatheon conjugens*, but with somewhat paler flowers, sometimes even white, is found in the foothill grasslands and mountain meadows.

FRINGED LOOSESTRIFE

Photo. p. 260

Lysimachia ciliata   *Perennial*

FLOWERS:	Bright yellow; showy; ¾ - 1 inch across; in twos or threes in the leaf axils; calyx 5 - 6-parted; corolla wheel-shaped, 5-cleft; 5 fertile stamens and 5 sterile; 1 pistil.
FRUIT:	A many-seeded capsule.
LEAVES:	Opposite, with fringed petiole, oval lance-shaped, sharp-pointed, 2 - 6 inches long.
HEIGHT:	1 - 3 feet.
HABITAT:	Moist places.
DISTRIBUTION:	Fairly common throughout wooded regions of Alberta. July.

The Fringed Loosestrife is found commonly in moist thickets and roadside woods and very often in marshy ground along with sedges, burreeds and the Common Skullcap. It is a tall, almost smooth, soft-stemmed plant with light green opposite leaves. The descriptive term, "fringed" refers to a shadowy row of fine hairs that extends along the short slender petioles of the leaves. The flowers are bright yellow and wheel-shaped and grow out on long slender stalks from the axils of the upper pairs of leaves.

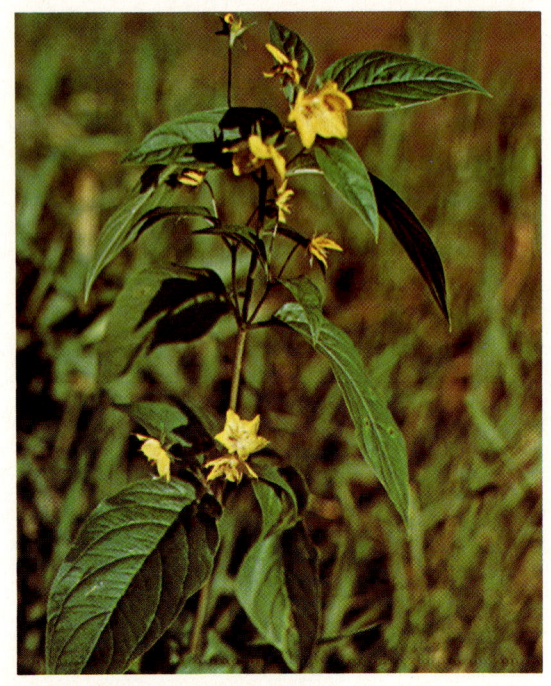

FRINGED
LOOSESTRIFE
(Text p. 259)

JANETTE GOODWIN

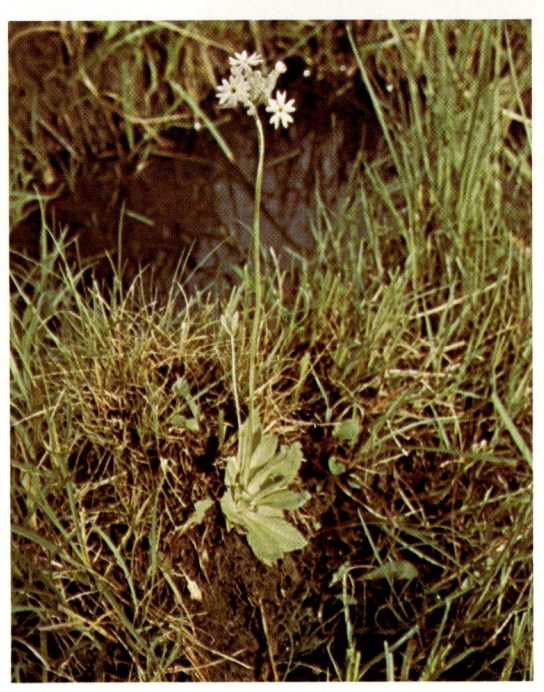

MEALY
PRIMROSE
(Text p. 262)

R. C. SWEET

260

DWARF
CANADIAN
PRIMROSE
(Text p. 262)

R. N. SMITH

NORTHERN
GENTIAN
(Text p. 263)

R. C. SWEET

261

MEALY PRIMROSE
Primula incana

Photo. p. 260
Perennial

FLOWERS:	Lavender with a yellow centre; showy; small, about ¼ inch across; several in a terminal cluster; calyx tubular, 5-cleft; corolla-tube salver-shaped, 5-lobed; 5 stamens; 1 pistil.
FRUIT:	A small capsule.
LEAVES:	Simple, usually oval, 1 - 4 inches long in a basal rosette, green above and yellowish-mealy beneath.
HEIGHT:	Flower stalk 4-16 inches.
HABITAT:	Moist fields, lakes shores and sides of springs and streams.
DISTRIBUTION:	Locally abundant and widespread. June.

The Mealy Primrose is one of the old-fashioned favourites that grows in moist fields, on marshy shores and along the sides of calcareous springs. A yellowish, dense, mealy substance appearing on the under surface of the leaves, on the bare flower stalks and on the flower clusters is the main feature of this plant. This gives to the plant a silvery appearance which attracts almost as much attention as do the dainty lavender flowers. Attached to the top of the flower stalk in a small open cluster, the individual flowers look like little pin wheels with their five lavender lobes and contrasting yellow centres.

DWARF CANADIAN PRIMROSE
Primula mistassinica

Photo. p. 261
Perennial

FLOWERS:	Lilac or pink with an orange centre; showy; small, about ½ inch across; several in a terminal cluster; calyx cup-shaped; corolla-tube salver-shaped, 5-lobed, spreading and notched; 5 stamens; 1 pistil.
FRUIT:	A small capsule.
LEAVES:	Simple, oblong lance-shaped, often toothed, not mealy, ½ - 1 inch long.
HEIGHT:	2 - 4½ inches.
HABITAT:	Wet calcareous shores, and meadows.
DISTRIBUTION:	Occasional. May-June.

The Dwarf Canadian Primrose is similar in general appearance to the Mealy Primrose and grows in the same damp places in forested areas. However, it is a much smaller plant, rarely grows five inches tall, but makes up in beauty what it lacks in size. The leaves are seldom mealy and the bluish-lavender flowers have deeply cleft wedge-shaped lobes and yellowish-orange centres. A favourite haunt is the wet marly shore of a bog or pond where it is often found behind a sheltering reed or sedge.

GENTIAN FAMILY — *GENTIANACEAE*

The gentians comprise a small family of annual, biennial or perennial herbaceous plants renowned for the beauty of their large showy flowers. The flowers are borne either singly or in tight clusters and the corollas are wheel-shaped, bell-shaped or funnel-shaped. About a dozen members of this family grow in Alberta and most of these are found in Western Alberta and in the Rocky Mountains.

NORTHERN GENTIAN. FELWORT   Photo. p. 261
Gentianella amarella   *Annual*

FLOWERS:	Pale violet, pale blue, greenish-yellow or white; showy; 3/8 - 1 inch long; numerous in small clusters; calyx 4 - 5-parted; corolla tubular, vase-shaped, 5-lobed; 5 stamens; 1 pistil.
FRUIT:	A dry capsule.
LEAVES:	Opposite, simple, no petiole, narrowly lance-shaped.
HEIGHT:	6 - 18 inches.
HABITAT:	Moist grassy places.
DISTRIBUTION:	Common and widely distributed. June - September.

The gentians are some of our most beautiful wild flowers and are easily recognized by their bottle or vase-shaped corollas. A most variable species, and, the most widely spread of all Alberta gentians is the Northern Gentian or Felwort. Wherever it is found, in fields and thickets or in the grassy borders of woods and streams, it grows in abundance. It is a bunchy plant, the numerous flowers growing in dense clusters on short stalks in the axils of the paired leaves. The vase-shaped corolla-tube is rimmed at the narrow mouth by a thin fringe of fine hairs and opens out into five short sharp-pointed lobes. Unlike most gentians, the flower colours are weak and range from greenish-violet to pinkish-violet or from greenish-yellow to white. The Northern Gentian blooms from June until September, the lower blossoms setting mature seed before the uppermost blossoms have opened.

WESTERN FRINGED GENTIAN   Photo. p. 264
Gentianella crinata ssp. *macounii*   *Annual*

FLOWERS:	Deep blue; large, 5/8 - 1½ inches long; solitary at the top of the leafy stem; calyx 4-lobed; corolla tubular, 4-lobed; 4 stamens; 1 pistil.
FRUIT:	A dry, urn-shaped capsule.
LEAVES:	Opposite, simple, somewhat clasping, 1 - 2 inches long.
HEIGHT:	4 - 12 inches.
HABITAT:	Low moist ground.
DISTRIBUTION:	Not common, but locally abundant. August - September.

The Western Fringed Gentian has the largest flowers and is the most beautiful of all the Alberta gentians. They grow in little groups along stream banks and in calcareous bogs where their leafy stems and gorgeous single flowers add colour to the autumn vegetation. Towards the end of August, the long slender sapphire blue corolla-tube emerges from its pale green sheath, the calyx. The four large dark blue lobes of the expanded corolla-tube are diffused with silver and are toothed at the apex and fringed along the sides.

WESTERN
FRINGED
GENTIAN
(Text p. 263)

SMOOTH ALPINE GENTIAN
(Text p. 266)

MOUNTAIN
GENTIAN
(Text p. 266)

MARSH FELWORT
(Text p. 267)

SMOOTH ALPINE GENTIAN

Photo. p. 264

Gentiana glauca   *Perennial*

FLOWERS:	Greenish-blue; large, ½ - ¾ inch long; several in a tight cluster at the top of the stem; calyx 4 - 5-lobed; corolla tubular, 4 - 5-lobed, 4 - 5 stamens; 1 pistil.
FRUIT:	A dry urn-shaped capsule.
LEAVES:	Basal leaves in a rosette, simple, oval, somewhat succulent, about ½ inch long; stem leaves, 2 - 3 pairs, similar.
HEIGHT:	1 - 4 inches.
HABITAT:	Damp, stony ground.
DISTRIBUTION:	At high elevations in the Rocky Mountains. August.

One charming, very small plant to watch for at very high altitudes is the Smooth Alpine Gentian. It grows in damp, mossy, stony places and can be distinguished from other alpine gentians by the over-all glossy smoothness of its leaves and stems. The beautiful, dark greenish-blue flowers are grotesquely large in relation to the smallness of the plant. Another dwarfed gentian, the Moss Gentian, *Gentiana fremontii*, with creeping stems, grows in the same damp mossy places. Each short stem is covered with tiny overlapping leaves and ends in a solitary pale greenish-blue flower.

MOUNTAIN GENTIAN

Photo. p. 265

Gentiana calycosa   *Perennial*

FLOWERS:	Blue; large, 1⅛ - 1⅝ inches long; solitary at the top of the leafy stem; calyx 4 - 5-lobed; corolla oblong funnel-form, 5-lobed with extensions on the folds; 4 - 5 stamens; 1 pistil.
FRUIT:	A dry urn-shaped capsule.
LEAVES:	Opposite, crowded on the stem, thickish, dark shiny green, smooth, 3/8 - 1 1/8 inches long.
HEIGHT:	4 - 12 inches.
HABITAT:	Damp, mossy, stony ground.
DISTRIBUTION:	At high elevations in the Rocky Mountains. August.

This gentian grows in the same damp, mossy, stony places and at the same high altitudes as the Smooth Alpine Gentian. It also has the same leafy smooth stems but its flowers are entirely different. These are much larger, are a truer blue and grow in a solitary fashion at the point where the top two broad leaves join the stem. A distinctive feature of the flower is the small often shredded outgrowths of the folds which grow between the five lobes of the long funnel-shaped corolla. Although seen only by alpinists, this gentian is one of the most beautiful of them all.

MARSH FELWORT
Lomatogonium rotatum

Photo. p. 265
Annual

FLOWERS: White or bluish-white; showy; ½ - ¾ inch across; borne singly or in clusters in the axils of the leaves; calyx deeply 4 - 5 cleft; corolla wheel-shaped, 4 - 5 lobed; 5 stamens; 1 pistil without style.

FRUIT: A dry 2-valved capsule.

LEAVES: Basal leaves, spatula-shaped, simple, petioled; upper leaves narrow to lance-shaped, ½ - 2 inches long.

HEIGHT: 4 - 16 inches.

HABITAT: Marshy wet places.

DISTRIBUTION: Rare, Western and Northern Alberta. August - September.

The Marsh Felwort is a slender annual which from a distance looks like the Northern Gentian or Common Felwort, but at close quarters, it is found to be quite different. The flowers are mainly confined to the axils of the upper leaves and instead of being blue and funnel-shaped they are white or bluish-white and are strikingly wheel-shaped. Although somewhat rare in Alberta, the Marsh Felwort is occasionally found in saline flats and wet marshy places where its white wheel-like flowers are easy to spot against the dark green of reeds and sedges.

BUCK-BEAN
Menyanthes trifoliata

Photo. p. 268
Perennial

FLOWERS: White within, pink without, showy; about ½ inch long; crowded in a leafless spike; calyx-tube deeply 5-parted; corolla-tube funnel-shaped with 5 lobes; 5 stamens; 1 pistil.

FRUIT: A dry capsule.

LEAVES: All basal, clasping, long-petioled, compound of 3 thick smooth shiny green leaflets, each 2 - 4 inches long.

HEIGHT: Flower stem 4 - 12 inches.

HABITAT: Boggy ground, wet swampy places.

DISTRIBUTION: Not common, but locally abundant throughout the wooded regions of Alberta. June.

The Buck-Bean grows in the shallow water in ditches and at the sides of boggy pools where its short spikes of gloriously beautiful flowers have a back-ground of floating mats of submerged rootstocks and dark green foliage. The leaves spring from the creeping spongy rootstock and consist of a long succulent petiole and a three-parted blade. The flowers are funnel-shaped with a wide open mouth and are pinkish outside and pure-white inside. The interior of the flower tube is lined with soft white hairs which give the flowers a feathery appearance while the five red anthers add a bright spot of colour to the sides of the tube.

BUCK BEAN
(Text p. 267)

SPREADING DOGBANE
(Text p. 270)

SHOWY MILKWEED
(Text p. 270)

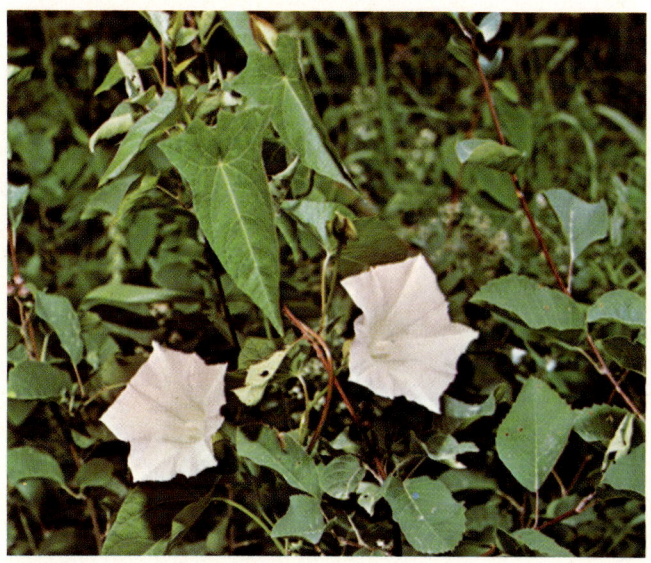

WILD MORNING GLORY
(Text p. 271)

DOGBANE FAMILY — *APOCYNACEAE*

The Dogbane Family is found mainly in the tropics but it is represented in Alberta by four species all in the same genus, *Apocynum*. All of these are perennial herbs with an acrid milky juice called latex and all have opposite simple leaves. The flowers are small but dainty and bell-shaped and are arranged in loose clusters. Each flower has five sepals, five partly-joined petals, five stamens joined to the corolla-tube and a rather complex pistil.

SPREADING DOGBANE

Apocynum androsaemifolium

Photo. p. 268

Perennial

FLOWERS:	Pink; fragrant; small, ¼ - ⅓ inch long; several in small terminal clusters; calyx 5-lobed; corolla bell-shaped, 5-lobed; 5 stamens; 2 ovaries.
FRUIT:	2 long, round, many-seeded pods.
LEAVES:	Opposite, simple, oval to oblong, smooth dark green above, paler beneath, 1 - 3 inches long.
HEIGHT:	1 - 4 feet.
HABITAT:	Dry sandy soil and thickets.
DISTRIBUTION:	Fairly common throughout wooded regions. July-August.

The Spreading Dogbane is a familiar woodland perennial, recognized by its erect forked branches, blue-green foliage, clusters of small, pink, bell-shaped flowers and, if bruised, by its milky juice. The flowers droop in small clusters at the ends of the leafy stems and are a delicate shade of pink, streaked with darker pink on the inside. Pairs of long slender red pods filled with many hair-tipped seeds soon replace the small flowers.

MILKWEED FAMILY — *ASCLEPIADACEAE*

The Milkweed Family is characterized by milky-juiced plants which have large, opposite leaves and five-parted flowers. An unusual feature of the flowers is that the five stamens are united into a tube with the anthers joined to the stigma.

SHOWY MILKWEED

Asclepias speciosa

Photo. p. 269

Perennial

FLOWERS:	Purplish or pinkish; showy; ⅓ - ½ inch across; numerous in dense rounded umbels, 2 - 3 inches across; calyx 5-lobed, turned downwards; corolla 5-parted, turned downwards; 5 stamens; 2 ovaries with short styles.
FRUIT:	A large, soft, many-seeded pod.
LEAVES:	Opposite, simple, oval, broad, 3 - 6 inches long.
HEIGHT:	1 - 2½ feet.
HABITAT:	Thickets, roadsides and moist grassland.
DISTRIBUTION:	Southern Alberta. June - July.

This plant is easily recognized by its tall coarse stem, its large leaves, its round tight clusters of purplish or pinkish flowers, its fat soft hairy seed pods and its copious supply of milky sticky juice which spurts out when the stems or leaves are wounded. The flowers which are of the typical milkweed structure described above have a strong sweet smell that has a slightly stupefying effect on insects. The Low Milkweed, *Asclepias ovalifolia*, a much smaller species with greenish-white flowers, grows in thickets and gullies and the Green Milkweed, *Asclepias viridiflora*, a rare species with whitish-green or yellowish-green flowers has been reported from one locality in Southern Alberta.

MORNING-GLORY FAMILY — *CONVOLVULACEAE*

The description of the Wild Morning-Glory will serve to illustrate the chief features of this small but well known family of twining and climbing plants.

WILD MORNING-GLORY. HEDGE BINDWEED   Photo. p. 269
Convolvulus sepium   *Perennial*

FLOWERS:	White or pink; showy; large, 1½ - 2½ inches across; funnel or trumpet-shaped; calyx deeply 5-parted, enclosed by 2 large bracts; corolla 5-lobed; 5 stamens; 1 pistil.
FRUIT:	A 4-seeded capsule.
LEAVES:	Alternate, simple, spear-shaped, 2 - 5 inches long.
HEIGHT:	Climbing vine.
HABITAT:	Thickets, banks, waste places.
DISTRIBUTION:	Common. June - August.

Two species of the Morning-Glory Family grow in Alberta: one is the Wild Morning-Glory or Hedge Bindweed and the other is the Field Bindweed, *Convolvulus arvensis*. The former is an extremely variable species which twines and climbs over the underbrush of thickets and river banks and sometimes behaves as a weed in cultivated fields and gardens. Its individual flowers have the same trumpet-shaped tubular corollas as the garden climbers but they are smaller and are either white or pink. It also has two large green leaf-like bracts which enclose the calyx and it produces jet black smooth seeds. The latter, an introduced noxious weed, lacks the two leaf-like bracts and produces grey rough seeds.

PHLOX FAMILY — *POLEMONIACEAE*

In Alberta, the Phlox Family is represented by about ten species of annual or perennial herbs of which the phloxes and the jacob's ladders are the best known. They all have an abundance of green foliage, often tufted, and a profusion of showy five-parted flowers.

MOSS PHLOX   Photo. p. 272
Phlox hoodii   *Perennial*

FLOWERS:	White; small, about 3/8 inch across; numerous among the matted leaves; calyx 5-lobed, hairy; corolla-tube 5-lobed, salver-shaped; 5 stamens; 1 pistil with a 3-lobed style.
FRUIT:	A small dry capsule enclosed by the calyx.
LEAVES:	Densely overlapping, firm, narrow, awl-shaped, sharp-pointed, grayish-green, fine hairy, 1/8 - 3/8 inch long.
HEIGHT:	Tufted, mat-forming.
HABITAT:	Open prairie and dry, eroded hillsides.
DISTRIBUTION:	Common throughout Southwestern Alberta. April-June.

As its name suggests this is a low-tufted, mat-forming plant with a coarse woody stem-base and tough woody roots. In early spring, a mass of small white flowers make their appearance above the innumerable, short, spiny, sparsely woolly leaves. The flowers are rolled up longitudinally in the bud but soon unfold and flatten out to form the five-lobed, wheel-shaped corolla-tube typical of all phloxes. In the heat of August, the Moss Phlox presents an almost lifeless, dry, drab cover of stems, prickly leaves and papery seed capsules often intermingled with the prostrate stems of both the Creeping and Common Juniper.

MOSS PHLOX
(Text p. 271)

BLUE PHLOX
(Text p. 274)

WESTERN JACOB'S LADDER
(Text p. 274)

SKUNKWEED
(Text p. 275)

BLUE PHLOX
Phlox alyssifolia

Photo. p. 272
Perennial

FLOWERS:	Pale bluish-purple or white; small, ½ - 5/8 inch across: borne in a dense tufted cluster; calyx 5-lobed, glandular-hairy; corolla-tube 5-lobed, salver-shaped; 5 stamens; 1 pistil with a 3-lobed style.
FRUIT:	A small dry capsule enclosed by the calyx.
LEAVES:	Narrowly oblong, firm with sharp-pointed tips, ¼ - ½ inch long.
HEIGHT:	Prostrate.
HABITAT:	Rocky and gravelly slopes.
DISTRIBUTION:	Occasional. Southern Alberta. May-June.

The Blue Phlox, *Phlox alyssifolia,* is very similar to the Moss Phlox in size and general appearance but its flowers are slightly larger and range in colour from white to pale bluish-purple. Both plants grow in the same regions but the Blue Phlox is not nearly so common. It covers many slopes and screes and its low thick cushiony mat of branches, leaves and flowers conceals the stony surface on which it grows.

WESTERN JACOB'S LADDER
Polemonium occidentale

Photo. p. 273
Perennial

FLOWERS:	Blue; showy; 3/8 - ½ inch long; several in a narrow cluster; calyx cup-shaped, 5-lobed; corolla bell-shaped, 5-lobed; 5 stamens; 1 pistil.
FRUIT:	A 3-valved capsule.
LEAVES:	Alternate, compound of 15 - 27 oval to lance-shaped leaflets.
HEIGHT:	1 - 3 feet.
HABITAT:	Moist open woods, boggy places.
DISTRIBUTION:	Western and Northern Alberta. June-July.

Though not common in Alberta, the Western Jacob's Ladder is widely distributed in valleys and open woods in the foothills and in the Rocky Mountains. It is the tallest of the three species of the genus *Polemonium,* about three feet high and at the end of each stem, clusters of dark blue bell-shaped flowers appear. Its leaves, which are compound, are as attractive as it flowers and the leaflets are so evenly spaced that they look like little ladders. Another similar but much smaller plant, *Polemonium pulcherrimum,* has dark cobalt blue flowers and beautiful fern-like leaves.

274

PHLOX FAMILY — *POLEMONIACEAE*

SKUNKWEED   Photo. p. 273
Polemonium viscosum   *Perennial*

FLOWERS:	Blue or violet; large, 5/8 - 1¼ inches long; several in a crowded cluster; calyx 5-lobed; corolla funnel-shaped, 5-lobed; 5 stamens; 1 pistil.
FRUIT:	A 3-valved capsule.
LEAVES:	Alternate, compound of many small leaflets.
HEIGHT:	4 - 6 inches.
HABITAT:	Loose rocky slopes.
DISTRIBUTION:	High areas. Rocky Mountains. July.

On loose rocky slopes, in high alpine places, the Skunkweed forms scattered low mounds of solid blue. The flowers grow in graceful clusters on short stalks and these are so dense that they spill over each other partially concealing the closely packed whorls of dark green fern-like leaves. Single flowers have funnel-shaped corollas which when fully open expose a circle of yellow stamens and a long thread-like style. Although the flowers are beautiful, the plant is covered with sticky hairs which give off an offensive odour.

WATERLEAF FAMILY — *HYDROPHYLLACEAE*

This family of annual or perennial herbs has hairy, watery stems and lobed or dissected leaves. The parts of the flowers are in fives and when fertilized develop into small dry capsules.

SCORPION WEED   Photo. p. 276
Phacelia sericea   *Perennial*

FLOWERS:	Violet-blue; small, about 3/8 inch long; numerous in a crowded spike; calyx 5-cleft; corolla tubular, 5-lobed; 5 stamens; 1 pistil; style 2-cleft.
FRUIT:	A small dry capsule.
LEAVES:	Alternate, deeply cleft or divided, silvery-hairy, usually petioled.
HEIGHT:	6 - 18 inches.
HABITAT:	Open slopes and rock crevices, often at high altitudes.
DISTRIBUTION:	Rocky Mountains. July-August.

The Scorpion Weed, with its densely flowered spikes and silvery hairy foliage, is often found at the side of gravelly roads, in screes or rock crevices high up in the Rocky Mountains. It grows in clumps or small patches and although the violet-blue flowers are small they are so closely clustered that they make the plant conspicuous. The individual flowers have five widely spreading lobes and these together with the long protruding stamens and styles produce a fluffy effect which softens the rough hairy stiffness of the stems and leaves. Several other scorpion weeds, including *Phacelia lyallii* with dark blue flowers and *Phacelia heterophylla* with white or pinkish flowers are also found on the mountain slopes.

SCORPION WEED
(Text p. 275)

CRYPTANTHA
(Text p. 278)

HOUND'S TONGUE
(Text p. 278)

VIPER'S BUGLOSS
(Text p. 279)

BORAGE FAMILY — *BORAGINACEAE*

This is a family of annual or perennial herbs distinguished by its coarse, hairy stems and leaves, the intense colour of its flowers and by its bur-like fruits. The flowers are perfect and regular with a five-parted calyx-tube and either a wheel-shaped, bell-shaped, salver-shaped or tubular corolla. There are five stamens attached to the corolla-tube and a single pistil. There are about twenty members of the Borage Family in Alberta, some of them introduced weeds.

CRYPTANTHA   Photo. p. 276
Cryptantha bradburiana   *Biennial*

FLOWERS:	White; small, about ¼ inch across; many in compact terminal clusters; calyx 5-parted; corolla salver-shaped, 5-lobed; 5 stamens; 1 pistil.
FRUIT:	4 small nutlets.
LEAVES:	Alternate, simple, narrow, white bristly hairy, about 1 inch long.
HEIGHT:	4 - 12 inches.
HABITAT:	Dry hillsides and prairies.
DISTRIBUTION:	Common throughout Southern Alberta. May - June.

This familiar prairie plant has no well established common name and until recently went by another scientific name. It is a short-lived perennial and grows on dry plains and rolling hillsides. It appears early in the spring and is found growing with the Prairie Yellow Violet, the Prairie Onion and some of the goosefoots, pigweeds and locoweeds. It is easy to recognize as one of the Borage Family because of its short hairy stem, bristly leaves and salver-shaped flowers. The individual white flowers are small, but crowded together on a short stout spike at the top of the leafy stem they have the appearance of a hyacinth.

HOUND'S TONGUE   Photo. p. 277
Cynoglossum officinale   *Biennial*

FLOWERS:	Reddish-purple; small, 1/4 - 3/8 inch across; many drooping in dense open clusters; calyx 5-parted; corolla 5-lobed, funnel-formed; 5 stamens; 1 pistil.
FRUIT:	4 small prickly nutlets.
LEAVES:	Lower leaves, simple, petioled, oblong, lance-shaped, 6 - 12 inches long; upper leaves, smaller, clasping, soft hairy.
HEIGHT:	1½ - 3 feet.
HABITAT:	Dry fields and waste places.
DISTRIBUTION:	Common, particularly in Southern Alberta. June.

The Hound's Tongue is a coarse unattractive plant with stems, leaves and flower-stalks densely covered with fine downy hairs. The petals are a beautiful maroon, but as they extend scarcely beyond the rim of the calyx-tube they do not attract much attention. However, after fertilization, each flower is replaced by a pyramid of four bur-like nutlets and these attract attention by catching in one's clothing or in the fur of animals. It is an introduced weed and is fast becoming widely distributed in waste places and in neglected pastures.

VIPER'S BUGLOSS
Echium vulgare

Photo. p. 277
Biennial

FLOWERS:	Bright blue; showy; about 5/8 inch long; numerous in short branches; calyx 5-parted; corolla tubular, 5-lobed; 5 stamens; 1 pistil; style 2-cleft.
FRUIT:	4 nutlets.
LEAVES:	Alternate, simple, narrowly lance-shaped, bristly.
HEIGHT:	1 -2½ feet.
HABITAT:	Roadsides and waste places.
DISTRIBUTION:	An introduced weed. Occasional throughout Alberta. July-August.

The Viper's Bugloss is a biennial which forms a flat rosette of leaves the first year and a flowering stalk the second year. It has a rough bristly stem from which grow silvery light green hairy leaves and many small bright blue flowers. The flowers are closely packed together in numerous recurved spikes and each has the five-lobed tubular corolla which is characteristic of most members of the Borage Family. In the bud, the flowers are a purplish-red which changes to blue when they open.

STICKSEED
Hackelia floribunda

Photo. p. 280
Biennial

FLOWERS:	Pale blue; small, about 3/16 inch broad; in numerous erect clusters; calyx 5-parted; corolla 5-lobed, salver-shaped; 5 stamens; 1 pistil.
FRUIT:	A barbed nutlet.
LEAVES:	Alternate, simple, narrowly lance-shaped, rough hairy.
HEIGHT:	1½ - 3 feet.
HABITAT:	Moist woodlands and thickets.
DISTRIBUTION:	Fairly common. July.

The Stickseed is another familiar member of the Borage Family. The rough, hairy stems grow stiffly erect and support at their tops several loose clusters of small pale blue flowers. After fertilization, these flowers are replaced by small nut-like fruits rimmed around with a row of very flat prickles. It is often mistaken for the true Forget-Me-Not or for the Blue-Bur as the blue salver-shaped flowers in all three are very much alike. However, in Alberta, the true Forget-Me-Not is a low tufted plant and grows only at high altitudes in the Rockies, while the Stickseed is fairly wide-spread and grows in thickets and on wooded banks. The Blue-Bur grows in open fields and waste places and has smaller flowers which are very pale blue or almost white.

STICKSEED
(Text p. 279)

WESTERN BLUE-BUR
(Text p. 282)

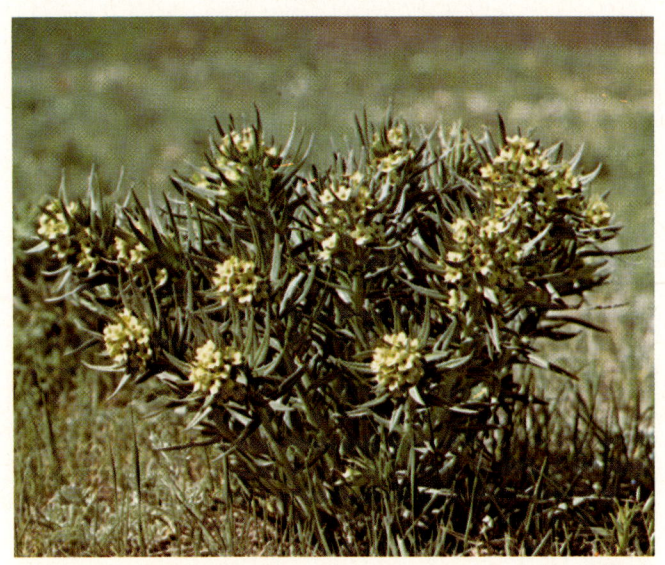

YELLOW PUCCOON
(Text p. 282)

TALL LUNGWORT
(Text p. 283)

BORAGE FAMILY — *BORAGINACEAE*

WESTERN BLUE-BUR
Lappula redowskii var. *occidentalis*

Photo. p. 280
Annual

FLOWERS:	Pale blue or white; tiny, less than 1/8 inch across; many in several leafy, bracted, rough, hairy clusters; calyx 5-parted; corolla 5-lobed, salver-shaped; 5 stamens; 1 pistil.
FRUIT:	4 small spiny nutlets.
LEAVES:	Alternate, simple, narrowly spatula-shaped, stiff hairy, ¾ - 1½ inches long.
HEIGHT:	4 - 18 inches.
HABITAT:	Light sandy soils. Dry prairie.
DISTRIBUTION:	Common throughout Southern Alberta. June - July.

The Western Blue-Bur, commonly but mistakenly called Forget-Me-Not, is a well-known native annual which grows in gravelly sandy soils, along roadsides, railway grades and in abandoned fields. The rough hairy leafy stem ends in several loose clusters of small, pale blue, salver-shaped flowers which resemble those of the true Forget-Me-Not. However, these flowers are very tiny, no larger than the head of a pin and when the petals fall off they are replaced by small, spiny, bur-like fruits.

YELLOW PUCCOON. WOOLLY GROMWELL
Lithospermum ruderale

Photo. p. 281
Perennial

FLOWERS:	Yellow; showy; about ½ inch across; crowded in a leafy terminal cluster; calyx 5-lobed; corolla salver-shaped, 5-lobed; 5 stamens; 1 pistil.
FRUIT:	4 white hard small nutlets.
LEAVES:	Numerous, alternate, simple, no petioles, narrow, stiff hairy, 2 - 4 inches long.
HEIGHT:	8 - 20 inches.
HABITAT:	Prairie grassland.
DISTRIBUTION:	Common throughout Southwestern Alberta. June-August.

The Yellow Puccoon or Woolly Gromwell is found mainly in the rolling foothills and bunch-grass grazing country of Southern Alberta. As the grasses bend and sway with every breeze that blows, the stout, leafy, stiff-hairy stem, firmly anchored by a thick tap root, keeps the Yellow Puccoon erect. The small, lemon-yellow, sweet-scented, salver-shaped flowers are borne among the leaves at and near the top of the stem. They open a few at a time from below upwards, so by the end of summer, when the uppermost flowers are still in bloom, the lowermost have given place to four small hard white shining nutlets. The name of the genus is from the Greek *lithos*, a "stone" and *sperm*, a "seed" in allusion to the nutlets which are as hard as little stones. The long thick roots were used by the Plains Indians for food and as a source of a red dye for staining the skins of animals. A narrow-leaved species, *Lithospermum incisum*, grows in the same region.

TALL LUNGWORT. BLUEBELLS
Mertensia paniculata

Photo. p. 281
Perennial

FLOWERS:	Purplish-blue; showy; about ½ inch long; several in loose, drooping clusters at the end of the stems; calyx small, deeply 5-cleft; corolla 5-lobed, funnel-shaped; 5 stamens; 1 pistil.
FRUIT:	Four small nutlets.
LEAVES:	Alternate, simple, oval to lance-shaped, hairy on both sides; basal leaves long-petioled, 2-5 inches long; stem leaves not petioled.
HEIGHT:	1 - 3 feet.
HABITAT:	Open woods and shady stream banks.
DISTRIBUTION:	Common throughout the wooded regions of Alberta. June - July.

In June, the Tall Lungwort or Bluebells is one of the beauties of poplar woods and shady stream banks. It is found too in damp, shady thickets and roadsides. It has an airy grace with its tall, curving stem and dark green foliage and its drooping clusters of blue flowers add to its attraction. The beautiful lance-shaped leaves, however, make the plant conspicuous long after the flowers have faded and given way to small, nut-like fruits. The corolla is funnel-shaped with the lobes of the five, joined petals not flaring out but cup-shaped.

ALPINE FORGET-ME-NOT
Myosotis alpestris

Photo. p. 284
Perennial

FLOWERS:	Bright blue with yellow centre; showy; small, about 3/16 inch across; many in dense clusters; calyx 5-parted; corolla 5-lobed, salver-shaped; 5 stamens; 1 pistil.
FRUIT:	Four, small, smooth nutlets.
LEAVES:	Alternate, simple, hairy, oblong, narrow.
HEIGHT:	3 - 9 inches.
HABITAT:	Moist mountain meadows.
DISTRIBUTION:	High elevations. Rocky Mountains. June - August.

Of all our high mountain wild flowers, the Alpine Forget-Me-Not is the most easily recognized because it resembles so closely our well-known garden favourite. During July and August, it combines with the Alpine Blue Bell, Blue Beard Tongue, Alpine Speedwell and Blue-Eyed Mary to make an Alpine meadow or rocky slope into a sea of misty blue. It could only be mistaken for an Alpine Speedwell because both have the same dwarfed form and appearance and both flowers are the same size and shape. However, they differ in the number of lobes of the corolla: there are five lobes in the Alpine Forget-Me-Not and only four in the Alpine Speedwell. The corolla of the Forget-Me-Not is further distinguished by a bright yellow spot in the centre.

ALPINE FORGET-ME-NOT
(Text p. 283)

FALSE GROMWELL
(Text p. 286)

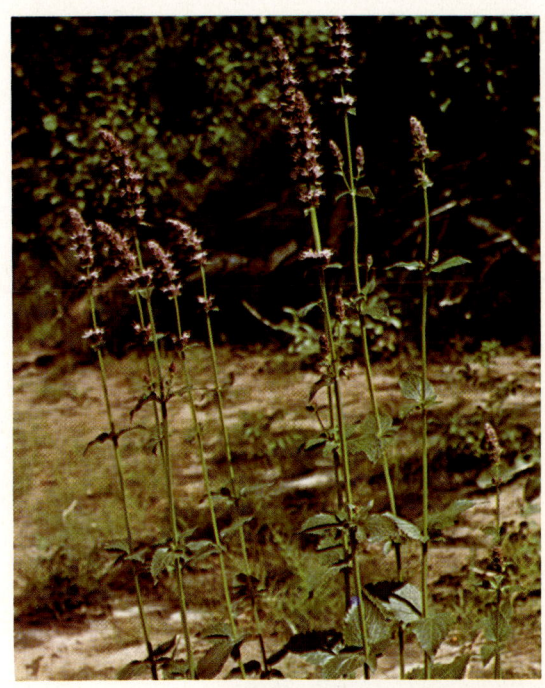

GIANT HYSSOP
(Text p. 286)

FALSE
DRAGONHEAD
(Text p. 287)

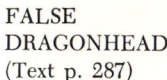

FALSE GROMWELL
Onosmodium occidentale

Photo. p. 284
Perennial

FLOWERS:	Yellowish-white or greenish; showy; ½ - ¾ inch long; many borne in leafy-bracted curved clusters; calyx 5-parted; corolla-tube salver-shaped; 5 stamens; 1 pistil.
FRUIT:	4 shiny smooth brownish-white nutlets.
LEAVES:	Simple, oval to lance-shaped, coarse hairy, conspicuously veined, 2 - 3 inches long.
HEIGHT:	1 - 2 feet.
HABITAT:	Light soil on prairie and grassy thickets.
DISTRIBUTION:	Occasional in Southern Alberta. July - August.

The False Gromwell is very similar to the Yellow Puccoon or Woolly Gromwell in general appearance and it grows in the same localities. Its flowers, however, are yellowish-white or greenish and are two to three times longer than those of the Yellow Puccoon. They are arranged in leafy densely hairy terminal spikes which are curled up in the bud but straighten out during growth. The nutlets are also similar to those of the Yellow Puccoon but are dull white or brownish and are somewhat larger.

MINT FAMILY — *LABIATAE*

This is a well-known family of annual or perennial herbs with a strong and pungent odour. Many plants important in medicine and in flavouring and seasoning belong to this family: peppermint, spearmint, thyme, basil, marjoram and others. However, most of the volatile oils produced by these plants are now prepared synthetically. The mints are characterized by square or angular stems, opposite, usually toothed leaves and perfect irregular flowers. Each flower consists of a cup-shaped calyx, a two-lipped tubular corolla, four or two stamens and a four-lobed ovary. About twenty members of the Mint Family are found in Alberta and about one-quarter of these are introduced weeds.

GIANT HYSSOP
Agastache foeniculum

Photo. p. 285
Perennial

FLOWERS:	Blue; small, 1/4 - 3/8 inch long; many in a dense, sometimes interrupted, spike, 1 - 4 inches long; calyx cup-shaped; corolla tubular, 2-lipped; 4 stamens protruding; 1 pistil.
FRUIT:	Four small nutlets.
LEAVES:	Opposite, simple, short-petioled, oval, coarsely-toothed, green above, whitish beneath, 1 - 3 inches long.
HEIGHT:	2 - 3½ feet.
HABITAT:	Thickets and open woodlands.
DISTRIBUTION:	Common throughout semi-wooded regions of Alberta. July - August.

Throughout July and August, the tall, erect, leafy stems of the Giant Hyssop may be seen at the edge of thickets, in thin open poplar woods and on river banks. It is the tallest of our native mints and has the square stem, opposite leaves and irregular flowers characteristic of the Mint Family. Although only about one-quarter of an inch long, the flowers are typically mint-shaped, two-lipped blossoms and are densely crowded onto a long, sometimes interrupted, spike. It is an attractive plant and has a pleasant odour of anise.

FALSE DRAGONHEAD Photo. p. 285
Dracocephalum nuttallii *Perennial*

FLOWERS: Rose-pink or purple; showy; about ½ inch long; numerous in a long terminal spike; calyx inflated; corolla tubular, two-lipped; 4 stamens; 1 pistil.

FRUIT: 4 small nutlets.

LEAVES: Opposite, simple, no petiole, oblong lance-shaped, coarsely-toothed, 3-4 inches long.

HEIGHT: 1 - 3 feet.

HABITAT: Stream banks and moist places.

DISTRIBUTION: Fairly common but very local. June-July.

Often when wandering along the side of a slow-moving stream or a marshy pond margin, we are likely to spy the rose-purple flowers of the False Dragonhead appearing with the sedges and the reeds. The flowers are crowded on a terminal leafless spike, those at the bottom opening first and often setting seed while those at the top are still in bud. Individual flowers are typical of the mints. They have a funnel-shaped, two-lipped corolla-tube greatly enlarged at the throat. The False Dragonhead is sometimes mistaken for the Hedge Nettle as both plants grow in wet places and both have rose-purple flowers but those of the latter are definitely mottled with dark purple.

HEMP NETTLE Photo. p. 288
Galeopsis tetrahit *Annual*

FLOWERS: Pink or whitish; showy; ⅝ - ⅞ inch long; in dense terminal whorls; calyx-tube with 5 sharp points; corolla-tube 2-lipped; 4 stamens; 1 pistil.

FRUIT: 4 small nutlets.

LEAVES: Opposite, simple, petioled, oval or lance-shaped, hairy, coarsely toothed, 1½ - 4½ inches long.

HEIGHT: 1 - 2½ feet.

HABITAT: Waste places, thickets and roadsides.

DISTRIBUTION: Common. Introduced weed. July-August.

The Hemp Nettle is a mint and has the characteristic square stem and numerous small flowers which have two-lipped tubular corollas. The distinguishing feature of the Hemp Nettle is the close arrangement of the pink flowers among the upper pairs of coarse hairy leaves. Another feature is the prominent sharp-pointed calyx which gives this plant the name nettle.

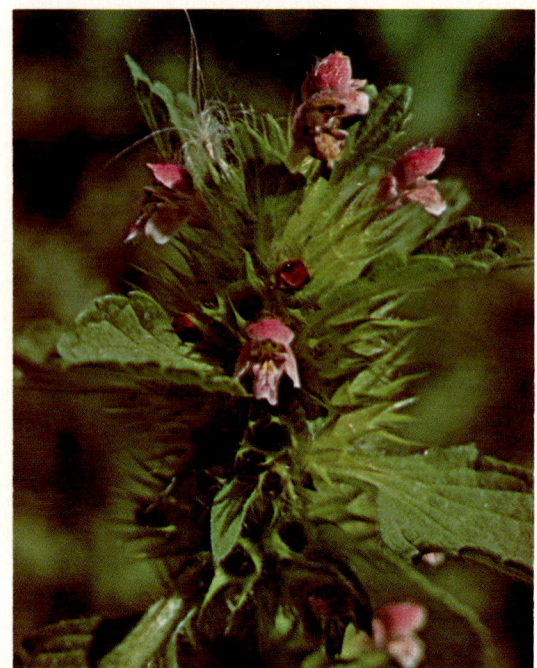

HEMP NETTLE
(Text p. 287)

A. KARVONEN

WILD MINT
(Text p. 290)

J. CLAESSEN

R. C. SWEET

WESTERN WILD BERGAMOT
(Text p. 290)

JANETTE GOODWIN

HEAL ALL
(Text p. 291)

WILD MINT   Photo. p. 288
Mentha arvensis var. *villosa*   *Perennial*

FLOWERS:	Pinkish-purple or white; tiny, 1/8 inch long; many in a whorled cluster; calyx tubular; corolla 4 - 5 lobed; 4 stamens; 1 pistil.
FRUIT:	4 small nutlets.
LEAVES:	Opposite, simple, short-petioled, oval to lance-shaped, ½ - 2 inches long.
HEIGHT:	4 - 18 inches.
HABITAT:	Sloughs and wet places.
DISTRIBUTION:	Common. Locally abundant. June-July.

The Wild Mint is one of our most familiar native plants and can be identified immediately by its pungent odour. It grows with reeds and sedges, often in the water at the edge of sloughs and in other wet places. The tiny pinkish bell-shaped flowers are tightly packed in circles around the main stem and appear at the base of each pair of leaves. The Wild Mint, well-known to the Plains Indians, was used as medicine and as a savory for dried meats.

WESTERN WILD BERGAMOT   Photo. p. 289
Monarda fistulosa var. *menthaefolia*   *Perennial*

FLOWERS:	Mauve; large, ¾ - 1¼ inches long; numerous in a terminal head-like cluster, 1½ - 2½ inches across; calyx tubular, toothed; corolla 2-lipped, hairy; 2 stamens; 1 pistil.
FRUIT:	Four small nutlets.
LEAVES:	Opposite, simple, short-petioled, triangular-oval, hairy, 1 - 4 inches long.
HEIGHT:	1 - 2½ feet.
HABITAT:	Edge of scrubby woods and sides of coulees.
DISTRIBUTION:	Common throughout prairie and thinly wooded regions. July-August.

The Western Wild Bergamot surpasses all other native mints in the size and brilliance of its flowers and is one of our most beautiful prairie plants. It grows on dry banks, on the sides of coulees and along the edge of shrubby poplar thickets. It is similar in every respect to the old-fashioned bergamot of our gardens except in the colour of its flowers which is an unusual shade of mauve rather than red. It differs from all other native mints in that the flowers are crowded onto a single, flat-topped cluster at the top of the leafy stem. These tall, showy flower-heads stand out like gay-feathered plumes. The Western Wild Bergamot is a true mint; it has square stems, opposite leaves, two-lipped corollas and a sweet-smelling minty odour.

HEAL ALL. SELF HEAL   Photo. p. 289
Prunella vulgaris   *Perennial*

FLOWERS: Purplish-blue; small, ⅓ - ½ inch long; many in a short,
                    dense, terminal, bracted spike; calyx tubular, 2-lipped;
                    corolla tubular, 2-lipped; 4 stamens; 1 pistil.

FRUIT: 4 smooth nutlets.

LEAVES: Opposite, simple, petioled, oval lance-shaped, 1 - 4
                    inches long.

HEIGHT: 4 - 12 inches.

HABITAT: Woodlands, moist places, roadsides.

DISTRIBUTION: Occasionally throughout Alberta. July - August.

Although the Heal All or Self Heal is not common, it is sometimes very
abundant in damp fields, open woods, thickets and along roadsides. It is
a low growing perennial and has all the characteristics of a typical mint;
square stem, opposite leaves and tubular, two-lipped flowers. The flowers
are a deep purplish-blue and are closely set in a thick terminal spike, interspersed with small brownish-green, bract-like leaves at the top of the stem.
The individual flowers are small and a very noticeable feature is a tuft of
hairs on the three-lobed lower lip. This plant, as its common name
indicates, was at one time highly valued as a medicine for internal bleeding
and for external wounds.

COMMON SKULLCAP   Photo. p. 292
Scutellaria galericulata   *Perennial*

FLOWERS: Blue; showy; 5/8 - 3/4 inch long; borne singly in the
                    axils of the leaves; calyx tubular; 2-lipped; corolla
                    tubular, 2-lipped; 4 stamens; 1 pistil.

FRUIT: 4 small nutlets.

LEAVES: Opposite, simple, oblong lance-shaped, wavy margined,
                    1 - 2½ inches long.

HEIGHT: 1 - 3 feet.

HABITAT: Wet places, lake shores, stream banks.

DISTRIBUTION: Fairly common in Alberta. July - August.

In low marshy ground and around the wet muddy shores of sloughs,
lakes and slow moving streams and in company with sedges, reeds and
swamp grasses, one is almost certain to find the Common Skullcap. It
would go unnoticed were it not for its beautiful blue flowers. These are
borne singly on short slender stalks in the axils of the oppositely placed
leaves, but because they face in the same direction and are so close
together, they become a pair. The calyx is tubular and two-lipped and a
special distinguishing feature is a broad hollow pouch on the upper lip,
from which the plant gets its scientific name. The corolla is also tubular
with two lips and these are wide enough apart to reveal a pale blue
interior which contrasts with the darker blue of the outside.

**COMMON
SKULLCAP**
(Text p. 291)

DORTHEA CALVERLEY

**HEDGE
NETTLE**
(Text p. 294)

KATHLEEN HODGES

292

BLACK
HENBANE
(Text p. 294)

WILD TOMATO
(Text p. 295)

MINT FAMILY — *LABIATAE*

HEDGE NETTLE   Photo. p. 292
Stachys palustris var. *pilosa*   *Perennial*

FLOWERS:	Magenta, dotted with purple; showy; 3/8 - 1/2 inch long; many in a leafy terminal spike; calyx 5-toothed; corolla tubular; 2-lipped; 4 stamens; 1 pistil.
FRUIT:	Four, small, brown nutlets.
LEAVES:	Opposite, simple, short-petioled, lance-shaped, to oblong, toothed, 1 - 5 inches long.
HEIGHT:	1 - 3 feet.
HABITAT:	Moist fields, waste places and wet shores.
DISTRIBUTION:	Common throughout Alberta. June - August.

The Hedge Nettle has a preference for moist waste places, disturbed soil and thickets where it is often found growing with the Stinging Nettle, Cow Parsnip, coarse sedges and weedy grasses. With its erect, square stem, opposite, toothed, hairy leaves, terminal spike of many, whorled, small, two-lipped flowers and pungent odour, it could be classed as the typical mint. Its flowers are an unusual shade of magenta, marked with darker spots and this beautiful colour gives distinction to the drab surroundings where it thrives.

NIGHTSHADE FAMILY — *SOLANACEAE*

This family of herbaceous plants is represented in Alberta by only a few species, all of them introduced weeds. Strongly scented foliage and salver-shaped, wheel-shaped or bell-shaped corollas are the chief characteristics. Two well-known members of this family are the potato and the tomato.

BLACK HENBANE   Photo. p. 293
Hyoscyamus niger   *Biennial*

FLOWERS:	Greenish-yellow, lined with purple; large, 3/4 - 1 1/4 inches long; several in drooping clusters; calyx-tube cup-shaped, persistent; corolla-tube funnel-shaped, 5-lobed; 5 stamens; 1 pistil.
FRUIT:	A dry capsule, opening by a lid.
LEAVES:	Lower leaves, simple, short-petioled, irregularly lobed, glandular-hairy, 4 - 10 inches long; upper leaves, smaller and not petioled.
HEIGHT:	1 - 4 feet.
HABITAT:	Waste places.
DISTRIBUTION:	Occasional. Southern Alberta. July - August.

All the members of the Nightshade Family found in Alberta are weeds, most of them introduced from Europe. One of these is the Black Henbane, a poisonous, ill-scented herb with a stout branching stem and large clammy-hairy leaves. The flowers are borne on short one-sided spikes in the axils of the upper leaves. They are funnel-shaped with five broad greenish-yellow lobes which are streaked with purple. After fertilization the ovary ripens to form a thin papery seed-capsule, while the persistent calyx-tube forms a dry, sharp-pointed, shell-like sheath around it. The Black Henbane thrives in overgrazed rangeland and in dry gravelly roadsides and is a fit companion for the coarse, hairy Common Mullein with which it often grows.

WILD TOMATO
Solanum triflorum

Photo. p. 293
Annual

FLOWERS: White; small, 1/4 - 3/8 inch across; borne in clusters of 3; calyx 5-cleft; corolla 5-lobed, wheel-shaped; 5 stamens; 1 pistil.

FRUIT: A small, round, green, poisonous berry.

LEAVES: Alternate, simple, deeply lobed, 1 - 3 inches long.

HEIGHT: Mat-forming.

HABITAT: Disturbed soil, waste places.

DISTRIBUTION: Locally. Southern Alberta. June - July.

The Wild Tomato is a low-spreading leafy annual commonly found in disturbed soil of the southern prairies. The flowers, though white, so closely resemble those of the cultivated tomato that the plant is easily recognized. They have the same wheel-shaped corolla and the anthers of the five stamens form around the short style in the same cone-shaped fashion. The fruits are typical small round tomatoes about half an inch in diameter. However, they remain green when mature and are poisonous to most people when eaten, especially children. Another species, Black Nightshade, *Solanum nigrum*, a cosmopolitan weed has small white flowers and small round fruits which turn black or yellow at maturity. They too are considered to be poisonous.

FIGWORT FAMILY — *SCROPHULARIACEAE*

The Figwort Family is made up of soft-stemmed herbs which includes many familiar garden plants as snapdragon, nemesia, pentstemon and foxglove. A characteristic shared by them all is a beautiful irregular corolla of diverse form and shape; wheel-shaped, bell-shaped or strongly two-lipped. The stamens vary in number from two to five and are attached to the corolla-tube. The single pistil develops into a dry many-seeded capsule. Some of our best known and most beautiful wild flowers belong to this family. They are the paint brushes, pentstemons and the louseworts.

CLAMMY HEDGE HYSSOP
Gratiola neglecta

Photo. p. 296
Annual

FLOWERS: Pale yellow or whitish; small, 1/4 - 3/8 inch long; numerous on slender stalks in axils of leaves; calyx 5-lobed; corolla tubular, 2-lipped; 2 stamens; 1 pistil.

FRUIT: A small dry capsule.

LEAVES: Opposite, simple, without petioles, narrow to lance-shaped, ½ - 2 inches long.

HEIGHT: 4 - 8 inches.

HABITAT: Wet muddy places.

DISTRIBUTION: Found occasionally in wet localities. July.

Although the common name Hedge Hyssop suggests that it is one of the mints, this plant belongs to the Figwort Family and is found occasionally in wet ditches and in mud flats. It is a greatly branched, somewhat straggling plant and its many small pale yellow or whitish flowers are pouch-shaped and two-lipped and look like miniature snapdragons. The upper parts of the plant are densely covered with soft glandular hairs and they feel cold and clammy to the touch.

P. D. SEYMOUR

CLAMMY HEDGE HYSSOP
(Text p. 295)

H. A. MacGREGOR

YELLOW TOADFLAX
(Text p. 298)

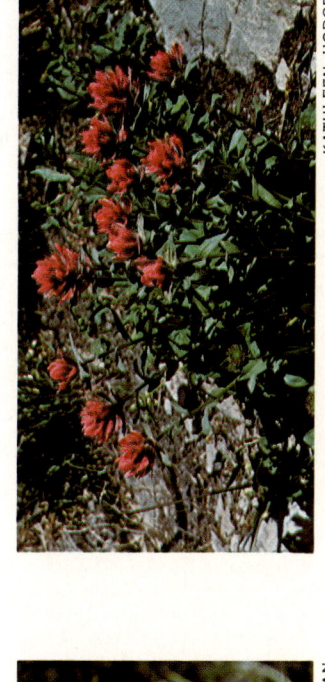

COMMON RED PAINTBRUSH (Text p. 298)

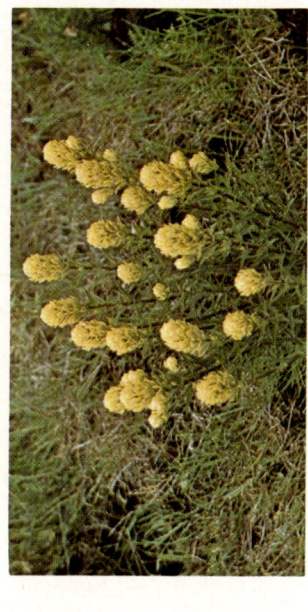

COMMON YELLOW PAINTBRUSH (Text p. 298)

PAINTBRUSH, VARIETY

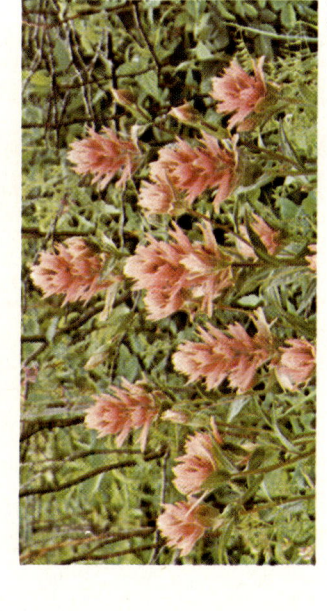

PAINTBRUSH, VARIETY

297

COMMON RED PAINT BRUSH

Castilleja miniata

Photo. p. 297

Perennial

FLOWERS:	Pale green; ¾ - 1¼ inches long; partly enfolded in a showy red, pink or orange coloured bract almost as long as the flower; many in a long terminal spike or brush; calyx tubular, laterally flattened, 4-lobed; corolla tubular, 2-lipped; 4 stamens in 2 pairs, enclosed; 1 pistil with protruding style.
FRUIT:	A small, dry, many-seeded capsule.
LEAVES:	Alternate, simple, no petiole, narrow, 1 - 2 inches long.
HEIGHT:	1 - 2 feet.
HABITAT:	Open woodlands, meadows and slopes.
DISTRIBUTION:	Common in the mountains, foothills and wooded regions of Alberta. June - September.

Alberta has a wealth of paint brushes of almost every colour of the rainbow: red, scarlet, purple, magenta, pink, orange, yellow and greenish-white. The best known species is the Common Red Paint Brush whose beautiful, torch-like flower-stems or so-called brushes set mountain slopes, foothills and open woodlands ablaze with colour from June to September. It is a most variable species with brushes of red, pink or orange and is sometimes separated into several species by colour. The colour of the brush is not due to the flowers themselves, but to the floral leaves or bracts which enfold them—one coloured bract below each pale green flower. The flowers are narrow and tubular, with four enclosed stamens and a long protruding style and they emerge here and there among the bracts. Like most of the paint brushes, it is parasitic on the roots of other plants. The Common Yellow Paint Brush, *Castilleja septentrionalis*, is another variable species that grows in mountain and foothill grasslands of Southern Alberta. The corolla is greenish but the showy bracts are sulphur yellow. Another species, *Castilleja raupii*, found only in the bogs, stream banks and stunted woods of Northern Alberta has spectacular violet-purple brushes. The paint brushes are one of our greatest tourist attractions and one of the cheapest.

YELLOW TOADFLAX. BUTTER AND EGGS

Linaria vulgaris

Photo. p. 296

Perennial

FLOWERS:	Yellow, tipped with orange; large, 1 - 1¼ inches long; many in a dense spike; calyx 5-cleft; corolla 2-lipped, spurred; 4 stamens; 1 pistil.
FRUIT:	An oval, dry capsule.
LEAVES:	Alternate, simple, no petiole, narrow, ¾ - 3 inches long.
HEIGHT:	1 - 2½ feet.
HABITAT:	Roadsides and waste places.
DISTRIBUTION:	Common throughout Alberta. June - July.

The Yellow Toadflax is an introduced plant from Europe, long established as a troublesome weed in Eastern Canada and becoming more and more common along roadsides and in fields and waste places throughout Alberta. Despite its reputation as a weed, it is a striking looking plant and its bright yellow flowers are most attractive. These, with their two-lipped, pouch-shaped corollas look like snapdragons at first glance but differ in having a long spur. The lower lip is furnished with a swollen orange-coloured palate which nearly closes the throat of the corolla. The lips of the corolla are so firmly compressed that only long-tongued bees and certain butterflies are able to reach the nectar at the base of the spur.

FIGWORT FAMILY — *SCROPHULARIACEAE*

RED MONKEY FLOWER   Photo. p. 300
Mimulus lewisii   *Perennial*

FLOWERS: Rose-red; showy; large, about 1 - 2 inches long; several
                  in leafy clusters; calyx tubular, 5-pointed; corolla
                  tubular, 2-lipped; 4 stamens in 2 pairs; 1 pistil.

FRUIT: A 2-valved many-seeded capsule.

LEAVES: Opposite, simple, lance-shaped to oblong, thin,
                  irregularly toothed, 1½ - 3 inches long.

HEIGHT: 1 - 2 feet.

HABITAT: Wet mossy ground along mountain streams and lakes.

DISTRIBUTION: Rocky Mountains. Southwestern Alberta. July-August.

The Red Monkey Flower is a Rocky Mountain plant and must be
looked for in the deep forest and at higher elevations, usually at timberline.
It prefers the sunny open places on the mossy sides of springs and small
streams, where it grows in dense clumps tumbling over moss-covered stones
and windfalls. Another favourite haunt is a sunny moss-lined hollow or a
pot-hole formed by an up-rooted tree. Its charm lies in its luxuriant dark
green foliage and its showers of rose-red flowers. The corollas are so
strongly two-lipped that only the strong-bodied bumble-bee can force a
passage between them.

YELLOW MONKEY FLOWER   Photo. p. 300
Mimulus guttatus   *Annual*

FLOWERS: Bright yellow, usually spotted with red; showy; large,
                  ¾ - 1¼ inches long; few on long slender stalks; calyx
                  tubular; corolla tubular, 2-lipped; 4 stamens in 2 pairs;
                  1 pistil.

FRUIT: A 2-valved, many-seeded capsule.

LEAVES: Opposite, simple, commonly toothed, oval to rounded,
                  ½ - 2 inches long.

HEIGHT: 3 - 24 inches.

HABITAT: Wet mossy places and sides of streams.

DISTRIBUTION: Rocky Mountains. Southwestern Alberta. June-July.

This is a rarer species which has bright yellow flowers and crisp
green foliage and it makes a colourful showing along the mossy sides of
springs and small mountain streams. It is very similar to the Red Monkey
Flower, but somewhat smaller. The corolla-tube is short and distinctly two-
lipped with prominent ridges in the throat. Although our Alberta monkey
flowers are plants of the sunny openings and mossy springy places, they
are forest plants too and depend upon the trees for the damp mossy conditions they prefer.

RED MONKEY FLOWER
(Text p. 299)

YELLOW MONKEY FLOWER
(Text p. 299)

OWL CLOVER
(Text p. 302)

WESTERN
LOUSEWORT
(Text p. 302)

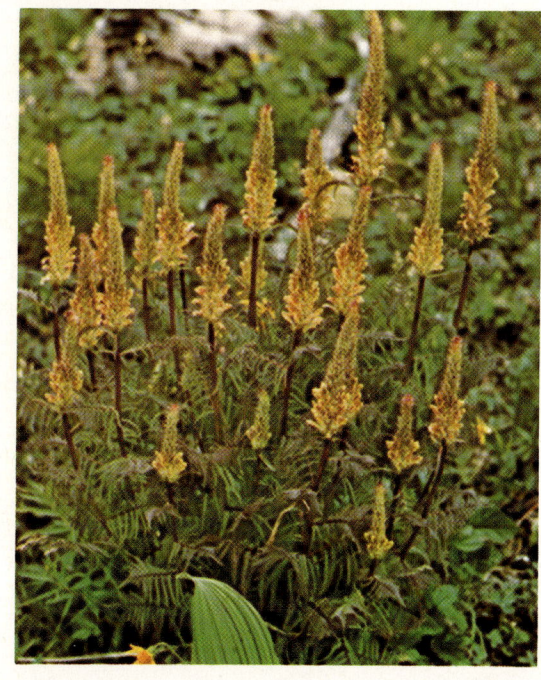

301

FIGWORT FAMILY — *SCROPHULARIACEAE*

OWL CLOVER Photo. p. 301

Orthocarpus luteus *Annual*

FLOWERS: Yellow; small, ⅜ - ⅝ inch long; numerous in very leafy narrow terminal spikes; calyx 4-cleft; corolla tubular, 2-lipped; 4 stamens; 1 pistil.

FRUIT: A small flattened capsule.

LEAVES: Alternate, simple, narrow, not petioled, ½ - 1½ inches long.

HEIGHT: 6 - 18 inches.

HABITAT: Dry prairie grassland.

DISTRIBUTION: Common throughout Southern and Southwestern Alberta. June-August.

Owl Clover is the common name for Yellow Orthocarpus. It grows mostly in the open dry prairie but is found also on mountain slopes. It is closely related to the Yellow Rattle which it faintly resembles. The small narrow leaves grow close together and seem to zig-zag up the slender glandular hairy stem. From the axils of all the top leaves, small yellow flowers appear. Like most of the figworts the corolla is tubular in shape, the tube opening out just beyond the rim of the calyx into two widely separated lips. The Plains Indians used this plant as the source of red dye.

WESTERN LOUSEWORT Photo. p. 301

Pedicularis bracteosa *Perennial*

FLOWERS: Yellow or purplish; showy; ⅝ - ¾ inch long; numerous in a dense bracted terminal spike; calyx tubular; corolla tubular, 2-lipped, slender; 4 stamens; 1 pistil.

FRUIT: A dry capsule.

LEAVES: Alternate, deeply cleft, margins toothed, 4 - 12 inches long.

HEIGHT: 1 - 3 feet.

HABITAT: Shrubby thickets and thin woods.

DISTRIBUTION: Fairly common in foothill and mountain regions. July-August.

The louseworts make up a distinct group of the Figwort Family, distinguished by fern-like leaves and odd-shaped flowers. The Western Lousewort, a perennial species which grows in the foothills and mountains, is one of the best known. The flowers are yellow or yellow tinged with purple and are borne in a dense terminal spike interspersed with narrow leaf-like bracts. The corolla tube is strongly two-lipped; the lower lip is divided into three lobes, while the upper lip is long and flattened at the sides and arched at the apex enclosing the stamens. Like all the louseworts, it is an unusual looking plant and one to look for in moist places and in open pine woods.

CONTORTED LOUSEWORT
Pedicularis contorta

Photo. p. 304
Perennial

FLOWERS:	Yellowish-white; showy; numerous on a long spike; calyx 2 - 5-lobed; corolla 2-lipped, beak coiled downwards; 4 stamens; 1 pistil.
FRUIT:	A flattened capsule.
LEAVES:	Feathery or fern-like.
HEIGHT:	8 - 12 inches.
HABITAT:	Alpine meadows and slopes.
DISTRIBUTION:	Rocky Mountains. July-August.

This group of plants, commonly called louseworts, is noted for the unusual shape of its flowers. The Contorted Lousewort is possibly the most spectacular of the whole group. It is a Rocky Mountain species and is found in alpine meadows well above timberline. It grows in clumps and its fern-like leaves and spikes of showy yellowish-white shell-shaped flowers make it most attractive. At a distance these flowers might be mistaken for small pea blossoms but on closer view what at first sight might be taken for a keel is actually the long downward coiled upper lip of the corolla-tube, partially enclosed by the two lobes of the lower lip.

ALPINE LOUSEWORT
Pedicularis arctica

Photo. p. 304
Perennial

FLOWERS:	Rose or purple; large, about ¾ inch long; densely set on a stout leafy terminal flower-spike; calyx 5-lobed; corolla 2-lipped; 4 stamens; 1 pistil.
FRUIT:	A dry many-seeded capsule.
LEAVES:	Both basal and stem leaves greatly divided.
HEIGHT:	2 - 6 inches.
HABITAT:	Rocky slopes above timberline.
DISTRIBUTION:	Rocky Mountains. July-August.

This lousewort grows in high alpine places and is one of the dwarfs of this genus. Although its leaves and flowers are different, it looks very much like a hyacinth growing straight out of the ground. The flowers are a beautiful rose-purple and are closely set on a thick flower-spike at the top of a short stout stem. They have a long narrow, two-lipped corolla-tube, typical of all the louseworts, but in this case the upper lip is strongly arched. The leaves are small and fern-like and extend from the base to the very tip of the flower-stem.

CONTORTED
LOUSEWORT
(Text p. 303)

AILEEN HARMON

P. D. SEYMOUR

ALPINE LOUSEWORT
(Text p. 303)

HEAD-SHAPED LOUSEWORT
(Text p. 306)

ELEPHANT
HEAD
(Text p. 306)

305

HEAD-SHAPED LOUSEWORT
Photo. p. 305

Pedicularis capitata
Perennial

FLOWERS:	Yellow tinged with lavender; large, 1 - 1¼ inches long; very few in a very short terminal flower-spike; calyx 5-lobed; corolla 2-lipped; 4 stamens; 1 pistil.
FRUIT:	A dry many-seeded capsule.
LEAVES:	Few, almost all basal, greatly divided.
HEIGHT:	2 - 6 inches.
HABITAT:	Rocky slopes above timberline.
DISTRIBUTION:	Rocky Mountains. July-August.

This lousewort is very similar to the preceding species, *Pedicularis arctica*, and grows in the same high alpine places. It has the same short stout unbranched flower stem and the same short spike of flowers, but differs from it in that the flower stem is leafless or almost so, and the flowers are a trifle larger and are a dull yellow tinged with lavender. The leaves are small and fern-like and are closely clustered around the base of the erect flower stem.

ELEPHANT HEAD
Photo. p. 305

Pedicularis groenlandica
Perennial

FLOWERS:	Reddish-purple; showy; about ⅜ inch long; numerous on a long 2 - 6 inch purple spike; calyx 5-lobed; corolla 2-lipped, resembling the head of an elephant; 4 stamens; 1 pistil.
FRUIT:	A dry many-seeded capsule.
LEAVES:	Both basal and stem leaves, greatly divided, often purplish, 2 - 8 inches long.
HEIGHT:	1 - 1½ feet.
HABITAT:	Stream margins, marshy ground and wet meadows.
DISTRIBUTION:	Common in Western Alberta, foothills and Rocky Mountains. June-August.

The Elephant Head, next to the Paint Brush, is possibly our most conspicuous Rocky Mountain and foothill wild flower. The various shades of purple run the gamut of lavender to maroon not only in the flowers but also in the stems and fern-like leaves. Its colour attracts attention from a distance and its unusual flower arouses curiosity from close quarters. It is the odd shape of the corolla-tube that has suggested a likeness to an elephant's head, complete with high smooth forehead, big ears, long upturned trunk and small tusks. It grows in great abundance in bogs, damp marly shores, stony river bottoms and in wet meadows.

SMOOTH BLUE BEARD TONGUE
Pentstemon nitidus

Photo. p. 308
Perennial

FLOWERS:	Blue; showy; about ¾ inch long; numerous in a short, dense, leafy spike; calyx deeply 5-parted; corolla tubular, 2-lipped; 5 stamens (4 fertile, 1 bearded sterile); 1 pistil with long style.
FRUIT:	A small, dry, many-seeded capsule.
LEAVES:	Opposite, simple, oval to lance-shaped, smooth, 1 - 2 inches long.
HEIGHT:	8 - 12 inches.
HABITAT:	Dry eroded banks and hillsides.
DISTRIBUTION:	Common throughout Southern Alberta. May - June.

The beard tongues, about a dozen species in Alberta, constitute one of the largest and most distinctive groups of plants belonging to the Figwort Family. The beard tongues are among our most beautiful prairie, foothill and mountain plants with attractive flowers ranging in colour from white, yellow, blue through every shade of violet and purple. All of them are characterized by a two-lipped tubular corolla and five stamens, one of which is sterile and which has a tuft of hair near the apical end. The corolla tube has the added distinction of being open at the mouth, expanded in the throat and the interior of the lower lip thickly bearded with soft hairs. One of the most striking is the Smooth Blue Beard Tongue, a short, stout, leafy-stemmed, early blooming plant of the dry prairie. It is distinguished from the other prairie beard tongues by its vivid sky-blue flowers and by its smooth stem and leaves which are covered with a blue-grey bloom like the skin of a grape.

WHITE BEARD TONGUE
Pentstemon albidus

Photo. p. 308
Perennial

FLOWERS:	White; showy; sticky-hairy; about ¾ inch long; numerous in a short dense leafy spike; calyx deeply 5-parted; corolla tubular, 2-lipped; 5 stamens (4 fertile, 1 bearded sterile); 1 pistil with long style.
FRUIT:	A small dry many-seeded capsule.
LEAVES:	Opposite, simple, lance-shaped, hairy, 1 - 3 inches long.
HEIGHT:	6 - 12 inches.
HABITAT:	Dry hillsides and prairie.
DISTRIBUTION:	Common in Southern and Southwestern Alberta. May-July.

Like the Smooth Blue Beard Tongue, the White Beard Tongue is a plant of dry prairie hillsides and in early summer adds a touch of white to the variegated hue of the rolling grasslands. It also has the same short stout leafy type of flower-stem but the stem itself and the leaves are somewhat hairy and the flowers are slightly larger. The latter are white but sometimes are tinged with lilac. The corolla is of the two-lipped tubular type, characteristic of all the beard tongues, but it is widened at the throat and glandular hairy within.

SMOOTH BLUE BEARD TONGUE
(Text p. 307)

WHITE BEARD TONGUE
(Text p. 307)

SLENDER BLUE BEARD TONGUE
(Text p. 310)

YELLOW BEARD TONGUE
(Text p. 310)

309

FIGWORT FAMILY — *SCROPHULARIACEAE*

SLENDER BLUE BEARD TONGUE
Pentstemon procerus

Photo. p. 309
Perennial

FLOWERS:	Purplish-blue; small, about 3/8 inch long; in dense whorls on upper part of stem; calyx 5-parted; corolla tubular, 2-lipped; 5 stamens (4 fertile, 1 bearded sterile); 1 pistil with long style.
FRUIT:	A small dry many-seeded capsule.
LEAVES:	Opposite, simple, oblong to lance-shaped, 1 - 3 inches long.
HEIGHT:	4 - 12 inches.
HABITAT:	In damp thickets, low meadows and open woodlands.
DISTRIBUTION:	Common throughout Central and Southern Alberta. June-August.

The Slender Blue Beard Tongue is a rather weak-stemmed species that blooms most of the summer in low meadows, open woodlands, on grassy hillsides and lower mountain slopes. Possibly it is the most common and most widely distributed of all our Alberta beard tongues. The individual flowers are small, scarcely one-third of an inch long and have the typical two-lipped tubular corollas. They are coloured a deep purplish-blue. These are densely arranged in multiple whorls around the upper part of the stem. These whorls are about one inch or so apart and look like sapphire bands. This particular arrangement of the flowers in separate whorls distinguishes this Beard Tongue and the Yellow Beard Tongue from all the other Alberta species.

YELLOW BEARD TONGUE
Pentstemon confertus

Photo. p. 309
Perennial

FLOWERS:	Yellow; small, about ½ inch long; in dense whorls on upper part of stem; calyx 5-parted; corolla tubular, 2-lipped; 5 stamens (4 fertile, 1 bearded sterile); 1 pistil with long style.
FRUIT:	A small dry many-seeded capsule.
LEAVES:	Opposite, simple, lance-shaped or narrow, 2 - 5 inches long.
HEIGHT:	4 - 20 inches.
HABITAT:	Dry grassland, thin woodland and hillsides.
DISTRIBUTION:	Fairly common, Southern Alberta. June-August.

This is another slender-stemmed beard tongue. It has the same general form and size as the Slender Blue Beard Tongue and grows on the same dry grassy hillsides and thinly wooded slopes. The flowers of both species are almost identical. They too are arranged in multiple whorls around the upper part of the stem, but are sulphur-yellow. These rings of small yellow flowers stand out in sharp contrast to the dark green leaves.

310

LILAC-FLOWERED BEARD TONGUE
Pentstemon gracilis

Photo. p. 312
Perennial

FLOWERS:	Lilac or dull white; large, ¾ - 1 inch long; numerous in a loose open spike; calyx deeply 5-parted; corolla tubular, slender, 2-lipped, 5-lobed; 5 stamens (4 fertile, 1 bearded sterile); 1 pistil with long style.
FRUIT:	A small dry many-seeded capsule.
LEAVES:	Opposite, simple, oblong to lance-shaped, 1 - 3 inches long.
HEIGHT:	8 - 16 inches.
HABITAT:	Moist prairie grassland.
DISTRIBUTION:	Fairly common throughout Southern and Central Alberta. June-July.

The Lilac-Flowered Beard Tongue is somewhat like the Slender Blue Beard Tongue and the Yellow Beard Tongue but has much larger lilac-coloured flowers. These are borne in interrupted rings or circles or sometimes in a more or less continuous spike. The flowers are not as numerous as in the other two species and droop slightly on short thread-like stalks. At the edge of woods and thickets, but usually preferring a damp spot, the Lilac-Flowered Beard Tongue often grows in company with some of the other beard tongues which are found in the foothills, lower slopes and prairie grasslands.

LARGE PURPLE BEARD TONGUE
Pentstemon fruticosus

Photo. p. 312
Perennial

FLOWERS:	Lilac-purple; large, 1¼ - 1¾ inches long; in dense clusters; calyx 5-parted; corolla tubular, 2-lipped; 1 bearded sterile and 4 fertile stamens; 1 pistil.
FRUIT:	A dry oval capsule.
LEAVES:	Opposite, simple, narrowly lance-shaped.
HEIGHT:	4 - 16 inches.
HABITAT:	Rocky slopes and stony ground.
DISTRIBUTION:	Rocky Mountains. July-August.

The beard tongues make up a distinct group of the Figwort Family. But the Large Purple Beard Tongue, because of its large trumpet-like blooms, is the most beautiful and most conspicuous. These flowers grow in such profusion that the prostrate stems and leaves are often hidden. The corolla-tube is two-lipped with the long yellow-bearded sterile stamen protruding at the widened throat. Several other very similar species, also having large purple or lavender flowers, are found in the Rockies.

311

JANETTE GOODWIN

DORTHEA CALVERLEY

LARGE PURPLE BEARD TONGUE
(Text p. 311)

LYALL'S BEARD TONGUE
(Text p. 314)

CRESTED
BEARD
TONGUE
(Text p. 314)

LYALL'S BEARD TONGUE

Pentstemon lyallii

Photo. p. 313
Perennial

FLOWERS:	Pale purple or light lavender; large, 1 - 1½ inches long; numerous in dense clusters; calyx 5-lobed; corolla tubular, 2-lipped, 5-lobed; 5 stamens (4 fertile, 1 smooth sterile); 1 pistil with long style.
FRUIT:	A small dry many-seeded capsule.
LEAVES:	Opposite, simple, narrowly lance-shaped.
HEIGHT:	12 - 20 inches.
HABITAT:	Open rocky slopes, at fairly high altitudes.
DISTRIBUTION:	Rocky Mountains. Southwestern Alberta. June - August.

Another mountain species, Lyall's Beard Tongue has flowers which are quite similar to those of the Large Purple Beard Tongue, but they are slightly smaller. Permanently bent over by the wind, the slender stems spread over the loose stony ground to form dense mats of dark green leaves and purple flowers. Purple is the predominant colour of many alpine Beard Tongues but the shade of purple of Lyall's Beard Tongue is almost a lavender and is possibly the most beautiful. Clumps of this spectacular plant are most often found on open rocky slopes and shale slides.

CRESTED BEARD TONGUE

Pentstemon eriantherus

Photo. p. 313
Perennial

FLOWERS:	Rose-purple; large, about 1 inch long; numerous in a fairly dense leafy spike; calyx deeply 5-parted; corolla tubular, 2-lipped, 5-lobed; 5 stamens (4 fertile, 1 bearded sterile); 1 pistil with long style.
FRUIT:	A small dry many-seeded capsule.
LEAVES:	Basal leaves simple, oblong to spatula-shaped, petioled; upper leaves narrower, smaller, clasping the sticky-hairy stem; all leaves ¾ - 2½ inches long.
HEIGHT:	6 - 18 inches.
HABITAT:	Dry open places.
DISTRIBUTION:	Open prairie and foothills. Southern Alberta. June.

This is one of the first beard tongues to appear in early summer and is found chiefly on the open prairie and on dry rolling foothills. It has the same general appearance and the same stout erect leafy hairy stem as the White Beard Tongue but the flowers are a little larger, more densely clustered and are a beautiful deep rose-purple. Although characteristically two-lipped, the corolla-tube is greatly enlarged in the throat and densely bearded within. In no other Alberta species is the common name, beard tongue, more appropriate, because the conspicuously hairy sterile stamen projects far beyond the wide-open mouth of the corolla-tube.

YELLOW RATTLE
Rhinanthus crista-galli

Photo. p. 316
Annual

FLOWERS:	Pale yellow; small, ¼ - ½ inch long; numerous in a one-sided, leafy, terminal spike; calyx tubular, inflated; corolla tubular, 2-lipped; 4 stamens; 1 pistil.
FRUIT:	A dry, round capsule, enclosed in calyx-tube.
LEAVES:	Opposite, simple, no petiole, toothed margins, lance-shaped, 1 - 2 inches long.
HEIGHT:	1 - 2 feet.
HABITAT:	Moist meadows, open woodlands.
DISTRIBUTION:	Not common, in semi-wooded regions. July.

The Yellow Rattle is an annual that grows in meadows and at the edge of damp woods and thickets. From its two-lipped flowers and general appearance, it is sometimes mistaken for one of the mints but it can easily be distinguished by its calyx-tube. This is yellowish-green, flattened along two sides and drawn together at the top like a bag where it is split into a fringe of four short teeth. The corolla forms a narrow tube ending in two pale yellow lips, which barely protrude beyond the fringed mouth of the calyx-tube. The fruit is a small, dry capsule which is completely enclosed in the enlarged and inflated calyx-tube. When mature, the seeds are loose in the capsule and rattle when the wind blows the withered stems. It is partially parasitic on the roots of other plants and although not common, it is often locally abundant.

COMMON MULLEIN
Verbascum thapsus

Photo. p. 316
Biennial

FLOWERS:	Bright yellow; large, ¾ - 1 inch across; numerous, borne in a dense woolly spike 4 - 24 inches long; calyx deeply 5-cleft; corolla wheel-shaped, 5-lobed; 5 stamens; 1 pistil.
FRUIT:	A dry, round capsule.
LEAVES:	Alternate, simple, elliptical to lance-shaped, densely covered with felt-like hairs, 4 - 12 inches long.
HEIGHT:	2 - 6 feet.
HABITAT:	Roadsides, waste places and dry stony fields.
DISTRIBUTION:	Occasional in Southern Alberta. June - September.

An introduced European weed and for a long time a scourge in run-down stony fields and pastures in Eastern Canada, the Common Mullein is now well established at scattered points in Southern Alberta. Here, it may be found growing in waste places, dry stony ground and along roadsides. Its presence in fields and rangeland indicates impoverished soil and over-grazing. The Common Mullein requires two years to grow from seed to seed, producing a low rosette of leaves in the first year and an erect, sometimes branched, stem, 3 - 6 feet tall, in the second year. The stem bears many large, thick leaves and ends in a long, stout flower-spike. The whole plant is densely covered with soft woolly hairs which give it a velvety appearance. The bright yellow flowers open a few at a time, the lower ones opening first. The flower is wheel-shaped, the five lobes of the corolla bending backwards and exposing the stamens and receptive stigma to a visiting insect. The Mullein is a grotesque, picturesque plant and once recognized is seldom forgotten.

315

YELLOW RATTLE
(Text p. 315)

R. N. SMITH

COMMON MULLEIN
(Text p. 315)

JULIE HRAPKO

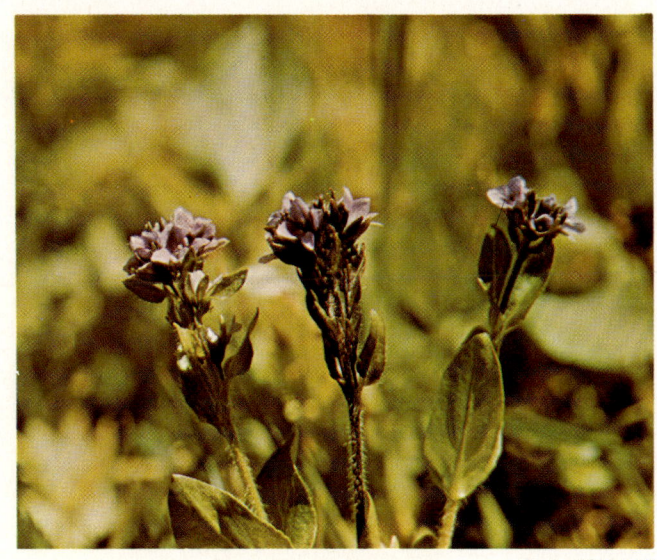

ALPINE SPEEDWELL
(Text p. 318)

COMMON
BUTTERWORT
(Text p. 318)

ALPINE SPEEDWELL   Photo. p. 317
Veronica wormskjoldii   *Perennial*

FLOWERS:	Blue; showy; small, 1/8 - 3/16 inch across; several in a loose cluster; calyx 4-cleft; corolla wheel-shaped, 4-lobed; 2 stamens; 1 pistil.
FRUIT:	A small flattened capsule.
LEAVES:	Opposite, simple, oval to oblong, without petioles, 1/2 - 7/8 inches long.
HEIGHT:	3 - 8 inches.
HABITAT:	Moist heathy meadows, boggy ground and river flats.
DISTRIBUTION:	Not common but often locally abundant in the Rocky Mountains. July - August.

The speedwells or veronicas make up a small group of low-growing plants which belong to the Figwort Family. These are characterized by weak stems, dark green foliage and small blue flowers of a distinctive shape. These flowers have a corolla which is tubular but not two-lipped and the upper portion of the tube is deeply cleft into four spreading lobes. Although these plants bloom most of the summer, the individual flowers are short-lived and are soon replaced by a small locket-like seed-capsule. The one shown in the photograph, the Alpine Speedwell, is a dwarfed species with brilliant blue flowers and grows in high alpine meadows. The most common speedwell, the American Brooklime, is widely distributed along marshes, stream sides, ditches and sloughs. In the wetter places, it is often found growing with the Skullcap among the reeds and sedges.

BLADDERWORT FAMILY — *LENTIBULARIACEAE*

The Bladderwort Family is one of small carnivorous herbaceous plants that grow in shallow water or marshy wet places. Only four members of this family are found in Alberta. Like the sundews, they are all green plants and capable of manufacturing their own food but supplement the meagre amounts of nitrogen their environment supplies by trapping small insects and other tiny organisms. They do this by means of a sticky leaf surface or by small underwater bladders. The flowers are noteworthy for the beauty of their two-lipped colourful corolla and characteristic spur.

COMMON BUTTERWORT   Photo. p. 317
Pinguicula vulgaris   *Perennial*

FLOWERS:	Purple; showy; ½ - ¾ inch long; solitary at the end of the leafless stalk; calyx 5-cleft; corolla, irregular, 2-lipped with a tapering slender spur; 2 stamens; 1 pistil.
FRUIT:	A 2-valved many-seeded capsule.
LEAVES:	Several, simple, elliptical, about 2 inches long, in a tightly appressed basal rosette.
HEIGHT:	Flower-stalk, 3 - 4 inches.
HABITAT:	Boggy places, wet rocky banks, and mossy streamsides.
DISTRIBUTION:	Occasional, in the wooded areas and foothills. June-July.

The Common Butterwort grows in wet bogs, moist rocks and wet calcareous springy soil. It is easily recognized by its beautiful purple irregular-shaped flowers that somewhat resemble a violet and pale green leaves. The latter are succulent and tongue-shaped and overlap each other in a tight basal rosette. The upper surface of the leaves is covered with glandular hairs which secrete a greasy sticky fluid. Seeds, pollen, small insects and other small organisms that become attached cause the margins of the leaf to roll over them, and an acid juice is secreted which slowly digests these objects.

BLADDERWORT FAMILY — *LENTIBULARIACEAE*

COMMON BLADDERWORT   Photo. p. 320
Utricularia vulgaris var. *americana*   *Perennial*

FLOWERS:	Bright yellow; showy; ½ - ¾ inch long; several in a long leafless spike; calyx 2 - 5-cleft; corolla, irregular, 2-lipped, short spurred; 2 stamens; 1 pistil.
FRUIT:	A 2-valved many-seeded capsule.
LEAVES:	All submerged, finely divided, ¾ - 2 inches long, bearing numerous bladders 1/8 - 3/16 inch long.
HEIGHT:	Submerged stems, 1 - 3 feet long; aerial flower-stem, 4 - 12 inches high.
HABITAT:	In shallow water in lakes and sloughs.
DISTRIBUTION:	Fairly common throughout Alberta. June - July.

The Common Bladderwort is found in shallow water in lakes, sloughs and ditches and is one of our most interesting water plants. It floats beneath the surface in a tangle of coarse stems and leaves. These long branching stems and finely divided leaves spread out under the water like miniature fish nets. Attached to the leaves are countless little bladders hanging out like little floats. These bladders are actually traps, for when tiny water organisms brush against them they open suddenly and the minute creatures are swept in. When they die their decomposing remains are absorbed by the plant as food. In July, spectacular golden yellow flowers are produced on long stems several inches above the water. In the fall, the plant disintegrates, thick leafy buds form and these sink to the bottom of the slough and grow into new plants the following year.

PLANTAIN FAMILY — *PLANTAGINACEAE*

This is a family of unattractive predominantly green annual or perennial herbs with a cluster of coarse conspicuously ribbed basal leaves, an elongated flower-spike and with no apparent stem. Seven species, all belonging to the genus *Plantago,* grow in Alberta.

COMMON PLANTAIN   Photo. p. 320
Plantago major   *Perennial*

FLOWERS:	Greenish-white; tiny; densely set on a long leafless flower-stem; calyx 4-lobed; corolla 4-lobed; 4 stamens; 1 pistil.
FRUIT:	A small dry seed-capsule.
LEAVES:	All basal, numerous, broadly oval, prominently veined, 1 - 10 inches long.
HEIGHT:	Flower-stem, 4 - 20 inches.
HABITAT:	Lawns, gardens, waste places.
DISTRIBUTION:	Introduced weed. Common everywhere. June - July.

Next to the Common Dandelion, the Common Plantain is our most familiar and most widely spread weed. Although the large green leaves lying flat on the ground are conspicuous, the plant does nothing to attract attention either in flower or in seed. In early summer, a long green flower-stem springs from the centre of the rosette of leaves and is covered from top to bottom with innumerable tiny white flowers. In August, this flower-stem turns into a long stiff spike of very small seed-capsules.

COMMON
BLADDERWORT
(Text p. 319)

R. C. SWEET

H. A. MacGREGOR

COMMON PLANTAIN
(Text p. 319)

SALINE PLANTAIN
(Text p. 322)

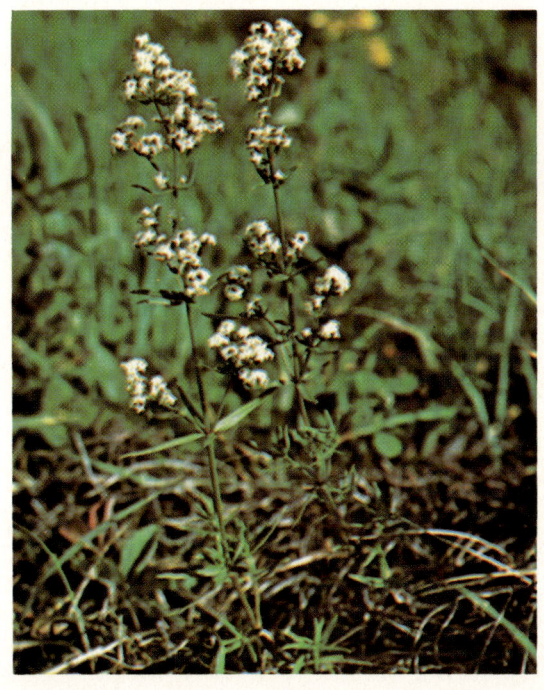

NORTHERN
BEDSTRAW
(Text p. 322)

321

PLANTAIN FAMILY — *PLANTAGINACEAE*

SALINE PLANTAIN   Photo. p. 321
Plantago eriopoda   *Perennial*

FLOWERS:	Greenish-white; tiny; densely set on a long leafless flower-stem; calyx 4-lobed; corolla 4-lobed; 4 stamens; 1 pistil.
FRUIT:	A small dry seed-capsule.
LEAVES:	All basal, numerous, narrowly lance-shaped, prominently veined, erect, brown woolly at base, 2 - 8 inches long.
HEIGHT:	Flower stem, up to 18 inches.
HABITAT:	Saline or alkaline soils.
DISTRIBUTION:	Common, particularly in Southern Alberta. June.

If we can recognize the Common Plantain, it is not difficult to spot the other members of this family as they all have the same general appearance. The Saline Plantain, as its common name suggests, grows in alkaline flats and sloughs and in salt meadows. The long lance-shaped leaves, instead of lying flat on the ground like those of the Common Plantain, grow almost erect in a dense rosette from a brown-hairy stout rootstock. It is a coarse, somewhat fleshy, unattractive plant and seldom is given a second glance.

MADDER FAMILY — *RUBIACEAE*

This small family of annual or perennial herbs derives its name from a European plant which has been cultivated for hundreds of years in order to produce a dull red dye called "Madder" or "Turkey Red". In Alberta, it is represented chiefly by the bedstraws, a group of plants characterized by slender weak four-sided stems, whorled leaves and clusters of four-parted flowers.

NORTHERN BEDSTRAW   Photo. p. 321
Galium boreale   *Perennial*

FLOWERS:	White; tiny, 1/8 inch across; many in a branched leafy cluster; calyx absent; corolla 4-lobed, wheel-shaped; 4 stamens; 1 pistil with 2 styles.
FRUIT:	2 rounded densely hairy nutlets.
LEAVES:	In whorls of 4, simple, narrow, 1 - 2½ inches long.
HEIGHT:	8 - 24 inches.
HABITAT:	Borders of woods, thickets and in moist meadows.
DISTRIBUTION:	Common throughout the wooded regions of Alberta. July - August.

The Northern Bedstraw is the most common of six native bedstraws and is one of our most familiar woodland and roadside plants. It grows in clumps and is recognized easily by its small narrow leaves which are arranged in whorls of four around a rather weak square stem. It is most conspicuous in July, when its sprays of tiny flowers stand out like white lace against the dark green of the underbrush. Like many other members of this family, the roots on boiling with various reagents yield a red dye know as "Madder" or "Turkey Red". Both Plains and Northern Indians used this dye to stain porcupine quills.

MADDER FAMILY — *RUBIACEAE*

SWEET-SCENTED BEDSTRAW
Galium triflorum

Photo. p. 324
Perennial

FLOWERS:	Greenish-white; small; long-stalked; borne in clusters of 3; calyx absent; corolla 4-lobed; 4 stamens; 1 pistil with 2 styles.
FRUIT:	2 rounded bristly nutlets.
LEAVES:	Generally in whorls of 6, simple, narrowly oval with a sharp-pointed tip, 1 - 2½ inches long.
HEIGHT:	Trailing, 1 - 3 feet long.
HABITAT:	Moist woodlands.
DISTRIBUTION:	Fairly common throughout the wooded regions of Alberta. July - August.

The Sweet-Scented Bedstraw is also found in moist woodlands but is not quite as common as the Northern Bedstraw. Unlike the Northern Bedstraw, which grows erect, it has a weak trailing stem which spreads over the underbrush. The small greenish-white long-stalked flowers are borne in clusters of three and the leaves are in whorls of five or six.

HONEYSUCKLE FAMILY — *CAPRIFOLIACEAE*

The Honeysuckle Family is a large and well known family of shrubs and vines and sometimes perennial herbs. These plants have opposite leaves and flat-topped or cone-shaped flower clusters. The flowers are usually small, with a three to five-lobed calyx-tube and a corolla-tube varying from bell-shaped to wheel-shaped. There are usually five stamens or occasionally four and a single pistil that develops into a berry, a stone-fruit or a dry capsule. About a dozen species and several varieties of this family grow in Alberta and found among them are the honeysuckles, the bush cranberries and that well-known woodland favourite, the Twin Flower.

TWIN FLOWER. LINNAEA
Linnaea borealis var. *americana*

Photo. p. 324
Perennial

FLOWERS:	Pink; small, about 3/8 inch long; in pairs, nodding; fragrant; calyx 5-parted; corolla bell-shaped, 5-lobed; 4 stamens; 1 pistil.
FRUIT:	A small oval dry sticky-hairy 1-seeded capsule.
LEAVES:	Opposite, simple, short-petioled, broadly oval, evergreen, small, 3/8 - 5/8 inches across.
HEIGHT:	Stems creeping; flower-stalks 3 - 4 inches.
HABITAT:	Rich moist mossy woods.
DISTRIBUTION:	Common throughout the cool moist forest region of Alberta. June - July.

Named in honour of Linnaeus, the great Swedish botanist, the Twin Flower is one of the most graceful and most charming of our woodland plants. It makes its home in the cool moist northern forest that extends across the top of both old and new world continents like a green belt. Under the shade of spruce and pine it forms a matty growth of trailing evergreen leafy stems and at intervals sends up delicate flower-stalks, each bearing two pink bell-shaped flowers. Hanging down in pairs, these look like tiny lamps on a miniature lamp-post.

SWEET-
SCENTED
BEDSTRAW
(Text p. 323)

G. W. MACHELL

TWIN FLOWER
(Text p. 323)

A. KARVONEN

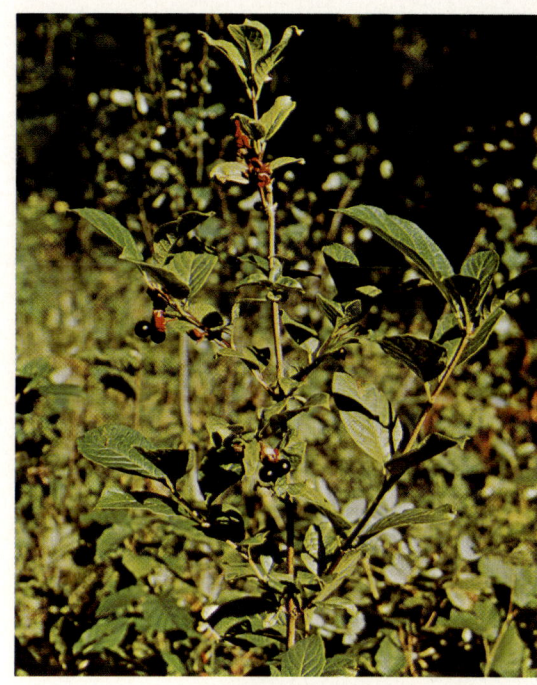

**BRACTED
HONEYSUCKLE**
(Text p. 326)

H. PEGG

**TWINING
HONEYSUCKLE**
(Text p. 326)

R. C. SWEET

BRACTED HONEYSUCKLE
Lonicera involucrata

Photo. p. 325
Perennial

FLOWERS:	Yellow; small, about ½ inch long; in pairs; bracted; calyx-tube short; corolla-tube funnel-shaped, 5-lobed, hairy; 5 stamens; 1 pistil.
FRUIT:	A twin black-purple juicy inedible berry with 2 large purple bracts.
LEAVES:	Opposite, simple, oval to oblong, more or less downy beneath, 2 - 6 inches long.
HEIGHT:	3 - 10 feet.
HABITAT:	Moist woods and stream banks.
DISTRIBUTION:	Common throughout the wooded areas of Alberta. June - July.

The Bracted Honeysuckle grows in moist ground under the shade of spruce and poplar trees. It is a bushy shrub with several erect downy stems and an abundance of dark green foliage. It is easily recognized by the dull yellow of its flowers which are borne in pairs and are flanked below by two green leaf-like bracts. The corolla-tubes are funnel-shaped and five-lobed, the lobes bending back away from the protruding stamens and long bulb-tipped style. After fertilization, the flowers develop into twin inky-black berries which stand out sharply against the greatly enlarged wing-like bracts that, by this time, have changed to a deep red-purple.

TWINING HONEYSUCKLE
Lonicera dioica var. *glaucescens*

Photo. p. 325
Perennial

FLOWERS:	Yellow to orange-red; showy; ¾ - 1 inch long; several in a terminal cluster; calyx-tube 5-cleft; corolla-tube 2-lipped, 5-lobed; 5 stamens; 1 pistil.
FRUIT:	A round red berry.
LEAVES:	Opposite, simple, short-petioled, oval, smooth above, pale hairy beneath, 2 - 3½ inches long.
HEIGHT:	A climbing or trailing vine.
HABITAT:	Open woods and thickets.
DISTRIBUTION:	Common throughout the wooded regions of Alberta. July - August.

Flowering vines form a most colourful and dense part of the vegetation of tropical countries but they are rare in Alberta. The Twining Honeysuckle is a woody vine or sprawling shrub that climbs by twining itself around the trunks of trees or other low growing shrubs. It is a robust grower and is widely distributed in deciduous and coniferous woods. The flower buds grow in clusters at the stem tips and open a few at a time. The flowers are a bright yellow when they first open but they change gradually to an orange-red before they fall. Each individual flower is a single hairy slender two-lipped tube, often swollen on one side, its tip curving back into four or five lobes. This vine attracts attention not only by its sweet-scented beautiful flowers but by the two leaves just below the flower-cluster which, united, form a shallow protective cup.

HONEYSUCKLE FAMILY — *CAPRIFOLIACEAE*

SNOWBERRY　　　　　　　　　　　　　　Photo. p. 328
Symphoricarpos albus var. *pauciflorus*　　　　　　*Perennial*

FLOWERS:	White tinged with pink; small, about 3/16 inch long; few in usually terminal clusters; calyx-tube 5-parted; corolla-tube bell-shaped, 5-lobed; 5 stamens; 1 pistil.
FRUIT:	A round white berry.
LEAVES:	Opposite, simple, short-petioled, thin, wavy-margined, green above, white hairy beneath, ¾ - 1¼ inches long.
HEIGHT:	1½ - 3 feet.
HABITAT:	Rich poplar-spruce woods and thickets.
DISTRIBUTION:	Common throughout the wooded regions of Alberta. July.

The Snowberry is a low growing shrub that is better known for its berries than its flowers. The Snowberry most commonly found in Alberta is the variety *pauciflorus,* and as the name suggests, it is distinguished from the species by having very few flowers in a cluster. It is further distinguished by having leaves that are dull blue-green above and that are covered with fine white hairs underneath. It is found in open aspen groves and shrubby thickets where it grows beside the Wild Rose. In summer it may go unnoticed as the pinkish bell-shaped flowers are so small and are partially covered by the leaves. However, in September, its round waxy-white berries stand out vividly against the bright yellow of its leaves and the scarlet fruits of the Wild Rose.

BUCKBRUSH. WOLFBERRY　　　　　　　Photo. p. 328
Symphoricarpos occidentalis　　　　　　　　　　*Perennial*

FLOWERS:	Pinkish-white; small, about ¼ inch long; several in dense axillary clusters; calyx-tube 5-toothed; corolla-tube funnel-shaped, 5-lobed; 5 stamens; 1 pistil.
FRUIT:	A round dull greenish-white berry.
LEAVES:	Opposite, simple, oval to oblong, short-petioled, thick and leathery, soft hairy beneath, 1 - 3 inches long.
HEIGHT:	1 - 4 feet.
HABITAT:	Prairies, thickets and borders of poplar woods.
DISTRIBUTION:	Very common and widely spread throughout Alberta. July.

The Buckbrush or Wolfberry grows almost everywhere in Alberta and is so common and so widely spread that it often goes unnoticed. On the open prairie it forms dense patches in gullies, coulees and on stream banks, either by itself or mixed in with Sagebrush, Silverberry or scrubby aspen. In wooded regions, together with Choke Cherry, Saskatoon, Wild Rose and a variety of herbaceous plants, it makes up the vegetation of thickets and open poplar woods. It is a stocky shrub and its numerous upright greyish-brown leafy stems spread freely from creeping roots and bear along their entire length tight clusters of small funnel-shaped pinkish-white flowers. Later on, bunches of dull greenish-white berries replace the flowers and these along with dense shrubby growth provide food and cover for small animals and birds.

SNOWBERRY
(Text p. 327)

BUCKBRUSH
(Text p. 327)

LOW BUSH CRANBERRY
(Text p. 330)

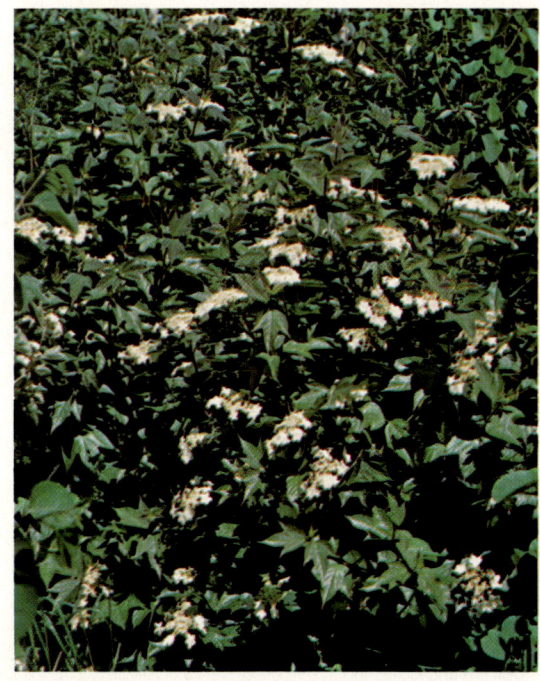

HIGH BRUSH
CRANBERRY
(Text p. 330)

LOW BUSH CRANBERRY. MOOSEBERRY

Viburnum edule

Photo. p. 329
Perennial

FLOWERS:	White; small, about ¼ inch across; many in flat-topped showy clusters; calyx 5-toothed; corolla 5-lobed; 5 stamens; 1 pistil.
FRUIT:	A red berry-like stone-fruit.
LEAVES:	Opposite, simple, shallowly 3-lobed, coarsely toothed, 1½ - 4 inches across.
HEIGHT:	2 - 6 feet.
HABITAT:	Rich soil in woods and thickets.
DISTRIBUTION:	Common throughout wooded region of Alberta. June-July.

In Alberta, woody shrubs are one of the constant features of the vegetation of open mixed woods, scrubby aspen groves and thickets. The Low Bush Cranberry is one of the best known and most widely distributed. It is a rather straggly shrub and can be easily recognized by its flat-topped clusters of small white flowers, set among the dark green maple-like leaves, and by its clusters of bright red shining berries. It is not a true cranberry but goes by that name because of the acid quality of its fruits. The true cranberry is a member of the Heath Family and grows in boggy coniferous woods and muskegs. The so-called berries of the Low Bush Cranberry are actually stone-fruits and contain a single large flattened stone, while those of the Bog Cranberry are true berries made up of mealy pulp and many small black seeds. The fruits of both plants are "dessert" for the birds and also make excellent jelly.

HIGH BUSH CRANBERRY

Viburnum trilobum

Photo. p. 329
Perennial

FLOWERS:	White; inner flowers of cluster small and perfect; marginal flowers larger and neutral with wheel-shaped corollas, ½ - ¾ inch across.
FRUIT:	A red berry-like stone-fruit.
LEAVES:	Opposite, simple, deeply 3-lobed, 2 - 4 inches across.
HEIGHT:	3 - 12 feet.
HABITAT:	Woods and moist thickets.
DISTRIBUTION:	Fairly common throughout the wooded regions of Alberta. June-July.

The High Bush Cranberry is enough like the Low Bush Cranberry to be easily recognized. It is a much taller shrub, sometimes almost a small tree, and has larger three-lobed leaves and wider white flat-topped flower-clusters. The marginal flowers are another notable feature. These are neutral (neither stamens nor pistils) and they have showier and much larger wheel-shaped corollas than the centrally placed fertile flowers.

HONEYSUCKLE FAMILY — *CAPRIFOLIACEAE*

RED ELDERBERRY   Photo. p. 332
Sambucus pubens   *Perennial*

FLOWERS: Creamy-white; very small; many in cone-shaped termi-
                      nal clusters; calyx lobes minute; corolla open, urn-
                      shaped; 5 stamens; 1 pistil.
FRUIT: A small round red berry.
LEAVES: Opposite, large, compound of 5 - 7 toothed leaflets.
HEIGHT: 3 - 10 feet.
HABITAT: Damp places, at the edge of woods and thickets.
DISTRIBUTION: Wooded regions in Western Alberta. June - July.

The Red Elderberry is a conspicuous and locally abundant mountain
shrub that grows in moist soil, in forest clearings and along roadsides. It
is an open rather bushy and leafy shrub and the skeletal remains of last
year's stems often give it an unkempt look. Cone-shaped dense clusters of
small creamy flowers, held erect like torches, appear on this shrub in July
and these have a strong scent which attracts insects. The individual flowers
are urn-shaped with three or five spreading lobes. In August, the cone-
shaped flower clusters change to bunches of flaming-red berries. Another
native species, and one seen less frequently, is the Black Elderberry,
Sambucus melanocarpa. It has the same general appearance but the flower-
clusters are wider and flatter and give place to large bunches of black-
purple berries. The berries from this shrub are used for making pies, jelly
and wine.

VALERIAN FAMILY — *VALERIANACEAE*

There are only two members of this family in Alberta. They are both
herbaceous perennials with stout rootstocks, an abundance of dark green
foliage and dense clusters of tiny white or pinkish flowers. The flowers are
funnel-shaped or wheel-shaped and when mature give rise to flat one-
seeded fruits.

WILD HELIOTROPE   Photo. p. 332
Valeriana sitchensis   *Perennial*

FLOWERS: White or pinkish-white; small; many in flat-topped
                      clusters; calyx 5-parted; corolla funnel-shaped, 5-lobed;
                      3 stamens; 1 pistil.
FRUIT: A small dry achene.
LEAVES: Opposite, commonly 3 - 5 divided, petioled, smooth
                      margined or variously toothed.
HEIGHT: 1 - 3 feet.
HABITAT: Streamsides and moist meadows.
DISTRIBUTION: At lower altitudes in the Rocky Mountains. South-
                      western Alberta. June - August.

The Wild Heliotrope is one of many wild flowers we take for granted
and one we make little effort to know its name. It is an erect smooth soft-
stemmed perennial with dark green foliage and showy clusters of small
fluffy white flowers. Where the soil is rich and moist, in clearings, at the
edge of woods and beside streams, it often grows in great profusion, filling
the air with a sweet fragrance. The thick rootstock of this plant, and that
of a very similar species, was used by the Plains Indians as food and as a
medicine for stomach ailments.

RED
ELDERBERRY
(Text p. 331)

A. KARVONEN

J. CLAESSEN

WILD HELIOTROPE
(Text p. 331)

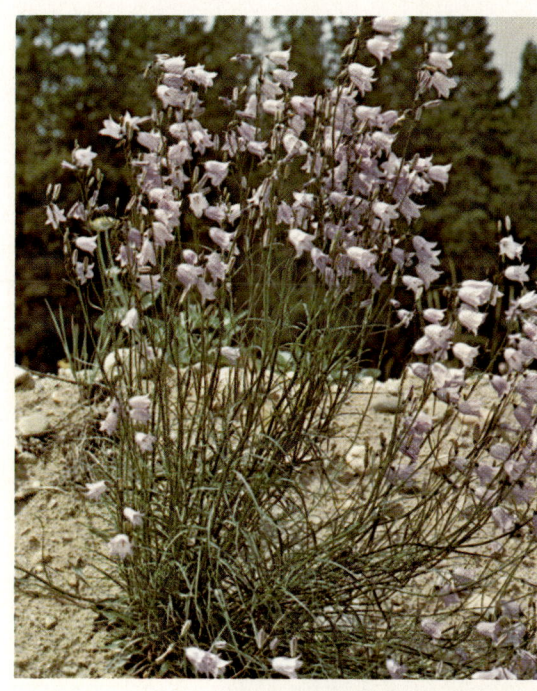

COMMON
BLUEBELL
(Text p. 334)

ALPINE
HAREBELL
(Text p. 334)

BLUEBELL FAMILY — *CAMPANULACEAE*

The Bluebell Family is one of the best known families of flowering plants. It is a family of perennial herbs and both wild and cultivated species are renowned for their beautiful blue, purple or sometimes white bell-shaped flowers. Three species are native to Alberta, but the Garden Bluebell often escapes and is found growing in lanes and in waste places.

COMMON BLUEBELL. HAREBELL
Campanula rotundifolia

Photo. p. 333
Perennial

FLOWERS:	Purplish-blue; large, ½ - ¾ inch long; calyx 5-parted; corolla bell-shaped, 5-lobed; 5 stamens; 1 pistil, inferior, with 1 style and 3-lobed stigma.
FRUIT:	An oval papery many-seeded capsule.
LEAVES:	Basal leaves round; stem leaves narrow, very variable, ½ - 3 inches long.
HEIGHT:	4 - 18 inches.
HABITAT:	Almost anywhere.
DISTRIBUTION:	Very common throughout Alberta. June - September.

Along with the Common Dandelion, Early Blue Violet and Wild Rose, the Common Bluebell is one of the first flowers to be recognized by a child. And why not? It is blue and it is bell-shaped. The Common Bluebell is a native of both the old and new worlds and is as closely associated in song and story with Scotland as the Scotch Thistle. It is found almost everywhere; in shade or in sunshine, in rich soil, gravel, barren sand or rocky crevices, in the mountains, foothills or prairie grasslands. Beginning in June and ending in September, the tall wiry stems give rise to a succession of graceful, rich, deep blue bells, these swinging in the lightest breeze from thread-like flower-stalks. The stout style ending in a conspicuous 3-lobed stigma simulates the clapper of a bell and accentuates the bell-like structure of the whole flower.

ALPINE HAREBELL
Campanula lasiocarpa

Photo. p. 333
Perennial

FLOWERS:	Bright blue; large, ¾ - 1 inch across; solitary at the end of the stem; calyx 5-parted; corolla bell-shaped, 5-lobed; 5 stamens; 1 pistil with 1 style and 3 stigmas.
FRUIT:	An oval hairy papery many-seeded capsule.
LEAVES:	Alternate, simple, petioled, slightly toothed, oval to spoon-shaped, ¾ - 1½ inches long.
HEIGHT:	1 - 6 inches.
HABITAT:	Mountain summits.
DISTRIBUTION:	Rocky Mountains. July - September.

The Alpine Bluebell or Harebell is remembered by anyone who climbs above timberline as a plant that by its dwarfed stature defies the rigors of the harsh mountain climate. Here, scattered Alpine Harebells may be found growing in thin mossy stony ground, in alpine meadows or behind a sheltering ledge. It can be recognized at once by its single blue bell-shaped flower which looks grotesquely large in comparison to its short stem, sometimes scarcely an inch high. The leaves are also small and grow often among the moss at the base of the slender stem. The name harebell which is also given to the Common Bluebell is a contraction of heatherbell.

LOBELIA FAMILY — *LOBELIACEAE*

In North America, the Lobelia Family is well known for the beauty of its irregularly shaped flowers and it includes some of our most beautiful wild flowers and garden ornamentals. Only one species is found in Alberta, the beautiful Brook Lobelia.

BROOK LOBELIA
Lobelia kalmii

Photo. p. 336
Biennial

FLOWERS: Blue or mauve; showy; about 3/8 inch long; several in a loose cluster; bracted; 5 partly united sepals; corolla tubular, 2-lipped, 5-lobed; 5 stamens; 1 pistil.

FRUIT: A pod-like capsule.

LEAVES: Alternate, simple, narrow, short-petioled, ½ - 1 inch long.

HEIGHT: 4 - 20 inches.

HABITAT: Bogs and wet meadows.

DISTRIBUTION: Fairly common. July-August.

The Brook Lobelia is found growing with grasses and sedges in calcareous bogs or along the banks of streams. Its graceful slender stem emerges from a rosette of dark green leaves and along its end appear several showy blue or mauve flowers. The corolla-tube is strongly two-lipped and five-lobed and is split down one side. The smaller upper lip has two small lobes bent backwards like two small horns, while the three lobes of the larger lower lip bend down at a sharp angle. The Brook Lobelia is closely related to the cultivated lobelias which decorate our window boxes and garden borders.

**BROOK
LOBELIA**
(Text p. 335)

H. PEGG

A. H. DICKSON

COMMON YARROW
(Text p. 339)

LARGE-
FLOWERED
FALSE
DANDELION
(Text p. 339)

AILEEN HARMON

ORANGE-
FLOWERED
FALSE
DANDELION
(Text p. 342)

DORTHEA CALVERLEY

337

DAISY FAMILY — *COMPOSITAE*

The Daisy Family or Composite Family is a very large and varied one and is world-wide in its distribution. Well over two hundred species, making up about sixty genera, are found in Alberta. Of this number, a few are woody or semi-woody perennials but most are annual, biennial or perennial herbs. Let us consider what is commonly called a "Daisy". The so-called flower is actually a collection of many small individual flowers called florets arranged in a compact head on a common receptacle surrounded by a supporting structure (involucre) made up of several leaf-like involucral bracts. It is from this compact flower-head of many small florets that the family derives the name *Compositae* and members of this family are often called composites. The flower-heads range in size from tiny ones of the sage and goldenrod, through larger ones of the daisy, fleabane and thistle to the huge blooms of the cultivated sunflower, dahlia and chrysanthemum. The florets are of two types: ray-florets or ligulate-florets with a conspicuous strap-shaped corolla, commonly called rays (the erroneously called "petals" of the daisy) and disk-florets or tubular-florets with a straight five-lobed corolla. The structure of the flower-head is extremely variable, but in each genus, the flower-heads of all the species are constructed in the same manner. In some plants, e.g. thistle, all the florets are disk-florets (tubular), in others, e.g. dandelion, all the florets are ray-florets (ligulate), and in still others, e.g. daisy, the centre of the flower-head is filled with disk-florets (tubular) and there is a row of ray-florets (ligulate) on the margin. The matter of stamens and pistil is also a variable feature. In flower-heads with both disk and ray-florets (radiate), e.g. daisy, the disk-florets have both stamens and pistil while the ray-florets have either a pistil or neither pistil nor stamens. In some flower-heads there are bracts or scales among the florets on top of the receptacle and these are commonly called the "chaff", while in other flower-heads there are none. The fruit is always a one-seeded achene; sometimes smooth, e.g. sunflower, and sometimes with a tuft of hairs (pappus), e.g. dandelion. Some of our most beautiful wild flowers and cultivated plants belong to this family and others are very important producers of food, oils, dyes, tonics, medicines and poisons.

COMMON YARROW. MILFOIL   Photo. p. 336
Achillea millefolium   *Perennial*

FLOWERS: Ray-florets white or rarely pinkish, 5, with a pistil; disk-florets yellowish, 10 - 30, with both stamens and pistil; involucral bracts overlapping in 3 - 4 rows; flower-heads small, about ¼ inch across, numerous in a flat-topped cluster, receptacle chaffy.

FRUIT: A dry small flattened achene, no pappus.

LEAVES: Alternate, very finely dissected, 1½ - 6 inches long.

HEIGHT: ½ - 2 feet.

HABITAT: Roadsides, prairie and waste places.

DISTRIBUTION: Common throughout Alberta. June-August.

The Common Yarrow or Milfoil is so well known by sight and scent that it requires little describing. It is recognized easily by its flat-topped cluster of many small white or sometimes pinkish flower-heads, by its feathery carrot-like leaves and by its strong aromatic smell. Its scientific name is in honour of Achilles, who is said to have made an ointment from the juice of this plant to heal the wounds of his soldiers. Today, it is still used mainly as a tonic and as a cure for stomach disorders.

LARGE-FLOWERED FALSE DANDELION   Photo. p. 337
Agoseris glauca   *Perennial*

FLOWERS: Ray-florets yellow with both stamens and pistil; disk-florets none; involucral bracts overlapping in several series; flower-heads borne singly at the end of a long stalk, 1 - 2 inches across.

FRUIT: A dry beaked achene with white pappus.

LEAVES: Several in a basal rosette, lance-shaped to narrow, sometimes toothed, 4 - 8 inches long.

HEIGHT: Flower-stalk 4 - 16 inches.

HABITAT: Moist grassland, open forest.

DISTRIBUTION: Fairly common in prairie and foothills regions. July-August.

The Large-Flowered False Dandelion is a familiar plant on the prairies, the foothills and the mountain slopes but like so many yellow composites it is usually passed over as just another dandelion. It has many characteristics of the Common Dandelion, a long tap-root, a rosette of basal leaves, a large single yellow flower-head borne singly on a long stalk and milky juice. But the leaves are long and very narrow and stand erect, while the leaf blades are only faintly toothed rather than deeply incised. It is a variable species and several varieties have been described.

PEARLY EVERLASTING
(Text p. 342)

SMALL-FLOWERED EVERLASTING
(Text p. 343)

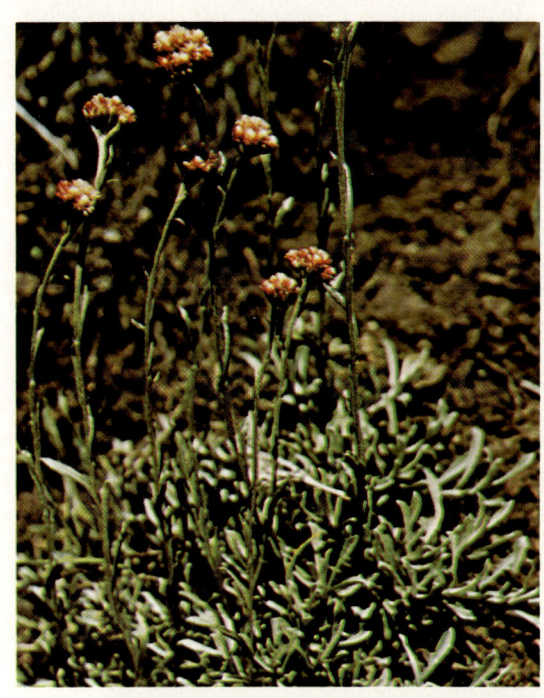

ROSY
EVERLASTING
(Text p. 343)

DORTHEA CALVERLEY

DORTHEA CALVERLEY

LOW EVERLASTING
(Text p. 346)

341

ORANGE-FLOWERED FALSE DANDELION
Agoseris aurantiaca

Photo. p. 337
Perennial

FLOWERS:	Ray-florets burnt orange with both stamens and pistil; disk-florets none; involucral bracts overlapping; solitary on a long stem, about 1 inch across.
FRUIT:	A narrow achene with white bristly pappus.
LEAVES:	All basal, simple, tufted, narrowly oblong, slightly toothed, up to 10 inches long.
HEIGHT:	Flower-stem 6 - 19 inches.
HABITAT:	Open slopes and alpine meadows.
DISTRIBUTION:	Fairly common. Mountains and foothills. June-August.

Only two of our Alberta composites have orange-coloured flower-heads; the Orange-Flowered False Dandelion and the Orange Hawksweed. The former is a native species and grows on open slopes and mountain meadows, while the latter is an introduced weed which occurs locally in fields and roadsides. The former is very similar to the Large-Flowered False Dandelion, but the flower-heads are burnt orange and the leaf blades are somewhat wider and a little more hairy.

PEARLY EVERLASTING
Anaphalis margaritacea

Photo. p. 340
Perennial

FLOWERS:	Ray-florets none; disk-florets yellow, several, with either stamens or pistil; involucral bracts overlapping in several rows, pearly white, thin, translucent; flower-heads small, ¼ - ⅓ inch across, many in a broad cluster.
FRUIT:	A dry warty achene, no pappus.
LEAVES:	Alternate, narrowly lance-shaped, densely white-hairy below, not petioled, 2 - 5 inches long.
HEIGHT:	12 - 30 inches.
HABITAT:	Open woods.
DISTRIBUTION:	Mountain and foothill slopes. July-August.

The Pearly Everlasting is the most beautiful of all the everlastings and if picked will remain fresh-looking for many a long day. It is a white-woolly stemmed perennial with many long leaves and these are densely white-woolly beneath and greyish-green above. At the end of the stem there is a broad cluster of many pearly-white flower-heads. These owe their long-living quality to the dry paper-thin nature of the involucral bracts. Unlike the Pussy-Toes that prefers dry open places, the Pearly Everlasting grows in open woods and on thinly wooded mountains and foothill slopes.

SMALL-FLOWERED EVERLASTING. PUSSY-TOES
Antennaria nitida

Photo. p. 340
Perennial

FLOWERS:	Ray-florets none; disk-florets whitish, with either stamens or pistil; involucral bracts overlapping, thin, white, translucent; flower-heads several, in a usually compact cluster.
FRUIT:	A dry achene, with white pappus.
LEAVES:	Basal leaves small, spatula-shaped, white or greyish woolly on both sides; stem leaves small, narrow, scattered.
HEIGHT:	Flower-stem 4 - 10 inches.
HABITAT:	Dry open places.
DISTRIBUTION:	Common on the prairies and in the foothills. June-July.

As a group, the antennarias or everlastings are characteristic of dry places in the prairies, foothills and mountains where they form narrow to wide silvery-grey patches on grassy hillsides and dry exposed denuded slopes. The Small-Flowered Everlasting is remarkable for its mats of tough fibrous creeping stems and rosettes of small soft grey-woolly leaves. The plant derives one of its common names, Pussy-Toes, from the fanciful resemblance of the rounded cluster of small hairy flower-heads to a kitten's paw. The flower-heads have long-lasting qualities and when mature they become so dry and papery that they crackle and rustle at the slightest touch.

ROSY EVERLASTING. PUSSY-TOES
Antennaria rosea

Photo. p. 341
Perennial

FLOWERS:	Ray-florets none; disk-florets whitish, with either stamens or pistil; involucral bracts overlapping, pinkish; flower-heads several, in a narrow cluster.
FRUIT:	A dry flattish achene, without pappus.
LEAVES:	Alternate and basal, mat-forming, densely white woolly on both sides.
HEIGHT:	Flower-stem 6 - 8 inches.
HABITAT:	Open areas, moist meadows and hillsides.
DISTRIBUTION:	Common. Prairie, foothill and mountain regions. June-August.

The Rosy Everlasting is another mat-forming species which grows in open places and in moist meadows. It is very similar to the Small-Flowered Everlasting, or Pussy-Toes, but its rosettes of white woolly basal leaves do not hug the ground so closely and its small dry paper-thin bracts are tipped with pink. Twelve species of this genus grow in Alberta but they are so similar they are hard to identify.

HEART-
LEAVED
ARNICA
(Text p. 346)

ALPINE ARNICA
(Text p. 347)

LAKE LOUISE ARNICA
(Text p. 347)

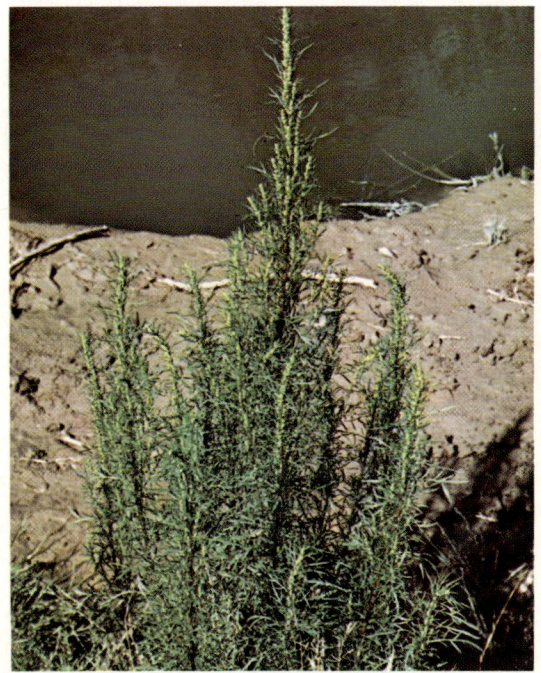

BIENNIAL
SAGEWORT
(Text p. 350)

LOW EVERLASTING. PUSSY-TOES　　　　　　　Photo. p. 341
Antennaria aprica　　　　　　　　　　　　　　　　　*Perennial*

FLOWERS:　　　　Ray-florets none; disk-florets whitish, with either sta-
　　　　　　　　　mens or pistil; involucral bracts whitish or pinkish;
　　　　　　　　　flower-heads several, in a compact cluster.

FRUIT:　　　　　　A dry achene, with white pappus.

LEAVES:　　　　　Basal leaves small, wedge-shaped, densely whitish
　　　　　　　　　woolly on both sides, 3/8 - 1¼ inches long; stem
　　　　　　　　　leaves narrow and smaller.

HEIGHT:　　　　　2 - 6 inches.

HABITAT:　　　　　Dry open places.

DISTRIBUTION:　　Common on the prairie and in the foothills. June-July.

　　The Low Everlasting or Pussy-Toes grows on thin often bare stony
ground baked hard by the sun's rays and dried out by strong winds where
few other plants save drought-resistant grasses can survive. Here, it forms
thin to dense silvery patches of mat-forming leaves and short erect flower-
stems. The whole plant from top to bottom is covered with a felt-like coating of soft woolly hairs. The compact cluster of short-stalked flower-heads
are white and woolly and always appear dried out and lifeless.

HEART-LEAVED ARNICA　　　　　　　　　　Photo. p. 344
Arnica cordifolia　　　　　　　　　　　　　　　　　*Perennial*

FLOWERS:　　　　Ray-florets many, lemon-yellow, with pistil; disk-
　　　　　　　　　florets many, yellow, with both stamens and pistil; in-
　　　　　　　　　volucral bracts white-hairy and glandular; flower-heads
　　　　　　　　　usually solitary, 1½ - 3 inches across.

FRUIT:　　　　　　A dry hairy achene, with white pappus.

LEAVES:　　　　　Basal leaves long-petioled, heart-shaped, 1 - 3 inches,
　　　　　　　　　long; stem leaves heart-shaped but smaller.

HEIGHT:　　　　　8 - 24 inches.

HABITAT:　　　　　Rich moist coniferous woods.

DISTRIBUTION:　　Common in forestlands. Western Alberta. June-August.

　　The Heart-Leaved Arnica is the most common of all the arnicas in the
mountains and is the one most easily recognized because of its conspicuous
heart-shaped leaves and its bright yellow daisy-like flowers. It is usually
found in mossy coniferous woods where it takes full advantage of clearings
and any sunny openings. There are fifteen species of arnica native to Alberta
and it requires a botanical key to distinguish one from another and to
distinguish it from some other groups of the Composite Family which also
have yellow flower-heads.

DAISY FAMILY — *COMPOSITAE*

ALPINE ARNICA Photo. p. 344
Arnica alpina *Perennial*

FLOWERS:	Ray-florets about 12, yellow, with pistil; disk-florets many, yellow, with both stamens and pistil; involucral bracts white-woolly, often purplish; flower-heads usually solitary, about 1¼ inches across.
FRUIT:	A dry hairy achene, with pappus.
LEAVES:	Basal leaves short-petioled, smooth-margined; stem leaves 1 - 3 pairs, smaller
HEIGHT:	4 - 12 inches.
HABITAT:	Mountain slopes and rocky ridges.
DISTRIBUTION:	At high elevations in the Rocky Mountains. July-August.

Three species of Arnica grow at high elevations in the Rocky Mountains. They all have conspicuous yellow daisy-like flower-heads and to most people they look essentially alike. However, botanists are able to separate them on minor differences of leaves and flower-parts. This particular species, the Alpine Arnica, can be distinguished by its soft densely hairy stems and leaves and by its white woolly involucre. The long yellow rays, toothed at the tips, are another characteristic feature. In bud the very short flower-stem is bent double and the solitary flower-head opens about an inch or two from the ground.

LAKE LOUISE ARNICA Photo. p. 345
Arnica louiseana *Perennial*

FLOWERS:	Ray-florets about 10, yellow, with pistil; disk-florets many, yellow, with both stamens and pistil; involucral bracts smooth; flower-heads 1 - 3, about 1¼ inches across.
FRUIT:	A smooth or sparsely hairy achene, with pappus.
LEAVES:	Basal leaves short-petioled, oblong to lance-shaped, often toothed; stem leaves 1 - 2 pairs or none.
HEIGHT:	2 - 10 inches.
HABITAT:	Open slopes and rock slides.
DISTRIBUTION:	At high elevations in the Rocky Mountains. July-August.

The Lake Louise Arnica is a tiny alpine plant which grows in rock crevices or in loose stony ground at extremely high altitudes. It is recognized easily as an arnica by its large yellow daisy-like flower-heads. These are borne singly or in twos or threes at the top of a short stout flower-stem and are held at an unusually sharp angle only a few inches from the ground. However, its involucral bracts are smooth and its long yellow rays are not toothed.

347

SAGEBRUSH HABITAT

HERRIOT'S
SAGE
(Text p. 350)

SAGEBRUSH
(Text p. 351)

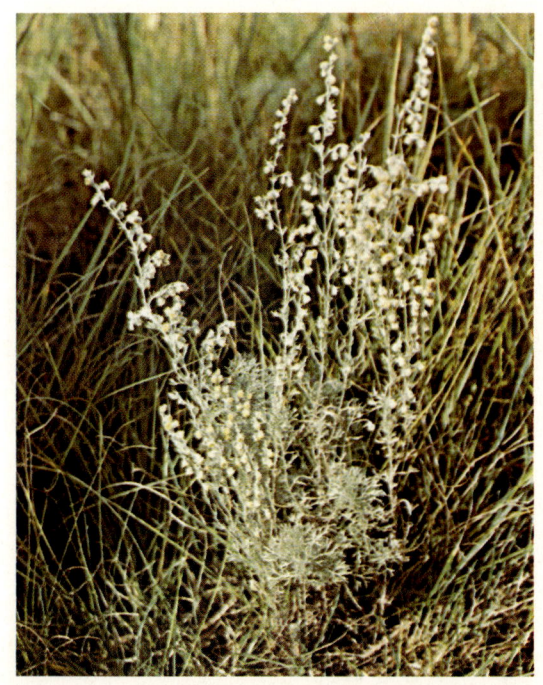

PASTURE SAGE
(Text p. 351)

BIENNIAL SAGEWORT. WORMWOOD   Photo. p. 345
Artemisia biennis   *Biennial*

FLOWERS: Ray-florets none; disk-florets greenish, usually with both stamens and pistil; involucral bracts smooth, greenish, overlapping; flower-heads small, numerous in dense spikes.

FRUIT: A small smooth achene, no pappus.

LEAVES: Alternate, green, smooth on both sides, divided into several narrow toothed segments, 1 - 3 inches long.

HEIGHT: 1 - 4 feet.

HABITAT: Slough margins, roadsides and cultivated fields.

DISTRIBUTION: Common in moist places. July-August.

The Biennial Sagewort or Biennial Wormwood grows along the damp sides of streams and sloughs but often goes unnoticed because of its nondescript weedy appearance. It is a tall rank growing herb and bears a leafy spike-like cluster of small flower-heads typical of the sages but unlike most of them, it has only a faint aromatic smell. It can be distinguished by its smooth often reddish stems and smooth green leaves which are cleft into several narrow toothed segments.

HERRIOT'S SAGE   Photo. p. 348
Artemisia herriotii   *Perennial*

FLOWERS: Ray-florets none; disk-florets yellowish, usually with both stamens and pistil; involucral bracts densely woolly, overlapping; flower-heads numerous, erect in a long cluster.

FRUIT: A small smooth achene, no pappus.

LEAVES: Alternate, simple, generally narrow, sometimes lobed, smooth, green above, densely white-woolly beneath, 2 - 6 inches long.

HEIGHT: 1½ - 3 feet.

HABITAT: Moist places.

DISTRIBUTION: Occasional. July-August.

Herriot's Sage is a tall single-stemmed herb which is often found growing along the side of a woodland path or a shady river bank. The stem which is densely covered with white soft hairs grows from a stout woody stem-base and ends in a spike-like cluster of many small flower-heads. It can be recognized easily by its leaves which are green and smooth above and white and densely woolly beneath, and when blown in the wind, make the plant conspicuous.

SAGEBRUSH
Artemisia cana

Photo. p. 349
Perennial

FLOWERS:	Ray-florets none; disk-florets yellow, usually with both stamens and pistil; involucral bracts small, thin, dry, overlapping; flower-heads small, crowded in a leafy cluster.
FRUIT:	A small smooth achene, no pappus.
LEAVES:	Alternate, simple, narrow or narrowly lance-shaped, silvery hairy on both sides, rarely toothed, ½ - 1½ inches long.
HEIGHT:	1 - 4 feet.
HABITAT:	Lighter soils, on plains and hills.
DISTRIBUTION:	Common in the prairie region. Southern Alberta. July-August.

The blue-grey of the Sagebrush is famous in song and story and the shrub itself is as characteristic of the great North American plains as the heather is of the Scottish hills. With its branches withered by drought, twisted by wind and broken by drifting snow, the Sagebrush is a familiar sight on dry exposed hillsides and in sheltered coulees. The small narrow leaves and young twigs are densely covered with fine hairs which give this shrub its characteristic silvery-grey or bluish-grey colour. Another woody but much rarer species, *Artemisia tridentata*, has silvery three-toothed wedge-shaped leaves and has a strong aromatic odour.

PASTURE SAGE
Artemisia frigida

Photo. p. 349
Perennial

FLOWERS:	Ray-florets none; disk-florets yellowish, usually with both stamens and pistil; involucral bracts small, hairy; flower-heads numerous, in a narrow leafy cluster.
FRUIT:	A small smooth achene, no pappus.
LEAVES:	Alternate, finely dissected, silvery hairy on both sides, ½ - 1½ inches long.
HEIGHT:	6 - 20 inches.
HABITAT:	Dry plains, hills and mountain slopes.
DISTRIBUTION:	Common in the prairie region and on south-facing slopes. July-August.

Next to the Prairie Sage, the Pasture Sage is the most common and widespread of all our Alberta sages. In company with the everlastings, various goosefoots, fleabanes and groundsels, it grows on dry prairie grasslands, along the sides of coulees and on warm exposed south-facing slopes. It is a soft-hairy silvery-grey perennial with a somewhat woody stem-base and tufts of finely dissected feathery leaves. It is the leaves that distinguish it from all our other Alberta sages and these give off a strong aromatic smell if bruised or crushed between the fingers. The Pasture Sage is unpalatable to livestock and therefore increases quickly on overgrazed rangeland.

PRAIRIE SAGE
(Text p. 354)

BALSAM ROOT
(Text p. 354)

ASTER

ASTER

ASTER

ASTER

PRAIRIE SAGE Photo. p. 352
Artemisia gnaphalodes *Perennial*

FLOWERS: Ray-florets none; disk-florets brownish, usually with both stamens and pistil; involucral bracts densely hairy; flower-heads small, numerous in a narrow spike-like woolly cluster.

FRUIT: A dry small smooth achene, no pappus.

LEAVES: Alternate, simple, occasionally lobed, densely white-woolly on both sides, ½ - 3 inches long.

HEIGHT: ½ - 4 feet.

HABITAT: Grassy plains and hillsides.

DISTRIBUTION: Very common throughout the prairie region. July August.

The Prairie Sage is probably the most common and the most widespread sage in Alberta and is one of our most beautiful prairie plants. It forms silvery-grey clumps or patches of erect densely hairy leafy stems which grow from a creeping somewhat woody rootstock and which end in slender leafy clusters of small brownish-coloured flower-heads. The beautiful silvery-grey densely woolly leaves are as soft to touch as velvet and when rubbed between the fingers give off a pleasant aromatic odour. When growing in profusion among the waving grasses, the Prairie Sage gives a bluish-grey haze to the prairie scene.

BALSAM ROOT Photo. p. 352
Balsamorhiza sagittata *Perennial*

FLOWERS: Ray-florets yellow, without stamens or pistil; disk-florets numerous, with both stamens and pistil; involucral bracts large, densely grey-woolly; flower-heads borne singly at the end of a long stalk; 2 - 3 inches across.

FRUIT: A dry achene, without pappus.

LEAVES: Mostly basal, long-petioled, arrow-shaped, white woolly on both sides, 4 - 8 inches long.

HEIGHT: 1½ - 2½ feet.

HABITAT: Dry hillsides.

DISTRIBUTION: Fairly common. Southwestern Alberta. May - July.

The Balsam Root is a true western species and is characteristic of the dry prairie hillsides and the denuded exposed slopes. It is the only Alberta species of this genus and it can be identified immediately by its clump of large densely grey-woolly arrow-shaped leaves, its numerous bright yellow sunflower-like blossoms and by its thick tuberous strong-smelling root. It is a coarse conspicuous plant and because it is shunned by cattle and horses, it tends to increase on overgrazed rangeland.

DAISY FAMILY — *COMPOSITAE*

ASTERS

Aster spp.

Photo. p. 353

Perennials

Throughout Alberta the asters are one of our most ornamental wild flowers. There are twenty-one native asters and they usually come into bloom in late summer and early fall. Asters come in white, pink, blue, lavender or purple, every colour of the rainbow except yellow. The so-called Golden Aster is not a true one. Asters have the same colours and the same daisy-like flower-heads as the fleabanes. They can be distinguished from the fleabanes by their rays which are fewer and much broader and by the fact that they bloom later in the season. It is easy to recognize an aster but it is very difficult to tell one from another in the field without the aid of a botanical key and it is still more difficult to identify one from a photograph unless it has been accurately identified at the time the photograph was taken. To avoid making a mistake of identity a brief description will be given of a few of our most common species without reference to the accompanying photographs. One photograph is a close-up of a single flower-head and shows the solid centre of yellow disk-florets and the blue rays of the ray-florets.

There are many species of blue or lavender asters in Alberta and none is more common than the Smooth Aster, *Aster laevis* var. *geyeri*, whose large bright flower-heads measure about an inch across. It is a perennial with a stout smooth stem, two to four feet in height, and, with numerous smooth, blue-grey, thick leaves, the lower ones narrowed into winged petioles and the upper ones without petioles and more or less clasping the stem. The Smooth Aster is widely distributed and its gay star-shaped flowers brighten roadsides, fields and open woods just before the poplar leaves begin to show their autumn colours.

Another common woodland species of the late summer is the Showy Aster, *Aster conspicuus*. It is an erect coarse species with a rough hairy stem and it grows about two feet high. It has dense dark green foliage and beautiful wide-spreading clusters of violet or blue flower-heads. Each flower-head is about one and one-half inches in diameter and has earned for this aster the descriptive name of "showy".

Lindley's Aster, *Aster lindleyanus*, is another common aster of open woodlands and scrubby thickets and it blooms in August and well into September. It is a stout straight-stemmed plant, sometimes reaching a height of four feet and is densely covered with dark green oval or lance-shaped leaves. Like the Smooth Aster, the lower leaves have petioles with winged-margins while the upper leaves are often without petioles. The flower-heads are fairly large but few in number, each with a conspicuous yellow centre and a fringe of blue or violet rays.

There are several white asters in Alberta but the Many-Flowered Aster, *Aster ericoides*, is the one we see most often. It is common on the prairie and other open places. The stems reach a height of one to two and one-half feet and are fine-hairy and very much-branched. The leaves are narrow and relatively long and have smooth margins. As the name suggests, the flower-heads are numerous and are borne generally on one side of recurved branches. Compared to most asters the flower-heads are small, each about one-half inch in diameter with a showy fringe of short white rays.

R. C. SWEET

J. CLAESSEN

OX-EYE DAISY
(Text p. 358)

GOLDEN ASTER
(Text p. 359)

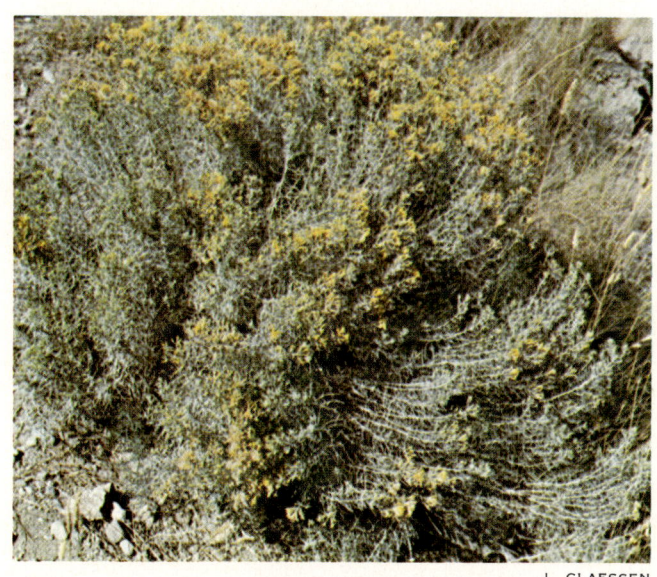

RABBIT BRUSH
(Text p. 359)

DAISY FAMILY — *COMPOSITAE*

NODDING BEGGAR TICKS   Photo. p. 356
Bidens cernua   *Annual*

FLOWERS:	Ray-florets yellow, 6 - 8 or absent, neither stamens nor pistil; disk-florets numerous, with stamens and pistil; involucral bracts rough, leafy; flower-heads several, nodding, chaffy, ¾ - 1¼ inches across.
FRUIT:	A dry 4-barbed achene.
LEAVES:	Opposite, simple, without petiole, narrowly lance-shaped, 2 - 6 inches long.
HEIGHT:	1 - 2½ feet.
HABITAT:	Very wet soil.
DISTRIBUTION:	Fairly common in wet places. August-September.

The Nodding Beggar Ticks is a familiar plant found in roadside ditches and along the marshy margins of sloughs and slow-moving streams. It has a perfectly smooth stem, opposite dark green leaves and several nodding somewhat bristly flower-heads. Individual flower-heads have a somewhat ragged appearance as the yellow ray-florets are not uniformly spaced and are sometimes missing. The disk-florets are numerous and after fertilization grow into bur-like fruits which catch in one's clothing and in the fur of animals.

OX-EYE DAISY   Photo. p. 356
Chrysanthemum leucanthemum   *Perennial*

FLOWERS:	Ray-florets white, with pistil; disk-florets yellow, with both stamens and pistil; involucral bracts overlapping, narrow; flower-heads borne singly at the end of a long flower-stem, 1 - 2 inches across.
FRUIT:	A dry ribbed achene, without pappus.
LEAVES:	Basal leaves petioled, oblong to spatula-shaped, coarsely toothed or divided, 1 - 3 inches long; stem leaves not petioled, clasping, toothed margins.
HEIGHT:	1 - 2 feet.
HABITAT:	Meadows and moist roadsides.
DISTRIBUTION:	Local in distribution. June-August.

The Common or Ox-Eye Daisy, although a native of Europe, has spread across Canada and into Alberta where it is now a familiar roadside and much beloved wayside wild flower. It often grows in wide patches and is regarded in some localities as a troublesome weed. It is a perennial herb with a single leafy stem which springs from a short rootstock and which ends in a single showy flower-head. The Common Daisy is a good example of the radiate type of flower-head which has a solid centre of yellow disk florets surrounded by a row of white ray-florets.

GOLDEN ASTER   Photo. p. 357
Chrysopsis villosa   *Perennial*

FLOWERS:	Ray-florets golden yellow, with pistil; disk-florets with both stamens and pistil; involucral bracts overlapping, somewhat hairy and glandular; flower-heads solitary to several at the end of branches.
FRUIT:	A dry flattened hairy achene, with double pappus.
LEAVES:	Numerous, alternate, short-petioled, oblong to lance-shaped, hairy, 1 - 2 inches long.
HEIGHT:	6 - 24 inches.
HABITAT:	Dry sandy soil.
DISTRIBUTION:	Common. Prairie region in Southern Alberta. July-September.

The Golden Aster is another familiar yellow-flowered composite which is common in dry open places generally, but is found more abundantly in the southern part of the province. It is a low-growing, almost creeping, perennial, has several leafy much-branched hairy stems, and a few golden yellow flower-heads. The leaves are numerous and are covered with short stiff somewhat sticky hairs. Although it is called the Golden Aster, it is not a true aster, for all the members of that genus have flower-heads which are various shades of blue, violet, pink and white, but never yellow.

RABBIT BRUSH   Photo. p. 357
Chrysothamnus nauseosus   *Perennial*

FLOWERS:	Ray-florets none; disk-florets yellow, with both stamens and pistil; involucral bracts in distinct vertical ranks, hairy; flower-heads dense, in terminal rounded clusters.
FRUIT:	A dry slender hairy achene, with bristly pappus.
LEAVES:	Alternate, almost thread-like, not petioled, erect, usually covered with matted hairs, ½ - 2 inches long.
HEIGHT:	8 - 24 inches.
HABITAT:	Very dry localities.
DISTRIBUTION:	Abundant locally. Southern Alberta. July - August.

The Rabbit Brush is strictly a plant of the dry open prairie and it thrives under conditions too dry for most plants. It is of local occurrence and is found in abundance on badlands, eroded hillsides, coulee slopes and on dry saline flats. It grows in large clumps from a very thick woody root which is often exposed by erosion. From a distance it could be mistaken for a patch of greasewood or sage, for all three plants grow in clumps to about the same height and all have the same greyish colour. However, its typical composite flower-heads distinguish it from the greasewood and its lack of aromatic odour distinguishes it from the sage.

CANADA
THISTLE
(Text p. 362)

W. H. VANDEN BORN

WHITE
THISTLE
(Text p. 362)

JANETTE GOODWIN

360

BULL THISTLE
(Text p. 363)

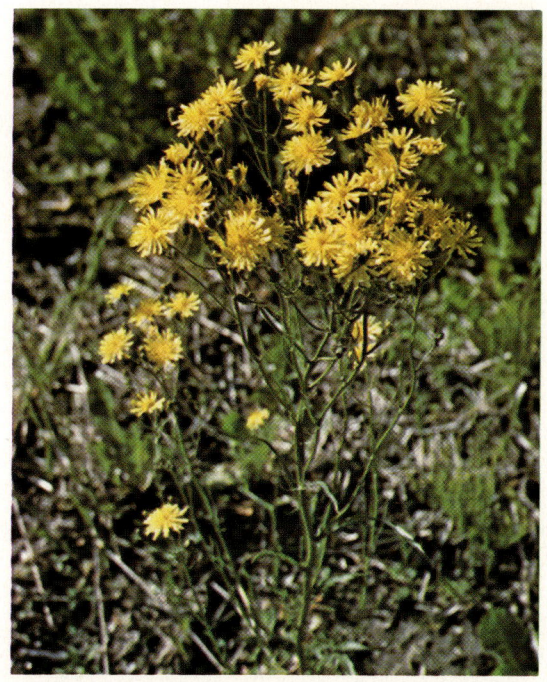

**ANNUAL
HAWKSBEARD**
(Text p. 363)

CANADA THISTLE   Photo. p. 360
Cirsium arvense   *Perennial*

FLOWERS: Ray-florets none; disk-florets pinkish-purple, occasion-
                  ally white, with both stamens and pistil; involucral
                  bracts usually spineless; flower-heads relatively small,
                  about ½ inch across, numerous in loose clusters.

FRUIT: A small dry achene, with white pappus.

LEAVES: Alternate, roughly lance-shaped, deeply divided into
                  many prickly segments, not petioled, 2 - 5 inches long.

HEIGHT: 1 - 3 feet.

HABITAT: Waste places, fields and roadsides.

DISTRIBUTION: Common introduced weed. July - August.

The Canada Thistle is one of our worst perennial weeds and is familiar in the country as well as in the city where it is a constant irritation to any gardener. It is the most common of six species of thistle found in Alberta. A native of Europe, it has not only taken this country's name but, given half a chance, it would take over much of its cultivated land. It is a prolific seed-producer but it spreads chiefly by means of long, deep-seated, white fleshy roots. If these roots are broken into small segments by plough or spade, each small piece sprouts into a new plant. The showy pinkish-purple flower-heads are borne in loose clusters at the top of the stem, the florets emerging a few at a time from the cup-shaped involucre.

WHITE THISTLE   Photo. p. 360
Cirsium hookerianum   *Perennial*

FLOWERS: Ray-florets none; disk-florets white or cream-coloured;
                  with both stamens and pistil; involucral bracts cob-
                  webby, woolly, spine-tipped; flower-heads few to
                  numerous, 1¼ - 1½ inches across.

FRUIT: A dry achene, with whitish pappus.

LEAVES: Alternate, narrowly oblong, lobed or narrowly toothed,
                  white woolly beneath, smooth above, not petioled,
                  4 - 10 inches long.

HEIGHT: 1 - 3 feet.

HABITAT: Woods and open places.

DISTRIBUTION: Uncommon. Western Alberta. July - August.

This thistle is found in the foothills and on the lower slopes of the Rocky Mountains. It is a tall sturdy plant and is similar to the Bull Thistle, except that the flower-heads are a white or a creamy-white colour. Another feature to note is that the leaf bases do not continue down the stem in wing-like spiny extensions as they do in the Bull Thistle. The whole plant, and especially the spine-tipped cup-shaped involucre, is covered with loose-spreading white hairs.

BULL THISTLE
Cirsium vulgare

Photo. p. 361
Perennial

FLOWERS: Ray-florets none; disk-florets rose-purple, rarely white, with stamens and pistil; involucral bracts hairy, with slender spines; flower-heads several, 1½ - 2 inches across and about 2 inches high.

FRUIT: A dry flattish achene, with bristly pappus.

LEAVES: Alternate, dark green, hairy on both sides, deeply cleft and very prickly, 3 - 6 inches long.

HEIGHT: 3 - 5 feet.

HABITAT: Waste places and borders of fields.

DISTRIBUTION: Fairly common. Southern Alberta. July - August.

The thistles with their prickly stiff leaves and their prickly flower-heads are a familiar but a hated weed. The Bull Thistle, commonly called the Scotch Thistle because of its similarity to the Scotch emblem, is the prickliest of all and has leaf bases extending down the sides of the stem in two prickly wing-like lobes. The flower-head looks like a silky rose-coloured shaving brush, with its rose-purple florets emerging from a green prickly cup-shaped involucre. A native of Europe, it is now well established in thickets and pastures in Southern Alberta.

ANNUAL HAWKSBEARD
Crepis tectorum

Photo. p. 361
Annual

FLOWERS: Ray-florets yellow, several to many, with both stamens and pistil; disk-florets none; involucral bracts, 1 or 2 rows; flower-heads numerous, about ½ inch across.

FRUIT: A small purplish achene, with whitish pappus.

LEAVES: Basal leaves petioled, lance-shaped, slightly toothed, 4 - 6 inches long; upper leaves narrow, not petioled.

HEIGHT: 6 - 18 inches.

HABITAT: Light soils, clearings.

DISTRIBUTION: Common. Introduced weed. June - July.

The Annual Hawksbeard is an introduced weed and the only justification for including it in this book is the fact that it shows the chief features of this group of composites and is common in waste places and along roadsides. It is a short-lived annual and this feature alone distinguishes it from the other members of this genus. It is a tall smooth leafy stemmed plant with milky juice and many small yellow dandelion-like flowers. Like many annuals, the seeds germinate soon after they mature, form rosettes of leaves which over-winter, and from these rosettes flowering stems develop the following spring.

ALPINE HAWKSBEARD
(Text p. 366)

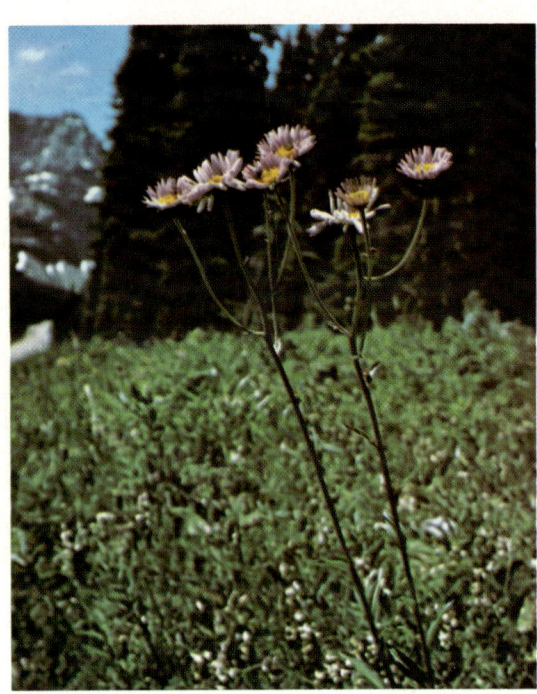

SMOOTH
FLEABANE
(Text p. 366)

TUFTED FLEABANE
(Text p. 367)

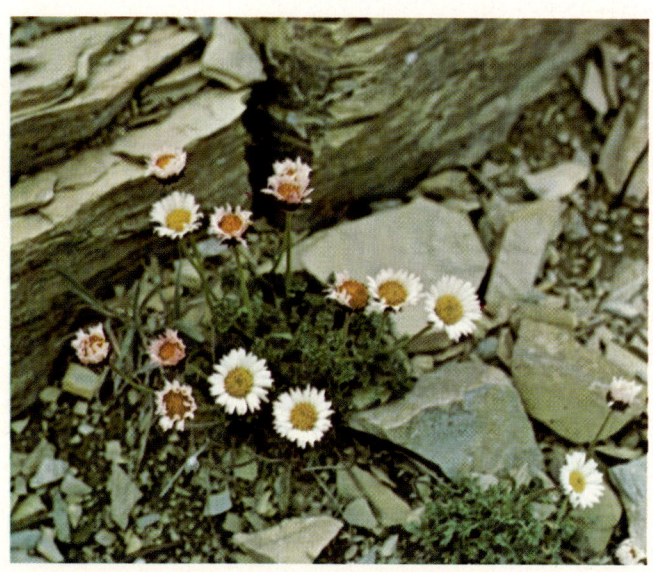

DAISY FLEABANE
(Text p. 367)

ALPINE HAWKSBEARD   Photo. p. 364
Crepis nana   *Perennial*

FLOWERS: Ray-florets yellow, with both stamens and pistil; disk-
                    florets none; involucral bracts in 1 - 2 rows; flower-
                    heads several to numerous on short stalks, about ¼
                    inch across.

FRUIT: A brown dry achene, with pappus.

LEAVES: Mostly basal, tufted, narrowly spatula-shaped, smooth
                    and somewhat purplish, 1 - 2 inches long.

HEIGHT: 2 - 4 inches.

HABITAT: Stony slopes and moraines.

DISTRIBUTION: High altitudes. Rocky Mountains. June - July.

The Alpine Hawksbeard is a sturdy stunted perennial which grows
in loose rock, in rock crevices or on gravel bars and at most is only four
inches high. It has tufts of smooth bluish-grey spade-shaped leaves and
numerous bright yellow flower-heads. The flower-stems are stunted but
grow from a strong stem-base which in turn is attached to a long fibrous
tap root and this prevents it from being blown away by the wind. Though
small and borne on short stalks among the leaves, the flower-heads are
very like those of the taller Many-Flowered Hawksbeard, *Crepis elegans*,
which grows on river-bars and rocky slopes but at a much lower elevation.

SMOOTH FLEABANE   Photo. p. 364
Erigeron glabellus var. *pubescens*   *Perennial*

FLOWERS: Ray-florets blue, pink or white, 125 - 175, with pistil;
                    disk-florets yellow, with stamens and pistil; involucral
                    bracts hairy; flower-heads 1 - 3 on stem, ½ - ¾ inch
                    across.

FRUIT: A dry achene, with bristly pappus.

HEIGHT: Basal leaves oblong to lance-shaped, sometimes toothed,
                    usually hairy, 2 - 4 inches long; stem leaves small.

HEIGHT: 6 - 20 inches.

HABITAT: Hillsides and grassy mountain slopes.

DISTRIBUTION: Fairly common. Western Alberta. July.

The fleabanes, or wild daisies as they are commonly called, make up
the largest genus of the Daisy Family in Alberta. The most conspicuous
difference between the fleabanes and the asters is that the former have very
numerous and very narrow rays while the latter have rays which are
broader and much fewer in number. The Smooth Fleabane is one of
twenty-seven species of this genus that brighten the prairies, the foothills,
the valleys and the slopes of the Rockies in spring and early summer. The
flower-heads are very showy with a thick finely cut blue or purple fringe
of ray-florets and a flat bright yellow centre of disk-florets. Although it is
called the Smooth Fleabane, stems, leaves and involucral bracts are sparsely
covered with appressed stiff hairs.

TUFTED FLEABANE
Erigeron caespitosus

Photo. p. 365
Perennial

FLOWERS: Ray-florets white, blue or pink, 30 - 100, with pistil; disk-florets yellow, many, with both stamens and pistil; involucral bracts overlapping; flower-heads few or solitary; ¾ - 1¼ inches across.

FRUIT: A dry achene, with pappus.

LEAVES: Basal leaves clustered, somewhat spatula-shaped, 1 - 3 inches long; upper leaves small and not petioled,

HEIGHT: 6 - 10 inches.

HABITAT: Dry open places.

DISTRIBUTION: Common on the prairie. June - July.

The Tufted Fleabane is a common prairie species and is abundant on dry hillsides and eroded slopes. It is a deep-rooted, low-growing perennial with tufted leaves, a tough branching stem-base and several single-headed leafy stems. The flower-heads are built on the open-faced daisy plan with a solid centre of yellow disk-florets surrounded by a conspicuous fringe of white, blue or pink ray-florets. Both leaves and flower-stems are covered with fine spreading hairs. With few exceptions, one fleabane is difficult to distinguish from another without the aid of a botanical key.

DAISY FLEABANE
Erigeron compositus

Photo. p. 365
Perennial

FLOWERS: Ray-florets white, pink or blue, with pistil, many; disk-florets yellow, many; involucral bracts overlapping, glandular-hairy; flower-heads solitary, ½ - ¾ inch across.

FRUIT: A dry achene, with coarse pappus.

LEAVES: Basal, tufted, erect, divided into 3 narrow segments, more or less glandular-hairy, ½ - 2 inches long.

HEIGHT: 2 - 5 inches.

HABITAT: Rocky soil.

DISTRIBUTION: Rocky Mountains. June - July.

The Daisy Fleabane is commonly found growing on the slopes of the Rocky Mountains and on dry hillsides and plains as far east as the Cypress Hills. It is a charming little plant and growing as it does with its white, pink or blue flower-heads a bare two or three inches from the stony soil, it brings to mind the short-stemmed English Daisy. The leaves are crowded at the base and their three-lobed leaf blades help to distinguish this plant from the other dwarfed species of fleabane which grow in the same locality.

WOOLLY FLEABANE
(Text p. 370)

ALPINE FLEABANE
(Text p. 370)

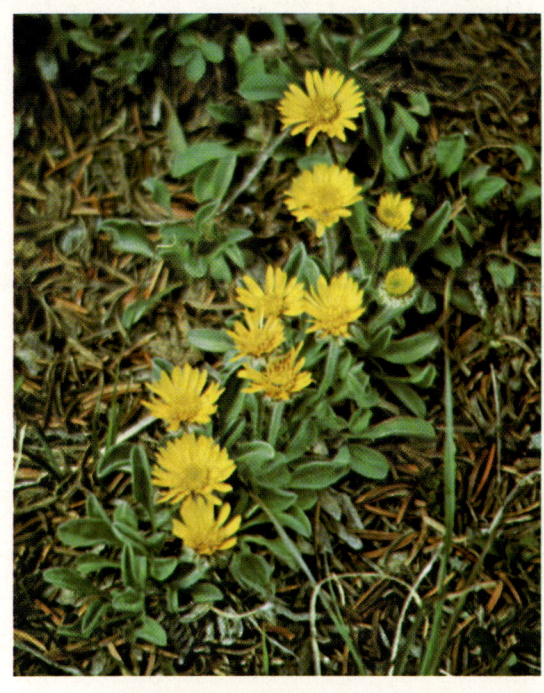

GOLDEN
FLEABANE
(Text p. 371)

R. N. SMITH

AILEEN HARMON

LARGE-FLOWERED FLEABANE
(Text p. 371)

WOOLLY FLEABANE
Erigeron lanatus

Photo. p. 368
Perennial

FLOWERS:	Ray-florets usually white, sometimes blue or pink, with pistil; disk-florets yellow, with both stamens and pistil; involucral bracts purplish, very woolly; flower-heads solitary, ¾ - 1¼ inches across.
FRUIT:	A dry achene, with bristly pappus.
LEAVES:	All basal, oblong lance-shaped, loosely woolly, ½ - 1¼ inches long.
HEIGHT:	2 inches or less.
HABITAT:	High alpine areas.
DISTRIBUTION:	Rocky Mountains. July.

About five species of fleabane grow in high places in the Rocky Mountains. All of them have a long taproot, a stout branching stem-base, tufts of smallish leaves and short-stemmed solitary daisy-like flower-heads. They differ only in minor details of flowers and leaves. The one shown in the photograph is the Woolly Fleabane, an extremely low squat plant with unusually long white rays. The leaf blades are short and often three-toothed at the tips and these and the single-headed flower-stems are covered with loose soft branching hairs.

ALPINE FLEABANE
Erigeron pallens

Photo. p. 368
Perennial

FLOWERS:	Ray-florets pinkish or white; disk-florets yellowish, with stamens and pistil; involucral bracts sticky-hairy; flower-heads solitary.
FRUIT:	A dry achene, with pappus.
LEAVES:	Mostly basal, spatula-shaped, 3-lobed, hairy, about 1 inch long.
HEIGHT:	Flower-stem 1 - 2 inches.
HABITAT:	Rocky slopes at high elevations.
DISTRIBUTION:	Rare. Rocky Mountains. July-August.

One mountain plant which has adapted itself to its windy icy environment is the Alpine Fleabane. It has a creeping stem-base and an inch-high flower-stem which is leafless and which often bends over so that the solitary flower-head lies on the ground. The flower-head is relatively large for the size of the plant and the ray-florets are a pinkish-white. In addition to its dwarfed size, all parts of the plant are covered with soft long and somewhat sticky hairs. The Alpine Fleabane is a rare mountain wild flower and well worth a stiff climb to see.

GOLDEN FLEABANE Photo. p. 369
Erigeron aureus *Perennial*

FLOWERS: Ray-florets yellow, 25 - 70, with pistil; disk-florets yellow, with stamens and pistil; involucral bracts loose, green with purple tips; flower-heads solitary, about 1 inch across.

FRUIT: A dry achene, with a double pappus.

LEAVES: Basal leaves with oval shaped blades, somewhat hairy; stem leaves few, small and narrow.

HEIGHT: ¾ - 6 inches.

HABITAT: Rocky or peaty places.

DISTRIBUTION: Rocky Mountains. Southwestern Alberta. July-August.

The Golden Fleabane like the Alpine Fleabane grows at great elevations in the Rocky Mountains. It is a tiny low perennial with a branched stem-base that gives rise to a very short flower-stem and to a tight cluster of small hairy leaves. The solitary flower-head is a beautiful golden yellow and appears incongruously large for the small size of the plant. It is regarded by many as the loveliest of the fleabanes and it is a favourite of all the mountain climbers and alpine photographers.

LARGE-FLOWERED FLEABANE Photo. p. 369
Erigeron grandiflorus *Perennial*

FLOWERS: Ray-florets blue or lavender, 100 - 125, with pistil; disk-florets yellow, with stamens and pistil; involucral bracts loose, often purplish and glandular-hairy; flower-heads solitary, 1 - 1½ inches across.

FRUIT: A dry achene, with bristly pappus.

LEAVES: Basal leaves oblong to lance-shaped, hairy, 1 - 2¼ inches; stem leaves several, smaller.

HEIGHT: 1½ - 10 inches.

HABITAT: High alpine areas.

DISTRIBUTION: Rocky Mountains. July-August.

Another alpine species, the Large-Flowered Fleabane is found growing at higher altitudes among rocks and on bare stony ground. It grows from a spreading stem base, sending up tufts of small dark green leaves and several short flower-stems. Each flower-stem ends in a single large flower-head which has a thick fringe of blue or bluish-lavender rays and a big golden yellow disk. Like many other low growing fleabanes, it resembles one of the small cultivated English daisies.

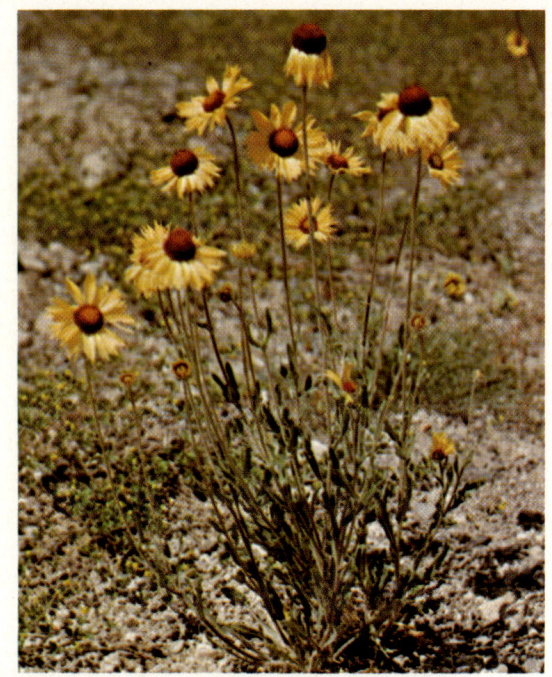

WILD
GAILLARDIA
(Text p. 374)

DORTHEA CALVERLEY

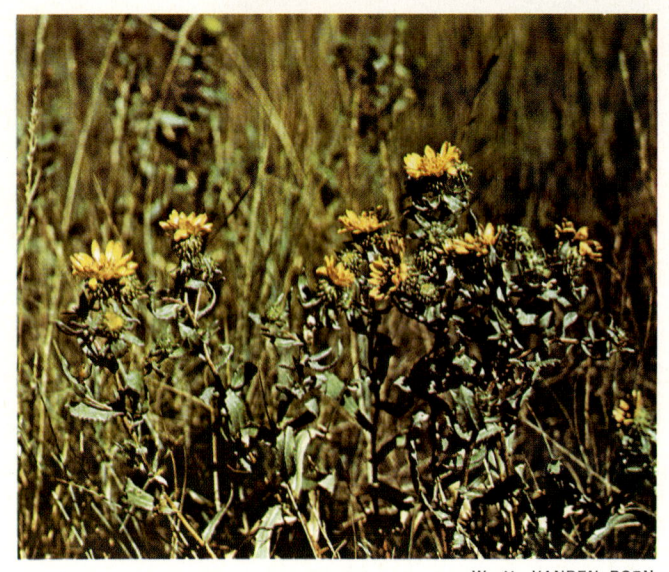

W. H. VANDEN BORN

GUMWEED
(Text p. 374)

BROOMWEED
(Text p. 375)

SPINY IRON PLANT
(Text p. 375)

WILD GAILLARDIA   Photo. p. 372
Gaillardia aristata   *Perennial*

FLOWERS: Ray-florets yellow, streaked with purple, 10-18, with
                wedge-shaped 3-cleft rays; disk-florets purplish-brown,
                numerous, with both stamens and pistil; involucral
                bracts hairy; flower-heads large, showy, solitary or
                few, long-stalked, 1¾ - 2½, inches across.

FRUIT: A dry hairy achene, with scaly pappus.

LEAVES: Basal leaves oblong with lobed margins, long petioled,
                2 - 5 inches long; stem leaves hairy, smaller, not
                petioled.

HEIGHT: 8 - 24 inches.

HABITAT: Dry prairie plains and hillsides.

DISTRIBUTION: Common in prairie grassland. July - August.

Whether the Gaillardia or Brown-Eyed Susan, as it is commonly but incorrectly called, grows in the garden or on the dry prairie it is always a favourite. It is an erect-stemmed perennial with a slender taproot and an abundance of greyish-green hairy leaves. Even from a distance it is recognized easily by its large purple-brown bull's-eye, surrounded by a gay fringe of pale yellow wedge-shaped rays. After the rays fall, the bull's-eye becomes a dry hairy head of small scaly achenes.

GUMWEED   Photo. p. 372
Grindelia squarrosa   *Biennial or Perennial*

FLOWERS: Ray-florets bright yellow, with pistil; disk-florets yellow,
                with both stamens and pistil; involucral bracts very
                resinous and sticky; flower-heads ¾ - 1¼ inches across,
                numerous at the ends of the stems.

FRUIT: A small dry achene, without pappus.

LEAVES: Alternate, narrowly oblong, stiff, smooth, finely toothed,
                ½ - 1½ inches long.

HEIGHT: 8 - 24 inches.

HABITAT: Dry places on the prairie.

DISTRIBUTION: Common. Southern Alberta. August - September.

When the hot dry winds of August blow across the prairies, the delicate plants of the early season die down and the hardy drought-resistant yellow-flowered composites come into their own. One of the most common of these is the Gumweed, a plant found on dry coulee slopes, on roadsides and on saline flats. The photograph shows the characteristic daisy-like flower-heads with bright yellow rays and dull yellow centre. However, it is recognized more easily by its gummy involucre, which on a very hot day oozes a sticky kind of resin. It grows in the company of the Tarweed, *Madia glomerata*, a very similar composite with very sticky but much smaller flower-heads. The sticky substance of the Tarweed has a strong smell suggesting tar or creosote. Gumweed and Tarweed both have appropriate names.

DAISY FAMILY — *COMPOSITAE*

BROOMWEED
Gutierrezia sarothrae

Photo. p. 373
Perennial

FLOWERS:	Ray-florets yellow, few, with pistil, disk-florets yellow, several, with both stamens and pistil; involucral bracts leathery, sticky; flower-heads small, very numerous, 1/8 inch across in tight clusters.
FRUIT:	A dry achene, with scaly pappus.
LEAVES:	Alternate, very narrow, thread-like, usually hairy, ½ - 1½ inches long.
HEIGHT:	8 - 20 inches.
HABITAT:	Dry prairie lands.
DISTRIBUTION:	Common. Southern Alberta. August - September.

In spite of their rather rough coarse appearance, the hardy composites add a bright patch of yellow to the prairie landscape when the heat and strong winds of August begin to wither the grasses and when the plants of the early season have gone to seed. One of these bright yellow composites is a low-growing tufted perennial whose numerous erect slender brittle stems have suggested the common name Broomweed. It is extremely drought-resistant and has a deep woody taproot, a woody branching stem-base and wire-like leaves. The very numerous small yellow flower-heads are borne in tight clusters at the top of the stems. It is a common dry prairie composite that tends to increase on overgrazed rangeland, as it is unpalatable to cattle.

SPINY IRON PLANT
Haplopappus spinulosus

Photo. p. 373
Perennial

FLOWERS:	Ray-florets yellow, 15 - 50; disk-florets yellowish, many with both stamens and pistil; involucral bracts overlapping, bristle-tipped; flower-heads numerous, ¼ - ¾ inch across.
FRUIT:	A dry achene, with soft pappus.
LEAVES:	Bluish-green, hairy, deeply dissected into narrow bristle-pointed teeth, ½ - 1½ inches long.
HEIGHT:	6 - 18 inches.
HABITAT:	Dry plains and hillsides.
DISTRIBUTION:	Common. Southern Alberta. June - August.

The Spiny Iron Plant grows plentifully in dry places on the prairie, on eroded coulee slopes and on saline flats. Like the Broomweed, the rubber weeds and many other low yellow-flowered composites, it has a woody rootstock and a thatch of erect stiff rough green stems. The bluish-grey leaves are rather stiff and hard and are divided into several bristle-pointed segments. The bright yellow flowers are daisy-like and very showy. Another very similar low-tufted species, the Toothed Iron Plant, *Haplopappus nuttallii*, has undivided leaves with short spiny teeth and is also common on dry eroded hillsides and hard clay knolls.

375

**LYALL'S
IRON PLANT**
(Text p. 378)

AILEEN HARMON

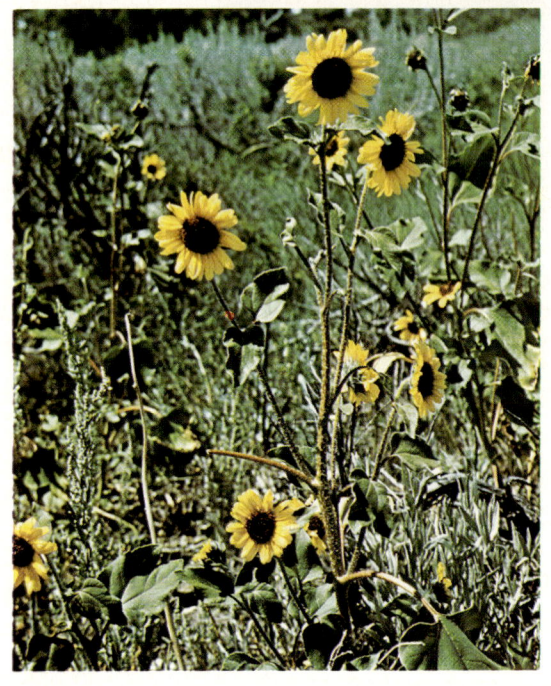

**SHOWY
SUNFLOWER**
(Text p. 378)

R. N. SMITH

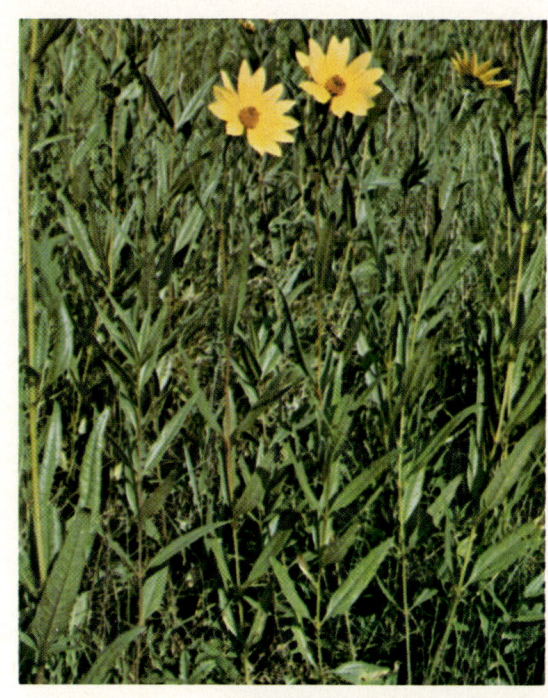

TUBEROUS-
ROOTED
SUNFLOWER
(Text p. 379)

R. C. SWEET

CANADA
HAWKWEED
(Text p. 379)

A. KARVONEN

377

LYALL'S IRON PLANT
Haplopappus lyallii

Photo. p. 376
Perennial

FLOWERS: Ray-florets yellow; disk-florets yellowish, with both stamens and pistil; involucral bracts glandular-hairy, purple-tipped; flower-heads solitary, about 1 inch across.

FRUIT: A dry achene, with whitish pappus.

LEAVES: Leaves mainly basal, oblong to lance-shaped, glandular-hairy, ¾ - 2½ inches long.

HEIGHT: 5 - 6 inches.

HABITAT: Alpine meadows.

DISTRIBUTION: Rocky Mountains. July-August.

Lyall's Iron Plant is another dwarf mountain wild flower which is found growing in a rocky ridge or in a mossy mountain meadow near timberline. Only climbers are likely to see it and few of these will know its name. It grows close to the ground from a branched stem-base and this gives rise to one or two short flower-stems, each bearing a solitary relatively large flower-head. The small somewhat soft-hairy leaves are clustered mainly around the base of the flower-stem and in no way resemble those of the Spiny Iron Plant that grows on the dry prairie.

SHOWY SUNFLOWER
Helianthus lenticularis

Photo. p. 376
Annual

FLOWERS: Ray-florets yellow, large, without stamens or pistil; disk-florets brownish-purple, numerous, with both stamens and pistil; involucral bracts hairy; flower-heads solitary or several, 3 - 6 inches across.

FRUIT: A dry smooth achene, without pappus.

LEAVES: Mainly alternate, simple, oval with usually a heart-shaped base, petioled, coarsely toothed, 4 - 8 inches long.

HEIGHT: 3 - 6 feet.

HABITAT: Roadsides and waste places.

DISTRIBUTION: Fairly common. Southern Alberta. July-August.

The Showy Sunflower is a plant of moist meadows, slough margins and roadsides. It is a coarse annual with a slender rootstock, thick fleshy roots, large hairy leaves and one to several relatively large flower-heads. There are five species of sunflower in Alberta, three are perennials and two are annuals. The cultivated sunflower is taller, has thicker stems, has larger showier flower-heads and of course has larger oil-rich seeds.

TUBEROUS-ROOTED SUNFLOWER
Helianthus subtuberosus

Photo. p. 377
Perennial

FLOWERS:	Ray-florets yellow, showy, without stamens or pistil; disk-florets yellow, numerous, with stamens and pistil; involucral bracts numerous; flower-heads on long stalks, 1½ - 2½ inches across.
FRUIT:	A dry smooth achene, without pappus.
LEAVES:	Mainly opposite, simple, not petioled, narrow, rough on both sides, 2 - 6 inches long.
HEIGHT:	3 - 7 feet.
HABITAT:	Moist, saline lowlands and roadside ditches.
DISTRIBUTION:	Fairly common. Southern Alberta. August - September.

The name sunflower is given to many a yellow-flowered composite, but this plant is the perfect one for the name, as the whole flower-head is a sunny hue. But it is the cluster of spindle-shaped fleshy roots which is the characteristic feature of this sunflower and from which it takes its common name, Tuberous-Rooted Sunflower. Long before the first settlers arrived, the wild sunflowers were growing as a seed crop for the Plains Indians. The small seeds were treated in two ways; boiled in water to obtain oil and ground between stones to make flour. The oil was used for cooking or for oiling their hair while the flour was used to make a kind of bread or to thicken their thin vegetable soups. Today, the much larger seeds of the cultivated sunflower form one of our most important oil crops.

CANADA HAWKWEED
Hieracium canadense

Photo. p. 377
Perennial

FLOWERS:	Ray-florets yellow, many, with stamens and pistil; disk-florets none; involucral bracts in 1 - 3 rows; flower-heads numerous, about 1 inch across.
FRUIT:	A dry achene, with rough pappus.
LEAVES:	Alternate, narrowly oblong, more or less hairy, somewhat toothed, 1 - 3 inches long.
HEIGHT:	1 - 4 feet.
HABITAT:	Dry woodlands.
DISTRIBUTION:	Fairly common. Wooded regions. July - August.

There are seven species of hawkseed in Alberta and of these the Canada Hawkweed is the most common. It grows in thickets, open woods and in waste places. The small yellow dandelion-like flower-heads are borne in a many-branched cluster at the top of a tall leafy stem. The yellow hawkweeds are often confused with the hawksbeards. However, the former have one to three rows of involucral bracts with a few smaller bracts at their base, while the latter usually have one row only.

HEART-LEAVED ARNICA
(Text p. 346)

STEMLESS RUBBER WEED
(Text p. 382)

COLORADO RUBBER WEED
(Text p. 383)

COMMON
BLUE LETTUCE
(Text p. 383)

ORANGE HAWKWEED
Hieracium aurantiacum

Not Illustrated
Perennial

FLOWERS: Ray-florets red-orange, with both stamens and pistil; disk-florets none; involucral bracts with dark glandular hairs; flower-heads ¾ - 1 inch across, several in a compact cluster.

FRUIT: A dry achene, with brownish pappus.

LEAVES: Basal leaves in rosettes, spatula-shaped with winged-petioles, sparingly hairy, 2 - 5 inches long; stem leaves few and small.

HEIGHT: 6 - 20 inches.

HABITAT: Roadsides and fields.

DISTRIBUTION: Introduced weed of local occurrence. July - August.

Of the seven hawkweeds found in Alberta only one has an orange flower-head and is therefore called the Orange Hawkweed. It is an introduced weed from Eastern Canada and is found locally in weedy pastures. In spite of its brilliant orange-red flower-heads, it is a rather coarse plant with a single, somewhat sticky flower-stem and a rosette of basal leaves. The Orange Hawkweed has a tight terminal cluster of several flower-heads while the Orange-Flowered False Dandelion, with which it is often mistaken, has a single flower-head.

STEMLESS RUBBER WEED. BUTTE MARIGOLD
Hymenoxys acaulis

Photo. p. 380
Perennial

FLOWERS: Ray-florets 10 - 15, bright yellow, 3-toothed, with pistil; disk-florets yellowish, with both stamens and pistil; involucral bracts soft hairy; flower-heads solitary on long stems, ¾ - 1¼ inches across.

FRUIT: A dry achene, with bristly pappus.

LEAVES: All basal, tufted, narrow lance-shaped, greyish-green, silvery-woolly, ½ - 2 inches long.

HEIGHT: 4 - 8 inches.

HABITAT: Dry sandy soil.

DISTRIBUTION: Fairly common. Southern Alberta. May - June.

We have two species of rubber weed in Alberta, the Stemless Rubber Weed and the Colorado Rubber Weed. In general apparance they are very similar and they are often found growing together in the same dry places. The Stemless Rubber Weed, as its name suggests, has no true stem. Both the leaves and the flower-stems grow in tufts from the crown of a coarse woody taproot. The bright yellow daisy-like flower-heads are borne singly on leafless flower-stems which rise only a few inches above the tufts of the grey-green silky-hairy leaves. This plant is sometimes called the Butte Marigold and it is as decorative in the dry prairie as the cultivated marigolds are in our own gardens.

COLORADO RUBBER WEED
Hymenoxys richardsonii

Photo. p. 381
Perennial

FLOWERS: Ray-florets bright yellow, 3-toothed, with pistil; disk-florets yellowish, with both stamens and pistil; involucral bracts with rough margins; flower-heads few in a flat-topped cluster, about ¾ inch across.

FRUIT: A dry achene, with pappus.

LEAVES: Mostly basal, tufted, 2 - 4 inches long, divided into 3 - 7 narrow rubbery wire-like segments.

HEIGHT: 4 - 12 inches.

HABITAT: Dry light soil.

DISTRIBUTION: Common on dry prairie. Southern Alberta. June-July.

The Colorado Rubber Weed is another low-growing yellow composite that arises from a branched and somewhat woody stem-base which is covered with last year's dead leaf bases. The bright yellow flower-heads resemble those of the Stemless Rubber Weed but they are somewhat larger and are borne in a flat-topped cluster. The chief difference between the two plants is the leaves; in the Stemless Rubber Weed they are all basal and covered with fine silvery hairs, while in the Colorado Rubber Weed they are divided into several narrow rubbery and usually smooth segments. This plant will grow in the dryest soil and since it is unpalatable to cattle it tends to increase with heavy grazing.

COMMON BLUE LETTUCE
Lactuca pulchella

Photo. p. 381
Perennial

FLOWERS: Ray-florets blue, with both stamens and pistil; disk-florets none; involucral bracts overlapping; flower-heads about 1 inch across, few in a loose cluster.

FRUIT: A dry achene, with soft white pappus.

LEAVES: Alternate, smooth, narrowly lance-shaped, with backward directed lobes, 2 - 7 inches long.

HEIGHT: 1 - 3 feet.

HABITAT: Heavy moist soil.

DISTRIBUTION: Common as a weed in fields and in roadsides. July-August.

The Common Blue Lettuce is closely related to the dandelions, goatsbeards, sow thistles, hawksbeards and hawkweeds and like them, its stems and leaves contain a milky juice and its flower-heads are made up only of ray-florets. In fact, the showy flower-heads look like bright blue dandelions. It is a tall smooth plant and is common on stream banks, at the edge of thickets, in roadside ditches and is often found in cultivated fields.

BLAZING STAR
(Text p. 386)

JULIE HRAPKO

S. SMOLIAK

SKELETON WEED
(Text p. 386)

384

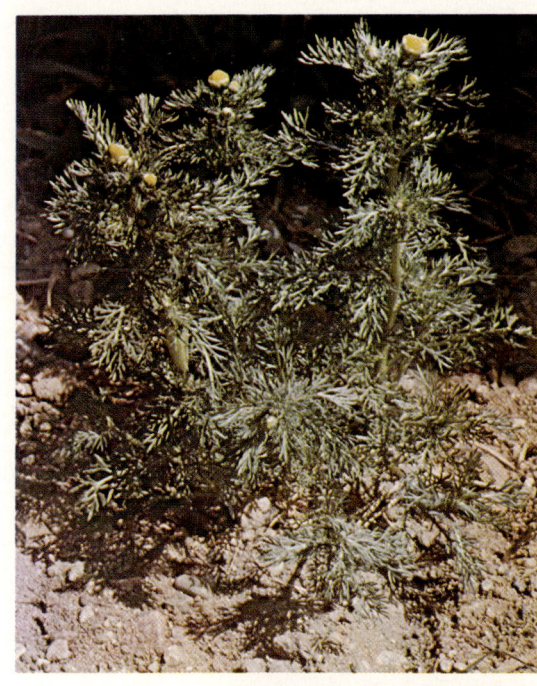

PINEAPPLE
WEED
(Text p. 387)

SCENTLESS
CHAMOMILE
(Text p. 387)

BLAZING STAR   Photo. p. 384
Liatris punctata   *Perennial*

FLOWERS:	Ray-florets none; disk-florets rose-purple, with both stamens and pistil, style feathery; involucral bracts purplish; flower-heads about ½ inch across, several in a crowded spike.
FRUIT:	A dry ribbed hairy achene, with feathery pappus.
LEAVES:	Alternate, numerous, narrow, stiff, rather thick, dotted, 2 - 6 inches long.
HEIGHT:	4 - 18 inches.
HABITAT:	Dry hillsides and prairies.
DISTRIBUTION:	Common. Southern Alberta. August-September.

The beautiful bright rose-purple Blazing Star is the show-piece of the dry prairie in August just as the Showy Locoweed was in July. It comes into its own when the earlier blooming plants have gone to seed and then it stands out in sharp contrast to the drab grey-green of the withered grasses. The flower-heads have a soft feathery look due to the branching of the long delicate styles. The Blazing Star is a hardy perennial whose very thick tuber-like rootstock and very narrow stiff leaves enable it to withstand long periods of drought on the dry grassy plains and hills of Southern Alberta.

SKELETON WEED. PRAIRIE PINK   Photo. p. 384
Lygodesmia juncea   *Perennial*

FLOWERS:	Ray-florets pink, 5, with stamens and pistil; disk-florets none; involucral bracts few; flower-heads solitary at the ends of branches, ½ - ¾ inch across.
FRUIT:	A dry achene, with a soft bristly pappus.
LEAVES:	Lower leaves narrow and short; upper leaves scale-like or absent.
HEIGHT:	6 - 18 inches.
HABITAT:	Dry open places. Sandy soil.
DISTRIBUTION:	Common throughout Southern Alberta. July.

The Skeleton Weed is a bizarre skeleton-like plant that is common on the dry prairie and on light sandy soils. The distinguishing feature is its rigid fibrous green stems which grow stiffly erect from the crown of a deep tough perennial rootstock. The stems branch freely at the base and are almost leafless. Each branch ends in a single flower-head whose wheel-shape and pink colour have suggested the common name Prairie Pink. A rarer species, the Annual Skeleton Weed, *Lygodesmia rostrata*, is very similar but has long narrow wire-like leaves and grows abundantly on sandy soil in Southern Alberta. Both species have milky juice.

PINEAPPLE WEED Photo. p. 385
Matricaria matricarioides *Annual*

FLOWERS: Ray-florets none; disk-florets yellowish, with stamens and pistil; involucral bracts dry, in 2 - 3 series; flower-heads numerous, about ¼ inch across.

FRUIT: A small dry achene, without pappus.

LEAVES: Very dense, finely divided, ½ - 2 inches long.

HEIGHT: 4 - 16 inches.

HABITAT: Waste places, yards.

DISTRIBUTION: Common throughout Alberta. July-August.

An introduced weed from Europe, the Pineapple Weed is commonly found in roadsides, waste places, farm yards and in city alleys. It is not a pretty plant, the flower-heads being rayless and the somewhat cone-shaped disk a dull greenish-yellow. Despite its drab unattractive weedy appearance, the abundant lacey foliage is remarkable for its strong pineapple odour which is most noticeable when the leaves are bruised or rubbed between the fingers.

SCENTLESS CHAMOMILE Photo. p. 385
Matricaria maritima var. *agrestis* *Annual*

FLOWERS: Ray-florets white, with pistil; disk-florets yellow, with both stamens and pistil; involucral bracts dry, in 2 - 3 series; flower-heads ½ - 1 inch across, numerous at the ends of branches.

FRUIT: A small dry achene, without pappus.

LEAVES: Numerous, not petioled, divided into many thread-like segments, ¾ - 3 inches long.

HEIGHT: 8 - 30 inches.

HABITAT: Roadsides and waste places.

DISTRIBUTION: Locally abundant. July-August.

The Scentless Chamomile is another introduced composite which is found growing locally in waste places and roadsides. The daisy-like flower-heads with their yellow centres and white rays are sometimes confused with the Ox-Eye Daisy. However, the flower-heads are only half as large and the two plants can be distinguished easily by their leaves. Those of the Scentless Chamomile are divided into numerous narrow thread-like segments, while those of the Ox-Eye Daisy are spatula-shaped with toothed margins. It is closely related to the Pineapple Weed but its leaves have no odour.

ARROW-
LEAVED
COLTSFOOT
(Text p. 390)

A. G. PORCHER

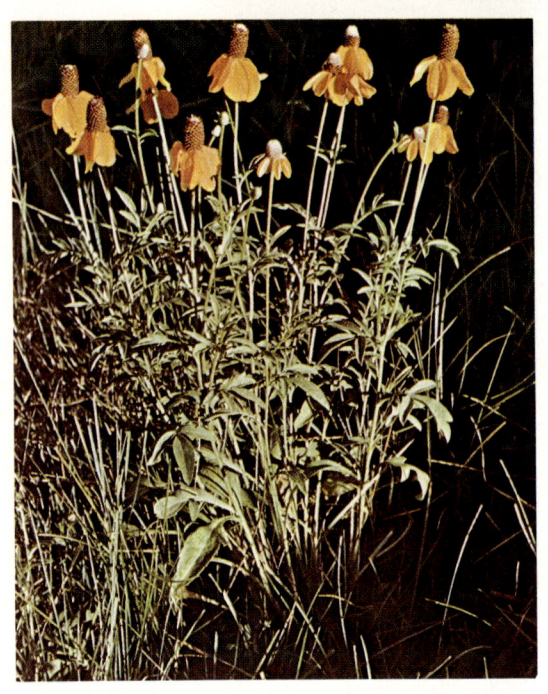

PRAIRIE
CONE-FLOWER
(Text p. 390)

G. W. MACHELL

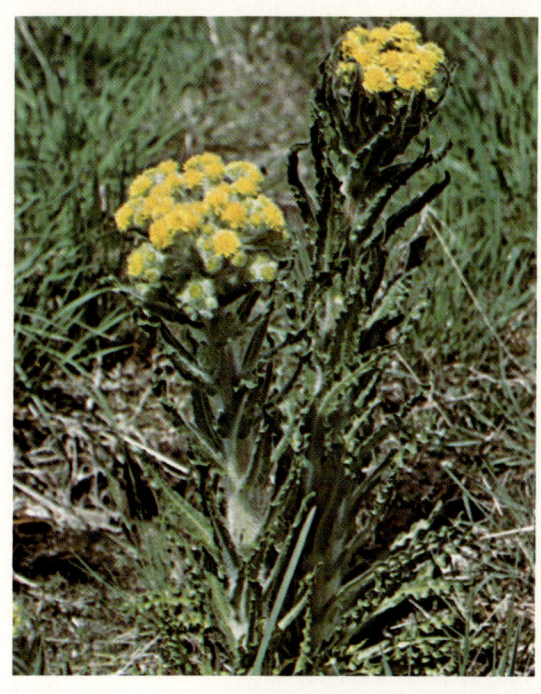

MARSH
RAGWORT
(Text p. 391)

A. KARVONEN

TRIANGULAR-
LEAVED
RAGWORT
(Text p. 391)

JULIE HRAPKO

ARROW-LEAVED COLTSFOOT
Petasites sagittatus

Photo. p. 388
Perennial

FLOWERS:	Ray-florets white, small or lacking; disk-florets whitish, with either stamens or pistil; involucral bracts in 1 series; flower-heads numerous, small, in a dense terminal cluster.
FRUIT:	A dry achene, with white pappus.
LEAVES:	All basal, long-petioled, arrow-shaped, greyish-green above, densely white-woolly beneath, 4 - 10 inches long.
HEIGHT:	Flower-stem 8 - 12 inches.
HABITAT:	Wet places, ditches, and slough margins.
DISTRIBUTION:	Common in forested and parkland regions. April - May.

The thick coarse hairy flower-stem of the Arrow-Leaved Coltsfoot always appears before the leaves and sometimes comes through patches of late snow. This stem, together with several huge basal leaves, grows from a thick creeping rootstock and ends in a torch-like cluster of white flower-heads. The leaf blades are arrow-shaped and are so densely woolly that they look as though they had been cut from a piece of stiff grey flannel. Another species, the Palm-Leaved Coltsfoot, *Petasites palmatus,* with palm-shaped leaf blades, grows in the same wet places.

PRAIRIE CONE-FLOWER
Ratibida columnifera

Photo. p. 388
Perennial

FLOWERS:	Ray-florets yellow, with pistil; disk-florets yellow to purple-brown, with both stamens and pistil; involucral bracts leaf-like; flower-heads several, on long stalks, cone-like disk, ½ - 2 inches high.
FRUIT:	A grey-black flattened achene, no pappus.
LEAVES:	Alternate, deeply divided into narrow segments with stiff hairs, 2 - 4 inches long.
HEIGHT:	1 - 2 feet.
HABITAT:	Dry prairie and roadsides.
DISTRIBUTION:	Fairly common. Southern Alberta. July - August.

In warm dry Southern Alberta many unusual composites flourish but do not grow in any other part of Alberta. One of these is the Prairie Cone-Flower that thrives on dry gravelly soil and is found along roads and coulees. It is a rough-stemmed perennial, grows from a strong tap-root and has numerous deeply segmented leaves. However, its most notable feature is its several showy flower-heads, each one borne at the end of a long stalk. A long brown-purple cone-shaped central disk, surrounded at the base by about ten pale yellow downward-directed rays, explains the popular name of the Prairie Cone-Flower.

DAISY FAMILY — *COMPOSITAE*

MARSH RAGWORT
Senecio congestus var. *palustris*

Photo. p. 389
Annual

FLOWERS:	Ray-florets pale yellow, short, with pistil; disk-florets yellow, with both stamens and pistil; involucral bracts hairy; flower-heads ½ - ¾ inch across, several in a tight hairy cluster.
FRUIT:	A small dry achene, with pappus.
LEAVES:	Basal leaves lance-shaped to spatula-shaped with wavy margins, 2 - 6 inches long; upper leaves much smaller, clasping the stem.
HEIGHT:	8 - 30 inches.
HABITAT:	Wet marshy places.
DISTRIBUTION:	Fairly common throughout Alberta. May-June.

The nineteen species of ragwort or groundsel found in Alberta have yellow daisy-like flower-heads. The leaves and stems are the distinguishing feature in this group and vary by being hairy or not and in other minor respects. The Marsh Ragwort is the most distinctive of them all. It is a tall, very leafy, densely soft-hairy plant and has a preference for wet marshy places. Here it often forms a solid ring of yellow gold around the edge of a pond or slough.

TRIANGULAR-LEAVED RAGWORT
Senecio triangularis

Photo. p. 389
Perennial

FLOWERS:	Ray-florets yellow, with pistil; disk-florets yellow, with stamens and pistil; involucral bracts smooth; flower-heads ½ - ¾ inch across, few or many in a flat-topped cluster.
FRUIT:	A small dry achene, with pappus.
LEAVES:	Alternate, numerous, mostly petioled, triangular-shaped, thin and shining, coarsely toothed, 2 - 6 inches long.
HEIGHT:	1 - 5 feet.
HABITAT:	Wet marshy ground.
DISTRIBUTION:	Occasionally. Rocky Mountains. July-September.

This ragwort goes by many common names: Giant Ragwort, Triangular-Leaved Ragwort and, because it is often found at the edge of a stream or in wet places, it is sometimes called Brook Ragwort. It is a coarse perennial with several tall erect very leafy smooth stems and few to many showy yellow flower-heads which grow in an open flat-topped cluster. Were it not for the triangular-shaped leaves and shiny smooth stems, it could be easily mistaken for the Marsh Ragwort.

**THIN-LEAVED
RAGWORT**
(Text p. 394)

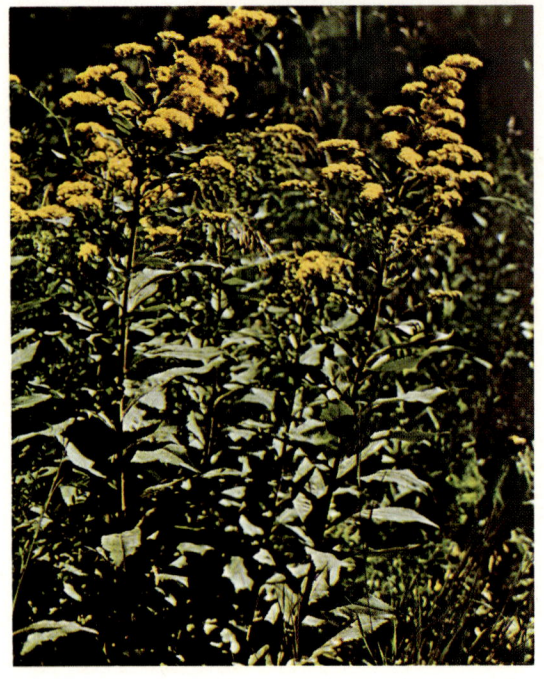

**TALL SMOOTH
GOLDENROD**
(Text p. 394)

MOUNTAIN
GOLDENROD
(Text p. 395)

PERENNIAL
SOW THISTLE
(Text p. 395)

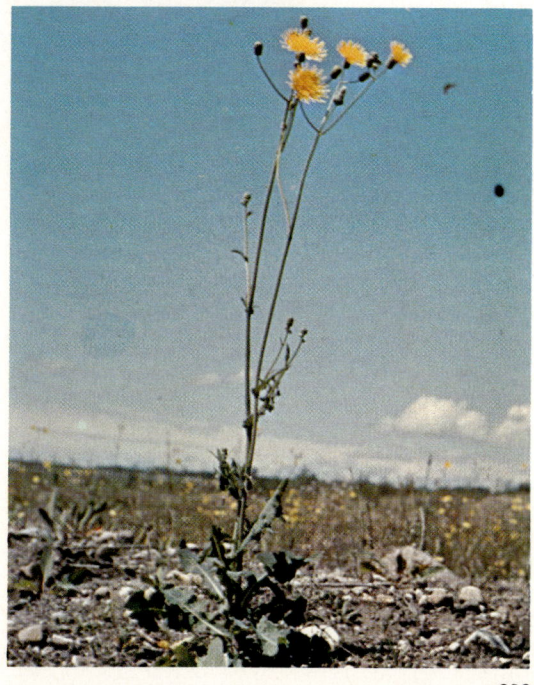

THIN-LEAVED RAGWORT

Senecio pseudaureus

Photo. p. 392
Perennial

FLOWERS:	Ray-florets golden yellow, showy, with pistil; disk-florets yellow, with both stamens and pistil; involucral bracts green, in one row; flower-heads ½ - ¾ inch across, several to many in a terminal cluster.
FRUIT:	A small dry achene, with white pappus.
LEAVES:	Basal leaves thin, mostly oval, saw-toothed, long-petioled, 1 - 2½ inches long; upper leaves not petioled.
HEIGHT:	1 - 2½ feet.
HABITAT:	Moist woods and swamps.
DISTRIBUTION:	Occasional. Wooded regions. May-June.

This species of ragwort or groundsel is often seen in moist woodlands and wet meadows chiefly in Western Alberta and in the Rocky Mountains. It is a hairless perennial and grows from a creeping rootstock and to a height of one to two feet. Like many other ragworts, this plant has two kinds of leaves, basal and upper. The former have long petioles and thin heart-shaped saw-toothed leaf blades while the latter cling closely to the stem and have small finely dissected leaf blades. The flower-clusters make a showy sight with all the yellow flower-heads spread out on the same level.

TALL SMOOTH GOLDENROD

Solidago gigantea

Photo. p. 392
Perennial

FLOWERS:	Ray-florets yellow, with pistil; disk-florets yellow, with stamens and pistil; involucral bracts overlapping; flower-heads small, very numerous in a pyramidal cluster.
FRUIT:	A small dry achene, with pappus.
LEAVES:	Alternate, thin, lance-shaped, somewhat saw-toothed, not petioled, 1 - 6 inches long.
HEIGHT:	2 - 5 feet.
HABITAT:	Woodlands, thickets, river flats.
DISTRIBUTION:	Common throughout wooded and semi-wooded regions. August-September.

In Alberta, in woods, fields and along roadsides, the ten species of goldenrod give the countryside a continuous golden glow in August and September. The Tall Smooth Goldenrod with its tall smooth leafy stems and broad plume-like flower-clusters is one of the showiest. What appears from a distance to be one huge flower is actually hundreds of very small flower-heads crowded into a spectacular cluster. On close examination, each small flower-head is found to be a miniature daisy with several very short wide-spreading yellow rays and a solid yellow centre of disk-florets.

MOUNTAIN GOLDENROD
Solidago decumbens

Photo. p. 393
Perennial

FLOWERS:	Ray-florets yellow, short, with pistil; disk-florets yellow, with stamens and pistil; involucral bracts narrow, overlapping; flower-heads small, densely numerous in a long narrow cylindrical cluster.
FRUIT:	A small dry achene, with white pappus.
LEAVES:	Basal leaves spatula-shaped, wavy-margined, petioled, 1 - 4 inches long; stem leaves smaller, with smooth margins.
HEIGHT:	4 - 16 inches.
HABITAT:	Prairie grassland, open woods and mountain slopes.
DISTRIBUTION:	Fairly common. Central and Western Alberta. August-September.

The popular name goldenrod describes this particular species perfectly, for from a distance the upper half of the slender often reddish stems look like sticks of pure gold. The stems bend slightly near the ground before growing erect and are very leafy at the base. This species is extremely variable. In the dry prairie and western foothills the stems appear as in the photograph with the small flower-heads arranged in an elongated cluster, while in the mountains the stems are less than six inches high with the flower-heads much more compactly arranged.

PERENNIAL SOW THISTLE
Sonchus arvensis

Photo. p. 393
Perennial

FLOWERS:	Ray-florets yellow, numerous, with both stamens and pistil; disk-florets none; involucral bracts hairy; flower-heads several, in an open cluster.
FRUIT:	A dry flattened achene, with pappus.
LEAVES:	Lower leaves with backward-pointing lobes, prickly-margined, petioled, 4 - 10 inches long; upper leaves less lobed, not petioled.
HEIGHT:	1 - 5 feet.
HABITAT:	Fields and waste places.
DISTRIBUTION:	Very common. A cosmopolitan weed. July - September.

The sow thistles are found growing along roadsides, in waste places and in neglected gardens. All four Alberta species are not true thistles for they have milky juice and their flower-heads are made up entirely of ray-florets while the true thistles have only disk-florets. Two species are annual, two perennial. This particular species, the Perennial Sow Thistle, has a smooth stem, many soft but spiny leaves and clusters of yellow flower-heads. Like many other troublesome weeds, it spreads and mutiplies by seeds and creeping roots.

SAW WORT
(Text p. 398)

TOWNSENDIA
(Text p. 398)

COMMON TANSY
(Text p. 399)

COMMON DANDELION
(Text p. 399)

SAW WORT   Photo. p. 396
Saussurea densa   *Perennial*

FLOWERS: Ray-florets none; disk-florets purple, many, with both
                stamens and pistil; involucral bracts in 4 - 5 rows,
                hairy; flower-heads very numerous, crowded on the
                end of the stem, ½ - ¾ inch across.

FRUIT: A dry achene, with double pappus.

LEAVES: Alternate, simple, lance-shaped, sharp-pointed, some-
                what toothed, hairy to smooth, 2 - 3 inches long.

HEIGHT: 4 - 8 inches.

HABITAT: Rocky slopes.

DISTRIBUTION: Rocky Mountains. July - August.

At high elevations in the Rocky Mountains, one often comes upon a
grotesque stunted plant that at first glance looks like a deformed thistle.
This is the Saw Wort. The thistle-like flower-heads are a beautiful dark
purple and they are so densely clustered at the top of the short stout stem-
base that quite often the dark green soft but sharp-pointed leaves are
scarcely visible. It is a spectacular plant and helps break up the dark-grey
monotony of the weathered rock.

TOWNSENDIA   Photo. p. 396
Townsendia sericea   *Perennial*

FLOWERS: Ray-florets white to pink, with pistil; disk-florets
                yellow, with both stamens and pistil; involucral
                bracts appressed and partially overlapping; flower-
                heads without stalks, about 1 inch across.

FRUIT: A dry achene, with pappus.

LEAVES: Alternate or basal, tufted, narrowly lance-shaped, with
                jagged margins, 1 - 1½ inches long.

HEIGHT: 1 - 1½ inches.

HABITAT: Dry open places.

DISTRIBUTION: Plains and mountains. Western Alberta. May - June.

Townsendia is a low squat composite that grows in dry open places,
on hillsides and on exposed mountain slopes. It is not a rare plant but it
is often passed over as one of the fleabanes because of its white, pink or
blue daisy-like flower-heads. However, its long tough fibrous root, short
branching stem-base, seldom more than an inch high, and its tufts of pale
green fine hairy leaves give it a character all its own. The showy flower-
heads are not stalked but grow directly on the top of the stem-base among
the leaves and come into bloom early in the spring.

COMMON TANSY
Tanacetum vulgare

Photo. p. 397
Perennial

FLOWERS:	Ray-florets none; disk-florets yellow, many, with pistil only or with both stamens and pistil; involucral bracts dry, leathery, overlapping; flower-heads ¼ - 3/8 inch across, many in a flat-topped cluster.
FRUIT:	A dry ribbed achene, usually without pappus.
LEAVES:	Very finely divided, aromatic, 2 - 10 inches long.
HEIGHT:	1 - 3 feet.
HABITAT:	Roadsides, waste places.
DISTRIBUTION:	Introduced weed. Common. July-September.

The Common Tansy is one of our most common roadside weeds. It is recognized easily by its strong aromatic scent when bruised or handled, by its flat-topped clusters of hard button-shaped flower-heads and by its finely dissected fern-like leaves. The latter are so characteristic of this plant that one of the mustards is called Tansy Mustard because it has the same lacey leaves. At one time it was grown in the garden as a savory, but today it has gone out of favour.

COMMON DANDELION
Taraxacum officinale

Photo. p. 397
Perennial

FLOWERS:	Ray-florets bright yellow, many, with both stamens and pistil; disk-florets none; involucral bracts dark green; flower-heads solitary, large, 1½ - 2 inches across.
FRUIT:	An elongated achene, with white pappus.
LEAVES:	All basal, coarsely toothed with triangular lobes, 2 - 16 inches long.
HEIGHT:	Flower-stem 2 - 16 inches.
HABITAT:	Fields, roadsides, lawns and waste places.
DISTRIBUTION:	A cosmopolitan weed. Common everywhere. April-September.

Whether it comes up in a vacant city lot, a well-cultivated garden, or along a country road the Common Dandelion is welcomed by all as the first flower of spring and is beloved by all children. It is one plant that needs no introduction. Its large flat rosette of deeply toothed leaves and bright golden flower-heads are familiar to everyone. It is the classical example of the composite type, where all the tightly packed florets are ray-florets. Remember too, the long hollow flower stems and the sticky milky juice.

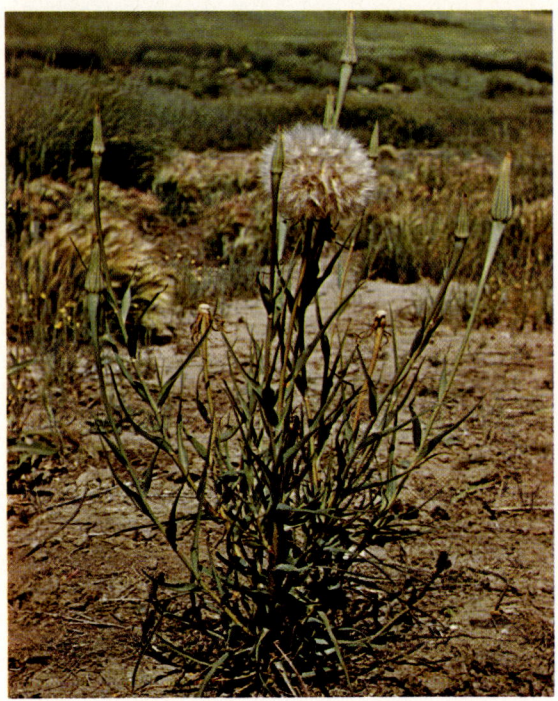

GOATSBEARD
(Text p. 400)

H. A. MACGREGOR

DAISY FAMILY — *COMPOSITAE*

GOATSBEARD   Photo above
Tragopogon dubius   *Biennial*

FLOWERS: Ray-florets greenish-yellow, with both stamens and
                  pistil; disk-florets none; involucral bracts very long, in
                  one row; flower-heads solitary, 1¼ - 2 inches across.

FRUIT: A narrow long-beaked achene, 1 - 1¼ inches long,
                  with plume-like pappus.

LEAVES: Alternate, narrow, erect, clasping the stem, grass-like,
                  4 - 12 inches long.

HEIGHT: 6 - 24 inches.

HABITAT: Roadsides, ditches and waste places.

DISTRIBUTION: An introduced weed. Common. June-July

The Goatsbeard is a giant-sized dandelion. This is the best way to
describe this tall green rank-growing biennial which has a deep fleshy tap-
root, grass-like leaves, huge greenish-yellow flower-heads and milky juice.
It is even more spectacular in seed when the flower-head turns into a symmetrical ball of fluffy achenes. The achenes are provided with a feathery
pappus which will carry them a great distance with a good wind. Although
the Goatsbeard falls into the category of an introduced weed, it is found
in abundance in fields and roadside ditches.

400

GLOSSARY

ABORTIVE—arrested in development.

ACHENE—a small dry hard 1-seeded fruit, not splitting open.

ANNUAL—a flowering plant that completes its life history in one season; from seed to seed in one season.

ANTHER—the pollen-bearing case of the stamen.

AWN—a bristle-like appendage.

AXIL—the upper angle formed by a leaf with the stem; where a bud originates.

BERRY—a fleshy or pulpy fruit formed from a single ovary and containing one to many seeds; loosely any juicy or pulpy fruit.

BIENNIAL—a flowering plant that lives for two growing seasons.

BLADE—the flat, broad part of a leaf.

BLOOM—a whitish powdery covering, often waxy.

BRACT—a scale or leaf, usually small.

BULBLET—a small bulb, often borne on the stem.

CALYX—the sepals, distinct or united.

CAPSULE—a dry fruit, opening at maturity.

CARPEL—a simple pistil or one member of a compound pistil.

CLUSTER—a number of structures, flowers, fruits etc., growing or grouped together.

COMPOUND—a leaf composed of two or more leaflets.

CONIFEROUS—referring to the conifers or evergreen trees.

COROLLA—the petals, distinct or united.

DECIDUOUS—falling away at the end of the growing season.

DIOECIOUS—unisexual with the staminate and pistillate flowers on separate plants.

DISK-FLORET—a single floret making up the central disk of a composite flower-head.

DISSECTED—divided, cut or cleft into segments.

DRUPE—a stone fruit, like a plum or cherry.

FERTILIZATION—the union of the male and female reproductive cells.

FLORET—the small flowers composing the head as in the *Compositae.*

FLOWER-HEAD—a terminal dense cluster of small flowers (florets); Composite Family.

FLOWER-STALK—the stem bearing the flowers.

FOLLICLE—a pod-like fruit which opens along one side.

FRUIT—the matured ovary, without or with other modified parts of the flower.

GENUS—a group of species which all agree in one important though minor structural feature, and all bear the same primary name, e.g. *Rosa.*

GLANDULAR—bearing secretory structures, producing sticky substances, volatile oils, or nectar, often referred to hairs.

GRAIN—the fruit of grasses and cereals, e.g. wheat.

GLOSSARY—Continued

HERB—a green soft-stemmed plant; the above ground stems living only one season.

HYPANTHIUM—a saucer-shaped, cup-shaped or tubular receptacle of the flower.

IMPERFECT FLOWER—wanting either stamens or pistil.

INFERIOR—an ovary situated below the level of the other flower parts.

INVOLUCRE—a collection of bracts surrounding a flower-head or a single flower.

IRREGULAR FLOWER—a flower in which all the sepals and petals are not the same shape and size.

LEAFLET—a single division of a compound leaf.

LINEAR—long and narrow.

LOBED—cut so as to leave prominent projections.

LOCULE—one of the compartments of the ovary.

MARGIN—the edge of the blade of the leaf.

MONOECIOUS—having stamens and pistils in separate flowers on the same plant.

NECTAR—a weak sugar solution produced in a gland or nectary of the flower.

NODE—the point on a stem where a leaf arises.

NUT—a one-seeded fruit with a woody, hard outer shell.

OVARY—the lowermost or swollen part of the pistil which contains the ovules and which on fertilization develops into the fruit.

PAPPUS—a whorl of bristles or silky hairs borne on the achene of a composite.

PARASITE—a plant which obtains nourishment from another living plant, e.g. mistletoe.

PEDICEL—the stalk of a single flower.

PERENNIAL—a plant that lives for several or many years.

PERFECT—a flower with both stamens and pistil.

PERIANTH—the combined calyx and corolla (sepals and petals).

PETAL—one of the showy inner leaf-like parts of a flower.

PETIOLE—stalk of a leaf.

PISTIL—the central ovule-bearing organ of the flower, made up of ovary, style and stigma, develops into the fruit.

PISTILLATE—with pistil or pistils but without stamens.

POLLEN—the powdery contents of the anther of the stamen; produce a pollen tube on the stigma.

POLLINATION—the transfer of the pollen grains from the anther to the stigma.

POME—a fleshy fruit containing a core and seeds, e.g. apple.

PROSTRATE—flat on the ground.

GLOSSARY—Continued

RACEME—an elongated flower-cluster.

RAY-FLORET—a strap-like marginal floret of many composites; often called the ray.

REGULAR—a flower in which all the sepals and petals are the same shape and size.

RHIZOME—an underground stem; a rootstock.

ROOTSTOCK—a more or less elongated, underground stem; rhizome.

ROSETTE—a cluster of leaves often basal in position.

SAPROPHYTE—a plant which obtains its food from non-living organic material, e.g. Indian Pipe.

SCAPE—a leafless flower-stalk arising from the ground.

SEPAL—one of the outer leaf-like parts of a flower, usually green.

SILICLE—a short pod-like capsule.

SILIQUE—an elongated pod-like capsule.

SIMPLE—a leaf not divided into leaflets.

SPADIX—a spike with a thick or fleshy axis.

SPATHE—a large bract enclosing a flower-cluster.

SPECIES—individuals that bear an almost absolute likeness one to another, varying only to a slight degree, e.g. *Rosa acicularis*.

SPIKE—a cluster of few to many individual flowers borne on a common stalk.

SPUR—a hollow, slender extension of the corolla.

STAMEN—the pollen-bearing organ of the flower.

STAMINATE—with stamens but without pistils.

STIGMA—the tip of the pistil, often sticky, on which the pollen grains land.

STIPULE—a leaf-like appendage at the base of a leaf.

STOLON—a creeping stem which takes root and produces new plants at the nodes.

STYLE—the part of the pistil connecting the stigma and ovary.

SUPERIOR—an ovary situated above the level of the other flower parts.

TENDRIL—a modified leaflet used in climbing.

TERMINAL—flower produced at or near the end of a stem or branch.

THALLUS—an undifferentiated plant body.

TREFOIL—a leaf divided into three leaflets, e.g. clover.

UMBEL—usually a flat-topped flower-cluster in which all flower stalks arise from a common point.

WHORL—a circle of leaves or flowers at the same joint or node.

WOOLLY—covered with long and matted or tangled hairs.

BIBLIOGRAPHY

Brown, Annora, *Old Man's Garden*. J. M. Dent and Sons (Canada) Limited, Toronto - Vancouver. 1954.

Budd, A. C., *Wild Plants of the Canadian Prairies*. Canada Department of Agriculture. Queen's Printer, Ottawa. 1957.

Clements, Edith S., *Flowers of Coast and Sierra*. The H. W. Wilson Company, New York. 1928.

Hardy, George A. and Winifred V. Hardy, *Wild Flowers in the Rockies*. H. R. Larson Publishing Company, Vancouver. 1949.

Henshaw, Julia W., *Mountain Wild Flowers of America*. Ginn and Company, Boston. 1906.

Morris, Frank and Edward A. Eames, *Our Wild Orchids*. Charles Scribner's Sons, New York. 1929.

Moss, E. H., *Flora of Alberta*. University of Toronto Press. 1959.

Neatby, K. W., *An Illustrated guide to Prairie Weeds*. Lake Elevators Farm Service, Winnipeg. 1941.

Rydberg, P. A., *Flora of the Rocky Mountains and Adjacent Plains*. 2nd Ed., New York Botanical Garden. 1922.

Turner, G. H., *Plants of the Edmonton district of the Province of Alberta*. Canad. Field-Nat., 63 : 1-28. 1949.

Herbarium. Department of Botany, University of Alberta, Edmonton.

INDEX OF COMMON NAMES

INDEX OF SCIENTIFIC NAMES

411